The Sources of Democratic Consolidation

The Sources of Democratic Consolidation

Gerard Alexander

Cornell University Press ITHACA AND LONDON

First published 2002 by Cornell University Press

Printed in the United States of America

Library of Congress Cataloging-in-Publication Data

Alexander, Gerard, 1965–
    The sources of democratic consolidation / Gerard Alexander.
      p. cm.
    Includes bibliographical references (p.) and index.
    ISBN 0-8014-3947-7
    1. Democratization.   2. Rational choice theory—Political aspects.
3. General will.   4. Democratization—Spain—History—20th century.   5.
Democracy—Spain—History—20th century.   6. Democracy—Europe—History—20th
century.   7. Political stability—Europe—History—20th century.   I. Title.
  JC423 .A495 2001
  321.8′094′0904—dc21   2001003578

Cornell University Press strives to use environmentally responsible suppliers
and materials to the fullest extent possible in the publishing of its books.
Such materials include vegetable-based, low-VOC inks and acid-free papers
that are recycled, totally chlorine-free, or partly composed of nonwood
fibers. For further information, visit our website at www.cornellpress.cornell.edu.

Cloth printing   10 9 8 7 6 5 4 3 2 1

To Greg, who does so much for so many
while asking so little in return

Contents

Acknowledgments

I have accumulated what feel like more than the usual debts. Research was made possible by generous funding from the Fulbright program, the Program for Cultural Cooperation between Spain's Ministry of Culture and United States Universities, and the invaluable pre-dissertation grant program of the Council for European Studies. My fieldwork debts are greatest in Spain. I am grateful to Patricia Zahniser and María Jesus Pablo of the Fulbright Commission; Rafael Cruz, Santos Juliá, and Mercedes Cabrera; and José Ramón Montero and Leopoldo Calvo-Sotelo e Ibáñez Martín of the Fundación Juan March. I am also grateful to the unfailingly hospitable personnel of the Fundación Pablo Iglesias and the staffs of the Biblioteca Nacional and a number of newspaper archives, including the Hemerotecas Nacional and Municipal in Madrid, and several regional and private newspaper archives I consulted, as well as América Saez de Ibarra of the Confederación Española de Organizaciones Empresariales (CEOE). Manuel Gómez-Reino of DATA, S.A., made survey data available.

I am grateful to interviewees in Spain, France, and Britain, including Fernando Abril, Julián Ariza, Leopoldo Calvo Sotelo Bustelo, Eduardo Carriles, Carlos Ferrer, Manuel Fraga, Enrique Fuentes Quintana, Ignacio Garcia Lopez, Antonio Garrigues Walker, Olivier Guichard, Quintin Hogg (Lord Hailsham), Landelino Lavilla, Laureano López Rodó, Francisco Lozano Vicente, José Lladó, Rodolfo Martín Villa, Michel Maurice-Bokanowski, Aurelio Menéndez Menéndez, Alberto Oliart Saussol, Alfonso Osorio, Carlos Pérez de Bricio, José Pedro Pérez-Llorca, José Prat García, Alvaro Rengifo Carderón, Miguel Primo de Rivera, Andrés Reguera, Ramón Serrano Suñer, José Félix Tezanos, and José María Zufiaur. Four

ix

people generously contributed to the design of the Spanish interviews: Manuel Gómez-Reino, José Ramón Montero, Robert Fishman, and Michael Mann, then resident at the Fundación Juan March. In Britain, France, Spain, and Italy, John Barnes, David Cannadine, Julian Jackson, Jose María Maravall, Gianfranco Pasquino, John Ramsden, Pietro Scoppola, Dennis Mack Smith, Javier Tusell, and Richard Vinen gave their time and research advice.

I am grateful for numerous improvements recommended by careful readers, Charles Tilly, David Waldner, Margaret Levi, Guillermo O'Donnell, Josep Colomer, Youssef Cohen, Douglas Chalmers, John Echeverri-Gent, Edward Malefakis, Consuelo Cruz, and Cornell's anonymous reviewers. Roger Haydon of Cornell University Press provided welcome encouragement and support. Several people, heavily engaged in their own work, offered more than professional advice. Engaging in some or all of this project would not have been nearly as enjoyable without the friendship and hospitality of, in rigorously alphabetical order, Brian Brivati, Laura Collura, David Waldner, and Bert Wicholas, as well as my family.

G. A.

Charlottesville, Virginia

Abbreviations

AP/PP	Alianza Popular/Partido Popular (conservative party, Spain)
CC.OO.	Comisiones Obreras (communist-aligned union, Spain)
CDU/CSU	Christlich Demokratische Union/Christlich Soziale Union (center-right parties, [West] Germany)
CEDA	Confederación Española de Derechas Autónomas (conservative Catholic party, Spain)
CEOE	Confederación Española de Organizaciones Empresariales (employers' association, Spain)
CNT	Confederación Nacional del Trabajo (anarchosyndicalist union, Spain)
DC	Democrazia Cristiana (Italy)
DNVP	Deutschnationale Volkspartei (right-wing party, Germany)
FDP	Freie Demokratische Partei (liberals, Germany)
FNTT	Federación Nacional de los Trabajadores de la Tierra (socialist-aligned rural laborers' union, Spain)
KPD	Kommunistische Partei Deutschlands
NSDAP	Nationalsozialistische Deutsche Arbeiterpartei (Nazis)
ORT	Revolutionary Labor Organization
PCE	Partido Comunista de España
PCF	Parti Communiste Français
PCI	Partito Comunista Italiano
PPI	Partito Popolare Italiano (Catholic party)
PSI	Partito Socialista Italiano
PSOE	Partido Socialista Obrero Español
PTE	Spanish Labor Party

SFIO	Section Française de l'Internationale Ouvrière (socialists)
SNF	Sindicato Nacional Ferroviario (socialist-aligned railway workers' union, Spain)
SPD	Sozialdemokratische Partei Deutschlands
UCD	Unión del Centro Democrático (center-right party, Spain)
UGT	Unión General de Trabajadores (socialist-aligned union, Spain)
USO	Unión Sindical Obrera (centrist union, Spain)

I THEORY

1

Rational Regime Preferences in Europe

> To the extent that beliefs do affect regimes, we shall want to know what factors determine beliefs.
>
> ROBERT DAHL, *Polyarchy*, 1971

On July 13, 1936, José Calvo Sotelo, the prominent leader of a hard-right political party, was kidnapped and killed by left-wing members of the state security forces. This murder escalated tit-for-tat violence in Spain's interwar democracy and provoked outrage among conservatives. Four days after his body was found dumped in a cemetery, a military coup against the left-dominated government began in Spain's Moroccan territories and swiftly spread to peninsular garrisons. Senior military officers planned the uprising, and military personnel maintained a commanding position both on the Nationalist side of the civil war that ensued and in the authoritarian regime that won, led by Francisco Franco. But what might appear at first glance to have been a purely military operation was the product of a complex interaction between the military's coercive resources and the massive civilian sympathy on the right on which the coup's plotters counted heavily. The conspirators had been affected profoundly by the social isolation and collapse of a previous dictatorship in 1930 and putsch in 1932; by 1936 even military figures who longed for conservative authoritarian rule would not participate in a project that faced the united opposition of the country and thus ran a high risk of failing.

Consequently, in the run-up to the 1936 coup, plotters carefully sought a consensus within the military, which in turn was predicated on prudent officers' expectations of widespread backing among civilian rightists. Crucially, in the summer of 1936, officers in many parts of Spain detected enormous potential sympathy from rightists at the mass level. Such calculations decisively influenced strategic action. The *pronunciamento* was carried off practically without a hitch in regions such as Navarre and large parts of Old Castile, where rightists made up the majority and where the coup could even draw on rightist paramilitary forces. In contrast, in left-dominated regions where a conservative coup promised to spark overwhelming mass opposition, plotters were much less sanguine about their chances, and only scattered officers and garrisons rebelled. Where they did, they were quickly bogged down in (or overwhelmed by) civilian opposition. The contrast between the two types of regions converted the coup into the three years of the Spanish Civil War.

Forty-five years later, the dispositions of rightists at the mass level again profoundly influenced a coup plot. On February 23, 1981, Leopoldo Calvo Sotelo, nephew of the assassinated interwar party leader, was being voted in as the second prime minister of the new democracy in Spain when a unit of the Civil Guard invaded the Chamber of Deputies. A cabal once again tried to overthrow a democratic government. But this time the plotters found it impossible to gain the support of many colleagues, even though most active officers had loyally served a dictatorship for most or all of their careers. The plot, bereft of mass support and hence of corporate consensus within the former regime's leadership, was isolated and suppressed. Leopoldo Calvo Sotelo, in an interview, remembers believing during the putsch that if it temporarily succeeded, within forty-eight hours millions of Spaniards would have been in the streets to demonstrate against it. He describes 1981 as the "Waterloo of Francoism," an offensive gambit in a contest that pro-authoritarian actors were bound to lose in the end.[1] After 1981, no serious plotters appealed for rightist support, marking what is commonly considered the consolidation of Spanish democracy.

In both 1936 and 1981, the Spanish military contained a notable number of conspirators who attempted to assemble what Guillermo O'Donnell has called a "coup coalition." But whereas in the first part of the century a variety of circumstances could generate rightist backing, emboldening plotters, by the 1980s no such mass support appeared likely, prompting officers to abstain from plots: a virtuous circle replaced the vicious one. What changed was the distribution of what different theoretical traditions describe as regime loyalty, support, commitment, legitimacy, or consent, and what I call in this book citizens' *regime preferences*. Instances of regime change (or regime maintenance) are not determined purely by regime preferences—citizens are often compelled to acquiesce publicly to specific regimes they do not prefer. But attitudes do matter.

---

1. Interview, Madrid, 1993.

Most recent theorizing about democratic breakdowns, transitions, and consolidation thus assigns a central role to the effects that the distribution of regime preferences *at the mass level* has on the choices of strategic regime contenders. Two main claims predominate. First, authoritarian coups and regimes typically are understood to require backing by what Juan Linz terms a "significant segment" of the mass population. O'Donnell and Philippe Schmitter argue that "in no case has the military intervened without important and active civilian support." Second, even theorists who accept Dankwart Rustow's view that a range of events can lead to the initial installation of democracy converge on agreement that a necessary if not sufficient condition for stable democracy is that most actors at the mass level (at least "politically significant groups") neither vote for antidemocratic parties nor offer other forms of support to pro-authoritarian projects.[2]

The influence of regime preferences on outcomes is thus mediated through the calculations of strategic actors whose decisions concerning balances of power include anticipation of likely patterns of resistance, support, or acquiescence. Coup plotters face important risks. The probability of winning or losing a bid to "pronounce" against the existing regime is determined by configurations of power. These configurations are shaped by the two interacting factors described earlier: the distribution of coercive resources and the distribution of mass support for competing regime alternatives. In most instances, neither factor alone is deterministic. While entrepreneurs with sufficient firepower may need no segmental mass support, more often challenges are based on a combination of segmental support and coercive resources. Pro-authoritarian entrepreneurs do not require majority sympathy or a social "consensus" (for reasons discussed in Chapter 3, coup constituencies are almost always a minority), but typically need to perceive that a significant segment of the population will at least not resist the overthrow. Thus, regime contenders seek to estimate the distribution of regime preferences before selecting their own strategies. Strategic actors have sampled public opinion either systematically or anecdotally in the lead-up to coups—"Over dinner, for example, people will begin asking the generals they have over as guests why the military does not take over"—and also during transitions to democracy.[3]

Yet despite acknowledgment that regime preferences at the mass level are causally crucial, no study has developed a full-blown explanation of them since the political culture research of the 1960s, research that was

2. Linz (1978a: 16–17, 85–86), O'Donnell and Schmitter (1986: 27, 31), Przeworski (1991: 26), O'Donnell (1992a: 48–49), Mainwaring (1992: 307), Rose, Mishler, and Haerpfer (1998: 11).

3. Alfredo Martínez de Hoz quoted in Erro (1993: 69n2), Stepan (1971: 95–98).

later abandoned by many regime-change theorists as the result of important predictive failures and theoretical shortcomings. The result is that the causal arguments of transition and consolidation studies crucially rely on regime preferences, but the latter remain largely unexplained, and influential studies rely on largely implicit, synthetic, and often inconsistent assumptions.

Regime preferences may be overlooked precisely because they influence regime outcomes only indirectly, via the calculations of strategic actors. Sidney Tarrow has critiqued analyses that focus on the final links in the causal chain: "because we can *see* [elite actors] making decisions affecting the prospect of democracy, [theorists assume] elite transactions must be given *causal* primacy," when in fact they are "only the culmination of a longer and broad-based process." Terry Karl warns of "the danger of descending into excessive voluntarism." The need to relocate the explanatory focus is captured directly by Alfred Stepan's suggestion that the role of the military interveners he interviewed be treated as "more a dependent than an independent variable." Juan Álvarez, an Argentine critic of his own period's theories about Latin American coups, made this point in 1936:[4]

> A good part of the error derives from attributing more importance to the visible aspects of the events than to their causes. It is as if a detonator were confused with the explosive. A military chief or *caudillo* almost always acts as the detonator, and those who follow him act out the proposition of elevating him to the highest office; because of this, it appears that the revolution is the result of the *caudillo*'s will. But by the same standard, we might say that the rise or fall of prices is determined solely by the eloquence of auctioneers.

Auctioneers anticipate and respond to consumer demand before raising or lowering prices, just as prospective electoral candidates in spatial models anticipate levels of support before deciding whether to run and on what platform. Accompanying the well-known "supply" side of regime changes is a "demand" side, which regime contenders in Europe acknowledged whenever they assessed distributions of regime preferences before selecting their strategies.

These regime contenders were typically on the political right. Insofar as segments of citizens have provided support for exclusionary entrepreneurs, they were conservative or rightist. And all nondemocratic regimes in modern Western Europe have been broadly rightist in nature or orienta-

---

4. Tarrow (1995: 205, 208), emphasis in original; Karl (1990: 6), Stepan (1971: 80), Álvarez (1936: 4).

tion. Rightist sectors also have numbered among the most committed supporters of democracies in the region. In all these senses, the regime preferences of the political right have been the single most decisive factor determining the fates of democracies in Europe, and they are consistently the primary focus in this study.

The Argument

In the following chapters I build on previous theorizing on transitions and basic rationalist principles to argue that people are neither born nor made democrats but rather choose democracy. I advance an argument about the conditions under which the right at the mass level formed *highly reliable* prodemocratic regime preferences, which I argue are characteristic of Western Europe's "consolidated democracies" (a term defined at the start of Chapter 3). In Chapter 2 I argue that peoples' regime preferences are driven by their expectations of the effects on their safety and well-being of overall political outcomes under democracy and authoritarianism. Democracy by definition prohibits state repression, but actors, in order to form expectations about all other political outcomes, require country- and time period–specific information that centrally concerns the preferences and behavior of the people who have the greatest influence on political outcomes under each regime. Actors can usefully be said to form regime preferences in response to the questions, "Democracy with whom?" and "Authoritarianism under whom?" Rational regime preferences are comparison-driven and context-specific.

This basic model of regime preferences has crucial implications for the study of democratic consolidation. Put most succinctly, variation in actors' regime preferences is caused by variation in their basic preferences and in their beliefs about political outcomes under regime alternatives. Manipulating this simple model generates three scenarios, which turn out to be central to patterns of regime preferences in twentieth-century Europe. The first scenario concerns us only in passing: two actors in the same country can form different regime preferences if they have different basic interests. This explains why actors on the left and right (with different basic preferences) have often preferred different regimes, because overall outcomes represent very different payoffs for each one. In the remainder of this study I explore the other two scenarios. All the chapters which follow hold constant one independent variable (actors' basic preferences) by limiting analysis to the political right, whose choices and strategies have determined regime outcomes in the region. Crucially, two actors with comparable basic preferences can nonetheless form different preferences if they possess sufficiently different beliefs about political outcomes under regime alternatives. This explains why European conservatives concerned with property and safety but located in different countries have often supported different regimes in the same time period, when democracy and authoritarianism were likely to generate sufficiently different outcomes. Third, actors' induced preferences may change even while their basic preferences remain the same, when expected outcomes under regime alternatives change sufficiently. As we will see, this explains why conservative sectors that once backed authoritarian regimes or at least maintained access to vehicles for exiting from democracy later became "committed" democrats.

In other words, a rationalist approach permits substantial flexibility in the relationship between actors' basic preferences, their beliefs about alternatives, and their induced preferences, but there is never a total disconnect. Regime preferences will change and will *only* change if a change in either basic preferences or beliefs (or both) warrants a shift in strategy or orientation. A causal logic is retained, which makes regime preferences susceptible to analysis.

In Chapter 3 I identify the conditions under which actors form highly committed support for democracy. Such support contrasts with uncertain or provisional support, which can crucially stabilize a democracy, at least for the short term, and which can be "crafted" through the use of political pacts, power-sharing, institutional design, and other devices. But committed support for democracy emerges only under more restricted conditions, ones for which factors such as pacts are neither necessary nor sufficient. Discussions of the conditions for long-term capital investment serve as a useful analytic starting point for our analysis. Discussions by Max Weber and others highlight the crucial role that juridical and administrative predictability play in capital-holders' decisions regarding whether or not to commit to long-term investments. Commitment to democracy develops under conditions of *low political risks or political predictability in democracy*, when actors perceive that expected payoffs from democracy are predictably higher than those from feasible authoritarian alternatives. As we will see, this occurs when conservatives perceive the left as predictably—and not merely tactically—moderate. The right's strategy toward democracy—and hence the prospects for democratic consolidation—are largely a matter of risk assessment.

When conservatives perceive the left as highly unpredictable, democracy might easily generate less threatening political outcomes than the most likely authoritarian alternative could, but might also generate *more* threatening outcomes in the course of plausible and readily identifiable events in democracy. As a result, actors on the right can know their present but not their future regime preferences. Their response is to "hedge" by maintaining access to coercive instruments for overthrowing democracy. High perceived risks and hedging do not deterministically lead to a breakdown at any given moment since power-sharing, pacts, and stakes-reducing institutions can help ensure that threatening outcomes do not materialize in democracy. But the right's support remains unreliable, and democracy remains unconsolidated.

In contrast, when conservatives believe the left is predictably moderate, democracy cannot result in threatening policies regardless of which parties hold office, whether or not assurances are extended or pacts are achieved or honored, and whether or not institutions are winner-take-all or instead are stakes-reducing. Conservatives' payoffs from democracy are then predictably higher than from authoritarianism, leaving the right with no incentives to maintain access to exit options. In order to conclude that the left is predictably moderate, conservatives must possess at least rudimentary "theories" of the left's political orientations. Chapters 3 through 7 discuss several common conservative theories from late-nineteenth- through twentieth-century Europe. However, this study is agnostic as to the causes of left moderation vs. potential radicalism. Like Margaret Levi in her study, in this text I am "concerned primarily with the effects of macro-level variables . . . rather than with the causes of the shifts in the macro-level variables," although it is difficult not to conclude that the great shift was related to substantial changes in the structures of economic conflicts.[5]

My argument relies on a series of assumptions that are non-obvious. In the previous section I made the case for one such assumption: that citizens' regime preferences are worth explaining because they go on to be an important independent variable in their own right. In this text I make the case for two further crucial assumptions. First, the highly reliable support for democracy that emerged in Western Europe after World War II is not persuasively accounted for by existing research, and for that reason remains perplexing in important ways. Second, as I argue in a portion of this chapter and then the bulk of Chapter 3, rational choices can be stable through time and even reliable, despite entrenched understandings to the contrary.

This argument differs from a number of others. It does not, by any means, always do so by displacing or rejecting competing frameworks outright. In many cases, it instead integrates them into a sustained discussion that attempts to identify when and how they matter. For example, I argue in Chapter 3 and in the empirical chapters that "crafted" devices such as power-sharing, pacts, and institutions can crucially stabilize democracy. But

5. Levi (1988: 33).

I also argue that they cannot consolidate it, a task that falls to a more "structural" factor. But this, in turn, is not one of the social, cultural, educational, or income-level "preconditions" classically invoked to explain regime outcomes. Instead, it is a political precondition: political predictability, caused by the stable narrowing of the political spectrum, ensures that political outcomes threatening to major groups are implausible in democracy, making even favorable authoritarian formulas the predictably worse (suboptimal) choice. It is crucial, however, that my focus is properly not on democratic consolidation as such but consolidation-causing *conditions*. I reject some frameworks, particularly diverse ideational assumptions concerning national and regional political cultures, international demonstration effects (IDEs), and zeitgeists. I discuss these competing approaches later in this chapter and in Chapter 2 and repeatedly revisit them in the empirical chapters. I test competing predictions through structured comparisons between democratic breakdowns, transitions, and consolidation across both countries and time in Spain, France, Britain, Germany, and Italy across the twentieth century.

Why Study Democratic Consolidation in Western Europe?

> Men have almost ceased to study its phenomena because these now
> seem to have become part of the established order of things.
>
> JAMES BRYCE, *Modern Democracies*, 1921

There are at least two compelling reasons to closely examine democratic consolidation in Western Europe: to better understand key political developments in that region, and to better inform debates about the prospects for consolidation in still-uncertain democracies. Despite the profound effects of consolidation in Europe, we possess neither a general theory of why exactly European democracies consolidated nor clear agreement as to when consolidation occurred in each country. This means, first of all, that rapidly expanding debates about the consolidation of Third Wave democracies in Latin America, Eastern Europe, East Asia, and elsewhere lack a crucial ingredient: a theory identifying the causes of consolidation in Western Europe, which contains the largest cluster of cases of once-precarious-now-consolidated democracies. Eugen Weber has suggested that "[b]ad ages to live through are good ages to learn from." The twentieth-century European experience suggests that the best classroom of all is comparisons between good and bad times. The study of Europe makes possible comparisons between cases of consolidated and unconsolidated democracies, critical to the challenge of advancing theoretically grounded and sharply delineated hypotheses about what causes consolidation, even while sharply mitigating the problems of teleological bias and isolating causal factors that would be encountered if cases of consolidated European democracies were instead compared directly to cases of unconsolidated Third Wave democracies. Indeed, comparisons within Europe could easily highlight reasons why cases of Third Wave democracies may be fundamentally different from their predecessors. We can agree with Samuel Huntington that "the experience of the consolidation of first and second wave democracies could yield lessons for the third wave."[6]

The fact that we currently operate without a general theory of European consolidation reflects neglect in the field of European studies. At one time, regime outcomes in Europe were a central focus of political analysis. James Bryce framed his influential 1921 study of democracy by noting "the universal acceptance of democracy as the normal and natural form of government." By the interwar period, several antidemocratic mass movements helped generate authoritarian regimes, and in the face of this tectonic shift, Karl Loewenstein inverted Bryce's analysis: "democracy is everywhere on the defensive, and the victory of autocracy seems hardly less inevitable than formerly the universal acceptance of democracy." Four years after that, Diana Spearman concluded that "[i]t appears . . . as if liberty has far less attraction and authoritarian government far more than has been usually supposed." Observers were particularly struck by the fact that several breakdowns were the work of substantial segments of the population, who chose to "escape from freedom" to authoritarianism. Within a single generation Europe had become what Ignazio Silone described as the preeminent classroom for "a man of good will who aspires to the dictatorship of his country."[7]

After 1945 the region underwent another great transformation, with the emergence of reliable, nearly universal support for democracy in Scandinavia, Great Britain, West Germany, France, and the Benelux countries. Sometime later, similar developments confirmed democratic success in Italy, Spain, and Portugal, producing the world's greatest concentration of highly stable democracies. If war, depression, and genocide were the region's central tragedies in the first half of the century, then peace, pros-

---

6. Weber (1994: 5), Huntington (1991: 270). O'Donnell (1996) has advanced perhaps the most powerful critique of the existing consolidation literature. Comparisons within the same countries across time generate new problems concerning changes in world-historical context and feedback or learning in individual countries. But patterns of regime preferences are sufficiently complex across cases in each time period to allow us to control for the former and within each country across time to control for the latter.

7. Bryce (1921: 4), Loewenstein (1935a: 574), Spearman (1939: 9), Silone (1962: 33).

perity, and democratic consolidation are its triumphs in the second half. And the crucial element of the twentieth-century European experience with democracy has been the movement of what had been substantial segments of the population from pro-authoritarian or fluctuating regime preferences to firmly prodemocratic ones. This change is so complete that it is difficult to remember that only sixty years ago it was Western Europe that evoked images of democratic precariousness and raw authoritarian power.

The unfamiliarity of such images may explain why ongoing regime outcomes in Europe have not remained the object of substantial attention. In 1935, Loewenstein assumed that future generations would probably consider "the battle waging between dictatorial and democratic rule . . . as the predominant political feature of our age."[8] And in the first two decades after World War II, scholars, many of them deeply affected by interwar traumas, attempted to explain especially the breakdown of Weimar and to compare broad background conditions with patterns of European regime outcomes. But these major studies, by such innovators as Gabriel Almond and Sidney Verba, Seymour Martin Lipset, and Barrington Moore, were generally written in years when "we still cannot be certain that the continental European nations will discover a stable form of democratic process."[9] In the following decades, when the full scope of Europe's democratic stabilization could be discerned, it has almost ceased to be an object of sustained analytic focus either in theoretical or in regionalist literature. Gregory Luebbert, Dietrich Rueschemeyer, Evelyne Stephens, and John Stephens, and Ruth Collier have produced major volumes on initial European democratization and divergent interwar experiences, but regional specialists have engaged in very limited discussion of the causes of postwar consolidation outside of Spain.[10] The vast majority of studies on post-1945 European politics focused initially on challenges of postwar reconstruction and later on voting and social movements, supranational unification, the rise of xenophobia, globalization, and the crisis of socialism. All of these events were monumentally important, but they also presupposed stable democracies that went unexplained. Mark Mazower is a

8. Loewenstein (1935b: 782).

9. Almond and Verba (1963: 1), Lipset (1959), Moore (1966), Rustow (1970), Dahl (1971). Innovative studies of Weimar continue to appear, including those by Abraham (1986), Hamilton (1982), and Childers (1983).

10. Luebbert (1991), Rueschemeyer, Stephens, and Stephens (1992), Collier (1999). In their combined first forty-two years of publishing, *West European Politics* and the *European Journal for Political Research* published a number of articles on southern European transitions in the 1970s, two on historic transitions to democracy and democratic experiences during the interwar period, and none that attempted to explain consolidation in any specific Western European democracy or in the region in general.

rare voice urging us to remember that it was "not preordained that democracy should win out" in Europe.[11]

Each wave of regime-change theorizing since the 1970s has made diminishing reference to Europe. Linz and Stepan analyzed several interwar European cases; O'Donnell, Schmitter, and Laurence Whitehead discussed successful transitions in southern Europe but hardly referred to other European cases; and the recent literature on democratic consolidation includes analyses of cases of apparent consolidation in southern Europe but is heavily focused on Third Wave democracies and makes no reference to France, Britain, Germany, Scandinavia, the Low Countries, or other cases of consolidation in Western Europe. Moreover, despite the intriguing juxtaposition of Europe's long history of authoritarian rule and democratic precariousness on the one hand and the relatively very recent outcome of high reliable support for democracy on the other, major studies of regime change are almost never organized around comparisons between breakdowns and consolidation.[12]

Justifying a New Explanatory Approach

It might be argued that scholars have not devoted monographs to this subject for the good reason that democratic continuity in Europe is historically overdetermined by a battery of factors of intuitive importance. But the factors most commonly cited or implicitly assumed do not, upon closer scrutiny, prove persuasive. This lack of persuasiveness does not mean that these factors are unimportant; it seems evident that postwar economic growth, elite choices, rising literacy, and interwar and wartime experiences influenced consolidation in the region. But instead of appearing overdetermined, Europe's democratic consolidation remains a perplexing puzzle. In this section I briefly examine five major categories of explanations for highly stable democracy in Western Europe: wealth, learning, mutual influence, habit, and containment of the right.

1. *Wealth.* At least since Lipset's influential 1959 article, the notion that wealth provides a ready soil for stable democracy remains a prevalent implicit assumption. Europe's trajectory, painted in broad strokes, seems

11. Mazower (1998: xii).
12. Linz and Stepan (1978), O'Donnell, Schmitter, and Whitehead (1986); e.g., Higley and Gunther (1992), Gunther, Diamandouros, and Puhle (1995), Linz and Stepan (1996). Historians have discussed postwar redemocratization in France and Germany, see, e.g., Herz (1982) and Merritt (1995). Among the few interwar/postwar comparisons are articles by Maier (1981) and Gunther and Blough (1981).

to reinforce this: its authoritarian backdrop coincides with preindustrial and industrializing poverty and then the Great Depression, while democracy has flourished amidst the post-1945 "miracle" economies. Recently, Przeworski and his coauthors concluded that "[a]bove $6,000 [adjusted annual per capita income], democracies are impregnable and can be expected to live forever."[13] But wealth appears to be neither a necessary nor a sufficient condition for democracy in general or its consolidation in particular. I argue that France had a consolidated democracy from the 1880s until 1914, when it was an overwhelmingly agricultural country. Democracy also appears to have consolidated in interwar Britain, Scandinavia, and the Low Countries when they were enjoying very modest levels of income (and even severe economic downturns).[14] Democratic support was strong in still-poor rural regions of postwar France and post-Franco Spain. At the same time, highly industrialized Weimar Germany experienced Europe's most spectacular democratic collapse. Finally, in each of the breakdowns examined here, it was the wealthiest (and most educated) sectors of the population that defected from democracy.

2. *Learning.* Mazower has articulated another widespread implicit assumption when he claims that "such was the shock of being subjected to a regime of unprecedented and unremitting violence that in the space of eight years [1938–46] . . . Europeans . . . rediscovered the virtues of democracy." Here, the monumental horror of World War II was a pivot point, giving Europeans powerful reasons to recall democracy's "quiet virtues" such as enforceable rights and governmental accountability.[15] This converts into an asset what many had taken as an unpropitious basis for democracy—a history of breakdowns and violence. But the war, while undeniably traumatic, appears to have been neither a necessary nor a sufficient condition for consolidation. Conservative sectors in Britain and Scandinavia committed to democracy substantially before the war began and without having undergone bitter violence. Nor did fascism and war abolish authoritarian impulses from the region. There is widespread agreement that Italian democracy did not consolidate for decades after the war, despite having undergone the longest totalitarian episode in the region. The Spanish right continued to support authoritarian rule for many years after 1945 despite not only having witnessed World War II but also directly experiencing its own civil war and harsh authoritarianism. There is also survey evidence (some of which is reviewed in Chapter 6) strongly suggesting

13. Lipset (1959), Przeworski et al. (1996: 41), Diamond (1992).
14. Zimmerman (1985).
15. Mazower (1998: 140); on learning generally, see Bermeo (1992).

that large sectors of the early postwar West German population were not "immunized" against authoritarianism under all circumstances. In other words, in a notable number of countries the right committed fully to democracy before World War II and in at least two major countries failed to do so afterward.

Other variations of the learning theme also are not persuasive. Major parties are sometimes said to have emerged from the war more committed to compromise. But consociationalism was rare. And formal pacts of the kind emphasized in transitions theorizing are prominent by their absence in the region after 1945; virtually none are present to explain the retention of democratic support in the 1950s, 1960s, 1970s, or beyond. Instead, a number of prominent governments—including Adenauer's, Felipe González's, and most British cabinets—pointedly flexed their majority powers and abstained from substantial cross-aisle cooperation. Such majorities also were often "manufactured" because opportunities for institutional redesign at war's end were not consistently used to adopt the low-stakes formulas preferred by many democratization theorists. Indeed, no single institutional or constitutional design is consistently associated with either regime outcome across time. For example, despite recent critiques of presidentialism, Matthew Shugart and John Carey have reminded us that the interwar breakdowns "claimed mostly parliamentary regimes."[16]

3. *Mutual influence: International demonstration effects and regional political culture.* Today, Western Europe evokes images of high and intensifying interdependence, suggesting that important outcomes in the region must be explained in terms of mutual influence. This assumption is only reinforced by the region's current homogeneity in regime type. But despite the heuristic value of the notion of regime change "waves," sharp divergences have been more common than synchronization. Conservatives in France (and Switzerland) committed to rare democracies at the end of the nineteenth and start of the twentieth centuries. The right's democratic support was eroding in France in the interwar years at a time when conservatives were defecting to authoritarianism in Italy, Germany, and Spain, but also at the same time that the right was increasingly committed to democracy in Britain, the Low Countries, Scandinavia, and Ireland. After 1945, Germany and France joined northern Europe as consolidated democracies, but Italy, and Portugal and Spain, did not. If the rise of Nazism did not cause the British, Dutch, or Irish right to defect from democracy, it is not clear why we should conclude that it inspired Spanish conservatives to

16. Lijphart (1977; 1984), Shugart and Carey (1992: 39), Przeworski (1991), Linz and Valenzuela (1994).

do so, nor why the Spanish right, having supposedly succumbed to authoritarian IDEs between the wars were impervious to democratic ones from 1945 to the 1970s.

4. *Habit*. Rustow and others suggest that democracy, regardless of original causes, becomes habitual with the passage of time, consistent with Robert Dahl's observation that breakdown is "extraordinarily rare" where democracy has "existed for as long as twenty years or more."[17] The notion that democracy, once firmly installed, is irreversible may derive from deeply embedded teleological assumptions described by Almond and Verba as an ubiquitous "faith of the Enlightenment in the inevitable triumph of human reason and liberty." Like any teleology, this one leaves its object underexplained. There are both empirical and epistemological reasons to be skeptical. First, enduring democracies have collapsed (in Chile and Uruguay) and in one major European case—interwar France—democratic support degenerated severely, two generations after democratic installation. More generally, Almond and Verba went on to note that assumptions about democracy's inevitability or irreversibility should have been badly shaken by regime reversals. Moore also criticizes the "widespread assumption in modern social science" that while change is problematic, "social continuity requires no explanation." If we take seriously Weber's view that the goal of social science is to explain why one outcome occurred and not "rather another," we must conclude that had specific identifiable factors taken on certain other values, Europe would have continued its familiar pattern of authoritarian dominance or democratic instability, and that those factors at those values could have recreated that pattern even in recent years. Hence, specific realized values of those factors both caused consolidation *and* regularly renew it.[18] For this reason, possibilities of deconsolidation are considered in Chapter 8.

5. *The Containment of the Right*: Rueschemeyer, Stephens, and Stephens, Göran Therborn, and Ruth Collier have connected democratization and the stabilization of democracy in Western Europe to (among other factors) key changes in the balance of power between rightist forces historically antagonistic to democracy and leftist forces committed to more inclusive political decision-making.[19] Specifically, the anti-democratic right became relatively less powerful in the 20th century as the result of long-term economic development and the growth of working-class organizations in particular. This made exclusion of the left substantially more costly to the right

17. Rustow (1970: 344–45), Dahl (1989: 313–15).

18. Almond and Verba (1963: 1), Moore (1966: 485–86), Weber (1949: 173, 187). France's degeneration may be indicated in its prominent absence from Dahl's (1989: 313–15) list of "stable" polyarchies displaced by the Nazi invasion in 1940.

19. Therborn (1977), Rueschemeyer, Stephens, and Stephens (1992: 58), Collier (1999).

than in the past. These claims are discussed at more length in Chapter 3 and evidence concerning them is considered there and in several other chapters, but we can anticipate those discussions here. Briefly, balances of power have certainly changed in the left's favor over the past few centuries, and it is highly plausible that this change played a crucial role in introducing democracy to Europe. But evidence considered in later chapters strongly suggests that the costs of excluding the left roughly leveled off at interwar levels, when rightists were often only provisional democrats and in some cases were actively pro-authoritarian. There appears to have been no important shift in left/right balances of power between that period and the post-1945 period, when more and more rightist sectors in Europe committed to democracy. Indeed, between these two periods, levels of working-class organizational mobilization remained roughly steady in some countries and actually *fell* in several others. In sum, consolidated democracies do not appear to be the result of the European right being "locked" into democracy by prohibitively high costs of excluding the left.

Rustow writes that "[a]ll scientific inquiry starts with the conscious or unconscious perception of a puzzle." To the then-recognized puzzle of contrasts between stable democracies and breakdowns in Europe, Rustow added a second puzzle, concerning "how a democratic system comes into existence."[20] This study is organized around a third puzzle: given the region's long inauspicious history on this score, why have Western European countries resolved upon democracies that are among the most reliable in existence? Addressing this puzzle requires answering other unanswered and puzzling questions. Did highly reliable support for democracy emerge in each West European country via similar pathways and according to a similar logic, or was it due to some subtle regional interdependence? Roughly when did it occur in each country? Answering such questions would offer crucial insights into Europe's past and its present: if the argument is correct that democratic consolidation in Europe was neither natural, normal, nor necessary but instead the result of intensive and extensive political change, then the renewal of consolidation requires regular renewal of those same political bases. It would also provide a crucial ingredient missing from debates about the prospects for consolidation in later Third Wave democracies.

The widespread conventions considered above, despite their sharp explanatory differences, have in common that they draw on implied theories of regime preferences in general. At the least, they build from implicit assumptions about the motivations that lead people to prefer democracy

20. Rustow (1970: 339).

or authoritarianism under any specific circumstances and then identify specific events that trigger these causal mechanisms into generating strong
democratic support. Use of these common conventions thus reinforces the
impression that the study of democratic consolidation cannot be separated
easily from the study of regime preferences in general, if for no other
reason than any theory that identifies stability in a phenomenon contains
the constitutive elements of a larger theory identifying the conditions of
its instability and its absence—in other words, a general theory of the phenomenon. Yet, since the heyday of political-culture theorizing, political scientists have operated without an elaborated or sustained theory of regime
preferences that makes its assumptions explicit, assembles these into a
more general causal argument about regime preferences in general, and
systematically tests predictions against evidence, particularly data concerning cases of democratic precariousness, breakdown, *and* consolidation.

Applied Rational Choice but Not Game Theory

The framework used to study these issues here is a rationalist one that
fits into an emerging research tradition known as "analytic narratives" or
empirically applied rational choice. Robert Bates and his coauthors
describe this tradition as problem-driven and seeking "to cut deeply into
the specifics of a time and place, and to locate and trace the processes
that generate the outcome of interest."[21] This overall approach is in part a
response to perceived failings in the way rational choice theory was long
utilized; even many rational choice advocates acknowledged Donald Green
and Ian Shapiro's claim that many rational choice practitioners had "paid
so little attention to empirical testing." But their further claim that "few
nontrivial applications of these models have been shown to withstand
empirical scrutiny" rings false because well before their critique, an important and fruitful shift toward empirical application had already begun.
Its most successful examples add innovative empirical research to rational
choice theory's powerful combination of flexibility in causal explanation,
strongly delineated independent variables, and high degree of susceptibility to testing. This has contributed to midrange theorizing, to the generation of new empirical knowledge, and to the rational choice tradition
itself, most obviously by improving its credentials as capable of powerfully
advancing "our understanding of how politics works in the real world,"
Green and Shapiro's yardstick of useful research.[22] Terry Moe argues that

21. Bates et al. (1998: 11–12).
22. Green and Shapiro (1994: 32, 11, 6).

rational choice (like all current social science theorizing) is "pre-scientific." But successful empirical applications suggest that if and when scientific explanations are achieved, rationally self-interested action will play a central role.[23]

Empirical application contextualizes and "historicizes" rational choice claims as well as seeks out evidence for testing. But both advances also raise important issues, addressed more specifically in several chapters below. First, empirical applications have generated useful explanations not by developing narrow understandings of decision situations but by using the core assumptions of rational choice theory to link abstract with contextual theorizing. Because actors' contexts structure the choices they make, empirical application if anything promises to move the rational choice tradition not so much away from a focus on decision-making processes as toward linking that focus with a complementary one on contexts, providing microfoundations that connect aspects of actors' environments to their strategies. Producing parsimonious explanations thus requires stylizing contexts: identifying which aspects of them are most relevant to outcomes. For example, Douglass North recomposes data by sorting contexts into ones with higher versus lower transaction costs. This categorization enables him to subordinate complex empirical data to the discipline of the "simple and compelling ideas," which Michael Hechter argues have always been present even in mathematically intense rationalist accounts.[24]

Rational choice might appear to play only a modest role in stylizing contexts in this way, since, as I make clear in Chapters 2 and 3, the task requires theoretical work that rational choice per se cannot offer. But rational choice adds substantial value because while its core assumptions are flexible enough to accommodate the notion that choices and outcomes are affected by a wide range of events (as experience suggests), they are not infinitely malleable. They serve as a crucial gateway, shifting attention away from factors that do not appear to matter to ones that do. We only know that we should focus on certain aspects of contexts, and not multitudinous others, by beginning with rationalist assumptions about what matters to people and basically how they operate. Thus, in Chapter 3 I sort democracies by levels of perceived risk and not according to many other possible criteria.

Second, empirical application raises several issues concerning the evidence appropriate for testing. To focus on the issue addressed at most length in this text, it is well known that rational choice theory treats actors' *basic preferences* as exogenous, but it also makes similar assumptions about

23. Moe (1979).
24. North (1990), Hechter (1987: 8n10).

their *beliefs* concerning the likely consequences of available options. Rationalist and game-theoretic accounts traditionally bypassed explicit discussion of beliefs and proposed to (or did) test claims by comparing actors'
choices to "objectively" assessed payoffs. At times this was amended to
salvage the framework from occasional conclusions that actors were irra-
tional because their decision proved to be suboptimal after the fact.[25]
Retrieving rationality in this way effectively acknowledges that predictions
all along have relied on assumptions about beliefs, both when actors were
correct about consequences and when they turned out to be wrong.[26]

Discussions by Josep Colomer and others make clear that data on subjective beliefs are often not only compatible with rational choice research
but also indispensable to it. If Russell Hardin is right that a "rational choice
explanation of behavior must often . . . take individual-specific knowledge
into account," then rational choice predictions necessarily concern actors'
beliefs about their options. Thus, some decision- and game-theoretic
accounts stipulate knowledge requirements in order for predictions to
obtain, and admit the possibility of actor error. In this sense, rational choice
can be understood to have not only a causal-explanatory ambition but also
an interpretivist agenda, one which, in John Ferejohn's words, "constructs
explanations by 'reconstructing' patterns of meanings and understandings
(preferences and beliefs) in such a way that agents' actions can be seen as
maximal, given their beliefs."[27]

Yet only a handful of studies have grounded empirical testing in such evidence. This may partly be because use of such evidence runs serious risks.
Among these may be, first, that tautologous deducing of rationality ex post
can be sneaked easily into the analysis not in the classic way (by permitting
actors to have any basic preferences whatsoever) but by attributing to actors
any beliefs, however unrealistic. Beliefs thereby can become an easy point
of entry for approaches attempting to hijack a rationalist framework for
their own purposes, approaches which might argue that, say, opinion

---

25. I am referring not to situations in which individuals contribute to collectively suboptimal outcomes or to decisions that merely appear to an observer to be suboptimal, but to decisions that actors would change if they could re-choose with greater information. On substantive
versus procedural rationality, see Simon (1976). Actors are concerned with both the course
of events that ultimately occur and ones that do not. The latter become counterfactual
scenarios later, but prior to decision-making simply number among several possible (and hypothetical) futures. In Bueno de Mesquita's (1996: 212) words, "what really happens is often—
perhaps always—the product of expectations about what would have happened had another
course of action been chosen."

26. It also raises the question of how much information it is rational to have before deciding; Elster (1986: 14).

27. Colomer (1995: ch. 7), Hardin (1995: 16), Ferejohn (1991: 281).

leaders manipulate mass actors' beliefs about alternatives. These discussions can make one wonder whether the real explanatory burden lies not in identifying subjective beliefs about available options, but in explaining the origins of those beliefs. In this study I try to have it both ways. I test predictions about choices by comparing actors' basic preferences and their subjective beliefs about regime alternatives on the one hand, with the regime preferences they form on the other. But I also argue that those beliefs were relatively accurate, and at any rate that ideational influences such as IDEs and opinion leadership do not appear to have determined beliefs.

Third, data concerning subjective beliefs may be suspect. Researchers have long been skeptical of actors' own accounts of their basic preferences. Barry Weingast has argued that more effective empirical evidence for rational choice predictions may be data that reveal whether actors changed strategies when relevant aspects of their contexts changed.[28] It is not clear to what extent we can place any greater trust in the versions actors offer concerning their own subjective beliefs. But actors may have less incentive to misportray their beliefs about options than their ultimate goals. Out of caution, and in order to explore the value of data on subjective beliefs, in Chapters 4 through 7 I combine different types of data on actors' subjective perceptions with data regarding changing contexts. Sources of evidence suitable for testing are discussed briefly at the beginning of Part II.

This book provides a rationalist account of the right's strategies toward democracy but not in a game-theoretic form. Game theorizations can be very productive when the factor most centrally explaining actors' (or groups') decisions is the choice of other actors. But game theory is not an appropriate tool when actors' decisions are not driven by this factor. That is the case here: the right's strategies either to hedge or to commit to democracy were driven not by the choices of the left but by the left's fundamental political identity as the right perceived it. This is evident in Chapter 3 when I discuss what I term high- and low-risk democracies. In the former, the right hedged against risks in democracy not based on decisions within the left to adopt radical versus moderate strategies but instead by the fact that the right believed the left to be weighing those options. In low-risk democracies, the right's commitment to democracy was a response not to the left's decision to moderate but to the right's belief that the range of the left's plausible behavior was abbreviated. In other words, the right's decision was a reaction to the degree of contingency that the right per-

28. Weingast (1996: 240–42).

ceived in the left's choices. This argument is not served by the types of game theorizations that have proved fruitful in many other contexts.

Outline of the Book

In this text, I integrate these questions about actors' beliefs, stylization of contexts, and evidence into an analysis of democratic consolidation. In the next two chapters of Part I. I develop one part of the theoretical argument. In Chapter 2 I analyze how rationally self-interested actors form induced preferences between democracy and authoritarianism. The model's independent variables are actors' basic preferences and their beliefs about how alternative regimes will affect them, and the main thrust of the chapter is to argue that these beliefs are informed by actors' answers to the questions, "Democracy with whom?" and "Authoritarianism under whom?" This model generates a series of predictions about real-world patterns of regime preferences crucial to an examination of democratic consolidation. In Chapter 3 I present a theory of commitment to democracy, the type of regime support characteristic of consolidated democracies. The discussion parallels Weber's argument that juridical predictability is a prerequisite for long-term capital investment. Actors' regime preferences are as reliable as they find predictable the matrix representing payoffs from democracy and authoritarian rule in their country. Their perceptions concerning predictability determine whether they hedge against risks in democracy or instead form reliable regime preferences. All this requires actors to forecast the future political behavior of specific other actors. Events and devices emphasized in transitions theorizing approximate but do not achieve the level of predictability required for long-term commitment to democracy. Actors abandon hedges only when they forecast that the political spectrum describing major political groupings is predictably compact.

In Part II, I argue that just such forecasts coincided with conservatives developing highly reliable prodemocratic regime preferences in the five largest countries in Western Europe, just as the development of predictable property rights coincided with the expansion of capital investment. I use empirical evidence to argue that no competing approach provides as effective an explanation for patterns of regime preferences and democratic consolidation in Spain, Britain, France, Italy, and Germany through the twentieth century. Because actors' beliefs about political outcomes in democracy, and especially the left's impact on those outcomes, are the main focus, evidence often parallels historian Richard Vinen's concern "not with the reality of the working class but with business's perception of it."[29] Vari-

---

29. Vinen (1991: 9).

ations across both countries and time provide crucial evidence for the claims made in the theoretical chapters. In Chapter 8 I place this evidence in the broader context of European political development and consider the theory's implications for both the future of currently consolidated democracies and the prospects for the consolidation of still-uncertain democracies in other regions.

2

Democracy with Whom? Authoritarianism under Whom?

> No one is foolish enough to think that he can fence off his family and his field of wheat and his flock of sheep and live isolated from the rest of the world.
>
> Laurence Wylie, *Village in the Vaucluse*, 1957

In his classic study of a French village, Laurence Wylie records that in the wake of World War II, farmers in Roussillon might have preferred to insulate themselves from war's ravages by retreating to subsistence agriculture. But they had "no illusion about the possibility of finding security in isolation" and believed that as long as they lived in a world in which foreign armies might invade France and intrude on their privacy and property, they were unavoidably exposed to risks.[1] We might conclude that these farmers understood that ostensibly secure lives (like ostensibly free markets) do not exist in the absence of politics but are instead created, enveloped, and maintained by specific political events. In their exposure to political risks, the farmers of Roussillon were analogues of every Western European in the twentieth century: embedded in communities, they were subjects of powerful state structures and of various political forces that attempted to manage and alter those structures. Because their countries were in turn embedded in regional and international state systems, they were exposed to the consequences, intended and unintended, of the choices and actions of other people—consequences that may be large or small, positive or nega-

---

1. Wylie (1957: 34).

tive, universal or selective. Some of these effects meant substantial advantages over isolation and were the very reasons they preferred to lead social lives. But at the same time, interdependence entailed risks of adverse policies, violence during the war, Vichy rule, direct Nazi occupation, and other events.

Factors believed to influence and organize the direction, size, and scope of the effects to which people are exposed are the focus of substantial portions of political science, including studies concerned, for example, with the effects of trade policies, welfare programs, and electoral laws and constitutional rules. These analyses do not assume that any one of these factors determines all outcomes or even that these factors necessarily either generate or abolish positive or negative effects de novo. Instead, they suggest these factors act as prisms or filters that alter, magnify, or mitigate, and perhaps most importantly, deflect, target, and redistribute the effects of ongoing events. Very often, these factors cause bundles of effects, and several may act simultaneously on overlapping events, making it difficult to study their influence in isolation.

Political regimes—democracy and authoritarianism—are among the most important factors that filter and bundle the effects of the actions and interactions of fellow citizens, national state structures, and international actors. Regimes are among the basic rules of the political "game" that produces binding outcomes. These rules of the game have only limited capacities to mitigate, amplify, or redistribute the effects of events, but they shape effects by establishing not so much what political decisions are made as the major features of the process governing *who* makes decisions and *how* they are made—in other words, where decision-making power is located and constraints on how it is exercised.[2] Helping govern the exercise of sovereign state power—both the power to make policy (David Easton's "authoritative allocation of values") and the command of the state's coercive agents (Max Weber's monopoly over the "legitimate" use of force)—regimes stand at the intersection of binding decision-making and the control and use of coercive power. They thus have the potential to profoundly affect both citizens' well-being and their security.

In this chapter, I argue that differences in expected outcomes under alternative regimes crucially influence the regime preferences that actors form, a classically outcome-oriented framework of analysis. The study of regime change (and especially of democratic consolidation) is an area of comparative politics that has proved highly resistant to causal arguments organized around rational or outcome-oriented actors. Yet traditional,

---

2. One attempt to define "regimes," and not simply regime types, is provided by Waldner (forthcoming).

often normative, theories of regime support often beg further explanation. For example, claims that actors may develop a normative "procedural consensus" for democracy typically do not identify the mechanisms that cause these norms. The need to explain *why* actors "value" one set of rules of the game over another is made pressing by the fact that, as the theoretical discussions and empirical chapters below repeatedly emphasize, actors in almost all cases are exposed to multiple normative or ideational factors. In this spirit, Barrington Moore argues that "[t]o explain behavior in terms of cultural values is to engage in circular reasoning . . . the problem is to determine out of what past and present experiences such an outlook arises and maintains itself." Applying a similar critique to regime questions, Samuel Huntington observes that "it is not perhaps tautological to say that democracy will be created if people want democracy, but it is close to that. . . . Inevitably, the mind wants to move further [back] along the causal chain."[3]

I begin this study from the premise that it is not reasonable to expect actors to care about outcomes in their lives that are crucially affected by regimes but to prefer a regime for purely aesthetic, normative, or other non-outcome-oriented reasons, any more than it would be reasonable to expect parties to compete for votes but not develop reasoned preferences over electoral rules, or for workers to care about welfare-state policies but not to develop preferences over which party holds office. As John Stuart Mill observed, it would be difficult to make a case "that a consideration of the consequences which flow from different forms of polity is no element at all in deciding which of them should be preferred." Regimes have multiple and often subtle effects on outcomes, and actors who care about outcomes thus care about regimes, too. A rational choice approach is well suited to asking not so much what follows when actors form (induced) preferences for democracy, but why and under what conditions they do so. In this sense this study parallels Michael Hechter's concern with the *emergence* of norms.[4] In the rest of this chapter I develop a basic model of regime preferences, and in Chapter 3 I use it to identify the conditions under which the right in Western Europe committed to democracy.

Competing Conceptualizations of Outcomes under Different Regimes

Under what conditions will outcome-oriented actors form prodemocratic or pro-authoritarian regime preferences? The answer is not self-evident;

3. Moore (1966: 486), Huntington (1991: 36).
4. Mill (1958/1861: 5), Hechter (1987: 54).

simply stipulating that actors prefer the regime that is "in their interest" generates very few useful conclusions about how actors either should or do act, suggesting that real-world choices between regimes are complicated and require elaboration. For example, a prediction that the stipulation might be understood to generate—that actors will prefer one regime because they fail to "win" at the other—does not prove particularly accurate. Coups sometimes do appear to be "the revenge of those defeated by universal suffrage," but just as often groups defeated in one election react by preparing for the next.[5] Nor are actors who gain "benefits" from a regime necessarily dependable supporters of it: powerful groups afforded privileges under authoritarianism have frequently supported democratization. One might conclude that given the diversity of events that can affect actors' interests and the wide diversity of forms assumed by both real-world democracies and authoritarian regimes, actors might form regime preferences only on such ad hoc bases as to produce no obvious patterns or generalizations across countries or across time within single countries.

However, much more common in contemporary democratization theorizing is the opposing assumption, that regimes are characterized by differences so systematic as to ensure that one regime's effects are consistently superior to the other's. Several assumptions of this kind are prevalent, at least in implicit forms, in comparative politics theorizing. Considering their prominence, it is worth briefly considering five such claims here.[6] Each conceptualization is at some level intuitive but is undermined ultimately by its systematic advantaging of one regime type over the other, which suggests that outcome-oriented actors should favor that one regime under all circumstances, leaving us poorly positioned to explain why both pro-democratic and pro-authoritarian regime preferences are common. The model presented in this chapter attempts to chart a course between these contending assumptions, proposing that while political outcomes under regime alternatives vary widely across countries and time periods—obviating the possibility of an analytic silver bullet—actors' regime preferences at the level of individual political systems are nonetheless structured in ways that render them highly susceptible to analysis and generalizations.

1. *Authoritarian effectiveness.* A number of theorists have argued that the centralized decision-making of authoritarianism generates more effective and farsighted policies, for example, suitable for economic development. Authoritarian South Korea and Taiwan appear as plausible examples.[7] But in other cases authoritarian regimes have proved indecisive, impulsive, slow

5. Makin (1983: 61).
6. Other comparable claims, e.g., that democracies are more violent or that absolute rulers distinctively govern for the general good, are no longer influential.
7. Haggard (1990: 254–64) reviews such claims.

to respond, beholden to powerful social and economic interests, or otherwise unable to formulate or implement long-term development strategies.[8] Similarly, some democracies have experienced cabinet instability and policy paralysis, but others appear highly effective. Perhaps most famously, the British government "wields vast amounts of political power" and its decision-making is considered worryingly rapid and potent by advocates of consensual decision-making.[9] The pattern is mixed enough to permit other theorists to conclude that it is democratic authorities who possess greater capacities for, for example, wartime exertion or withstanding the strains of economic restructuring.[10] Empirical evidence suggests that government stability, abilities to encourage investment or collect taxes, and propensities to select orthodox versus heterodox strategies of economic stabilization are the result of factors that cut across regime types.[11] Consequently, there is little evidence that actors are able to deduce likely patterns in these political outcomes from regime type alone.

2. *Democratic rights and personal safety.* Giovanni Sartori, Adam Przeworski, Scott Mainwaring, and others have emphasized the tangible value to actors of rights in democracy.[12] But democracy's ban on the use of state agents to arbitrarily coerce citizens does not determine a priori actors' short- and medium-term risks under either regime. First, while the reactionary shibboleth that democracy is anarchic has been debunked, levels of risk from civil violence are not fixed under either regime and have sometimes been high in democracy. Second, levels of authoritarian repression are neither fixed nor constant and instead vary from case to case and across time both in aggregate levels and in their distribution. In particular, selective repression (considered at greater length in later chapters) may create only ersatz rights that can be revoked at any time, but nonetheless frequently affords favored sectors highly confident expectations that they will be insulated from state violence. The combination of possible civil violence in democracy and frequent sectoral protections under authoritarianism mean that patterns of safety are much more complex than is suggested by a simple focus on democratic rights. While democratization meant reduced risks of violence for nearly all Germans after 1945, for certain Latin Americans in the 1980s and 1990s democratization has meant sharply reduced state repression but significantly higher risks from civil violence. Crucially, risks of violence experienced by different citizens can move in opposite directions in the course of a single regime change, as when one set of citizens

---

8. Waldner (1999), Cohen (1985).
9. Lijphart (1984: 6).
10. Maravall (1994), Lake (1992).
11. Cheibub (1998), Haggard and Kaufman (1992: 32–34).
12. Sartori (1987: 42), Przeworski (1991: 31), Mainwaring (1992: 306–07).

calculates that a military takeover will insulate them from repression but effectively deal with threatening civil violence—resulting in *lower* net risks to their safety than the risks in democracy—while another sector expects to be the target of severe repression under authoritarianism.

3. *Democracy's rule of law versus authoritarian arbitrariness.* A classic distinction between the rule of law and the rule of people suggests that authoritarianism is intrusive and capricious whereas democratic citizens are protected by privacy spheres and are equal before the law. But although democracies must respect core political rights (these are discussed later), policy under either regime can otherwise take as its subject all other areas of citizens' lives, including jobs, homes, the currency, the environment, education, and religious practice. And democratic decisions need not treat citizens fairly. Electoral and other decision rules typically favor certain groups over others. James Madison alluded to this ample room for bias when he wrote in the Federalist paper no. 10 that unlike a legal proceeding, democracy allows citizens to be both interested parties to a dispute and the judge. This permits sometimes shocking sectoral favoritism, especially when majorities impose their will on politically weak minorities or highly mobilized special interests achieve laws that favor them over a passive majority. Laws refracted through fully democratic and legal processes have profoundly unequally distributed tax burdens, spending benefits, and regulatory costs and neglects, have used taxes, subsidies, and protectionism to compel politically weaker groups to subsidize others, have expropriated the property of named individuals and entities, and have subsidized sports stadiums in one named city but not another. Citizens in democracies are treated equally by state policies only in the sense that they are treated consistently with the terms specified in policies, not in the sense that those terms are fair. In some cases, democratic policies are comparatively stable and egalitarian, but in others they are intrusive and biased. Similarly, authoritarianism has proved consistent with both general policies and highly arbitrary ones. Here, too, actors cannot predict political outcomes from regime type alone.

4. *Democracy's reduced negative externalities.* It has been argued that the individual's right to participate crucially allows that individual to influence events in democracy, reducing the risks of adverse policy outcomes. But an actor's individual participation has essentially no effect on policies, and James Buchanan and Gordon Tullock emphasized that while actors avoid negative externalities in a unanimous decision-making process, they risk them under majority rule democracy, as in a dictatorship.[13] Because democratic outcomes are decided by large groups, two actors with similar policy

13. Buchanan and Tullock (1962).

preferences may forecast very different risks of externalities in democracy if one of them expects to be politically isolated while the other detects influential allies. As a result, business people, for example, may expect lower negative externalities in democracy than under military rule in one case but higher ones in another. This may explain why Haitian elites remained pro-authoritarian in the 1980s and 1990s even as many Latin American business communities supported democratization.[14] While democracy offers members of isolated and threatened minorities the right to participate as individuals, they can still have reasons to prefer rule by specific authoritarian leaders who may be more sympathetic than the democratic majority. Their interests thus will be affected differently in different political contexts. For the same reason, representativeness of the electorate as a whole does not generate lower risks of negative externalities for all, as Sartori recognizes. In his example, widening decision-making from one person to ten in a population of one hundred has unknown effects on the risks of negative externalities facing the remaining ninety. Depending on the policy preferences of the one old and nine new deciders, their risks could even increase. Specifically, this increased risk could occur for a given sector as the result of democratization if power is transferred from authoritarian rulers sympathetic to their interests to voters hostile to them.[15] The risks of negative policy-related externalities in democracy are not fixed (at low or any other levels) and instead are based on decisions shaped by system-specific voters, parties, leaders, and institutions.

5. *Democracy's "institutionalized uncertainty."* Finally, Przeworski and others have suggested that actors may value the prospects for future winning definitional to democracy.[16] But the fact that no one set of actors can determine policies in democracy tells us nothing about the ability of actors to predict likely political outcomes under either regime. As Mainwaring has pointed out, definitional differences offer no grounds for assuming that authoritarianism generates higher degrees of ex ante certainty regarding political outcomes.[17] Przeworski acknowledges not only that authoritarian regimes may be characterized by greater ex post variation in policies but also that outcomes under it "can be predicted only by knowing the will of the dictator or the balance of forces among the conflicting factions." Knowing that what will happen is what the dictator *wants* to happen is very different from knowing what the dictator wants. Authoritarian leaders not only may have well-known and consistent "mentalities" but also can be so

---

14. O'Donnell (1992b: 43–44), Maxfield (1989: 82–84).
15. Sartori (1987: 218, 223). This transition would move toward maximum social welfare but would be Pareto suboptimal.
16. Przeworski (1991).
17. Mainwaring (1992: 313–17).

capricious and their decision-making so opaque that serfs are not the only actors who have maintained enduring beliefs that real or metaphorical czars will ultimately satisfy their policy preferences. Similarly, democracy is not characterized by an extreme value on the certainty/uncertainty continuum, as Przeworski also emphasizes: while actors may not know exactly "what will happen," they can "know what is possible and likely."[18] The entire range of electoral and policy outcomes is possible in a given democracy only in a purely technical sense; in reality this range is bounded effectively by local facts of political life. Because both regimes are compatible with either high or low levels of predictability over specific policies, actors have been able to predict respect for private property rights more clearly in some authoritarian regimes than certain democracies (e.g., Pinochet's Chile versus post-Soviet Russia) and in some democracies more clearly than other authoritarian systems (Switzerland versus Mobutu's Zaire).

"Electing" democracy, like electing a party, is "the final ceremony of a long process." Tracing that process from rationalist theoretical bases raises numerous questions: What basic preferences do actors try to secure? Which differences between democracy and authoritarianism matter? How can we operationalize the costs and benefits that serve as the bases on which actors prefer one regime to another? Is it realistic to assume that real-world actors are capable of reasoning about the effects of regimes in ways that justify calling their orientations "rational"? Finally, how can the conditions under which different types of actors prefer democracy or authoritarianism be described in terms general enough to travel across cases but local enough to organize data from specific countries? I address these questions in this chapter.

In the next section I contend that actors have basic preferences over personal safety and well-being, and that it is useful to portray them as having a dichotomous choice between democratic and authoritarian rules of the game. Regime preferences should be understood as "induced preferences" over these regime types. Then I argue that definitions of democracy and authoritarianism determine what information actors need to form expectations about political outcomes under alternatives. Actors require country-specific information concerning authoritarian leaders on the one hand, and democratic voters, parties, and institutions on the other. After that I contend that the cognitive and informational capacities of real-world actors make it possible to form what can be usefully termed rational regime preferences. In the last section of the chapter I show how this basic logic of regime preferences can be used to shed light on three patterns of regime

18. Przeworski (1991: 46–47, 12–13, 30).

preferences crucial to the right and democracy in twentieth-century Europe. I do so by using one of the strengths of a rationalist model: generating testable predictions or implications by holding constant one part of the causal argument while varying another in ways that mimic specific changes in politics. In Chapter 3 I use this basic model to address my central question: under what conditions do actors form the types of highly committed or reliable regime preferences characteristic of consolidated democracies?

Regime Preferences as Induced Preferences

> Material and other rewards—the "payoff" in the language of gangsters and game theory. . . .
>
> BARRINGTON MOORE, *Social Origins of Dictatorship and Democracy*, 1966

Basic Preferences and Induced Preferences

In all rationalist theories, people with "basic preferences" (often termed their interests or goals) form "induced preferences" for one course of action or events over another (or others) when they believe that option is likely to have the most advantageous (or least disadvantageous) consequences for their basic preferences; "being rational in a decision situation consists in examining the alternatives with which one is confronted, estimating and evaluating the likely consequences of each, and selecting that alternative which yields the most attractive set of expectations."[19] In this study, actors form an induced preference for the regime they believe will produce what can variously and interchangeably be described as the overall outcomes more advantageous to them, the outcomes closer to their "most-preferred" (or ideal) point, or the greater payoff to them (which need not be monetary). Actors form induced preferences in response to their beliefs about differences in the overall consequences of available options, as opposed to their beliefs about only some consequences or about the consequences of one option but not any other.

In terms of basic preferences, many rational choice models suggest that voters, for example, are motivated by economic goals alone, in part because of the microeconomic origins of the rational choice model. But when the state apparatus also can be used to engage in repression, actors are likely to care about more than one type of outcome. Thus, François Guizot wrote in 1849 that both "order" and "the regular protection of private interests"

19. Goldberg (1969: 5).

are "the daily bread of peoples" that regimes must satisfy to retain support. Similarly, Guillermo O'Donnell argues that Latin American workers suffered from both the repression *and* the disadvantageous economic policies of bureaucratic-authoritarian regimes; Mainwaring suggests that actors care about both policy *and* liberties; and Przeworski argues that people want "to eat and to talk—to be free from hunger and repression."[20] We can reasonably say, first, that actors care about their *well-being*: they want to advance their material and nonmaterial interests—for example, to preserve property rights or boost income, advance or restrain religious institutions, enhance or dilute ethnic identities, or reform education.

Second, actors care about their *security*: other things being equal, they want to experience the lowest possible risk of physical coercion, imprisonment, torture, murder, or any other form of violence. This basic preference does not appear in many rational choice analyses of political decision-making, but safety is in many ways a precondition for all other interests. It is difficult to achieve or enjoy any other benefit if one is terrorized, badly injured, or worse. Safety appears to be left out of explicit listings of actors' goals in many prominent rational choice analyses because studies of voting and candidates' and legislators' behavior assume that actors' safety is already assured by democratic rules of the game. In contrast, rationalist studies of situations in which violence is distinctly possible integrate interests in safety into the analysis; I do the same in this study.[21] I make several other assumptions, including that actors assign equal weight to these two basic preferences and meet several crucial technical criteria.[22]

A Dichotomous Choice between Democracy and Authoritarianism

Between what options are actors forming "regime preferences"? In this study I assume that actors face a dichotomous choice between democracy and authoritarianism. These regime alternatives are distinguished by the values they assume along three dimensions common to definitions of regime types: the extent of the right of political participation, the degree of availability of political rights, and the degree to which political decisions

---

20. Guizot (1974/1849) added that regimes' prosperity also requires "a little grandeur"; quoted in Woodward (1963: 201). O'Donnell (1979: 312), Mainwaring (1992: 306–07), Przeworski (1991: ix). Pairing these two interests is not novel. People engaging in protest activity are motivated by underlying grievances and also respond to risks of sanctions, which is why, in Charles Tilly's words, "repression works."

21. Results of several studies suggest that political protesters can see beatings and jail time as status-earning benefits.

22. Tsebelis (1990: 24–27) offers an accessible description of contradictions, transitivity, and probability. Crucially, people update beliefs as new information warrants.

result from formal popular and representative input rather than the influence of nondemocratic reserve domains of power. A dichotomous distinction obscures regimes that assume middling values on one or more of these dimensions, but it greatly simplifies my analysis without excessive distortion of the recent empirical record. In Western Europe for most years in the twentieth century and in most post-1945 cases worldwide, transitions produced regimes in which specific extreme values of these three dimensions run together, simultaneously featuring either the "democratic" values along all three dimensions (high liberty, extensive participation, and few or no reserve domains) or the "authoritarian" ones. As a result, nearly all modern studies of regime change, while not suggesting that variations within the two regime categories are distinctions without a difference, organize inquiry around a fundamentally dichotomous categorization: "breakdowns of democratic regimes" and "transitions from authoritarian rule."[23] I follow this example.

The two basic regime types are defined as follows. In *democracies*, nearly all adults have the right to participate in the making of binding political decisions by periodically casting votes. Groups' weights are refracted through party organizations, office-holders, and various political institutions, but voters can generate any policies that do not interfere with political rights and free competitive elections and can meaningfully be said to have the "last say" over those collective decisions. This right is necessarily accompanied by various political rights that state agents cannot violate.[24] Governing leaders may use state agents to enforce decisions made through democratic processes, but coercive acts cannot be arbitrary and must be the result of rule-bound processes devoted to that purpose. Democracy permits the mobilization of many groups but does not necessitate it, and other factors unique to specific political systems (and perhaps common to many of them) may actively favor mobilization by certain groups. While representative decision-making requires formal decision rules, no one set of arrangements is definitional to the regime type, and they can be changed without entailing a change of regime type.

In contrast, under *authoritarian rule*, binding political decisions are made by some small subset of the population.[25] The fact that authoritarian

23. For example, Valenzuela (1992: 98), Mainwaring (1992: 321). Wiarda (1981: 21–22) does not agree. A dichotomous distinction does not rule out more complex considerations: permitting nonextreme values along the dimensions (or relaxing the assumption of value isomorphism) would permit analysis of induced preferences between more gradated categories. Apartheid South Africa, portions of the U.S. South until 1964–65, and Latin American systems that excluded very large numbers of illiterates lay part way between the two basic regime types.

24. Sartori (1987: 32–33) argues that these rights are a "necessary condition of the democratic process itself." Dahl (1971: 3, 5) provides a widely cited list of such rights.

25. The most influential analysis remains that by Linz (1970).

decision-making is limited to a circumscribed subgroup—although it may not be valid to suggest that any single actor possesses a right to participate—means that there is only one possible democratic "decision body" in each given political system (the entire electorate) but many potential groups of authoritarian rulers. Authoritarian decision-making is created and maintained by coercive repression of behavior that might otherwise constitute or combine to produce effective political activity in the general population. Authoritarian regimes can vary sharply in decision-making procedures and in the degree and extension of the repression they apply. They may grant, for example, the functional equivalent of rights to most or selected citizens, but these are liberties not rights and they can be retracted, modified, or redistributed at any time.[26]

It is worth emphasizing the matter of selectivity in outcomes under both regimes. This selectivity is perhaps best recognized regarding economic policies, which often make finely graded distinctions among citizens and sectors and target benefits or costs under both regime types, but is particularly important regarding repression and personal safety. Certain forms of repression (such as censorship) take on public "goods" dimensions. But Tilly points out that many authoritarian regimes do not exercise their liberty to repress all citizens equally or even at all: "The repressiveness of a government is never a simple matter of more or less. It is always selective. . . . Sometimes the discriminations are fine indeed: the same government which smiles on church services bringing together a thousand people assembled to pray for salvation shoots without hesitation into a crowd of a thousand workers assembled to pray for justice."[27] This may not be true of truly murderous autocrats, but many, perhaps most, authoritarian regimes relax controls on political neutrals and especially civilians broadly sympathetic to the regime, whether defined by party, ethnic group, social class, or other bases of "groupness" that describe the characteristics of actors who are not exempt and those who are. This selectivity can create presuppositions of safety from repression among relevant actors.[28] As a result, it may

26. I do not consider democracies with (strong) adjectives here, with one exception: democracies with universal male suffrage; Collier and Levitsky (1997).

27. Tilly (1978: 106, also 56–57).

28. To accomplish this, authoritarian rule must persuade relevant sectors they will be protected. Irvine (1989: 173) quotes an anti-Semitic French politician at the end of the nineteenth century reassuring a correspondent who feared that steps taken against Jews would become universalized: "I would not have put the same argument to you a few years ago. At that time many people found anti-Semitism to be frightening. If you pillage the Jews, they said, we will end up being pillaged as well. . . . Today, such fears no longer exist. . . . Everyone has understood that we are struggling against a race." Sociological features of some countries may either facilitate or inhibit the selectiveness of repression. Rulers may find it relatively more costly to monitor sympathies and behavior in geographic peripheries and metaphorical underworlds,

be possible to overestimate the importance of aggregate outcomes such as aggregate (or average per capita) gross domestic product (GDP) or aggregate levels of violence.[29]

Comparing Political Outcomes: Authoritarianism under Whom? Democracy with Whom?

> We have advocated the goal of freedom for ourselves "and others," but we have not defined what "others" we had in mind. . . . Who are these others?
>
> ROBERT DAHL and CHARLES LINDBLOM, *Politics, Economics, and Welfare*, 1953

Actors will prefer democracy or authoritarianism if, and only if, they expect one regime to result in more attractive political outcomes (higher payoffs) than the other. On what basis could they form such expectations? We have already seen that they cannot do so on the basis of generic regime attributes, since these do not provide sufficient information about likely outcomes. Here I argue, however, that definitional attributes nonetheless perform a crucial function in the formation of rational regime preferences by directing actors' attention to consistent categories of system-specific information. This information permits actors in most circumstances to perceive that regime alternatives are likely to result in noticeably different effects on their well-being and security. It is this fact that permits analysts to identify important patterns in regime preferences despite variation across countries and time. In particular, regime attributes determine which *other* people have the greatest effect on actors' basic preferences. I argue that the actors' regime preferences derive from their assessment of those other people; these actors can usefully be said to compare "Democracy with whom?" with "Authoritarianism under whom?"

What are the essential differences between the two regime types? First, they assign state power to very different groups of people. Under authoritarianism it is assigned to a small group of leaders and in democracy, to the

---

whereas the relative ease of translating racial markers into differential treatment sharply reduced the transaction costs of enforcing both apartheid and Jim Crow. Regimes can also lower these costs, for example, in the way Nazis stigmatized Jews with markers on their outer clothing.

29. For example, O'Donnell (1992a: 24) usefully separated out authoritarian regimes in which "insecurity and fear affected broad sectors of the population, including many who supported the implantation of these regimes."

electorate, whose influence is refracted through patterns of mobilization, parties, and constitutional and other decision rules. Second, the location of decision-making power has the necessary collateral effect of either endowing rulers with substantial discretionary use of repression (under authoritarianism) or granting citizens extensive political rights vis-à-vis state agents (in democracy). Different regimes also can provoke different reactions from international actors and fellow citizens. International actors sometimes (but by no means always) either positively or negatively sanction countries with a specific regime type. And domestic political groups sometimes direct civil violence against regimes of one type, for example, when the African National Congress resisted apartheid but promised a return to peaceful politics in the event of a transition to majority rule.

These other people, then, may affect a citizen's basic preferences through what are here termed *political outcomes*: state policies (including, under authoritarian rule, policies of repression), civil violence from fellow citizens, and treatment of the country by international actors. For example, all other things being equal, an actor's payoffs are higher when state policies are closer to those he or she would most prefer. The fact that each actor's payoffs from a regime are defined in terms of the distance between political outcomes and the policies and levels of security *he* or *she* prefers means that different actors in the same country can associate the same regime with very different payoffs. As we will see, this variation is the basis of common divergences in left/right orientations toward regimes in the same country at the same time.

It is thus obvious why generic regime attributes do not render one specific regime preferable to all actors under all circumstances: political outcomes crucial to actors—state policies, strategies of civil violence, and international actions—are not definitionally fixed within or across regime types. Most political outcomes can take on almost any value under either regime. State policies on almost all issues can take on any value under both regimes. As Anthony Downs remarks concerning economic policy, a democratic government "can nationalize everything, or hand everything over to private parties, or strike any balance between these extremes. It can impose any taxes and carry out any spending" voters desire so long as policies do not interfere with political rights and elections. The same is obviously true of authoritarian regimes and their leaders.[30] It is also true of actors' overall levels of personal security, since civil violence is possible under both regimes and a given authoritarian project may effectively insulate a particular citizen from repression. Generic regime attributes do not enable actors to anticipate outcomes in these matters, because knowing whether a small

30. Downs (1957: 12).

number of authoritarian leaders or an entire electorate possess the power to make binding decisions is not the same as knowing what a specific group of either type of actor will do with that power. Similarly, regime definitions do not predetermine the behavior of international actors, who only sometimes discriminate between regime types, favoring different regimes in different time periods.

Consequently, "local" information—local to a specific country, time period, and international situation—is indispensable to forming beliefs about what political outcomes are likely under each regime in any given cases. Generic regime attributes determine a priori only one systematic difference in political outcomes: democracy prohibits arbitrary coercion by state agents. This is not trivial. Tilly concludes from the European historical record that "professional soldiers and police did the great bulk of the killing" in internal political conflicts.[31] Even actors who calculate that they are highly unlikely to be targeted with authoritarian repression in the short and even medium term run greater long-term risks of violence from the country's premier coercive instruments than they do in democracy. As a result, if all other political outcomes are expected to be equal, citizens will prefer democracy to authoritarianism. But even invoking this *ceteris paribus* prediction requires situation-specific information to establish the expectation of identicalness in all non-repression-related outcomes.

Thus, regime preferences are contextual. But while definitional attributes of authoritarian and democratic rules of the game cannot directly inform regime preferences, they perform a crucial function by focusing attention on which aspects of actors' political contexts matter, providing guidelines as to *what* system-specific information actors need in order to form regime preferences. To form expectations about likely political outcomes under regime alternatives, citizens must assess the likely behavior of the specific people who most decisively influence those outcomes under each regime, and regime definitions structure who these people are. As we have seen, the number of these other people may be large, including state rulers, democratic voters and parties, international actors, and fellow citizens as they may engage in civil violence. Because international sanctions and civil violence loom large in a small number of cases, they play roles in subsequent sections and later chapters. But the discussion that follows puts primary emphasis on the expected behavior of those who control state policy-making power in each regime: authoritarian leaders and democratic voters and representatives. It does so because civil violence and international action matter less than control of state power, for two reasons.

31. Tilly (1978: 101; 1986: 383).

Whereas state power is permanent and has pervasive impact on citizens' lives, civil violence and international actions for or against specific regime types tend to occur only episodically and very often have only marginal effects on actors' well-being and security. Civil violence targeted against one regime type has occurred in a number of cases but not in many others, and is often geographically circumscribed, directly affecting relatively few citizens. Similarly, international sanctions (such as bans on arms sales or loans by the International Monetary Fund) are generally limited rather than sweeping in nature and effects. More importantly, the international community has almost never systematically favored one regime type for long periods of time.[32]

Pride of place in the analysis therefore goes to the question of who controls state decision-making power and what they are likely to do with it. This means that forming rational regime preferences most centrally comes down to an actor answering the following question: would I prefer that state policy-making power be invested in all my fellow citizens, acting through local parties and representative institutions (a process which presupposes political rights), or would I prefer policy-making powers to be held by a specific small group of people (who are necessarily free to use repression to enforce their authority and policies)? Answering this question requires the actor to assess the likely behavior or political "identity" of authoritarian rulers and democratic voters and parties. A rational actor asks, "Democracy with whom?" and "Authoritarianism under whom?" Many analyses of politics use as their starting point a group that has already, in Douglas Rae's words, "decided which of its members are to participate directly in the making of collective policy." Regime preferences concern the prior issue of which members are to participate in decision-making to begin with. We can conceive of regime preferences in terms consistent with how Jack Knight portrays decision-making over alternative possible institutions in general, which he describes as "a product of the efforts of some to constrain the actions of others with whom they interact." He argues that "the main goal of those who develop institutional rules is to gain strategic advantage vis-à-vis other actors, and therefore, the substantive content of those rules should generally reflect distributional concerns."[33] To understand

---

32. In the interwar period, for example, both authoritarian and democratic regimes could reasonably hope for support from some great powers and sanctions from others. During the Cold War the United States discouraged authoritarianism in some cases but not numerous others. Even when the Organization of American States developed procedures for responding to "irregular" interruptions of democratic processes in member states, treatment was selective. Huntington (1991: 284–85) concluded that "American will to promote democracy . . . might or might not be sustained" after the Cold War.

33. Rae (1969: 40), Knight (1992: 19, 40, 73–80).

which institutional design a given set of actors prefers, we have to know something (or a few things) about their assessment of the "others with whom they interact."

Regime preferences are induced preferences between rule by two distinct sets of people. A given actor's induced preference for democracy is not a preference for universalized "rule by humanity" but for rule by the people who inhabit that specific political system at that time, just as a regime preference for authoritarianism is not for rule by "the few" in generic terms but for rule by a specific set of leaders. Thus, one conservative German's wish to replace Weimar's arrangements by which "everyone gets a say" with rule by "a real man" was crucially shaped by the political orientation of "everyone" in the Weimar electorate and of likely authoritarian leaders at the time. Similarly, a Spanish politician's support in 1976 for a transition from "a personal regime to a regime of participation" was influenced decisively by evaluations of the likely political identities of prospective authoritarian and democratic decision-makers at that time.[34] In the absence of an actor's local information about the likely political behavior of these other people, we should not assume that either regime is his or her natural "default." With such data, however, a great deal can be done analytically.

Realistic Assumptions about Decision-Making Capabilities

> Is it not patently unrealistic to suppose that individuals consult a
> wiggly utility curve before gambling or buying insurance?
>
> MILTON FRIEDMAN and L. J. SAVAGE, *Journal of*
> *Political Economy*, 1948

The above discussion might describe how well-informed actors *would* form regime preferences but not how they actually *do*. Anthony Downs recognized that "[a]t first glance, rational voting . . . appears to be a very simple matter. But its apparent ease is deceiving" due to its complex informational and computational requirements. Given real-world conditions, is it realistic to suggest that actors form regime preferences for the reasons outlined here? "Do real people make decisions the way the theory postulates?"[35] In

34. Turner (1985: 178); Miguel Primo de Rivera in *Diario de sesiones de las cortes* 29 (November 16–18, 1976), p. 7.
35. Downs (1957: 39), Monroe (1991: 13).

this section I argue that the answers to these two questions are that it more or less is and they more or less do. The problematic element here is not actors' basic preferences but their beliefs about regime alternatives. Even actors ignorant of their own basic preferences could still form induced preferences for the regime that is "socially efficient," whereas actors unable to detect differences in payoffs from regime alternatives will be unable to form rational regime preferences no matter how articulate and intense their basic preferences. Russell Hardin suggests it is a major obstacle for rationalist explanations "when the actor claims not to have the relevant intention"; it is also a problem when the actor has no idea how his or her intentions will be affected by alternatives. As Martin Shubik puts it, "Only by working through the intervening deterministic, probabilistic, or game-theoretic processes . . . can [the actor] translate his preferences among *outcomes* into preferences among *strategies*."[36]

Actors might be unable to form beliefs about alternatives for several reasons. People may lack the cognitive capabilities to analyze complex data. Or real-world actors simply may not possess the information needed to answer questions like "Authoritarianism under whom?" and "Democracy with whom?" Prospective authoritarian leaders may have vague political orientations that fall short of both ideologies and Linzian "mentalities." Theories of "pluralistic ignorance" suggest that democratic citizens routinely possess erroneous "beliefs about the beliefs of the public"; for example, there may have been no recent elections to provide benchmarks about the electorate's orientations.[37]

But there are several compelling reasons to believe that real-world actors can predict and reason in the ways suggested. First, definitional regime differences allow actors to focus on the consequences of granting policy-making powers to very different sets of people and permitting very different levels of state repression. This allows actors to concentrate on estimating what types of parties are likely to predominate in democracy and how potential military leaders are likely to legislate or repress. Second, while estimates of likely outcomes under regime alternatives cannot achieve exact numerical probabilities, they also do not need to. Economists distinguish between certainty (when outcomes are known a priori), risk (which can be measured in numerical terms), and uncertainty (which cannot be measured in numerical terms). Almost all important political decisions are made under uncertainty, as John Maynard Keynes suggested: "[T]he

36. Hardin (1995: 11), Shubik (1982: 82). In other words, my concern is not with what March and Olsen (1976: 12) called ambiguity of intention (i.e., their basic preferences) but instead with ambiguity of understanding and (insofar as the past is a resource for causal reasoning) ambiguity of history.

37. O'Gorman (1975).

prospect of a European war is uncertain, or the price of copper and the rate of interest twenty years hence, or the obsolescence of a new invention. . . . About these matters, there is no scientific basis on which to form any calculable probability whatever. We simply do not know!"[38] If decision-making required actors to calculate that land reform is 62 percent likely in democracy or that they run a 26 percent chance of severe repression under military rule—or that a given presidential candidate is 36 percent likely to reform public pensions in a specific way—people could make almost no outcome-oriented political choices. But what actors can do, and what is sufficient for many decisions, is to make what Margaret Levi terms "rough estimates . . . [but] fairly good estimates." Total ignorance can incapacitate choice; partial ignorance need not.[39] In only partial uncertainty, actors cannot measure probabilities numerically but can often predict that events are likely to lie within a diffusely bounded or "fuzzy" range. Thus, an actor might describe the probability of civil violence in a new democracy as "doubtful" and a specific policy as "very likely" or instead as having "no chance." Like many surveys, the interviews in Chapter 5 are designed to test opinion in just such terms.[40]

Finally, people have a wide array of sources of information for arriving at rough estimates of the likely behavior of democratic electorates and authoritarian rulers. Samuel Popkin argues that actors appear to retain more information when it involves comprehensible narratives, and a German in 1932 did not need to pore over Ministerial white papers to know that Franz von Papen's aristocratic and unaccountable "cabinet of barons" would be fundamentally conservative or that Felipe González's cabinets after 1982 would be moderate. Actors can even make complex electorates "legible" by organizing them into large groupings with basic political orientations; they may often form impressions of such orientations from directly observed local political experience.[41]

Given our concern here with actors' subjective perceptions, it is worth considering the forms their beliefs may take. Research has often identified large gaps in citizens' political knowledge, but Popkin argues that most surveys that set out to determine whether people know preselected facts miss "the many things that voters *do* know." Not only might some theories

38. Bernstein (1996: 228).

39. Levi (1988: 17). In Shepsle and Boncheck's (1997: 34) words, "It turns out . . . that many people do have hunches about likelihoods that they can associate with various actions." Popkin (1991) emphasizes that evidence that actors lack high-resolution information does not constitute proof they do not make decisions on the basis of what information they have.

40. Fuzzy sets have gradual not abrupt or precise boundaries. For example, exactly when do people become "old"? Wallsten (1990) describes experiments comparing the use of linguistic versus numerical descriptions of probabilities.

41. Popkin (1991: 22).

overestimate how much knowledge people need to make many decisions but we may also routinely underestimate how much information they possess. In particular, people's choices may be crucially influenced by information that respondents cannot (easily) articulate, what Michael Polanyi terms "tacit knowledge." The concept of at least quasi-tacit knowledge plays an important role in the interviews in Spain presented in Chapter 5. Respondents who repeatedly were unable to describe what they had believed was *likely* to happen in any new democracy after Franco's death were nonetheless able to describe what they had believed was highly *unlikely* to happen. They were in the habit not of predicting-by-including (specifying what lay within the fuzzy set of likely events) but of predicting-by-excluding (identifying what lay outside it). Hardin writes that some knowledge may be "irremediably non-verbal"; in this case, actors may possess knowledge that is remediably so.[42]

Disciplining Causal Complexity

Because actors' perceptions of payoffs from regime alternatives are likely to be influenced by diverse contextual events that assume very different values at different times and in different settings, it is highly unlikely that any analytic silver bullet or single type of event explains all or even most regime preferences. It is therefore not surprising that studies have generated intriguing correlations between regime preferences (or regime outcomes) and single categories of events such as income levels, income or property distribution, economic growth or recession, education, class location, and institutional arrangements, but that in each case the connection consistently proves far from definitive. Studies, both quantitative and qualitative, have drawn substantially different and even conflicting conclusions from similar samples of cases, suggesting not only that unambiguous indicators (of both independent and dependent variables) are difficult to construct, but also that regime preferences (and regime outcomes) are often caused by multiple factors acting together. Moreover, even specific combinations of variables believed to hang together (such as those associated with "modernization") generally produce only partial results, suggesting that no specific combination of events is either necessary or sufficient for specific regime preferences. Samuel Huntington summarizes a series of plausible conclusions: "No single factor is sufficient to explain the development of democracy in all countries or in a single country. . . . No single factor is necessary to the development of democracy in all coun-

42. Popkin (1991: 20), Polanyi (1966), Hardin (1982: 181).

tries. . . . Democratization in each country is the result of a combination of causes. . . . The combination of causes producing democracy varies from country to country."[43]

But rather than invalidating the relative simplicity of a rationalist framework for analyzing regime preferences, such causal complexity instead makes such a framework indispensable because it organizes discussion of inherently complex events around a common logic and causal mechanism. The contribution of such a framework is not to exclude as irrelevant specific factors emphasized by diverse transitions theorists, but instead to provide us with "handles" for identifying how diverse aspects of complex contexts matter and which appear to matter most. The fact that multiple types of events almost certainly affect actors' calculations does not mean that the dependent variable in our basic model is causally overdetermined or that testing of it is vulnerable to post hoc manipulations of data, because the model imposes substantial analytic discipline. Above all, the dependent variable (actors' regime preferences) must vary consistently, in ways susceptible to analysis, with the independent variables: actors' basic preferences and their beliefs about likely outcomes under regime alternatives. This permits us to manipulate the value of one component of the causal argument while keeping the other constant, producing predictions that are highly susceptible to testing.

Establishing Payoff Structures in Three Basic Scenarios for the European Right

"Expected payoffs" connect actors' basic preferences and perceptions of regime alternatives on the one hand, to the regime preferences they form on the other. Assigning specific numeric values to specific political outcomes inevitably would involve numerous arbitrary judgments across issues and across time; Guillermo O'Donnell and Philippe Schmitter emphasize that what is "regarded as an 'insult to the armed forces,' an 'act of secession,' or a 'threat to property' is hardly a constant" across historical periods.[44] Moreover, as we have seen, all people are incapable of estimating political outcomes with numeric precision. So how can I use expected payoffs—a crucial measure in my argument—in a rigorous way—that is, one that avoids risks of ex post manipulation of evidence concerning both independent and dependent variables? A fruitful and relevant method is to track actors' beliefs about the likely fate under regime alternatives of

---

43. Huntington (1991: 38).
44. O'Donnell and Schmitter (1986: 27).

their two basic preferences: their well-being and their safety. This approach proves effective because three relatively simple scenarios regarding these two types of basic preferences or interests can be discerned in each of the cases I examine in this study. Three permutations are relevant: actors can anticipate either that both their well-being and their safety will be better off in democracy, that both will be better off under authoritarian rule, or that regime alternatives will impose trade-offs between their two basic preferences. All three combinations appear in the cases covered in the chapters below.

In the first scenario, conservatives expected *both* their core policy interests *and* their personal safety to be effectively secured by the most likely authoritarian regime while expecting both to be threatened in democracy. In this case, the right's payoff structure clearly favors authoritarianism. This is the perspective of the European right (such as traditional aristocrats) who perceived that democracy was likely to lead to leveling and anarchy as the result of workers' and laborers' ambitions to seize their assets and income. In contrast, they had high levels of confidence in the favorable policies and personal protections offered by dynastic monarchies. In the cases covered here, this first scenario is most closely matched by Spain in 1936, when conservatives felt threatened by both proto-revolutionary expropriation of property *and* escalating civil violence in democracy but expected both threats to be suppressed by military rulers who would avoid exposing rightists to severe repression.

In the second scenario, conservatives perceived a specific pattern of trade-offs likely under regime alternatives. Specifically, they perceived greater threats to their well-being in democracy than under the most likely authoritarian formula but believed that democracy offered higher levels of safety than authoritarianism, since the latter inevitably generated at least some (even if low) risks of repression. If the risks these actors perceived under each regime (to their well-being in democracy and their safety under authoritarianism) were equal, this would induce indifference between regimes, since we assume actors weigh well-being and safety equally. Crucially, this was typically not the case because while democracy periodically exposed rightists to severe policy challenges, the most likely authoritarian alternatives to democracy in modern Western Europe consistently insulated the right from severe repression. Consequently, in this second scenario rightists faced a highly asymmetric trade-off: risks of repression under authoritarianism were substantially lower than threats to well-being in democracy. It is not a coincidence that conservatives opted for authoritarian projects in interwar Italy, Weimar Germany, and Spain in 1936, cases in which fascists, Nazis, and Spain's military plotters had developed—*before* they came to power—consistent track-records of insulating almost all rightists from the violence that they targeted against the left. As a result, the second scenario, like the first, favored rightist support for authoritarianism.

Finally, in the third scenario, conservatives expected *both* their well-being *and* their safety to be secured effectively in democracy while associating authoritarianism with favorable policies and modest (but inherent) risks of repression and regime/opposition violence. In this scenario, the payoff structure favors democracy, since it offers both favorable policies and the lowest possible risks to safety. Authoritarianism then cannot offer substantial policy gains over democracy that can compensate for its inevitable risks to safety, however limited the latter may be. It is of heuristic value to say that the long trajectory toward democratic consolidation in Western Europe represents movement from the first to the second to the third scenarios. Specifically, it involved the right coming to believe that the third scenario was not merely a stable but a predictable state of affairs. Chapters 3 through 7 identify the conditions under which this occurred.

Three Variations in Regime Preferences

Robyn Dawes remarks that a given model of rational decision-making in some ways "dictates what *cannot* be concluded, *not* what can."[45] But while it is valuable to eliminate patterns we should not expect to see, we can also go on to make a number of positive predictions. While we can acknowledge that no theory explains all aspects, even all major aspects, of a phenomenon as complex as consolidation, our model helps explain three variations in regime preferences central to the emergence of consolidated democracies in Western Europe. First, a given sector on the political right was often pro-authoritarian even while left forces favored democracy in the same country at the same time. This variation makes a focus on the political right crucial to any analysis of European regime outcomes in general and democratic stability in particular. Second, European rightists did not switch to prodemocratic strategies at the same time in all cases. Instead of synchronizing, conservatives in some countries came to support democracy even while their counterparts were still (or once again) backing authoritarian projects in others. The convergence on democracy since the 1970s represents the first time since before the 1870s that rightists in Western Europe's largest countries converged on support for the same regime type. Finally, rightist actors sometimes changed regime preferences—which permitted them to switch from support for authoritarianism to democracy—but at other times they formed stable regime preferences. The ability to

45. Dawes (1988: 10).

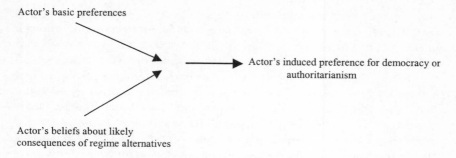

Figure 2.1 The Elements of Induced Preferences for Democracy or Authoritarianism

form both flexible and stable regime preferences enabled the same right-ist sector (and sometimes many of the same people) who had earlier supported authoritarianism to become democrats. Crucially, it also made possible the committed regime support that is the distinguishing characteristic of consolidated democracies, as I argue in Chapter 3. In the remainder of this chapter I apply our model to these three crucial but simple manipulations of the process by which actors form regime variations.

In each case, predictions of variations in regime preferences are generated when one of the model's independent variables (either an actor's basic preferences or beliefs about regime options) is kept constant while the other is varied.

Uniform versus Divergent Left/Right Regime Preferences

Whereas coups typically rely on support from antidemocratic social segments, stable democracy appears to require prodemocratic regime preferences among all major political groups. But while some cases manifest homogeneous regime preferences, others manifest divisions on regime matters, often along class and other cleavage boundaries, consistent with Huntington's description of authoritarian (one-party) regimes as "rule by one social force over another in a bifurcated" or even more fragmented society. Political culture approaches have noted these sometimes sharp divisions; Almond and Verba refer to sometimes opposing "subcultures."[46] In Western Europe across the twentieth century, these divisions tended to constitute leftist support for democracy but rightist support for authoritarian rule. Our basic model can be used to explain parsimoniously these intranational patterns by holding constant actors' beliefs about likely outcomes under regime alternatives but varying their basic preferences. Two actors with different basic preferences will associate specific democratic and

46. Huntington (1970: 11), Almond and Verba (1963: 26–29).

authoritarian regimes with different payoffs. They will form divergent regime preferences if their differentness is sufficient to result in a reversal of the payoff structure, specifically if the left expects higher overall payoffs in democracy than under authoritarianism while the right expects the reverse. This can be related to the scenarios described earlier. When democracy generates outcomes favorable to the left but threatening to the right, while the most likely authoritarian alternative is broadly conservative, actors on the left confront the third scenario discussed earlier: they can better secure both their well-being *and* their safety in democracy. But actors on the right may well confront the second scenario: under authoritarianism, they anticipate substantially more favorable policies than in democracy, and only modest threats to their safety from repression.

Example. In Italy early after World War I, workers and landless laborers pursued—through both direct action and numerous worker-controlled municipal governments—radically expanded worker control of workplace relations and wages and, in many regions, redistribution of agricultural property. Owners and employers perceived these outcomes as threats to their core interests and mounted vigorous opposition. In 1918–20, democratic processes at the national level created governments without clear mandates, which often failed to check widespread challenges by workers and retroactively ratified prominent land occupations. By 1921–22 the most likely authoritarian alternative to this democracy was the emerging force precariously led by Benito Mussolini, whose units violently suppressed unions, restoring employers' and owners' authority. The left therefore could anticipate even less favorable policies and higher risks to their safety under authoritarianism than in democracy. Democracy would generate favorable policies at least at times and limited protections from civil violence, whereas under fascist rule they could expect both highly adverse policies and systematic repression. Their expected payoffs from democracy were therefore notably higher than those from authoritarianism. They thus opposed the fasci's rise to national prominence and influence. In contrast, owners and employers, who could reasonably share these same predictions about likely outcomes under regime alternatives, could therefore anticipate a reversed payoff structure. In democracy their workplace authority and even property were likely to be challenged whereas the fascists had developed a substantial track-record not only of suppressing left demands and organizations but also of consistently using violence selectively against left activists. This was the second scenario described earlier: substantially more favorable policies under authoritarianism than in democracy, with the former imposing only modest increases in risks to conservatives' safety. The right's expected payoffs from authoritarianism were greater than from democracy, and employers and owners extensively supported the fasci.

This left/right divergence can be explained more richly by being placed in historical perspective. In the nineteenth and twentieth centuries, Europe's viable exclusionary entrepreneurs—entities and forces capable of excluding their opponents from state decision-making and establishing authoritarian rule—typically possessed broadly conservative political sympathies. The regimes they were likely to create were likely to protect existing property claims, maintain relatively low taxes on income and property, cooperate with owners and managers of large agricultural holdings and industries, control workers' organizations, and in most cases privilege traditional religious institutions. As a result, the most likely alternatives to democracy represented a much higher payoff for actors on the right than for the left. Often, actors on the left could specifically anticipate *less* favorable policies and patterns of safety under authoritarianism than in democracy. But actors on the right could often expect authoritarian regimes that protected conservatives' core interests and safety to be *more* advantageous than democracy if the latter began to generate highly threatening policies. This explains why European rightists much more often have supported authoritarian projects than their left counterparts. Since variation in basic preferences caused these variations in regime preferences, it is to be expected that class, status group, religiosity, and other markers of basic (in this case, policy) preferences frequently served as rough dividing lines between sectors with antagonistic regime preferences. This is consistent with such evidence as, for example, the fact that the *volkisch*—racist, nationalist, and authoritarian—values described by George Mosse were far more concentrated among German upper and middle classes than among workers.[47] A comparable pattern obtains in most Latin American cases, where viable exclusionary entrepreneurs (typically the military) have had similarly antileft orientations. David Collier and Deborah Norden and Laurence Whitehead identify a regional pattern similar to Europe's in which the Latin American "bourgeoisie" is "one of the most difficult sectors . . . to convince of the advantages of democracy," whereas it "may take very little . . . to 'purchase the loyalty' [to democracy] of the lower classes" in the region.[48]

Left/right variations of this kind also have been explained by an alternative ideational approach, arguing that rightist belief systems contain important elements favoring hierarchy and authority while left ideologies typically value inclusion and tolerance.[49] Such an approach predicts that left and right groups will consistently manifest distinct regime preferences

47. Mosse (1964: e.g., 7, 20–21, 262–63).
48. Collier and Norden (1992: 234), Whitehead (1989: 80).
49. McClosky and Brill (1983).

within a country, at least within the culture area(s) to which left/right cat-
egorizations apply. It therefore diverges from a counterintuitive prediction
generated by our rationalist model: historical left/right regime orientations
should "invert" if the most likely exclusionary entrepreneurs have broadly
leftist sympathies and it is the left that therefore associates authoritarianism with higher payoffs than democracy. Then rightists should be democracy's more fervent supporters. Survey evidence from two cases in which
military actors have been unusually left-oriented, Venezuela and post-1979
Nicaragua, suggests this is in fact the case.[50]

Crucially for the consolidation of democracies in Europe, differences
in basic preferences are not always sufficient to cause antagonistic
regime preferences. Left/right regime preferences will homogenize when
expected political outcomes under regime alternatives lead left and right
actors to associate regime alternatives with necessarily somewhat different
absolute levels of expected payoffs but nonetheless to rank regime options
in the same order. In Chapters 3 through 7 I argue that this is the case in
consolidated European democracies because the compacting of political
spectrums (left/right policy preferences) means that center-right and
center-left actors associate anticipated political outcomes in democracy
with only minor differences in payoffs. In this way, our model also provides
insight into change from a fragmented to a homogeneous regime "culture."
Profound change in actors' basic preferences helps explain why forces once
separated by antagonistic regime preferences come to prefer the same
regime.

Divergent versus Convergent Regime Preferences across Cases

Gradually, conservative sectors switched from support for authoritarianism to support for democracy. At times, different rightist sectors formed
the same regime preferences as each other in the same time periods. For
example, since the 1970s all significant European conservative sectors have
been committed to democracy. Such synchronization might be explained
in terms of international demonstration effects (IDEs), contagion or diffusion effects, or "snowballing."[51] But as we will see, just as often different

50. Seligson and Booth (1993: 789) show that in Nicaragua under the Sandinistas, centrist
and rightist voters expressed notably greater tolerance of dissent than did regime supporters.
In post-1945 Venezuela, military revolts with populist and leftist orientations were as common
as rightist ones, and survey research suggests that support for coups was as common among
left- as right-oriented citizens. More recent Venezuelan coup attempts (especially in 1992)
had distinctly left orientations, and survey respondents expressing strong support for them
identified with left parties. See Baloyra (1988: e.g., 212) and Myers and O'Connor (1998: 199–
201).

51. Huntington (1991: 33–34).

rightist sectors formed divergent regime preferences across countries, creating numerous exceptions to every "wave" of regime change. French conservatives supported democracy from the 1880s through the first part of the twentieth century, almost alone in the region. Their support then eroded during the interwar period, while Spanish and German rightists opted for authoritarianism but at the same time that British, Low Country, and Scandinavian conservatives were committing to democracy. After World War II, British, French, and German conservatives were committed to democracy. However, the Italian right maintained access to vehicles for exiting democracy and the Spanish right continued to support authoritarian rule, in both cases for several decades after 1945. These differences can be understood through a second manipulation of our model, one that holds constant actors' basic preferences while varying their beliefs about political outcomes under regime alternatives. Conservatives with similar basic preferences over safety, property, income, and religious institutions nonetheless form divergent regime preferences if their expectations over outcomes under regime alternatives are sufficiently different, specifically if one conservative sector expects higher payoffs in democracy than under authoritarianism and another expects the reverse. This divergence in strategies could arise, for example, when one conservative sector confronts the first scenario described earlier while another, sharing the same basic preferences, confronts the third scenario:

Example. Interwar Spanish and British conservatives shared the same basic preferences over safety, property, and income. But they confronted very different likely political outcomes under regime alternatives, particularly in democracy. Spanish rightists harbored enduring and intense concerns about potential radicalization of the left in democracy. This radicalization materialized during the Second Republic (1931–36), especially in 1936, when the left won office amidst a gathering social revolution threatening both the property and the safety of many rightists. Past military regimes and the reputations of prominent army officers strongly suggested that the most likely alternative to democracy in Spain would protect the right's property, income, and the Catholic Church, and would also shelter rightists from the high aggregate levels of repression needed to suppress massive workers' organizations and widespread violent direct action. By 1936, rightists thus could expect acute threats to both well-being *and* safety in democracy, whereas military rule credibly offered conservatives both favorable policies *and* reduced risks to their safety—in other words, higher expected payoffs from authoritarianism than from democracy. The Spanish right heavily backed the 1936 military coup. In contrast, in 1936 British conservatives, while sharing basic preferences with the Spanish right, perceived very different regime alternatives. Like in Spain, the most likely authoritarian alternative was highly likely to be rightist. But democracy was unthreatening. Instead of an acute challenge from the left in democracy, not only did the conservatives hold office in 1936 but also the Labour party, which overwhelmingly dominated the left, had a durable reputation for reformist moderation. British conservatives thus could expect to secure both core policy goals *and* safety in democracy, without running authoritarianism's inevitable risks of repression. While sharing basic preferences with the Spanish right, they anticipated higher payoffs in democracy than under authoritarianism. British conservatives, like conservatives in the Low Countries and Scandinavia, rejected authoritarian appeals and movements.

Such divergences in strategies were so common that it is not at all clear that rightist sectors can be said to have imitated each other, for example, as the result of zeitgeists or "prestigious" foreign models (IDEs). Instead, the region's conservatives were often happily, or painfully, aware of cross-national differences in context rather than similarities. On the eve of the 1936 Spanish coup, one leading conservative Catalan newspaper envied the situation of British conservatives who faced a moderate socialist opposition, lamenting that "here we are not English"; another editorialized that "we prefer that Catalonia resemble Norway" but knew that was not the case. Britain's conservatives were just as prepared to appreciate that their own situation did not warrant the same strategies adopted by their counterparts in more threatening democracies. Winston Churchill "endorsed" fascism by remarking, "If I had been an Italian I am sure that I should have been wholeheartedly with you from start to finish in your triumphant struggle against the bestial appetites and passions of Leninism. But in England we have not had to fight this danger in the same deadly form."[52]

As with occasional left/right divergences, the fact that rightist sectors can adopt divergent regime strategies does not mean they always will. The strategies of rightists in 1936 Spain and Britain diverged because the former expected higher payoffs from authoritarianism than democracy while the latter expected the reverse. But when they not only continued to share basic preferences but also formed roughly similar beliefs about expected political outcomes under regime alternatives (which occurred beginning

52. *La noche,* July 2, 1936, p. 8, and July 13, 1936, p. 8; *La veu de Catalunya,* July 18, 1936, p. 1; Cowles (1953: 271–72).

in the 1970s), they formed similar regime preferences. In Chapters 5 through 7 I argue that this convergence among rightists across Europe occurred at different points after 1945, creating the region's contemporary and distinctive pattern of homogeneously prodemocratic conservative strategies.

Stable versus Changing Conservative Regime Preferences

Given the right's history of variable support for democracy and authoritarianism, democratic consolidation required first a change in regime preferences (from pro-authoritarian to prodemocratic) and then a stabilization of them. In other words, regime preferences had to be capable of both change in one period and commitment in another. Political-culture approaches do not easily accommodate change because they are characterized by what Harry Eckstein terms an "expectation of continuity." Terry Karl emphasizes that changes in regime preferences have often taken place more quickly than culture shifts are generally understood to occur. These changes do not appear to be usefully explained through Eckstein's "culturalist theory of political change."[53] But our rationalist model can explain this complex pattern of both change and stability in regime preferences by, once again, holding constant actors' basic preferences while varying their beliefs. This framework assumes that democrats and authoritarians not only are not born but also are not indelibly "made," and that as a result people's regime preferences are neither automatic nor unchangeable. Actors will change their regime preference if a contextual change is sufficient to reverse their payoff matrices—in other words, if a rightist actor expects higher payoffs under authoritarianism than in democracy in one period but the reverse at a later point. One major example dealt with in this study involves a change from the first scenario discussed earlier to the third:

53. Karl (1990: 4), Eckstein (1988: 792, 796). Continuity is expected since normative approaches assume that actors do not continuously respond to developing circumstances. Eckstein argues that a gradual change in "attitudes" can occur, "so as to maintain optimally" more fundamental cultural "patterns and themes." This "culturalist theory of political change" initially approximates a rationalist model: actors, in service to their deepest values (basic preferences), change attitudes (induced preferences) as situations (beliefs about payoffs) change. But Eckstein specifies neither by what means some norms are identified as disposable and others fundamental nor how new attitudes are identified as optimal. In other words, Eckstein reinvents rational choice without the methodological individualism that locates agency or the rationality that provides the causal mechanism connecting contexts to final choices. Eckstein's use of the Tories' programmatic evolution as an analogy only highlights these gaps, since Tory leaders were the specified agents of programmatic change and they (consciously) treated as problematic the question of higher versus lower priorities.

Example. In 1936 the Spanish right faced acute threats to both their well-being *and* their safety in democracy but protection of both interests under conservative military rule. They thus heavily backed the military coup that year. But by the 1970s, conservatives had formed quite different expectations about likely outcomes in any new democracy. Authoritarian rule (including under Francisco Franco's chosen successor) appeared likely to continue to generate policies and patterns of (highly selective) repression favorable to conservatives. But rightists perceived that a new democracy was highly unlikely to generate policies more threatening than welfare-state reformism even while granting them political rights. This meant they could expect both favorable policies *and* the lowest possible level of threats to safety in democracy, lower even than under a sympathetic authoritarian regime. Unlike in 1936, they now expected higher payoffs from democracy, and many of the same rightists who backed military rule in 1936 voted for democratization in 1976. After the transition, this calculatory context stabilized as the left proved reliably unthreatening. As a result, the right's payoff matrix did not reverse and their support for democracy also stabilized.

Similarly, Brazilian business leaders recounted to Leigh Payne that in the early 1960s they perceived democracy as radical and military rule as protective, and favored military intervention. But in the 1980s military rule proved mediocre and democracy appeared far less threatening than before, and they favored redemocratization. In the words of one Chilean politician, "[w]e are grateful for what [Augusto Pinochet] did [in 1973], but we do not want a return to military rule."[54]

The role played by actors' beliefs about regime alternatives also explains why rational regime preferences do not inevitably change. Diverse changes in political, social, economic, and international events generally result in at least an incremental change in the absolute levels of the payoffs actors expect from regime alternatives. But change or stability in regime preferences depends on change or continuity not in the absolute level of expected payoffs from one or both regime alternatives but instead in the matrix representing payoffs from democracy and authoritarian rule. Significant continuity in choices is therefore possible, because many changes do not cause reversals of the actor's payoff structure, leaving the payoffs from one regime consistently higher than those from the other. In the

---

54. Payne (1994) Spooner (1994: 265).

Spanish example, this occurred because the conditions that led conservatives in the 1970s and 1980s to perceive democracy's payoffs as higher were unlikely to change. Differently put, the types of conditions that had led rightists to prefer authoritarianism beginning in 1936 were highly unlikely to be recreated. Consequently, the right was unlikely to experience a reversal in its prodemocratic strategy. Chapter 3 focuses on the conditions under which regime preferences become reliable through time and Chapters 4 through 7 examine the emergence of these conditions in Europe.

3

Predictability and Democratic Consolidation

> Politics means conflict.
>
> MAX WEBER, "Parliament and Government in a Reconstructed Germany," 1917–18

As late as 1950, the French farmers Laurence Wylie studied did not replace their grapevines with higher-yield apricot trees. They had substantial fears of another European war that might destroy themselves or the trees before the latter could mature and produce fruit, leaving the farmers less the costs, including opportunity costs, of planting but without any benefits. Wylie summed up the explanation they offered for their choice: "We know we should plant trees, but what's the use? Who knows if we and our children would be here by the time they started to bear?" The farmers of Roussillon did not know for a fact that there would be a war or that they would be unable to harvest any fruit, only that there was a significant enough risk as to make the investment unattractive. "In this situation the people of [Roussillon] do not act desperately. They simply plant no apricot trees."[1]

Their choice is a metaphor for the development of the regime preferences we associate with consolidated democracies. In the first section of this chapter I argue that actors' regime preferences are qualitatively very different in *uncertain* versus *consolidated* democracies. In the former, support for a regime is provisional or unreliable. In the latter it is reliable into the future as seen from any one point in time, and is highly unlikely to undergo reversal during the course of foreseeable events routine to democratic life. The metaphor of economic investment provides a starting

---

1. Wylie (1957: 33–34).

point for identifying the conditions under which nearly all actors in a political system form reliable regime preferences. In the same way that Max Weber and others have argued that specific types of political, economic, and juridical predictability are required for long-term capital investment, *political* predictability undergirds long-term commitment to democracy. In brief, and to use the terms developed toward the end of Chapter 2, when actors believe that outcomes under democracy are highly unpredictable, they can know if they are currently facing the first, second, or third scenario and therefore which regime they prefer at present. But they cannot know which scenario they will face in the foreseeable future and which regime they will prefer at that time. In several uncertain democracies I will examine, the right preferred democracy at a given time but could not know if it would prefer democracy or the most likely authoritarian alternative even in the near future. The right therefore had incentives to hedge against a reversal in their own regime preferences by maintaining access to coercive instruments for exiting democracy. In contrast, when actors perceive democracy as *predictably* the better choice, authoritarian alternatives cannot offer significant improvements on overall outcomes under democracy. Then, the right has incentives to abandon exit options and to commit to democracy.

This chapter is organized around the question, what leads the right to expect its well-being and safety to be predictably better secured in democracy than under authoritarian rule? I argue that this forecast cannot be created by "crafted" devices such as power-sharing, pacts, or institutional designs or by events such as raised barriers to imposing authoritarian rule. These devices and events have the vice of their virtues. They can be accomplished through short-term strategic action, and actors know they can also be reversed relatively easily too. The actors therefore retain incentives to hedge against their disappearance. European conservatives found democracy predictably more attractive only when they believed a change in a political "structural" factor had taken place—when they believed the left became predictably and not merely tactically moderate. This belief made democracy appear low risk regardless of which party was in office, whether pacts were present or absent, and whether or not institutions were stakes-reducing. In Chapters 4 through 7 I show that such calculations about politics were the basis of commitment to democracy by the right in Spain, Britain, France, Germany, and Italy.

Defining Democratic Consolidation in Terms of Committed or Reliable Support

> I can *predict* (with a fair degree of certainty) that in 1976, 1980, and
> 1984 there will be presidential elections in the United States, or that
> within every five years there will be at least one parliamentary
> election in Great Britain—no mean feat, since one cannot make such
> predictions about many countries.
>
> DANIEL BELL, *The Coming of Post-Industrial Society*, 1973

Defining *democratic consolidation* has proved to be a durable challenge, with theorists emphasizing attitudinal, behavioral, and institutional factors, and combinations of all three. Guillermo O'Donnell has argued that prominent existing definitions implicitly describe existing North Atlantic democracies and are thus vulnerable to teleological assumptions that democracies in the developing world should end up looking like existing consolidated democracies and arrive there via similar stages or pathways. Problems with definitions of *consolidation* have led some theorists to replace the (qualitative) concept of consolidation with (quantitative) differences in the chronological endurance of democracies as the relevant focus of research. But merely quantitative distinctions among democracies are also unsatisfactory. A number of democracies have endured for many years (or decades) but are regularly beset by subversion and extensive fears of breakdown, while others almost immediately develop high rates of intense support and shed perceptible "antisystem" challenges. As a result, other theorists have maintained that qualitative distinctions are indispensable. As Harry Eckstein argued nearly four decades ago:

> [A] definition of stability as mere longevity will not quite do. . . . Taking the
> term in this sense, a system may be stable because of its own effectiveness or
> simply because of the ineffectiveness (or bad luck) of its opponents; it may
> persist, as did the [French] Third Republic, for no better reason than that
> it never quite manages even to collapse, despite much opposition and many
> hairbreadth escapes.[2]

Recent theorizing on consolidation can be understood to approach the distinction between stronger and weaker democracies in two main ways.

First, theorists suggest that democracies vary by the degree to which significant antidemocratic groups are present. Some contain substantial

---

2. O'Donnell (1996), Eckstein (1966/1961: 228).

antiregime sectors while others contain almost none. Second, even democracies in which all groups overtly support democracy vary in the intensity of this support. In some cases, nearly all actors strongly support the regime, whereas in others significant sectors have only "weak allegiances" that might be "swiftly abandoned" by actors "tempted to roll it back when the occasion presents itself." Thus, James Gibson has discussed concerns that democratic support in Russia is "a mile wide but an inch deep," whereas Juan Linz and Alfred Stepan associated consolidation with support that is "habituated" and "deeply internalized" rather than brittle.[3] These formulations share a focus on present perceptions of the future, specifically the probability that democratic support (and thus democracy itself) will continue into the future as estimated from one point in time. Of course, no democracy is reliable under all circumstances and may "break down" as the result of an extraordinary event such as a foreign invasion. Regime support is "reliable" when it is highly unlikely to be reversed regardless of events *routine* to any democracy, such as electoral shifts, alternation in office, fluctuations in organizational strength, and the absence (or failure) of pacts. This approach suggests that the category of democracies, even democracies that might endure across a series of points in time, contains two qualitatively different subsets. I define the first, *uncertain* democracies, as ones in which a politically relevant sector either does not currently have prodemocratic regime preferences or has prodemocratic regime preferences with a significant probability of reversal in the foreseeable future as the result of routine events such as electoral defeat. François Guizot in effect described such regimes: "Tranquil on the surface and for the moment, the government was ardently being contested and attacked in people's minds and in the future."[4] Uncertain democracies evoke precariousness and reversibility, although a breakdown may not occur in any given year or for long periods. I define *consolidated* democracies as ones in which nearly all actors have prodemocratic regime preferences that are highly unlikely to be reversed as a result of routine events. To capture this distinction informally, democracy may well endure in any given year in Sweden, the United States, Russia, and Haiti, but at any given time most observers would probably be willing to gamble more heavily that the former two will remain democratic five or even ten years in the future than they would risk betting on the latter two.

Such subjective perceptions of what is likely to happen to regime preferences and regime outcomes are politically relevant rather than merely

3. Boron (1992: 90), Rueschemeyer, Stephens, and Stephens (1992: 57), Gibson (1996), Linz and Stepan (1996: 5–6).

4. Grubb (1996: 126).

illustrative, because protagonists' own expectations of future events have a multiplier effect on their present conduct. It is not only observers who assess possibilities that major groups' support for an existing democracy may be reversed in the foreseeable future—protagonists engage in these assessments as well. First, if actors know that their own regime preferences have a good chance of being reversed, they have strong incentives to hedge against such an eventuality by maintaining access to vehicles for exiting democracy. This can be illustrated in left/right terms. In modern Europe, the right typically has been recognized as the sector most capable of overthrowing democracy. When rightists knew their own support for an existing democracy might easily be reversed by routine events, they had incentives to maintain access to exit options. This hedging took a variety of forms:

- Rightists cultivated privileged personal and partisan ties within the military, what Stepan termed "co-opt[ing] the military."[5]
- When in office, they reorganized partisan sympathizers into key military commands and perhaps purged supporters of left parties from throughout the state security forces.
- They championed the budgetary resources needed to permit a politically sympathetic military to intervene effectively in political life.
- In the event the military was temporarily diminished or politically unreliable, they founded, funded, and staffed pro-authoritarian paramilitary organizations such as the Italian fascist squads, Weimar's Freikorps, and the Spanish Falange in 1936 (and, in other cases, Latin American paramilitary forces and Haiti's Tontons Macoutes).

In Chapters 4 through 7 I present evidence that in interwar France, Germany, Italy, and Spain, and in Italy from 1945 through the 1970s, the right hedged in one or more of these ways, combining—in insurance policy style—such forms of "disloyalty" with simultaneous support for mainstream conservative parties. In contrast, when such actors project continuity in their own prodemocratic regime preferences, they are like Alexis de Tocqueville's actors, who "could not imagine the possibility of putting anything else in [the] place" of their regime.[6] When this is the case, exclusionary entrepreneurs no longer have incentives to maintain networks of conspiracy and stockpiles of arms.

Similarly, the behavior of left groups is shaped by their perceptions of the likelihood that the right's current support for democracy might be

5. Stepan (1971: 62).
6. Tocqueville (1969: 398).

reversed. Several studies have focused attention on the behavior of leftist sectors "obsessed with [a possible overthrow] . . . [they] take steps to prevent such an outcome and avoid taking decisions which they feel might encourage it." For example, they may "limit the agenda of policy choice" when they are in office and their opponents appear threatened. In contrast, when the right appears committed to democracy, the left can afford to be "no longer dominated by the problem of how to avoid democratic breakdown" and can "relax" and pursue politics in office without self-censorship.[7] In sum, the qualitative distinction between uncertain and consolidated democracies can be discerned in the political behavior of major groups. This distinction poses the next question: what factors cause major groups to form committed, as opposed to merely provisional, prodemocratic regime preferences?

Political Conditions for Reliable Democratic Support

> A particular slave . . . may be lucky enough to escape such treatment but the sure knowledge that it *could* happen to her pervades the entire relationship.
>
> JAMES SCOTT, *Domination and the Arts of Resistance*, 1990

The assumption that regime preferences motivated by rational self-interest can never be stable dates at least from Max Weber's claim that "*[p]urely* material interests and calculations of advantages as the basis of solidarity between the chief and his administrative staff result, in this as in other connexions, in a relatively unstable situation."[8] Because norms are "not outcome-oriented," they appear suited to explaining stability in the face of widespread change.[9] But the notion that self-interested choices must be unstable misinterprets rationality, in the same way as the notion that rational choices always produce conflict and not cooperation. In this section I outline the calculatory context for rational commitment to democracy. Use of a rationalist framework to explain this commitment is attractive not only because it is theoretically feasible. Most research portrays choices made during transitions to democracy as calculated and even strategic, even if

7. O'Donnell and Schmitter (1986: 23, 41), Linz and Stepan (1996: 5–6), Valenzuela (1992: 69), Di Palma (1990: 142).

8. Weber (1978/1920: 213). This assumption is evident in the "legitimacy" theorizing that builds from Lipset (1959).

9. Elster (1989: 113) characterizes action "guided by social norms" as non-outcome-oriented; for a somewhat different view, see Hardin (1995: 114, 140).

they are based on limited information; this is captured in Guillermo O'Donnell and Philippe Schmitter's metaphor of a multilevel chess game. A number of theorists suggest that movement toward stable regime support after a transition requires a shift to normative modes of social action. It may be, as Dankwart Rustow suggests, that a burden of proof rests with "those who assert that the circumstances which sustain a mature democracy also favor its birth." But surely an even greater burden rests with those who assume an unexplained ontological shift in the underlying logic by which people form attitudes toward regimes. If major decisions made during transitions appear calculated, we should at least begin with the assumption that regime-related decisions made later are as well.[10]

Under most circumstances, it would not be rational to commit to one among several available options—to abandon access to others—in the absence of any information concerning future payoffs from them. The decision whether or not to commit is thus a function of forecasting. Briefly put, actors will commit to one option when they possess an expectation of what can be termed "rough" rigidity in the matrix representing payoffs from available options. This refers not to degrees of rigidity in the absolute levels of expected payoffs from any one option (or from both or all of them) but instead to degrees of rigidity in the relative relationship between the expected payoffs of different options—that is, in the matrix representing an actor's expected payoffs from options. This matrix (or payoff structure) is rigid when the actor expects payoffs from one option to remain relatively higher than those from the other, whatever their specific absolute levels at any given time. Some analyses suggest that actors will commit to an option in this manner only if they believe payoffs will favor that option throughout every one of a series of moments into the future—in other words, only if the actor forecasts what might be termed "strict rigidity" in his or her payoff matrix. Analyses of an actor's "trust" in another actor's promises or threats concerning future behavior often rely on such strict rigidity.[11]

Other analyses have relaxed this requirement somewhat. If actors face complex options that might be difficult to replace repeatedly, they may see overall outcomes of options bundled not only at any one time but also for

---

10. O'Donnell and Schmitter (1986), Rustow (1970: 341). Hirschman (1977) describes an inverted assumption from an earlier era that the "restlessness" of people driven primarily by passions could be stabilized through cultivation of their interests.

11. In these discussions, actors assume that others' promises or threats are credible only if the others' payoffs favor fulfilling the promise at all times; otherwise fulfilling it would be off the equilibrium path, and commitment to a strategy that required such behavior would be subgame imperfect. For discussions in these terms, see Coleman (1990: ch. 5) and Ziegler (1998).

perhaps extended periods of time. As a result they may be willing to foreswear exit options even if they believe that democracy, for example, could represent a lower payoff than authoritarianism for one or more brief periods, so long as they expect democracy's payoffs to average out at higher levels in the long run. In the same way, an actor may commit to fulfilling promises or threats even if they are not cost-effective when considered in temporal isolation, so long as the longer-term payoffs from doing so justify it, for example, if it helps to create a reputation for toughness that is cost-minimizing over the long haul. In this vein, Adam Przeworski emphasizes the importance of actors' present calculations of the prospects of advancing their interests in democracy in the future.[12] Exactly how far actors' time horizons must extend and how much the payoffs from democracy must average out above those from authoritarianism may be unclear. But even in the absence of answers to such questions, we can at least arrive at one conclusion. For actors to commit to one regime (to foreswear access to the other) assumes that they can forecast at least roughly the matrix representing their expected payoffs from democracy and authoritarianism.

If political outcomes under both regimes were radically uncertain, actors cannot know that periods of relatively lower payoffs from democracy are likely to be brief, that they will avoid irreversible losses under that regime, or that democracy's payoffs in fact will average out higher over time. Under radical uncertainty, actors have low time horizons, making present defeats loom large and commitment to one regime appear suboptimal. Such radical uncertainty does not determine all aspects of actors' choices, but it gives them strong incentives to keep their options open. Only actors who forecast at least rough rigidity in their regime-related payoff matrix will commit to one regime. In that sense, time horizons and discount rates are not simply an exogenous influence on choices but are themselves profoundly shaped by actors' forecasts. Actors' regime preferences are as reliable, and only as reliable, as they perceive their payoff matrix to be predictable. To foreswear exit options requires not uncertainty but on the contrary a certain type of predictability.

The effects of predictability are straightforward. When actors detect high variance or unpredictability in political outcomes under regime alternatives, a reversal (or more than one) of the matrix representing payoffs from democracy and authoritarianism is readily plausible. For example, rightists who perceive high degrees of variance in political outcomes in a democracy know not only that safety, property, and religious institutions may be protected but also that they could just as easily be threatened as political events unfold. If they perceive political outcomes under the most likely

12. Przeworski (1991).

authoritarian alternative as similarly unpredictable, they can know their present regime preferences but not their future ones. As a result, they have incentives to "hedge" against a possible reversal of the matrix and a switch in their regime preferences. The chances for commitment to democracy are enhanced by any events or factors that *predictably* (and not merely temporarily) reduce actors' expected payoffs from authoritarian rule or *predictably* increase expected payoffs from democracy. For their payoff matrix to be roughly rigid, actors must calculate that the bundle of overall political outcomes in one regime will be *predictably* closer to their preferred points than in the other regime.

Therefore uncertainty versus reliability in people's choices does not derive from any technical aspects of rational choice or game-theoretic principles but from people's contexts. "Games" are constituted by their rules, which identify the players, their available options, and the expected payoffs from combinations of them, and are at Nash equilibrium when payoffs are structured in such a way that no actor has an incentive unilaterally to change his or her strategy. However, changes in either actors' basic preferences or their (beliefs about) expected payoffs can cause changes in their choices. Where could such change emanate from? Michael Taylor emphasizes (regarding a specific game) that some discussions are limited by the assumption of staticness and that "a more realistic description of reality would require a *changing* payoff matrix," which is often "the result of influences external to the game."[13] The fact that rational choice is agnostic on the question of continuity or change in actors' payoffs means that the task of determining degrees of continuity and reliability into the future in their choices (if we hold their basic preferences and available strategies constant) requires a focus on degrees of continuity in those aspects of their contexts that structure their expected payoffs. To arrive at parsimonious conclusions about these aspects of their contexts entails stylizing the contexts. In most rational choice accounts, people's broader contexts are treated on an ad hoc basis, but Douglass North and others have used the rationalist framework to identify certain aspects of contexts (such as transaction costs) that shape the choices and behavior they are attempting to explain.[14] In our case, we must shift analysis to actors' forecasts of at least rough rigidity in the matrix representing payoffs from democracy and authoritarian rule. What conditions cause actors to forecast rough rigidity in the regime-related payoff matrix? Max Weber's discussion about the role that "predictability" plays in long-term capital investment provides a valuable starting point for our analysis, which will lead us to sort contexts into

13. Taylor (1987: 107).
14. North (1990).

democracies in which the right perceives high versus low risks to their core interests and values.

Risk, Long-Term Investment, and Commitment

Max Weber and others have argued that central to the history of capitalism is capital-holders' assessments of the political risks to which (nonsalvageable) long-term capital investments are exposed, such as expropriation or confiscation of either the investment or the income it produces. Weber argued that long-term investments are safe from political risk only if political and juridical practices are characterized by a high degree of "calculability" or "predictability," by which Weber meant low probabilities that rulers will exploit them in a predatory fashion. Two aspects of Weber's analysis are important for our purposes. First, Weber limited his discussion to the effects of risk on long-term investment, leaving implicit—but necessarily implied—that investors have the alternative of safely holding assets in more liquid forms with returns perhaps not as attractive as those from a successful long-term investment but also not as low as those resulting from any expropriation or other catastrophic loss of such an investment. Second, investors calculate political risks of long-term investment by assessing the likely behavior of the actor with the power to impinge the most on property and income: the ruler. In Weber's words, "[T]he patrimonial state lacks the political and procedural *predictability*, indispensable for capitalist development, which is provided by the rational rules of modern bureaucratic administration. Instead we find unpredictability and inconsistency on the part of court and local officials, and variously benevolence and disfavor on the part of the ruler and his servants."[15]

If capital-holders perceive the ruler as highly unpredictable—he or she might respect property rights but equally plausibly might expropriate them, impose confiscatory taxes, or tolerate bandits or other subsovereign predators—the investment situation appears ominous. Payoffs from long-term investment *might* be superior to those of retaining liquid assets but might just as easily fall below them. Without even rough rigidity in their investment-related payoff matrix, investors logically would hedge against risk, preferring investments that require only provisional participation, such as businesses with minimal up-front investment and short-term profits. In contrast, investors could become convinced, for whatever reasons, that

15. Weber (1978/1920: 237–40, 1095) suggests that corruption at constant levels will not inhibit investment, and pointed out that investment will be deterred by rigid (and thus predictable) feudal rules that severely restrict "acquisitive activity and the development of markets." Callaghy (1988) interprets "predictability" largely in terms of low risks of severe loss.

the range of the ruler's likely behavior does not include predatory exploitation. Then, perceived political risks are low. In sum, investors have to ask a situation-specific question concerning what game theorists term the future "type" of the ruler: is it plausible that the ruler will adopt very threatening policies toward (one's) property? Understanding this, rulers attempting to encourage long-term investment have offered assurances over their behavior. But not all steps taken with the aim of reducing perceived risks have that effect because investors are aware that the sovereign is not bound by precedent, promises, or contracts. Douglass North and Paul Thomas and E. L. Jones argue that European monarchs had to develop reputations for not expropriating property or goods, levying confiscatory taxes, debasing currencies, or repudiating public debts. Developing such a reputation was difficult when many had past records of, for example, reneging on loans. Issues of credibility play a comparable role in the experiences of Latin American economic reformers attempting to promote investment in the 1980s and 1990s. A similar line of reasoning sheds light on hedging in the form of capital flight, currency hedging, and insurance policies.[16]

The analysis of the right's commitment to democracy can be organized around these concepts. Actors perceive their regime-related payoff matrix as plastic or labile (and not rigid) when they perceive high degrees of variance or variability in payoffs from each regime.[17] If we assume that actors' basic preferences are stable, then perceived variance in payoffs occurs as the result of perceived variance in political outcomes in democracy or under authoritarianism. *Perceived variance* refers to the amplitude of the range in which actors expect outcomes to fall: it concerns not the actual distribution of outcomes known after the fact, but actors' present information about the degree of predictability of future events. Variance can assume values ranging from extremely high (when actors believe nearly anything can plausibly happen and predictions of almost any kind are impossible) to extremely low (when actors are highly confident that outcomes will lie within a narrow if perhaps diffusely bounded range).[18] Actors perceive variance as low when at a minimum they can confidently exclude certain outcomes (and hence certain levels of payoffs) as highly implausible.

Actors commit to democracy when they forecast that expected payoffs from democracy are predictably generally higher than those from author-

16. North and Thomas (1973), Jones (1981: 92), Maxfield (1989: 84), Mahon (1996: 162–66).

17. Since payoffs are measured by the distance between actors' most-preferred points and actual political outcomes, variance in payoffs is generated by variance in that distance.

18. The greater the level of variance, the greater the amplitude of expected political outcomes around the expected average.

itarianism—in other words, when they believe their well-being and safety are predictably better secured in democracy. Under what conditions will they make this forecast? Posing that question is as far as rational choice principles can take us, since those principles, while moving us a substantial distance, cannot tell us which types of events (if any) can lead to rough rigidity in actors' regime-related payoff structures. Instead, we must examine regimes and their contexts in more theoretically and historically grounded terms. Weber's reasoning concerning the conditions for commitment to long-term investment provides a valuable starting point for that examination as well as a close parallel for the line of argument I advance in the remainder of this chapter. That argument can be summarized here. Democratization theorists have emphasized several factors that reduce the right's expected payoffs from authoritarian projects or predictably raise their payoffs from democracy, or both, and they have connected these factors to (trends in) regime outcomes. In this chapter I argue that these factors *can* influence expected payoffs and hence regime preferences. But they can do so only on a basis actors perceive as temporary, and therefore they can induce *provisional* support for democracy. But they cannot influence expected payoffs in ways actors perceive as predictable and therefore cannot create commitment to democracy or democratic consolidation.

I make this argument in two steps. First, events that reduce the right's expected payoffs from authoritarianism have only limited effects because the right in modern Western Europe has always had a viable, if often mediocre, authoritarian option. For these actors in this region and time period, authoritarianism has played a role parallel to that played by liquidity or short-term investments for Weber's capital-holders. If the modern European right has neither been deprived of the authoritarian option nor confronted predictably prohibitively low payoffs from it, the right commits to democracy only if risks in democracy are low—in other words, if conservatives perceive political outcomes in democracy as predictably unthreatening. If political outcomes in democracy appear highly unpredictable, then the best plausible political outcomes under democracy may well be more attractive to rightists than those expected under authoritarian rule (in which case they prefer democracy) but democracy's worst plausible outcomes are less attractive to them than authoritarianism's (in which case they prefer authoritarianism). In these circumstances rightists will not have deterministic incentives to defect from democracy, but it leaves them able to know their present but not their future regime preferences. They have incentives to hedge. In contrast, when risks in democracy are low, that becomes the *predictably* better choice because democracy permits the right to secure its interests at the lowest possible level of threats

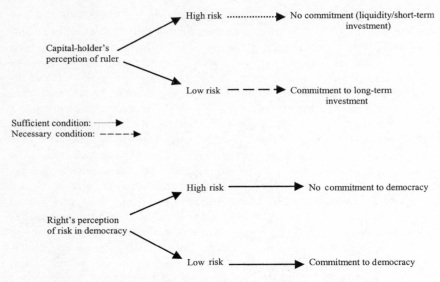

Figure 3.1 Weber's Investment Decision and Commitment to Democracy

to their safety. Then, authoritarianism at best can generate policies comparable to those the right expects in democracy anyway, and cannot compensate rightists for the risks of repression and conflict that authoritarianism inevitably imposes, however low these may be.

The parallel between Weber's depiction of the investment decision and this claim about commitment to democracy is illustrated in Figure 3.1.

In the following sections I consider factors often understood to reduce actors' risks in democracy: power-sharing, pacts, and protective decision rules. If we integrate these contingent protections, we can more fully approximate the European right's regime-related decision-making, as diagrammed in Figure 3.2.

Locking the Right into Democracy?

> The defence of democracy must consist in making anti-democratic
> experiments too costly for those who try them.
>
> KARL POPPER, *The Open Society and Its Enemies*, 1949

A number of theorists have argued that the solution to actors' defecting from democracy lies in events that reduce their expected payoffs from

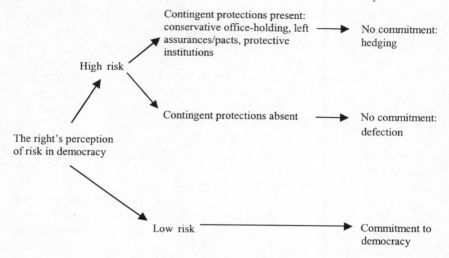

Figure 3.2 The Right's Regime Strategy

authoritarian projects. David Collier and Deborah Norden suggest that prodemocratic forces can raise the likely costs (and reduce the chances of success) of a coup attempt by aggressively monitoring conspiracies and punishing plotters, purging suspect officers, attempting to professionalize the military, and developing the organizational infrastructure of resistance. Prodemocratic international actors can reduce the right's military assets (as in Germany in 1945–49 and Haiti since 1994) or reduce expected payoffs from an authoritarian project by credibly threatening to impose sanctions in the event of a coup. Other theorists have argued that structural change can have the same effect. Theda Skocpol argues that the resistance of the British upper classes to middle-class demands for enfranchisement was hampered by the concentration of the state's coercive resources in naval forces unsuitable for internal repression. Göran Therborn, Dietrich Rueschemeyer, Evelyne Huber Stephens, and John Stephens, and Ruth Collier argue more generally that "[c]apitalist development is associated with the rise of democracy primarily because of two structural effects": it weakens politically antidemocratic landowners and "strengthens the working class" by encouraging the development of dense networks of workers' organizations. These claims suggest either that the "supply" of conservative authoritarian projects can be restricted or that "demand" can be undermined by conservatives' perceptions of adverse policies under authoritarian rule, severe international sanctions, or, perhaps especially, high levels of authoritarian repression or regime/opposition violence. O'Donnell argues that such developments can render authoritarian rule "too uncertain or risky for them, although they may prefer it in principle"—that is, in the absence of these specific costs.[19]

There is little doubt that these devices and conditions can affect expected payoffs sufficiently to induce prodemocratic regime preferences under certain circumstances. Examples include the very weak position the German right found itself in in 1918–19 and the calculatory context created for Haiti's economic and military elite by the severe sanctions and threat of invasion by the international community in 1993–94. But these devices and conditions can induce the right to *commit* to democracy only if they lead rightists to calculate that an authoritarian project is *predictably* not viable or that expected payoffs from such a project are *predictably* prohibitively low. In modern Western Europe (and arguably in most of Latin America) this is unlikely to be the case, for two reasons. For these reasons, rightists in modern Europe have rarely been deprived for long of a viable authoritarian option, and their expected payoffs from authoritarian rule, while perhaps fluctuating substantially in the short term, have never been predictably low.

First, the costs of authoritarian projects, rather than being uniquely determined by prodemocratic forces or fixed by "structural" conditions, are instead flexible and subject to competitive influence, especially by what may be termed exclusionary entrepreneurs on the right. Short-term crafting not only can create high barriers to coups but also can be "uncrafted" by both routine events and deliberate actions. Surveillance by prodemocratic governments fluctuates in extent and intensity and is often relaxed both when plots are rare and when rumors are so rife it is difficult to tell which if any should be taken seriously. Prodemocratic forces undergo periods of organizational disruption and distraction. International actors often weaken in their resolve to maintain and enforce sanctions. And exclusionary entrepreneurs, instead of remaining passive objects of prodemocratic crafting of this kind, frequently recuperate access to at least portions of professionalized militaries, laboriously reconstruct networks of conspiracy after investigation and exposure, pry at unity among prodemocratic groups, and circumvent international pariah status.

Second, the right in particular has repeatedly demonstrated a capacity to convert its structural advantages into superior coercive power. "Structural" barriers to exclusion are unlikely literally to prohibit the right from imposing authoritarian rule or make these costs predictably prohibitively high. There is something incongruous in referring to effective "structural" barriers to the right, whose defining characteristic is structural superiority.

---

19. Collier and Norden (1992: 236), Skocpol (1973: 22), Therborn (1977), Rueschemeyer, Stephens, and Stephens (1992: 58), Collier (1999), O'Donnell (1992a: 22).

Events that temporarily locked rightists into democracy thus typically provoked arms races that the right was favored to win, and did win. For example, few times in modern Europe has the right been as weak as in Germany after 1918, when the landed aristocracy was vastly weakened, left movements developed gargantuan national organizations, and the Allies fixed the army at only one hundred thousand lightly armed men and implicitly threatened to renew sanctions or hostilities in the event of authoritarian restoration. Yet within a short time, right-oriented paramilitary forces were prevalent, and by the early 1930s left power proved no match for massive exclusionary projects based on conservative middle-class support.

The enduring coercive superiority of the Western European right is indicated more systematically by the region's broader twentieth-century record. It is not simply that the left never overthrew a rightist authoritarian regime, as O'Donnell and Schmitter suggest: "no transition can be forced purely by opponents against a regime which maintains the cohesion, capacity, and disposition to apply repression."[20] Just as consistently,

- the left never successfully imposed an authoritarian regime of its own;
- whenever the left organized around a radical agenda, the result was a united right actively considering an authoritarian option; and
- (most important for our purposes) the left never successfully prevented a coup attempt organized by such a united right.

As we will see, leaders and commentators on the left often recognized the expanded options that the right possessed as a result of this underlying and enduring power imbalance. As one Spanish Socialist leader, Javier Solana, put it in the early 1980s, "[T]he Spanish right has shown that it can live very well under both authoritarian and democratic regimes, while the left can only survive within a democratic framework."[21] Conservatives did not always "live very well" under authoritarian rule, but as I show in Chapters 4 through 7, in no case in twentieth-century Western Europe has the right more than temporarily lacked the capability to translate economic and institutional resources into superior coercive capabilities. As a result, rightists could predict that authoritarianism consistently represented at least a mediocre option, never unattainable for long periods of time and generating broadly conservative economic policies while presenting them with modest risks of repression, opposition civil violence, and international sanctions.

---

20. O'Donnell and Schmitter (1986: 21); also Di Palma (1990: 37).
21. Share (1985: 92).

The record also does not sustain the more modest claim that high and rising costs of excluding the left rendered authoritarianism, if not impossible, at least decreasingly cost beneficial. If it had done so, levels of rightist commitment to democracy should vary with the left/right power balance. As we will see, this is not the case. In brief, the most prominent shift in levels of the right's commitment to democracy occurred from the interwar period, when a number of rightist sectors either hedged in democracy or backed authoritarian projects, to the post-1945 period, when the right in most cases committed to democracy. To explain this shift, a focus on power balances would suggest either that rightist forces such as agrarian elites were strong in the interwar period but weak after 1945, that working-class organizations were relatively weaker in the interwar period but strengthened substantially after 1945, or both. These claims are not persuasive. In many cases, it was during the interwar period that working-class organizational membership achieved what would prove to be historic peaks, leading many to conclude, in Mark Mazower's words, that the left was "never again as strong as in 1918–19."[22] And by the interwar period traditional agrarian elites were already profoundly weakened, as David Blackbourn and Geoff Eley emphasize even regarding the German case. As a result of this constellation of forces, interwar rightist exclusionary entrepreneurs offered viable exit options only by mobilizing unprecedented middle-class power. In other words, the costs of excluding the left were already extremely high in the interwar period, yet many rightist sectors nevertheless proved to be either unreliable democrats or pro-authoritarian. The transition to the post-1945 period reveals no sharp change in this power balance. Broad middle-class sectors remained intact. Postwar militaries if anything intensified their monopoly on coercive resources and generally retained distinctly antirevolutionary political orientations. And union power generally did not rise substantially.

A number of cases experienced what O'Donnell and Schmitter described as a postliberation "popular upsurge" in union membership, but this typically was followed by a slump, in many cases roughly to interwar levels and in several cases to *below* interwar levels, as shown in Table 7.3. Nor did rightist regime strategies after 1945 vary with the substantial variations in union strength across time and countries in postwar Europe. While there can be no doubt that excluding the left in postwar France, Italy, Germany, or France or post-Franco Spain would have been terribly costly, there is no evidence that it would have been any more costly—that a right united in that purpose would have been in command of fewer of the necessary resources—than between the wars. Yet in France, Germany, and Britain and

---

22. Blackbourn and Eley (1984), Mazower (1998: 24).

also Italy and Spain beginning in the late 1970s, conservatives did not even attempt to organize the coercive power needed to exclude the left.[23] Either crafted or "structural" barriers to coups have effects on political outcomes under authoritarianism too contingent or unpredictable to lead rightists to perceive a rigid payoff matrix and commit to democracy.

High- versus Low-Risk Democracies

If events cannot predictably reduce the right's expected payoffs from authoritarianism, commitment to democracy requires that the right anticipate predictably low risks that threatening political outcomes will occur in democracy. Under such conditions, democracy would be not the right's provisionally but its predictably better choice, since it would predictably offer the right protection of its core policy interests *and* the lowest possible levels of risks to safety. The right would lack incentives, not only in the present but also in the future, to defect from democracy and therefore would have no incentives to hedge against the risk of a reversal in its own regime preferences. The key difference, then, is between political contexts in which the right perceives democracy as low versus high risk.

Only one overarching development can lead the right to perceive democracy as predictably unthreatening or low risk. Just as Weber's capital-holders assessed the risks of long-term investments by forecasting the likely future behavior of the sovereign, the right—in order to estimate political risks in democracy—must assess the likely behavior of the people who ultimately make major policy decisions in democracy: that regime's "decision body," the electorate, operating through parties, representatives, and decision rules. Conservatives must extend the question, "Democracy with whom?" to scrutinize the likely *future* political behavior (or the future "type") of the left half of the electorate and party spectrum. When they engaged in such scrutiny, European conservatives mimicked the behavior Charles Tilly describes in a distinct (though not unrelated) context, in which people "scanned contentious events for political messages . . . interpreted the readiness of participants to commit themselves and to risk harm as signs

23. Comparable conclusions could be reached for the English case in an earlier era. Skocpol (1973) claims that English upper classes accepted inclusion in a context in which they lacked continental-style land armies. But Silver's (1971) data on debate over the 1832 reform bill leave the impression that elites were willing to commit resources to land forces *if*, in the words of William IV, "any augmentation of our military force should be considered necessary." This is consistent with Barrington Moore's (1966: 32, 444) claim that British land forces remained modest because while a strategy of mass militarization was feasible, elites judged it unnecessary. The same applies to the intraelite disputes over bureaucratic organization on which Silver focuses.

Example. In France from the 1880s until 1914, democratic political processes consistently generated parliaments dominated by parties of the center-right and center-left. Diverse socialists averaged less than 10 percent of the vote while the misleadingly named Radicals joined conservatives in the defense of private property, limitation of welfare-state measures, and control of union activities. As such, even the "worst" plausible events in democracy—center-left governments sincerely pursuing their agenda—generated policies regarding the basic political economy relatively close to those preferred by conservatives. Even the most favorable authoritarian regime could offer only modest improvements in policies while inevitably imposing at least modest risks of repression and regime/opposition violence. The right's expected payoffs from democracy were not only higher than those from authoritarianism but also predictably higher; its payoff matrix was roughly rigid. Consequently, conservative republicanism attracted the great bulk of right-of-center votes, while antidemocratic rightist parties and movements attracted only marginal electoral support and membership. But by the mid and late interwar period, a profound transformation on the left meant that electoral alternation entailed very different risks for the right. In 1928, the left coalition won over 50 percent of the vote, of which two-thirds was socialist or communist; in 1936, these numbers were 57 percent and three-fourths, respectively. Workers' organizations began to pose increasingly acute challenges to owners and employers' core interests. Conservatives began to express extensive fears of protorevolutionary threats and further radicalization by the left, especially when the 1936 general strike seemed to reveal widespread support by workers for direct action. In this context, conservatives could expect overall political outcomes to be more advantageous in democracy *if* conservatives or centrist parties won elections or *if* the left was in office but limited itself to moderate policies. But conservatives might prefer the most likely (broadly conservative) authoritarian regime in the event of such routine events in democracy as left parties winning office and sincerely pursuing their agendas, which many rightists believed included legislative assaults on property and income. Expected payoffs from democracy could plausibly be higher *or* lower than those from authoritarianism. Because rightists' payoff structures were no longer rigid, they could know their present but not their future regime preferences. They began to hedge by supporting diverse antileftist paramilitary organizations.

concerning the probability of new struggles for power, or new outcomes for old struggles for power. Open contention produced information about the intentions and capacities" of different groups.[24] If rightists perceive that the left is currently moderate but in the foreseeable future easily could switch to support highly threatening policies or civil violence, then rightists cannot predict with confidence whether their safety, property rights, fiscal and monetary orthodoxy, and traditional religious institutions will be protected in democracy or whether they will be threatened.

If this is correct, conservative commitment to democracy in modern Europe is based on the reliable narrowing of the left/right political spectrum, which ensured that outcomes in democracy were never highly threatening to conservatives regardless of election results and the presence or absence of pacts or protective institutional designs. In Chapters 4 through 7 I describe this narrowing, a process that was neither linear nor uninterrupted, just as European economies "neither modernised nor industrialised uniformly."[25] A simple periodization is not possible. While 1945 is usefully employed as a pivot point for heuristic purposes, it is empirically flawed. Reliable prodemocratic regime preferences emerged in France during the "golden" period of the Third Republic and in Britain in the late 1920s and 1930s, while segmental support for authoritarianism endured in Iberia well after 1945. Nor does the decline in the right's political risks in democracy appear to fulfill a teleology, since the French case shows that risk can rise from low levels, transforming a once-committed right into one that had incentives to hedge, just as investment conditions degenerated in some historical cases before recovering at later points. In fact, nonlinearity and nonsynchronization are valuable because variations in risk are crucial to demonstrating the causal influence of this factor.

In the rest of this chapter I conceptually sort democracies into two categories—high and low risk—that is, categories in which the right perceived the left as unpredictable versus predictably moderate. This dichotomous categorization parallels the emphasis of transitions theorizing on the utility of distinguishing between hard- versus soft-liners in authoritarian regimes. O'Donnell and Schmitter remark that the "Left too is likely to be divided into equivalents of soft-line and hard-line factions," although this has not been a major focus for theorizing.[26] A dichotomous sorting does not suggest that rightist perceptions of the left operated in only two modes or were otherwise simplistic. European rightists often appreciated that

24. Tilly (1986: 386).
25. Jones (1981: 104).
26. O'Donnell and Schmitter (1986: 63).

workers and left movements and parties were internally complex, and often were concerned precisely with whether left moderates or radicals had the upper hand. When rightists saw the left as unpredictable, this was either because they believed the whole left was potentially radical or because control of the left was contested and radicals were potential leaders. But the effect of rightists' forecasts is most visible when the contrast between risk levels is stark, and a dichotomous sorting helps to make sense of enormous detail and nuanced variation. Nor does this sorting produce a circular logic: evidence that rightists are hedging is not used as evidence that a democracy is high risk. How conservatives perceived the left can be established ex ante. The introduction to the empirical section of this book discusses measures for coding specific democracies as high or low risk.

Moreover, the notion of perceiving the left as either highly unpredictable or reliably moderate is not an abstraction but a meaningful description of sharp differences in rightists' answer to the question, "Democracy with whom?" Historically, European rightists were frequently unsure of what future political behavior to expect of workers and left movements and parties. They saw the range of possible political behaviors by the left as extremely wide and did not rule out extremely threatening behavior such as social and political violence as well as more legalistic but nonetheless radical or revolutionary agendas. These were assessments of ominousness, with severe threats perceived perhaps not in the present but as distinct possibilities in the foreseeable future. Rightists adopted different ways of describing this unpredictability. Lord Derby in 1867 was hardly the only one to refer to enfranchisement as "a leap in the dark"; others referred to anarchy or workers' psychological instability, or described the sensation of standing at the edge of a political precipice. As the French conservative leader François Guizot asked in 1849, "Which of us has not shuddered at the sudden discovery of the abyss over which we live . . . the destructive legions ready to rush forth upon society as soon as its jaws are unclosed?"[27] These situations had in common that rightists perceived the left as distinctly prone to pursuing

- extensive attempts to overturn the society's property regime, targeting not only the very largest holdings but also smaller (including much middle-class) productive property, either via expropriation or even compensated seizure, since the funds needed for sweeping socialization or redistribution could only come from current owners and employers through steeply progressive and very high tax loads;

27. Guizot (1974/1849: 9).

- what would amount to an undermining of a traditional church's role in both official and unofficial public life—for example, the banning of various public ceremonies, prohibitions on all church-related education, and attempts to harass, expel, or "unauthorize" the clergy as a whole; and
- possibly substantial civil violence against rightists.

Concluding that the left was fundamentally unpredictable or highly susceptible to radicalization required conservatives to develop what amounted to "theories" of political behavior by the workers and the left. Gustave Le Bon described the "extreme mobility of the opinions" of crowds—the "variability of their sentiments"—which by the early twentieth century were largely synonymous in rightist minds with workers and the poor, including landless agricultural laborers and poor peasants. Albert Hirschman has schematically analyzed comparable perceptions of workers, and Louis Chevalier analyzed them in detail in France and Don Herzog in Britain.[28] Rightists also argued that Marxism and other ideologies caused workers to harbor medium- and longer-term agendas of revolution even while acting reformist and legalistic at the moment. Finally, often, rightists explained leftist orientations in terms of social structure, arguing that workers and landless laborers were potentially revolutionary because they were economically desperate and lacked the inner (and social) stability that conservatives believed was engendered by property ownership. These explanations obviously are not incompatible. In fact, sometimes they overlapped and converged on an assessment that a radical threat was a distinct possibility in the foreseeable future. Such perceptions are not simply artifacts of famously ideological periods of European history and endured well after 1945 in Italy and outside Europe (an issue I address in Chapter 8).

However, in other circumstances European rightists calculated very differently, forecasting that workers and left movements were predictably moderate, very likely to

- oppose all forms of civil violence;
- pursue economic policies no more threatening than a welfare state and possibly nationalization of the very largest business concerns (or in some cases, the property of defined segments of the aristocracy); or
- pursue policies toward traditional religious institutions no more threatening than disestablishment of an official religion and perhaps the curtailing of public subsidies for the clergy.

28. Le Bon (1918: 24, 119, 131), Hirschman (1991), Chevalier (1958), Herzog (1998). Le Bon followed this with a study of the psychology of socialism.

Similarly, this is not a perception distinctive to one period, in this case advanced industrial Western Europe. In late-nineteenth-century France, such beliefs were a crucial element in the right's commitment to democracy. While historic conservative disdain for workers and the poor has been amply documented, this crucial shift in perceptions lacks a chronicler. Here, too, conservatives often invoked "theories" to explain the likely political behavior of the left in general and workers in particular. Conservatives in early Third Republic France frequently emphasized widespread rural property ownership, and those in Britain, a distinct national political culture. In Germany after the late 1940s, left moderation was often portrayed as one of many consequences of unprecedented prosperity combined with the profound trauma of dictatorship and war. Three decades later, Spanish conservatives believed profound class change and the welfare state eroded the historic social bases of revolutionary socialism. In this text, I am agnostic on both the causes of left behavior in Europe and the reasons why European conservatives explained it in the diverse ways they did. I am concerned solely with the effects of these conservative perceptions or beliefs on the right's strategies toward democracy.

A focus on these perceptions does not revive the classic proposition that polarization causes democratic breakdown while "consensus" leads to stability. First, whereas that classic formulation deterministically relates degrees of polarization to regime preferences, the claim here does not. As I highlight in the next section, when rightists perceive democracy as high risk, they have incentives not to defect but simply to hedge against the *potential* for left radicalization—that is, not to commit to democracy. Second, many traditional discussions subsume support for democratic procedures into the concept of "consensus," making a posited causal relationship between consensus and democratic support tautological.[29] Here, the two are clearly delineated. When the spectrum representing preferences over state policies and other political outcomes is predictably compact, significant segments will reliably prefer democratic to authoritarian rules of the game.

Devices for Raising Payoffs from Democracy

A number of transitions theorists have argued influentially that potential defectors can be inspired to remain loyal to democracy by devices that in effect raise their expected payoffs from democracy, in this case either by raising the right's chances of "winning" in democracy or by lowering the

29. Dahl (1956: 132–33) does not conflate these issues.

costs of losing. Office-holding, pacts and assurances, and protective institutional designs are prominent examples. Insofar as these devices have prevented democratic breakdowns, they are impressive and valuable. But they cannot lead rightists to perceive risks in democracy as *predictably* low so long as the right believes the left is fundamentally unpredictable. They cannot have this effect because these devices cannot effectively bind a radicalized electorate; instead each is a likely target of competitive or revisionist efforts when major political groupings have acute policy differences, as several theorists have noted. Consequently, conservatives have perceived each of these devices as themselves unreliable even when available. Assessing risks in democracy requires the right to look beyond office-holding, pacts, and institutions and to pose the system-specific question, "Democracy with whom?" As a result, these devices do not undermine the incentives to hedge possessed by rightists who perceive the left as fundamentally unpredictable. While potentially valuable for stabilizing an uncertain democracy, they cannot cause its consolidation.

Power-Sharing or Office-Holding

> A *coup d'etat* is something done by those who find themselves in the minority.
>
> José María Gil Robles, Spanish Catholic party leader, 1935

Actors' expectations about likely outcomes can be influenced substantially by which parties hold office. Consociational theorizing portrays grand coalitions as the central means of reducing groups' real and perceived risks in conditions of ethnic, linguistic, or religious conflict. Similarly, O'Donnell and Schmitter suggest that "the Right-Center and Right must be 'helped' to do well" in founding elections or granted positions disproportionate to their winnings, in order to ease their fears during transitions.[30] Rightist parties also may achieve electoral success under their own steam. If rightists control political outcomes in democracy, they do not have a problem for which relocating power to an authoritarian leadership would represent a solution, which is why antidemocratic movements nearly always appeal to minoritarian segments.

But as results of transitions studies have repeatedly indicated, election results are impermanent; Linz describes democracy as "government pro tempore."[31] Parties are well aware of the contingency of office-holding,

---

30. O'Donnell and Schmitter (1986: 62).
31. Linz (1998).

which helps explain why elections take on apocalyptic tones in polarized democracies. Office-holding via either an election victory or an agreement for power-sharing is unpredictable over anything beyond the short term. Events are least predictable in cases of power-sharing grand coalitions, since the invitation to join may have been the result of only short-term constraints, and continuing cooperation is not binding on any partner. In this regard, the frequent failure of oversized coalitions may be as important in its consequences as in its causes. Outright election victories by center-right or rightist parties create mandates lasting up to several years, but even then the duration of risk reduction is defined by the term of tenure, beyond which expected political outcomes become as high risk as the electorate is perceived to be, shortening time horizons as each election approaches. When highly threatening outcomes in democracy are held at bay only by office-holding, rightists retain incentives to hedge. The situation might be somewhat less risky if conservatives forecast that they are highly likely to win elections indefinitely. But of the cases discussed here, only in Italy during the 1950s to 1980s could participants confidently expect the left to be shut out of national office for at least two future mandates. More important, such a forecast requires system-specific information and invests causal influence on levels of risk not in office-holding but in the relative popularity of specific parties and the likely makeup of specific coalitions.

Pacts and Assurances

> In democracies, the rich should be spared.
>
> ARISTOTLE, *Politics*

Theorizing suggests that two crafted devices can reduce the risks actors associate with democracy by reducing not their chances but the costs of losing. The first is variously termed *garantismo*, pacts, or assurances of moderation. Terry Karl, O'Donnell and Schmitter, and John Higley and Richard Gunther argue that rightists who formerly backed coups have agreed to inclusion due to pacts and assurances.[32] It was in this spirit that Adolphe Thiers warned left and center-left deputies at the founding of the French Third Republic that "the Republic will be conservative or it will not exist at all."[33] If credible, assurances can lead potential defectors to predict that highly threatening outcomes are unlikely at least for as long as the promise obtains, undercutting any interest they might have had in relocating

32. Karl (1997), O'Donnell and Schmitter (1986), Higley and Gunther (1992).
33. Thompson (1946: 83).

decision-making to sympathetic authoritarian rulers. *Garantismo* is especially attractive because it is susceptible to short-term crafting; assurances can even be extended unilaterally without negotiations or even formal dialogue.

But assurances have the vice of their virtues. Since they are not binding and can be reneged on with impunity, recipients of political promises frequently have seen them as unreliable so long as they perceive the promise-maker as fundamentally unpredictable. This is the heart of Przeworski's critique of pacts. Because democracy permits ongoing contestation, it cannot guarantee any specific "substantive compromise" over policy. Parallels drawn from business and economics transplant poorly into regime matters. Unlike business, regime matters concern the rules of the sovereign political game; control of the regime involves the power to determine exactly what is binding and what is not. As Przeworski puts it, "[T]he Leviathan—an externally enforced cooperative agreement—is not democracy."[34] Entering into a binding contract or ceding control in other ways (offering someone "hostages" or "burning your bridges") binds actors' behavior regardless of possible changes in their preferences. But while the term *pact* connotes an enforceable contract of some kind, the promises are unilateral without any mechanism for preventing actors from reconstruing or violating them ex post, in the same sense that the "power to leave the wilderness is also the power to return" to it.[35] Even the judiciary cannot serve as a predictable guarantor in high-conflict political situations, since both judges' powers and the laws they enforce are shaped by ongoing political contestation and decision-making. *Garantismo* is no guarantee at all.

Rightists in a specific situation may conclude that the left will honor a given promise. But this assessment requires system-specific information, specifically concerning the left's likely future behavior, making clear that it is the left's future "type" and not the promise itself that is the guarantor. Recipients therefore tend to interpret assurances in one of three ways in high-risk democracies. First, the right at times has rejected assurances as noncredible on their face.[36] Second, they have concluded that while assurances are currently valid, they encapsulate a strategic misrepresentation of the left's "real" goals and are extended only because *current* political conditions do not favor radical agendas. They thus cannot be relied on to last longer than those conditions. Third, rightists have concluded that left leaders and negotiators, however sincere, may not be able to command

34. Przeworski (1986: 59–60; 1991: 22–23).
35. Grafstein (1991: 262). In economics, see Williamson (1983).
36. Allende's offer to include centrists in his cabinet in July 1973, like the Spanish Popular Front's proposals to moderate in July 1936, was dismissed.

their rank-and-file over time. For example, Samuel Huntington describes the contingency that characterized many amnesties offered to former military rulers.[37] Assurances over outcomes in democracy create a game in which the right's regime preferences remain a conditional or best-reply strategy, determined by whether or not the left honors its promises. The empirical record raises doubts of its own. No significant political pacts were present to explain the development and then renewal of conservative commitments to democracy in the long decades after 1945.

Protective Institutions

> In themselves, technical changes in the form of government do not
> make a nation vigorous or happy or valuable. . . . Perhaps it is
> regrettable that such bourgeois and prosaic matters . . . can be
> important at all. But this is the way things are.
>
> MAX WEBER, "Parliament and Government in a
> Reconstructed Germany," 1917–18

Finally, it has been argued that protective formal institutions—at the level of translating votes into seats and seats into decisions—can create a predictable payoff matrix favoring democracy. Recent transitions theorizing has suggested that proportional representation and parliamentarism favor democratic stability by ensuring that minorities retain enhanced blocking power and chances for turnover and entry into office.[38] Przeworski argues that loss-limiting designs "reduce the stakes of political battles," possibly enough to "make even losing under democracy more attractive than a future under nondemocratic alternatives." He concludes that democracies that constitutionalize loss limitation have a better chance to "last for a long time," and "solutions to the problem of democratization consist of institutions." Przeworski argues that institutions are capable of achieving this precisely because they overcome the weakness he identifies in pacts; they shape political decisions whoever is in office and whatever their program. As John Stuart Mill suggested, "All trust in constitutions is grounded on the assurance they may afford, not that the depositaries of power will not, but that they *cannot*, misemploy it." These solutions are also attractive because they, too, are highly susceptible to deliberate crafting; Giuseppe Di Palma celebrates the fact that "rules are adaptable."[39]

37. Huntington (1991: 211–31).
38. Linz and Valenzuela (1994), O'Donnell and Schmitter (1986: 59–61).
39. Mill (1958/1861: 128), emphasis added; Przeworski (1988; 1991: 30–33, 36, 39), Di Palma (1990: 129).

But adaptability exposes institutions to the same critique Przeworski levels against pacts. A protective design *predictably* reduces risks only if actors assume that a given set of institutions is likely to remain in place once installed. Formal political institutions fail this condition for the same reason they are attractive to crafters to begin with: actors can feasibly (re)design them to disperse losses and also can (re)redesign them at a later date to concentrate losses. This action is permissible because while each democracy must have some set of representative institutions, none is definitional to democracy, as Schmitter and Karl remind us.[40] Pacts cannot guarantee a "substantive compromise" over policies, but democracy also cannot guarantee "institutional agreements" because these, too, are contested and overturned frequently enough via institutional revision. To paraphrase Przeworski, any mechanism that rendered a given set of decision rules unchangeable would function as a Leviathan which "is not democracy."

This potential for redesign is not merely hypothetical, and the right has repeatedly demonstrated an awareness of the contingency of specific designs. Not surprisingly, actors either protected or blocked by existing decision rules have regularly battled over them with the knowledge that their survival was anything but predictable. As I show in the following chapters, almost all important political conflicts in twentieth-century European democracies included challenges to existing decision rules; such dynamics are also apparent beyond Western Europe.[41] Jack Knight's analysis of institutions helps us to understand why this is so. He argues that institutions are in large part the result of conflicts between groups engaged in distributional disputes, "a product of the efforts of some to constrain the actions of others with whom they interact." While there are costs to altering institutions, groups whose agendas are blocked by existing rules also bear costs of retaining them in their present form and can develop an interest in revision.[42] Consequently, institutions are path-dependent in the weak sense that how they are is affected by how they were in the past, but not in the stronger sense that they are challenged or changed only in extraordinary circumstances. This is true even when designs are loss (and hence

40. Schmitter and Karl (1991).
41. Skidmore (1967: 211–23) describes the Brazilian military and conservatives' attempt to protect themselves from João Goulart's assumption of the presidency in 1961 by switching to a form of parliamentarism. Over the next two years Goulart led an equally successful referendum effort to restore presidentialism. The postcommunist Hungarian Round Table agreement that the new president would be elected by the old regime's deputies was overturned by referendum even before it went into effect.
42. Knight (1992: 14, 19). Paralleling Elster (1993), Lijphart and Waisman (1996: 246) conclude that "the evidence . . . clearly points to the preponderance of self-interested motivations . . . in the design of democratic institutions" in Latin America and Eastern Europe.

win)-minimizing, because confident or stronger players can have incentives to make them more win (and loss)-concentrating.[43]

This does not mean that actors find institutional protections meaningless. In Stephen Krasner's words, "If institutions adjusted relatively quickly to societal changes . . . there was little point in making them an object of scholarly investigation," and actors also would not struggle to install rules favorable to them. Revision often requires supermajorities, ensuring that institutions generally last longer than the consensus that fashioned them. This relative durability encourages protected actors to discount the future at a less drastic rate than if they had been protected only by office-holding or assurances. But it does not necessarily follow that "citizens can count on the basic institutional framework remaining in place over reasonably long periods."[44] First, many electoral laws can be changed by a simple majority of representatives. Second, all other institutions can be changed either by qualified majorities of representatives or by democratic electorates. The time frame for revision is often only a few years, during which time there may be no guarantee as to how long the existing rules will last and if, when, or how they will be altered. If the majority is committed to revision, a minority's protection is contingent on whether it can maintain the vote share needed to veto, converting each election into a high-stakes referendum on control of the institutional agenda.[45]

Portraying constitutional designs as once-selected-never-changed may result in large part from the study of cases in which institutional arrangements happen to have endured. But institutions in many highly stable democracies are loss-concentrating. And institutional designs frequently stabilized only *after* democracy had already been stabilized for some time. Loss-limiting formulas may help reinforce uncertain democracies, but because they can be altered, are regularly challenged, and are often redesigned, they are not sufficiently predictable to inform long-term commitment to democracy. Institutions can be the solution to many problems of democratization and democracy but not to that of consolidation.

In sum, these crafted devices and contingent events are capable of inducing provisional prodemocratic regime preferences but not commitment, because the right cannot conclude from their presence alone that highly

---

43. The argument presented in this section is developed more fully in another publication by Alexander (2001).

44. Elster (1993: 175), Krasner (1984: 243).

45. North and Weingast (1989) argue that English monarchs became constrained by an institutional design allocating taxing power to parliament. But this means that confiscatory taxation was unlikely only because lords (who, joined with monarchs, did have sufficient power to be predatory) shared core interests with many other capital-holders. Here, too, actors' policy preferences were at least as important as the design of institutions.

threatening outcomes are precluded in democracy. Even if these devices are present, the right retains incentives to hedge and not commit so long as the left is unpredictable.

Commitment in Low-Risk Democracies

> . . . all bestir themselves within certain limits which they hardly ever pass.
>
> ALEXIS DE TOCQUEVILLE, *Democracy in America*, 1840

Low Risks and Commitment to Democracy

Calculations are dramatically different when rightists perceive that radicalization by the left is highly unlikely in the foreseeable future. When this is the case, enduring conditions accomplish what crafting cannot. When the moderation of their opponents is predictable into the future, conservatives can predict that future political outcomes in democracy stand to be unthreatening even if events in democracy are at their most perilous: if the most distant major party or coalition wins a legislative majority, is determined to implement its sincerely held agenda, and is not blocked by protective institutions. Then, even the most sympathetic possible authoritarian leaders can offer conservatives only modest improvements on the state policies they expect in democracy, even while generating increases in risk to conservatives' safety as the result of repression and possibilities of regime/opponent violence. Low political risks in democracy make authoritarianism the predictably worse choice. Rightists have no incentives to hedge against risks they do not perceive to exist.

The contrast between high- and low-risk contexts is most visible at the extremes. As quasi-revolutionary politics accelerated in Spain in 1936, the Popular Front government generated state policies (including toward civil violence) so threatening that many rightists perceived military rule as a plausible (if imperfect) net improvement *if* it shifted state policies dramatically to the right *without* exposing rightists to severe repression in the process. The record and reputation of military leaders suggested that would be the case. One need not share the right's support for the 1936 coup in order to accept that *these* actors found it preferable to democracy. But it would be implausible that conservatives losing to British Labour in 1964 or 1997 or the German Social Democrats in 1969 or 1998 would make the same decision. Electoral defeats for the right in these years inevitably meant some movement in state policies away from conservative ideals. But the distance likely to be covered—the distance that an ideal authoritarian regime might recover—was simply too modest to offset the risks inherent in exclusionary rules of the game.

Gabriel Almond suggested that in a "homogeneous" (Anglo-Saxon) political culture, an election "outcome is in doubt and . . . the stakes are not too high." The view advanced here is that risks (and stakes) are low when substantive political outcomes are *not* in doubt. In a sharp departure from Przeworski's formulation, democracy consolidates when it institutionalizes uncertainty only in a technical and *not* a substantive sense, when democratic competition takes place within boundaries so circumscribed that while people may not know exactly which party, candidate, or coalition will win a given election and by what margin, they possess relatively clear ideas about the diffusely bounded (or fuzzy) range that delimits the political outcomes likely to occur regardless of who wins. The emergence of reliable regime preferences and consolidated democracies is based on the "taming of chance" in a sense somewhat different from that meant by Ian Hacking; here, it is based on a reduction in the range of political events expected to occur at all. Robert Dahl describes conditions in which "disputes over policy alternatives are nearly always disputes over a set of alternatives that have already been winnowed down to those within the broad area of basic agreement." This describes the consolidated democracies discussed in Chapters 5 through 7. In contrast, in Italy in 1919–20, Germany in 1931–32, Spain in 1936, Chile in 1973, and many other cases, major groups differed sharply on issues fundamental to political economy or religion or both.[46]

To require that actors answer the question, "Democracy with whom?" in this way—by perceiving that the political orientations of the majority of the people with whom they participate in democracy not only *do* not but also *will* not radically differ from their own—may appear to be a dangerously narrow condition for consolidation. But consolidated democracies have consistently coincided with just such a compacting of the political spectrum representing major groupings' preferences over state policy and civil violence. This does not suggest that consolidated democracies are characterized by a complete overlap in opinions, nor even the unusual elite-level "consensus" that some researchers identified in postwar Britain. The compacting chronicled in the empirical chapters in this study is that complete only when it comes to the use of civil violence, which no significant political groups in consolidated Western European democracies employ as a political or social tool.[47] Compacting is not nearly as thorough in policy

---

46. Almond (1956: 398–99), Hacking (1990), Dahl (1956: 132–33).

47. The only sustained exceptions are Basque terrorists and the Irish Republican Army (IRA).

preferences. Notable differences continue to distinguish Social from Christian Democrats and conservatives and Gaullists from Laborites and Socialists. Smaller communist and extreme-right parties contribute to the diversity of political landscapes in consolidated democracies. But it is possible to discern (indeed it is difficult not to discern) a profound compacting that has restricted the boundaries of left/right competition and ensures that diversity exists within far narrower confines than actors had used to describe spectrums in other periods or cases. This underlying compacting in Britain, for example, both preceded and postdated the period of the so-called postwar consensus. Intriguingly, the consequent reduction in political risks in democracy occurred independently of trends in risk in other arenas—for example, at a time when economic life risks were being reduced by sustained growth and the systematization of welfare states, but ranges of possible military events were vastly expanding due to the deployment of thermonuclear weapons.

This relative consensus does not include every person in the political system. Small groups are located at substantial distances from the mean, and it may be because sympathetic exclusionary entrepreneurs *could* offer these actors substantial improvements on policy that they flirt the most often with antidemocratic possibilities. But generalized compacting means these groups are statistically marginal. The erosion of potential coup constituencies has critical implications for would-be exclusionary entrepreneurs. Without even the prospect of a future coup constituency, these entrepreneurs have no incentives to develop or maintain capabilities for exiting democracy. This lack of incentives does not mean that consolidated democracies do not generate isolated putsch attempts; the Spanish plotters in 1981 either may not have realized that they needed significant segmental support or mistakenly perceived they had it. How their decision to "pronounce" can be explained is an interesting question. But it does not eclipse the fact that almost no entrepreneurs bother to seek constituencies for the overthrow of low-risk democracies.

Office-Holding, Pacts, and Institutions in Low-Risk Democracies

A low-risk democratic context means that prodemocratic regime preferences survive even if conservatives' costs from authoritarian projects are low or declining, even if rightists remain an electoral minority for long periods, even if they fail to achieve pacts or explicit left assurances of moderation, and even if institutions are (or become) less protective of the right. This conclusion solves a series of otherwise puzzling patterns in contemporary Europe. Rightists in a low-risk democracy have no incentive to exclude their opponents by force even if that could be achieved at a reasonable cost, indeed even if it could be achieved at the same or *lower* cost than when the right may have favored authoritarianism in the past. This helps to explain why several rightist sectors committed to democracy after 1945 even though the costs of excluding the left were no higher than in the interwar period and indeed in several cases were lower than before.

In the same way, crafted devices that aim to raise payoffs from democracy are also irrelevant to the right's regime support when democracy is already perceived as low risk. Significant degrees of overlap between the agendas of the major parties reduce the importance to voters of exactly which party or coalition wins each election. Jon Elster notes that "[w]hen alternatives differ very little, the agent may be indifferent between them." While most voters in low-risk democracies voters are not indifferent, they have the luxury of something approaching indifference to election results. This indifference explains why groups have preferred democracy (and not hedged) even when their most-preferred political parties have no serious prospects of winning office for long periods. The British Liberals since the 1930s, Swedish conservatives from the interwar period to the 1970s, Spanish conservatives and British Labourites throughout the 1980s, and Japanese Socialists for almost the entire postwar period combined the prospect of indefinite opposition status with complete disinterest in authoritarian alternatives. Guillermo Makin's claim that coups are the "revenge of those defeated by universal suffrage" requires supplemental conditions to apply even in high-risk democracies; it does not apply at all to low-risk democracies. Elections are nonetheless always vigorously contested, since elections remain zero-sum and even all-or-nothing games for candidates and parties, though not for voters.[48]

Similarly, cross-aisle policy agreements may speed legislation or facilitate unpopular reforms in a low-risk democracy, but they do not serve the coup-averting function assigned to pacts in transitions theorizing. Specific assurances are redundant when the right already perceives the left as predictably moderate. As Gregory Luebbert puts it, when the distance between the major parties is modest, "failure to reach a broad cross-party agreement" does not threaten the "integrity of the regime."[49] This can explain why pacts, which figure so large in democratization theorizing, are prominent

---

48. Elster (1986: 20), Makin (1983: 61). Campaign coverage in the *New York Times*, March 11, 2000, pp. 13, 29, is illustrative of this difference in vantage points. Senate candidate Hillary Clinton declared that "you could not have a starker comparison" than the one between her and Al Gore on the one hand and Rudolph Giuliani and George W. Bush on the other. The same day, an opinion columnist remarked that "[t]he substantive disputes between [Gore and Bush] are, in truth, minimal."

49. Luebbert (1986: 18).

by their absence in Europe's consolidated democracies. Finally, institutional design takes on sharply reduced importance for regime survival in low-risk democracies. When actors perceive no plausible prospects for high political risks in democracy, even loss-concentrating institutions cannot result in highly threatening policies. This solves the puzzle of why democratic support has remained strong, in defiance of the expectations of a great deal of theorizing, in the face both of existing high-stakes designs in Britain and Fifth Republic France and of institutional revision in the direction of greater win and loss concentration in early postwar Britain, France in 1958, and Italy in the 1990s.

II CASES

Introduction to Part II

Case Selection and Measuring Independent and Dependent Variables

Testing the Theory

In Chapters 4 through 7 I demonstrate that influential, competing explanatory frameworks do not provide as effective an explanation for the emergence of rightist commitment to Western Europe's major democracies as the approach developed here. My approach connects, in a falsifiable manner, actors' perceptions of degrees of political risk in democracy to their attitudes and behavior toward regime options. Changes in the structure of their expected payoffs—regarding both safety and well-being—under regime alternatives cause specific changes in actors' attitudes and behavior. When conservatives perceive the left as potentially radical or revolutionary, they hedge by seeking and maintaining privileged relationships with the military or supporting paramilitaries. Rightists abandon such hedges and become reliable supporters of democracy when they perceive the left as predictably moderate and hence associate democracy with low risks. The theory would be falsified either if conservatives were shown to have perceived that the range of plausible political outcomes in democracy included ones highly threatening to their core interests and values yet abandoned all hedges, or if they forecast very low political risks in democracy yet maintained hedges or supported an exclusionary project.

The cases and evidence presented in Chapters 4 through 7 are designed to contrast this approach with common if often implicit assumptions about regional and national political cultures, international demonstration effects (IDEs), and zeitgeists, as well as claims about the ability of pacts and institutional design to not merely stabilize but consolidate democracies. In particular, comparisons both across countries at the same time and across time in several countries are crucial in helping to arbitrate between competing assumptions about regime support. For example, claims concerning IDEs make predictions about rough chronological synchronization across space, predictions that diverge from those of the rationalist model, making it useful to test against evidence concerning homogeneity versus heterogeneity in conservative regime projects across Europe in given time periods. Entirely beside its relevance for these purposes, Spain is accorded disproportionate space due to its value as the most recent consolidator in the region—Spanish conservatives, unlike their counterparts in the other cases, were widely available for interviews. Even with the limitations discussed earlier and subsequently, interviews represent a superior source of data on actors' beliefs about regime alternatives, moving us promisingly closer to tangible process-tracing. To maximize leverage from the Spanish case, extensive primary-source research was also conducted on Spain's interwar democracy, in order to use a "most similar systems" strategy to help arbitrate between competing theories about democratic failure in the 1930s and success since the mid-1970s. Nuanced data culled from these two cases in one country even permitted testing of claims about feedback effects and other factors that might portray Spain in two time periods as "dissimilar systems."

Connecting predictions to cases required the translation of key terms into indicators that can be measured. The three minimal elements of a rational choice theory are actors' basic preferences, their beliefs about (the consequences of) available options, and their induced preferences. These are addressed in turn.

The Right's Basic Preferences

Focusing on the political right simplifies testing by holding constant one of the two independent variables: actors' basic preferences. This leaves us free to manipulate the other variable—actors' beliefs about likely outcomes under (or payoffs from) regime alternatives—to see if the predicted variations in behavior match the available empirical evidence. But can we isolate a set of actors in modern Europe with basic preferences that are sufficiently similar to warrant labeling them "the right"? Clearly the right is not a simple category. Groups commonly assigned to it have been characterized by important policy differences and have undergone notable political and organizational change across the twentieth century. However, despite Kevin Passmore's just observation that "[d]isunity is a feature of conservatism in all countries," the next four chapters focus on actors whose basic preferences are nonetheless relatively consistently concerned with personal safety, maintenance of existing private property claims and income, relatively orthodox fiscality, and (in several cases) the protection of traditional religious institutions. These basic interests proved enduring and essential to the right's coordination and action, even when rightists were also distinguished from one another by economic disputes, party-political affiliations, status issues, and religion and other cultural factors.[1] Construed in this manner, the right is no more limited to landed aristocracies or big business than the authoritarian category is limited to monarchies. Even by the first third of the twentieth century, all significant conservative political projects, democratic or authoritarian, were based much more broadly than simply on classic social elites. Exactly how far into the ranks of the middle strata the right can be said to reach in each case is debatable. For example, why sharecroppers allied with the left in some instances and the right in others is of ongoing interest. The category of "the right" necessarily remains somewhat sloppy here. But I do not believe this sloppiness is the reason why the evidence supports the predictions to a greater or lesser extent.

Measuring Actors' Beliefs about Regime Alternatives

Our second independent variable concerns actors' expectations concerning political outcomes under regime alternatives. This variable can be sorted usefully into two components: actors' perceptions of authoritarianism and their perceptions of democracy in their country. I am effectively holding constant one of these two components. In Chapter 3 I argued that, unlike their leftist counterparts, rightists in twentieth-century Western Europe typically have had a viable authoritarian alternative to democracy, one that was often mediocre but likely to protect their core interests and values. The evidence presented in subsequent chapters broadly confirms that rightists only rarely (more accurately, only temporarily) perceived a rightist-oriented authoritarian option as unavailable or prohibitively costly. As a result, the decisive influence on the right's degree of commitment to democracy is variation in the levels of political risk they perceive in democracy. And levels of perceived risk in democracy were a product of their evaluations of the potential for radicalization by the left portion of the political spectrum.

Political scientists have generated a variety of measurements for "distance" or polarization in party systems. Unfortunately these existing

1. Passmore (1997: 5).

measures are not suitable for testing the causal argument developed here. Scholars have assembled "expert" scales of left/right placement of parties, and major efforts such as that by Stefano Bartolini and Peter Mair use content analysis to measure distance between the programs of major parties. Both of these approaches concern not actors' but rather observers' beliefs about the relative position of political parties. Giacomo Sani and Giovanni Sartori and others use surveys asking voters to place themselves on a left/right spectrum. This approach focuses on actors' subjective perceptions but typically establishes voters' perceptions of the notional position of themselves (or "their" parties), not of opposing parties—in other words, not conservatives' perceptions of the left. In addition, such surveys (like expert scales) are, as Bartolini and Mair point out, "available only for certain countries and over what is a very limited period of time."[2]

Ronald Inglehart and Dusan Sidjanski and several other (generally one-country) researchers asked survey respondents to "locate" all parties in their political system. But data of this kind are available for very few cases and time periods, and the fact that (with the exception of Sani) these studies rarely segregate respondents by political sector prevents us from measuring a crucial variable: how specifically right-of-center voters perceived specifically left parties. Moreover as Sani and Sartori note, "Direct comparison of left-right scores across countries would, of course, run squarely into the relativity issue."[3] Comparisons across time do the same. We simply cannot know if Italians in the 1970s and Danes in the 1950s meant the same thing when they located parties in the 20-point to 40-point "space" on a 100-point continuum, and especially if they meant the same thing as they would have in the 1930s when such surveys, moreover, were not conducted.

Perhaps most important, my causal argument concerns actors' subjective perceptions not of *present* "distances" between parties but their beliefs about the *potential* radicalization of the left captured in the notion of "risk." The two can be very different. For example, an examination of Popular Front manifestos in France and Spain in 1936 and Italy just after World War II suggests substantial left moderation. But no serious study of these cases would suggest that conservatives perceived the left as moderate. Instead, many believed that leftist programs were a public relations tactic, misrepresenting the left's true radical intentions. In such situations, only qualitative evidence can make sense of the right's strategies. The most effective manner in which to establish the relevant beliefs of actors in such a way as

2. For example, Huber and Inglehart (1995), Bartolini and Mair (1990: 196), Sani and Sartori (1983).

3. Sani and Sartori (1983: 309, 338n9), Sani (1975), Inglehart and Sidjanski (1974).

to permit comparisons across countries and time is to seek qualitative data concerning the range of specific strategies that conservatives believed the left might plausibly pursue in democracy.

This requires, first, establishment of criteria for coding specific democracies as low versus high risk (it is worth noting that the same challenge would be posed if quantitative data were to be used: how much "distance" would qualify a system as polarized?), and second, establishment of what types of qualitative data are appropriate for assigning cases to these categories.

Criteria for Coding Cases as High versus Low Risk

Obviously European conservatives did not uniformly assign the left in their countries dichotomously to the moderate or the unpredictable categories. Inevitably, their descriptions of the left often reflected "fuzzy" rather than precise thinking. However, these categories can be delineated relatively clearly to ensure meaningful distinctions within cases and comparability across them. In the analysis that follows I assume that rightists distinguished between moderate and radical lefts by the likelihood that "the left"—whether one party, several, or more amorphous movements based in the working classes—would pursue wide-ranging threats to conservatives' core interests and values. Rightists should be understood to perceive the left as predictably moderate, and hence democracy as politically low risk, when they believed they were highly *unlikely* to confront

- notable levels of civil violence against conservatives,
- economic policies any more threatening than the progressive taxation needed to fund a welfare state and possibly nationalization of the very largest business concerns (or in some cases, of defined segments of the aristocracy), and
- policies toward traditional religious institutions any more threatening than disestablishment of the state religion and perhaps the curtailing of public subsidies for the clergy.

In contrast, rightists perceived the left as potentially radical and democracy as high risk when they believed that one or more of the following political outcomes, even if currently absent, could relatively easily arise in the course of routine democratic political processes:

- extensive attempts to overturn the entire property regime—in other words, targeting not only the largest holdings but also smaller (including much middle-class) productive property—via either expropriation or even compensation, since the funds needed for such sweeping nationalization or redistribution (e.g., steeply progressive and very high taxes) could only come from current owners and employers themselves;

• not simply disestablishment of a state church but what would amount to an undermining of its role even in unofficial public life: the banning of ceremonies, prohibitions on all church-related education, and attempts to harass, expel, or "unauthorize" the clergy; and

• possibly but not necessarily, civil violence directed against rightists.

The dependent variable (hedging versus reliable support for democracy) is not overdetermined simply because conservative calculations concern several factors. Indeed, all rational choice explanations propose that actors compare at least two options, without risking causal overdetermination. They do so by maintaining a clear distinction between the singular causal mechanism (actors' cost-benefit analyses of regime alternatives) and the multiple factors that trigger that mechanism to produce one regime preference or the other. Proposing that multiple factors influence the causal mechanism is not an invitation to pick and choose the events the researcher finds most convenient. On the contrary, it imposes a significant discipline on the discussion: events in each case must be related consistently through the same prism. I do this here by, for example, always examining rightists' perceptions of likely outcomes under both authoritarian and democratic options, and never just one of the two.

Sources of Evidence on Actors' Beliefs

Most historiographical and other studies have focused on observable actions such as actors' behavior rather than their beliefs or perceptions, perhaps because protagonists themselves frequently fail to leave detailed records of their beliefs about options they faced in the past, most of which become counterfactual later. Other studies that seek to establish beliefs have relied on several possible sources, each offering problems as well as benefits. To reconstruct Swedish politicians' beliefs about legislative options, Leif Lewin uses parliamentary speeches and archival materials. These sources have the advantage of being insulated from retrospective revisionism, but tend to be elite-oriented, to contain limited information, and to be vulnerable to contemporaneous misrepresentation. For example, election-time rhetoric is often "speech . . . designed to conceal." This danger can be mitigated somewhat by privileging sources in which views were expressed privately.[4]

---

4. Cowling (1971: 9), Lewin (1988).

For many post-1945 cases, survey data are available. But surveys often fail to elicit systematic data on beliefs about options. Interviews can overcome this limitation by customizing questions; Leigh Payne uses them to establish Brazilian business leaders' perceptions of a changing political context. Unfortunately, interviews restrict research to recent events and are vulnerable on the scores of both sincerity and validity. Interviews seeking to establish present recollections of past beliefs permit a second opportunity for revision, whether deliberate or unconscious. Not only, as Duff Cooper remarked, is it "easier to remember events than to recall emotions" (and perhaps beliefs as well), but also events may have created incentives to bring memories into line with currently politically acceptable formulations about the past.[5] But interviews also offer devices for testing degrees of sincerity. The interviews used for Chapter 5 contain such devices. Interviews also offer a provocative possibility to test the counterfactual hypotheses that, as James Fearon emphasizes lie concealed in all causal claims. Interviews regarding Spain in the 1970s permitted a "test" of just such a hypothesis. In sum, for this study I rely on diverse sources, including interviews, newspapers, published diaries and letters, leaders' public statements and writings, and to a much lesser extent politicians' memoirs.[6]

This search for evidence forced me to take seriously the possibility that some knowledge is nearly "tacit." Michael Polanyi argues that people may often know, and presumably integrate into their decision-making, more information than they are capable of articulating. Perhaps as often, some knowledge is either difficult to articulate or not elicited in most conversations. For example, Louis Hartz remarks that the early leaders of the United States often lamented discord and division at home, until events prompted them explicitly to compare the United States to Europe, at which point they acknowledged that their disputes were limited.[7] Interviews are a nearly unique tool for accessing such quasi-tacit knowledge, and the Spanish interview format for this study was designed to establish normally unarticulated beliefs that appear crucial to the decisions actors made.

Chapters 4 and 5 draw on primary sources such as documents, newspapers, and interviews. Chapters 6 and 7, covering four countries over several decades, necessarily heavily rely on secondary sources, and for Germany, unhappily, on English-language sources alone. For these cases, I consulted primary sources where evidence was crucial and secondary data were especially thin. These sources included the posthumously published diaries of British politicians, private letters of Italian politicians, interwar and early

5. Payne (1994), Cooper (1954: 121).
6. Fearon (1991: 181).
7. Polanyi (1966), Hartz (1955: 81).

post-1945 French and British newspapers, and polling data and several interviews concerning France starting soon after Liberation in 1944. Secondary sources are sufficient to permit not only meaningful testing of competing predictions but also substantial reinterpretation of several cases. All translations are mine unless otherwise indicated. Historical sources intended for only private consumption are heavily privileged over public ones. It is well worth asking how representative are the rightists whose beliefs and perceptions were sampled, especially in the light of Ian Lustick's concerns about historical sources and selection bias. Perfect evidence is never at hand, and the best available response to Lustick's very valid concern is scholars' awareness of the problem and the casting of a deliberately wide and diverse research net. I have eschewed relying only on agreeable sources and regularly examined and addressed dissenting interpretations.[8]

Measuring the Dependent Variable

A series of sources, also imperfect, are used to establish rough distributions of actors' regime preferences and patterns of rightist hedging versus commitment. These include votes cast in elections, data on organizational membership, and results of public opinion surveys. Broad-based induced preferences for democracy thus can be discerned among French conservatives in the 1950s and 1960s by their consistent neglect of pro- (or proto-)authoritarian movements and parties and the scant antidemocratic sentiments expressed in numerous surveys. This contrasts sharply with, for example, the explosive surge of affiliation with the fascist Falange in Spain in 1936 and for the July military coup. Some Spaniards were prudently joining a bandwagon, but there can be little doubt that on the part of many others this outburst of enthusiastic activity was as close a *pro-authoritarian* version as any of the moments described by James Scott, when "the frontier between the hidden and the public transcripts is decisively breached." Scholarly attempts have been made to measure the distribution of regime support under authoritarianism. Since at least the 1970s limited survey research has been possible under some of these regimes.[9] Citizens in Spain in 1976 and Chile in 1988 essentially cast referendum ballots for their preferred regime. But not all possible indicators are credible, and in the analysis to come I attempt to identify such segmental regime support through

8. Lustick (1996).
9. For example, Myers and O'Connor (1998), Scott (1990: 202).

indicators other than the results of the distorted 1924 Italian and 1933 German elections and the 1947 and 1966 Spanish referenda.

Of course, while reifying both "the right" and a "moment" during which rightists make a decision to hedge or to commit to democracy, I cannot literally identify specific weeks or months in which complex calculations and processes occurred in that manner; the analyses in the subsequent chapters reflect this.

4

The Right and the Breakdown of Spanish Democracy, 1931–1936

> One can be very liberal and not at all democratic, or vice versa, very democratic and not at all liberal.
>
> José Ortega y Gasset, "Ideas de los Castillos," 1926

The last act of the Restoration monarchy in Spain was to oversee the dictatorship of General Miguel Primo de Rivera, beginning in 1923. In 1931, both gave way to Spain's first real democracy and its Second Republic (1931–36). At the start, rightists provisionally accepted democracy; by 1936, they supported a military coup. For Juan Linz this was the shift from the Republic's "great hopes" to its "civil war"; for Santos Juliá a shift from the "popular fiesta" of 1931 to the "class war" of 1936–39.[1] These events were of broader importance: if Spain's transition in the 1970s served as the "midwife" of many democratization theories, the collapse in the 1930s became perhaps the most emblematic interwar breakdown after Weimar's. As Linz has spent much of his career emphasizing, the breakdown was neither inevitable nor overdetermined. In this chapter I argue that despite the presence of several favorable conditions, the right did not commit to democracy, and the Republic never consolidated, because rightists detected high risks in democracy. These high risks were the result of the perceived susceptibility of millions of landless laborers and industrial and mining workers to revolutionary political appeals threatening the right's safety, property, income, control of the workplace, and church. Many on the right traced these risks to Spain's underlying social structure.

1. Linz (1978b), Juliá (1984).

The beliefs of those on the right had important consequences. As in all the cases considered in this study, high risks did not deterministically lead the right to defect from democracy. For the Republic's first four years, highly threatening outcomes were prevented by a series of contingent protections, especially the left's tactical moderation in 1931–33 and the right's office-holding in 1933–36. But this democracy could *never* consolidate because these protections were so contingent that they left intact the right's incentives to hedge against risk. The most likely authoritarian alternative to this democracy was one that credibly ensured owners' and employers' core policy interests, protected traditional religious institutions, and had a track-record of insulating rightists from repression. Democracy thus could offer superior outcomes *if* the right won office or *if* left parties won *and* were moderate *and* could control their rank-and-file, but democracy would be the worse choice if those events did not materialize. In other words, the right's payoff matrix could easily reverse as the result of readily identifiable and plausible scenarios. Since rightists could know their present but not their future regime preferences, they hedged from the start by a variety of means and particularly in the form of privileged access to the premier exit option: the military.

The right's strategies toward democracy evolved in a relatively straightforward manner. In 1931–33 the left's tactical moderation prevented the right's payoff matrix from reversing; in 1933–36 the right's office-holding had the same effect. But in 1936 the right's calculus changed dramatically. In the face of a left government, radicalized unions, and accelerating violence and direct action in many regions, even an authoritarian project that imposed some risks of repression and regime/opposition conflict was preferable. In particular, in Spain more than in any other case considered here, rightists' safety was threatened in democracy. Because of the military's history of insulating the right from severe violence, rightists had grounds for expecting both more favorable policies and *higher* levels of safety under authoritarianism. This evolving context is illustrated in Figure 4.1.

The Right's Beliefs in Interwar Spain

Who is the "right" whose beliefs we must establish? The term involves notable simplifications in interwar Spain as elsewhere. Religion does not suffice: some on the left were Catholic, and many secular economic conservatives supported the 1936 coup. But religion was clearly one of the major bases for conservative identity and mobilization, as the Catholic Church and Catholic associations created vast networks and provided many leaders for the parties opposed to the Republic's first, left-dominated, two years of

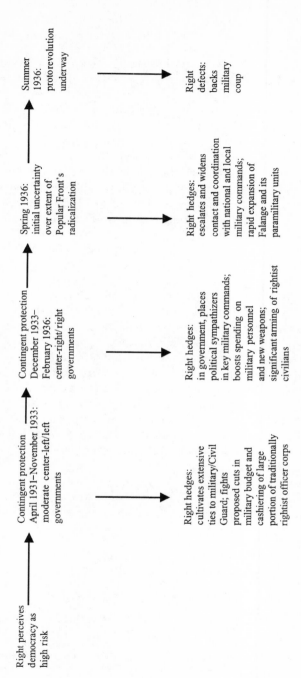

Right perceives
democracy as
high risk

Contingent protection
April 1931–November 1933:
moderate center-left/left
governments

Contingent protection
December 1933–
February 1936:
center-right/right
governments

Spring 1936:
initial uncertainty
over extent of
Popular Front's
radicalization

Summer
1936:
protorevolution
underway

Right hedges:
cultivates extensive
ties to military/Civil
Guard; fights
proposed cuts in
military budget and
cashiering of
traditionally
rightist officer corps

Right hedges:
in government, places
political sympathizers
in key military commands;
boosts spending on
military personnel
and new weapons;
significant arming of rightist
civilians

Right hedges:
escalates and widens
contact and coordination
with national and local
military commands;
rapid expansion of
Falange and its
paramilitary units

Right
defects:
backs
military
coup

Figure 4.1 Rightist Perceptions and Strategies in Spain, 1931–36

government (the first *bienio*). Property rights, orthodox fiscal policies, and a desire for public "order" united industrialists, estate owners, and owners of small businesses and farms, many of the latter organized by Catholic associations.[2] There was substantial overlap between religiosity and economic status, since many workers had abandoned regular practice, to the great consternation of the Church, leaving the middle classes as the backbone of the Catholic community. This analysis downplays orientations toward regionalism, which, while hotly debated at times, were never the basis of mass conflict except in the Basque Country and portions of Catalonia.

Rightists affiliated with such sectoral and religious organizations as chambers of commerce and Catholic Action were broadly organized into two political sectors. The first was generally secular, including mainly the no-longer-radical Radicals led by Alejandro Lerroux, as well as conservative republicans associated with Niceto Alcalá-Zamora and Miguel Maura and with the Liberal Democrats, and the Catalan Lliga. The second was the Catholic wing, overwhelmingly dominated by the Spanish Confederation of Autonomous Rightist Organizations (Confederación Española de Derechas Autónomas [CEDA]). This wing also included the Agrarians and several relatively small, explicitly antidemocratic parties: the Renovación Española monarchists and the Carlists. The fascist Falange stood somewhat apart. Internal complexity on the Right was evident; conservative Catholics despised Radical masons. Yet Radicals and *cedistas* (members and supporters of the CEDA) nevertheless allied on numerous antisocialist electoral slates, governed together in 1933–35, and often joined in support of the 1936 coup. In this chapter I focus especially on the CEDA, which alone represented over half the center-right's and the right's parliamentary seats in 1936. The movement of these groupings from acceptance of democracy in 1931 to support for the coup determined the Republic's fate.[3]

Only selected sources are available for establishing actors' beliefs about regime alternatives. A small number of diaries were published after the civil war, along with a limited number of biographies and (generally not useful) autobiographies. Exceedingly few opportunities existed for interviews.[4]

---

2. Castillo (1979).

3. For major studies, see the following: for the Radicals: Ruiz Manjón (1976); for the CEDA: Robinson (1970), Montero (1977), Preston (1978); for Renovación Española: Gil Pecharromán (1994); for the Carlists: Blinkhorn (1975); for the Falange: Payne (1961); for the Derecha Liberal Republicana: Avilés Farré (1976); for the Lliga: Molas (1972). On the right generally, see Montero (1988). Acción Nacional/Acción Popular/CEDA is referred to as the CEDA throughout.

4. Spaniards old enough to vote in 1936 would have been over eighty years old when fieldwork began in 1993. Two members of the Republic's parliament were interviewed: Ramón Serrano Suñer (CEDA) and José García Prat (PSOE), who has since died.

The evidence in this chapter relies instead on a range of both historiographical materials and especially on a diverse set of contemporaneously published sources. These sources include leaders' and political commentators' statements and speeches reported in the press or recorded during parliamentary debates, and editorial statements from numerous conservative newspapers. Not surprisingly, the large number of studies of the interwar Republic that have appeared in recent years have found the vibrant and diverse press of the period to be an indispensable source. Issues of external validity are raised in particular by the matter of interpreting editorial views in newspapers as representative of conservatives' perceptions. I partly addressed these issues by sampling hundreds of articles over a substantial period from more than a dozen regional and national newspapers affiliated with the hegemonic conservative party of the Republic, the CEDA. These sources make it possible to establish the crucial data for testing the theory: many rightists' beliefs about (1) major left parties and unions (2) the political desires and orientations of workers independent of their membership in one left organization or another (3) the ability of left leaders to exert organizational discipline over their rank-and-file, and (4) likely outcomes in democracy given different possible political scenarios, for example, in the event of left versus right victories in the 1931, 1933, and 1936 elections.

The Exclusionary Alternative to Democracy, 1931–33

What political outcomes could rightists expect in the most likely authoritarian alternative to democracy, both during its installation and afterward? One observer suggested in 1936 that rightist pro-authoritarians underestimated "the inconveniences of a dictatorship."[5] But they had experience with exclusionary rule as recently as five years earlier. The monarchy and then military rule under royal imprimatur (1923–31) managed a generally mediocre economy, but "Catholics found little to criticize and much to applaud," and the regime effectively restrained the quasi-revolutionary agendas that had erupted in 1917–20.[6] General Primo de Rivera's 1923 coup involved little violence, largely because the left was organizationally weak. This weakness also ensured that repression was not only selective but also relatively mild, earning the regime a reputation as a "soft" dictatorship (*dictablanda*). In such a context, a rightist like the Catalan conservative

5. Payne (1993: 448–47).
6. Lannon (1987: 175).

Francesc Cambó could assume that an authoritarian regime was capable of representing the "public interest" as well as or even more adequately than democracy.[7]

Actors had to engage in some updating since 1923–31. The exact identity of potential authoritarian leaders after 1931 could only be guessed at. But this was not so much the case in terms of likely policies. Even more than in the past, the military represented the most coherent potential exclusionary force and was predominantly conservative or at least anti-revolutionary.[8] A number of exclusionary entrepreneurs—hard-line monarchists and the fascist Falange—generally proposed to restore both "order" and Catholic values to the public arena, in large part by channeling class-based demands into state-managed corporatist institutions. To justify such a project, they invoked diverse nondemocratic components of Spain's political culture and made frequent reference to fascist Italy, Nazi Germany, and other models. José Calvo Sotelo, a senior figure in Primo de Rivera's regime before 1931, advanced a prominent and unambiguous line: "I think the Communist advance cannot be stopped by the instruments of a parliamentary democratic regime."[9]

But risks of resistance to an authoritarian regime expanded considerably in and after 1931 due to the spectacular expansion of working-class organizations. When Primo de Rivera seized power in 1923, the Socialist-affiliated union (the Unión General de Trabajadores, or UGT), had approximately two hundred thousand members; by 1933, it had well over one million.[10] Comparable expansions took place in anarcho-syndicalist and communist organizations. And these organizations had useful skills, possessing only modest coercive capacities but extensive networks of communication and mobilization, small arms, and underground experience sufficient to suggest to rightist coup plotters that a conservative coup attempt would meet resistance. There is no doubt that rightist leaders did not linearly project the past and instead took these developments into account. The main coup conspirator in 1936 argued that the military's initial move "must be violent in the extreme in order to crush the strong and well-organized enemy as soon as possible."[11]

---

7. He also acknowledged democracy had its benefits; *Diario de sesiones de las cortes* (hereafter *DSC*, including for the Cortes Constituyentes) 160 (February 15, 1935), p. 6361.

8. Lerroux remarked that only the socialists and the military were capable of ruling dictatorially; *El sol*, July 16, 1932, p. 8.

9. *ABC*, April 26, 1936, p. 35.

10. Contreras (1981: 55, 85).

11. Preston (1994: 129).

The Right's Political Risks in Democracy, 1931–33

High Risks to the Right's Basic Preferences

The familiar interpretation of the Second Republic emphasizes the moderation of the Republic's founding coalition and then radicalization of the left beginning only in 1933. But rightists perceived the Second Republic as high risk from the start because they perceived the left half of the political spectrum as highly unpredictable, for two reasons. First, working-class movements had direct access to power in democracy because the reformist Left-Republican parties consistently proved willing to ally with the Partido Socialista Obrero Español (PSOE) even when it was maximalist (just as the CEDA was willing to ally with monarchists and fascists). Second, as in interwar Italy and Germany, it was extremely unclear to rightists both whether moderates would retain control of the socialist party and whether the socialists would remain the dominant political option for workers. Rightists were well aware of the radicalizing pressures from below described by Edward Malefakis, Juliá, and others. These pressures were already evident in 1931–33 and raised the possibility that workers and landless laborers would pour support into the anarchosyndicalist Confederacíon Nacional de Trabajo (CNT) or even the fledgling Communist Partido Comunista de España (PCE).[12] This combination of perceived susceptibility of the left to radicalization and left access to power raised the specters of threats to the basic property regime, sweeping anticlericalism, and civil violence directed against rightists. These high risks did not mean the right had incentives to defect immediately, since contingent events could prevent threats from materializing at any given time. When such protections were present, the right's basic policy interests and safety were better secured in democracy. But if these contingent protections disappeared, the right would be better served by conservative military rule. Conservatives hedged.

The factor making this situation very different from that of Spain after the 1976–77 transition is the perceived likelihood of radicalization of the left and highly threatening outcomes in democracy, differences summarized in Table 4.1.

How did high risks during the Second Republic make themselves felt? The threats perceived by rightists were not new. They were part of a lengthy history of class-based dispute and confrontation that dated back decades and had reached one important peak in 1917–20.[13] Millions of workers

---

12. Malefakis (1970), Juliá (1984).
13. Calero (1976), Meaker (1974).

Table 4.1 Differences in the Right's Perceptions of the Left, 1931–36 and after 1977

	1931–36	After 1977
Largest left party had substantial prospects for winning?	Yes; held office 1931–33, 1936	Yes; held office 1982–96
PSOE largest party on the left?	Yes	Yes
PSOE ran on relatively moderate election manifesto?	Yes, especially in 1931 and 1936	Yes
Right perceived social basis for large radical movements?	Yes: millions of industrial workers and landless agricultural laborers	Small and diminishing further
Large revolutionary groups to PSOE's left?	Yes: CNT, PCE	No
PSOE leaders perceived as under extensive pressures from rank-and-file to radicalize?	Yes	No
Right believed that fundamental revision of property regime had wide appeal among masses on the left?	Yes	No
Estimated likelihood of widespread (e.g., class-based) civil violence	Very high from start, accelerating in 1936	Very low

lived in economically desperate conditions, and those in the latifundia in the south and southwest under conditions of durable quasi-feudal social domination. Observers thus could and did see continuities in social conflict before, during, and after the Republic. Luis Garrido González contends that the social revolution that broke out in the Republican south during the civil war was a sociopolitical project "which had been taking shape [*moldeando*] throughout the Republic, which was not born with it but which brought together a series of secular traditions of the Andalucían landless laborers."[14] It is no surprise that while many conservatives found monarchy untenable in 1931, they also faced democracy with great concern. Prior to the transition, the major conservative daily *El debate* expressed concern that democratization could lead to threats to "the fundamental institutions of society," and two weeks into the transition Angel Herrera, later a guiding spirit of the CEDA, described immediate dangers to the Church and "a serious threat, although not imminent, to the

14. Garrido González (1979: 8–9).

country, to order, to the family, to property."[15] Frances Lannon concludes that "it is evident from their correspondence that even the most politically sophisticated and flexible of the [Catholic] bishops faced the republican order with fear from the very beginning, and certainly before any anti-clerical measure was enacted." Bishops warned that "we have now entered the vortex" and "we have to be *ready for everything*," and considered how best to "avert radical measures, contrary to the interests of religion."[16] A leading reformist Socialist agreed: "No-one can believe that the change which occurred was a simple [formal] political change [alone]."[17]

Some on the right initially hoped the situation would parallel the early Third French Republic, with Lerroux playing Adolphe Thiers.[18] But if anything, high anxiety was soon reinforced, not defused. José Manuel Macarro Vera and Juliá emphasize that bottom-up radicalization of the PSOE began much sooner than previous studies suggested.[19] Moreover, dynamics within the left were regularly on public display. Socialist leaders struggled at great cost to maintain their organizations on a gradualist path, but what union leader Lucio Martínez Gil termed an "avalanche" of new members flooded the PSOE and UGT (PSOE membership rose seven and a half times in 1929–32), making top-down doctrinal and tactical discipline nearly impossible. Substantial pressure for far-reaching social change created a visible predicament, for example, for the UGT's sizable landless laborer, railway, and mining unions. In 1931–32, these organizations issued speeches, pamphlets, and newspapers ceaselessly urging workers to avoid direct action and await electoral and legislative progress, and constantly denouncing competing anarchosyndicalists and communists as unwitting allies of capital.

In other words, rightists were not the only ones detecting radicalization among workers. From the Republic's start, Socialist leaders regularly feared they were not successfully communicating their legislative accomplishments to their rank-and-file, and apparently delayed the PSOE's 1932 congress out of concern that it would become a forum for impatient protests and pressure.[20] Particularly contentious were the first *bienio*'s modest land reform, which deeply frustrated millions of landless laborers who had sup-

15. Vincent (1996: 146–47), Montero (1977, 2: 55).

16. Lannon (1987: 179–80), emphasis added.

17. Fernando de los Ríos in *El sol,* May 4, 1932, p. 2.

18. The Conde de Romanones in *El Castellano* (Toledo), April 12, 1933, p. 1; *El noticiero* (Zaragoza), September 15, 1933, p. 1.

19. That is, predating both the 1933 elections and the 1934–35 employer offensive; Juliá (1979: 67), Macarro Vera (1982).

20. See Largo's comments at the March 23, 1932, Madrid meeting of the PSOE Comisión Ejecutiva, Fundación Pablo Iglesias Archive. The predicament of the leadership became visible during the congress's debate over dissolving the Civil Guard; PSOE (1934).

ported the PSOE, and Socialist leaders' aggressive discouragement of strikes, which workers saw as among their only points of leverage. For example, Trifón Gómez was concerned that new members of his UGT-affiliated railway workers' union (Sindicato Nacional Ferroviario [SNF]) lacked the seasoned discipline needed to seek realizable goals in difficult circumstances. The union opposed a 1931 strike organized by the CNT, and attempted to generate tangible victories by calling on the government to nationalize the rails and provide for a substantial wage hike. But when the government (which included three PSOE ministers) lengthily debated the issue, the SNF held an extraordinary congress to pass pressure upward. Finally, the government rejected nationalization and found significant wage hikes financially inadvisable. PSOE Minister Indalecio Prieto became the target of open criticism by SNF locals. The next year, Prieto engineered a small raise, prompting the SNF to announce proudly, "[T]his is how workers' organizations earn their reputations." Throughout, leaders of the SNF felt the need to appeal repeatedly for members' loyalty, devoted substantial newspaper space to criticism of the CNT, denied that the SNF had any interests other than their members, and insisted the SNF was "profoundly revolutionary." But their commitment to reformism nonetheless resulted in angry workers, a membership that was sagging by 1932, and fears of organizational competition on their left flank.[21]

The contingency of the control which PSOE/UGT leaders had over workers was publicly discernible in two main ways. First, reformist socialist leaders regularly felt the need publicly to discourage rank-and-file defections to more radical competitors. Socialist publications devoted extensive space to criticizing the PCE for untrustworthiness and extremism and the CNT for seeking an "unrealizable utopia."[22] Nevertheless, the CNT remained the dominant working-class organization in industrial Catalonia and several provinces of the agrarian deep south, and by 1933, even the once-minuscule (and nationally still small) PCE nearly matched the PSOE's vote in Córdoba (the city), surpassed it in the cities of Seville and Málaga, and reached a quarter of the poll in the Asturian mining zone.[23] Second, PSOE leaders fought a running battle against workers' widespread use of direct action. Initially, most direct action emanated from the CNT and PCE,

21. *La unión Ferroviaria*, May 25, 1931; October 25, November 15 and 25, and December 5–15, 1931; July 5, 1932. See also *El socialista* through October, 1931; and December 24, 27, and 30, 1931. The centrist *El sol* found nationalization and raises imprudent: December 4, 1931, p. 1.

22. *El obrero de la tierra*, April 2, 1932, p. 1.

23. Results from Córdoba are partial; see *El sol*, November 21, 1933, pp. 4–5; and *Boletín oficial de la provincia de Córdoba*, December 4, 1933, pp. 20–39. Ward-level statistics for mining districts are in Asturias's *Boletín oficial.*

and the first *bienio* governments typically responded brutally. But gradually the line blurred between violence sponsored by the CNT (or PCE) and other workers' use of extralegal methods.

Much of the violence was "spontaneous" in that it required no organizers from outside a locality. Malefakis's analysis of events in the rural sector is unsurpassed: "Chaos frequently descended upon villages where organized labor units did not exist. It also visited villages affiliated with the Socialist UGT and FNTT [Federación Nacional de los Trabajadores de la Tierra]." Locals would disarm Civil Guards, burn property records, seize land, and declare a new society, even as troops were being dispatched. The CNT and PCE did not create this "war waged by the peasantry against its old enemies, the landlords and the Guardia Civil. . . . Their misery was too great, their hatred too intense, and their expectations too unlimited for them always to accept the spirit of restraint that guided the Socialist leadership prior to 1933." He concludes that "[i]t would be pointless to try to catalogue" the hundreds and perhaps thousands of confrontational incidents in 1931–33.[24] Unlike in the early Third French Republic, strife in interwar Spain proved widespread and ongoing.

Beginning in 1933, the Socialists began radicalizing at the national level. This accelerated after the conservative electoral victory in November 1933. The PSOE's old forms did not give way easily: Indalecio Prieto and Julián Besteiro remained associated with greater moderation, and the landless laborer union's Martínez Gil had to be overthrown by militants in an internal leadership challenge. But the trend was clear: moderates were weak counterweights to the PSOE/UGT's Francisco Largo Caballero, who declared on the eve of the 1933 elections that class struggle was "carrying us inexorably toward a violent situation."[25]

Claims that Socialist leaders were at heart reformist but were forced to radicalize could hardly be comforting to a right attempting to forecast outcomes in democracy, regardless of their origin. Rightists, appreciating that radicalism had wide social bases, reacted to where the left easily might go. They sometimes explained the potentiality for left radicalism in ideational terms, as the result of the erosion of Catholic faith. But they were also aware that this erosion was marked along class and occupational lines, and the famously unsuccessful social Catholic project was in many ways an attempt specifically to retrieve workers for the Church.[26] Rightists did not see scattered radical-

---

24. Malefakis (1970: 306–07, 310, 304). For leading local studies, see Macarro Vera (1985) and Pérez Yruela (1979).
25. *El socialista,* November 16, 1933, p. 4. Malefakis (1970: 317–42) and Juliá (1977) analyze the PSOE/UGT's radicalization.
26. Benavides (1973).

ism as a spasm, perhaps quick to subside. Like conservatives across Europe, they sometimes blamed class struggle on "agitators." But at the same time they repeatedly acknowledged that left organizations were able to dabble in the "troubled waters" (*ríos revueltos*) of enduring social conflicts, most obviously among the large working classes in industry and mining and on the agricultural estate regions employing landless laborers in the vast southern regions of Andalucía, Extremadura, and southern New Castile (La Mancha), regions with property structures comparable to great-estate Italy and southern Portugal. No one-to-one correspondence can be drawn between propertylessness and radicalism, and the politics of such categories as Catalan sharecroppers were as complex here as in other cases.[27] But numerous rightists believed rural revolutionary impulses were demarcated by class and fueled by landlessness, conditions likely to endure indefinitely.

A range of sources, including newspapers and other contemporaneous commentaries, reflect rightists' beliefs that high risks were a predictable companion of democracy. A CEDA newspaper in Extremadura warned that members of "the Extremeño proletariat," whether socialist or anarchist, were committed to "the calamity which a social revolution would be." *El debate* concluded that "revolutionary madness threatens to contaminate a considerable part of working-class Spain."[28] CEDA leaders José Maria Gil Robles, Luis Lucía, and Manuel Giménez-Fernández observed that middle classes and small-holders were moderate or conservative voters, and attributed political problems in many regions to a shortage of these social categories.[29] As one provincial rightist organization argued, "[T]here is nothing more conducive to social peace than augmenting, by all licit means, the number of small property owners."[30] The rightist *La región* in Galicia commented in early 1936 that in contrast to the latifundia south, "we have the security that all of Orense, both capital city and province, are of conservative tendencies. And it could not be differently: all of us or nearly all of us here have something to conserve. . . . There are a few hundred workers in the capital, and it is there that socialism will find some electoral support."[31] The Lliga's *La veu de Catalunya* argued slightly differently that the south

27. Balcells (1968).

28. *Hoy* (Badajoz), April 12, 1933, p. 1; *El debate*, May 20, 1934, p. 1.

29. *El debate*, February 27, 1936, p. 1; *Hoy*, October 19, 1933, p. 1. On Lucía and Giménez-Fernández, see Gil Robles (1968: 576); on Gil Robles, see Irwin (1991: 85).

30. Unión de Derechas Independientes de Jérez's 1932 petition to the Cortes concerning the pending land reform. See also the Badajoz landowners' association "Exposición y Enmiendas," p. 5. These and other declarations are in Cortes archive (Madrid), Comisión de Reforma Agraria, Serie General, Legajo 543/3.

31. *La región* (Orense), January 16, 1936, p. 1.

lacked the industrialization and strong bourgeoisie, the "proper social context," that democracy needed and Catalonia enjoyed. The political implications of this theory were the same.[32] The hard-rightist Calvo Sotelo took the analysis to one logical conclusion and dispensed with the cross-class One Nation rhetoric of so many European conservatives, simply aligning himself with the middle and upper classes.[33]

Consistent with this, many rightists did not attribute revolutionary agendas to a specific ideology or organization. In *El debate*'s words:

> the reality is, that between the "direct action" of Barcelona's anarchism . . . and the Marxism of other Spanish regions, whose opportunism permits it, simultaneously or in succession, to participate in legality and in armed revolts, in democracy and in murder . . . there may be profound differences in tactics, in nuance, at times in ideas, but they also conform absolutely in something which endangers the very life of society. And that is this: they want to incite revolution. They want to raze today's economic and social regime down to its foundations.[34]

The CEDA's *Hoy* concluded that "so long as the masses are hungry, prosperity and social peace will be impossible." The social Catholic Giménez-Fernández acknowledged that a Spain in which social peace was assured by "all the time fewer rich and fewer poor" was a long-term goal. In 1936, the conservative republican Maura believed that only "effective social justice" would permit "peace between Spaniards" and the Lliga's *La veu de Catalunya* estimated that it would take "many years" before regions with weak middle classes overcame the social bases of radical politics.[35]

There were different possible solutions to this problem. Revolutionary agendas fueled by economic insecurity and unemployment might be partially blunted by public works programs, which many rightists favored. But this was hardly a long-term solution to a profound political problem. Substantial wage and land reform concessions might win workers' hearts and minds but would mean sacrificing the core interests rightists were trying to preserve. Extensive irrigation of uncultivated areas might make vast quantities of land available on a non-zero-sum basis but was expensive and a

32. *La veu de Catalunya*, July 9, 1936, p. 8. The Lliga was aware that Catalan industrial workers were as prone to radicalism as rural laborers.

33. *ABC*, April 26, 1936, p. 35.

34. *El debate*, May 20, 1934, p. 1.

35. Respectively, *Hoy*, December 22, 1933, p. 1; *La gaceta regional* (Salamanca), February 26, 1935, p. 6; *El Sol*, June 23, 1936, p. 1; *La veu de Catalunya*, July 9, 1936, p. 8.

project effectively pursued by no government, left or right, democratic or authoritarian. In the end, radicalization of the left remained a distinct possibility. Short-term protections rendered democracy's payoffs higher for rightists at any given moment, but the unpredictability of the regime-related payoff matrix into the future made hedging the right's rational course of action.

Contingent Protections of the Right's Basic Preferences, 1931–33

Conservatives did not have incentives to defect from the Republic so long as contingent factors were present to prevent highly threatening outcomes from materializing in democracy. Formal decision rules were not in a position to accomplish that, since the 1931 constitution was designed to concentrate wins and losses. The PSOE successfully opposed a strong president and upper house, which they believed would become conservative bastions. Linz and others also criticize the electoral law that manufactured majorities by granting two-thirds to four-fifths of the seats in each province (and several large cities) to the leading single list of candidates, a system the center-left designed to undermine the electoral influence of conservative local notables.[36] Disproportionality meant both that the center-left and left won an enormous parliamentary majority in 1931 and that small swings in shares of the vote could (and did) result in wide swings in seats thereafter, although the parliament remained multiparty because of joint party lists. A 1933 reform reduced electoral stakes slightly.[37] Most telling, rightists could not rely on what institutional protections did exist. The supreme court emerged as a rare institutional protector of conservatives. The Popular Front responded by campaigning in 1936 for its fundamental revision. This lends little credibility to counterfactual hypotheses concerned with the democracy-reinforcing effects of a stakes-reducing design.[38]

Instead, protection was offered in 1931–33 by the left's tactical moderation and at least limited prevention of direct action and in 1933–35 by the

36. Gunther and Blough (1981), Linz (1978b: 168). The Agrarian leader Martínez de Velasco warned that the constitution, to be truly democratic, would have to be a "labor of transaction"; *El sol*, November 10, 1931, p. 5. But Prieto criticized a proposed upper house: "A brake on what? A counterweight to what? . . . I am not a proponent of constitutions of transaction"; *DSC* 63 (October 27, 1931), p. 1,958.

37. Critiques include *El debate*, May 6, 1931, p. 1; *DSC* 373 (July 19, 1933), pp. 14,224–27; Linz (1978b: 149, 168–69), Tusell (1974: 253). The 1933 reform essentially required a list to win 40 percent to earn the bonus, instead of 20 percent.

38. Bassols Coma (1981: 59–62). Carreras (1983: 167) notes that "for the whole Republican five-year period (*lustro*), proposals to reform [the electoral law] were constant."

Table 4.2 Spanish General Election Results, 1931–36

	Share of Votes (%)	Share of Seats (%)
1931		
Socialists	20	25
Left-Republican	31	34
Secular conservatives	26	29
Catholic right	11	11
1933		
Socialists	22	13
Left-Republican	11	6
Secular conservatives	21	28
Catholic right	33	48
1936, first round		
Popular front	47.2	56
Center	5.3	6
Center-right/right	45.7	39

right's office-holding. As already mentioned, left forces began the new democracy with moderation and appeals for calm.[39] For the first *bienio*, the government was made up briefly of a founding coalition (ranging from the PSOE to moderately conservative Catholics) and then a coalition of the PSOE and Left-Republicans, presided over by the center-left Manuel Azaña. This coalition, including its largest single (Socialist) member, was committed to incremental reformism and firmly opposed to direct action. Efforts were even made to include liberal-minded Catholics. This coalition won a parliamentary majority in 1931.

The 1931–33 coalition showed least restraint in its assault on the Catholic Church's traditional public role. The Church was disestablished, the Jesuits dissolved, divorce introduced, crucifixes removed from public classrooms, stipends to clergy set to be phased out, and traditional religious processions sometimes banned by local authorities. But on almost all other major issues, the Azaña governments drew back from fulfilling any of the right's worst fears. Despite concerns over expropriation via taxation, budgets proved highly orthodox, disappointing many union members and activists. The eventual land-reform legislation was limited and gradualist.[40] After an attempted putsch in 1932, the government called for confiscation of aristocrats' property but never suggested the same should be applied to other owners. Employers feared losing control of their businesses, but the government and the UGT urged wage restraint and accepted the death of a

39. For example, *El socialista*, April 15, 1931, pp. 1–2; also, Ben-Ami (1978).
40. Malefakis (1970) remains definitive; Lannon (1987: ch. 7).

proposed bill aimed at worker participation. While Socialist leaders publicly shared workers' frustrations, the government generally responded brutally to local direct action. In these senses, a clear distinction can be made between 1931–33, when conservatives perceived only the *potential* for radicalization, and 1936, when they perceived that radicalization was full blown and revolution was materializing.

By the time major leaders and organizations on the left radicalized in 1933, the right had won national elections and office (see Table 4.1). In sum, for the first several years of the Republic, rightists were protected from highly threatening outcomes in democracy, but they were protected by highly contingent factors and in particular believed that moderate leaders of the left were locked in an indefinite struggle to fend off powerful radicalizing impulses by the rank-and-file that were not easily dissolved or dissuaded. The right's victory in any given election was hardly a predictable protection. The logical response of the right was to hedge.

Hedging against Political Risk in Democracy

It bears repeating that high risks in democracy did not deterministically lead the right to defect to authoritarianism. The civilian right gave only modest support to explicitly antidemocratic parties, and there was no evident segmental support for General José Sanjurjo's abortive 1932 putsch. The single largest party on the right, the CEDA, was, in Stanley Payne's words, an example of "mass political Catholicism, something never before accomplished in the modern history of Spanish parliamentary regimes," and was not avowedly pro-authoritarian.[41] But high perceived risks in democracy led rightists to hedge aggressively from 1931 on, a development that has to be examined as a qualitative event taking place within parties operating in the democratic framework. Linz concludes that the Republic's "great question" is "why centrifugal tendencies rather than centripetal tendencies were reinforced in the major parties." Understanding dynamics within the CEDA is the most important task, since it was the single largest rightist party and its massive electorate formed the backbone of the constituency for the 1936 coup.[42] Rightist strategies can be discerned in widespread editorializing in the CEDA newspapers and in rightist behavior toward the military both in and out of office.

41. Payne (1993: 166).
42. Linz (1978b: 166).

Ambivalent Regime Discourses

Despite national traditions, monarchism was increasingly eclipsed in the mid-1930s as the plausible alternative to democracy by "republicanized"— though not truly fascist—authoritarian possibilities.[43]

The CEDA's commitment to the Republic is typically portrayed as shallow. After explicit Alfonsine monarchists decamped to form their own party in 1932, the CEDA was created and emphasized that Church teachings required respect for legally constituted authority. Whether the country was republic or monarchy was "accidental": "Before the form we defend the content."[44] "Accidentalism" could work to democracy's advantage. But *cedistas* also could easily imagine making the opposite choice in order to defend core interests against a radical left in democracy. Often they phrased these interests in terms of religion, family, property, and order. They may have omitted safety because it was too obvious to bear mentioning, or perhaps because they took it for granted in a country in which even military rulers had never targeted conservative citizens with violence. In considering the fundamentally instrumentalist nature of CEDA attitudes toward regime options, it is instructive for two reasons to consider CEDA responses to the Nazis' January 1933 assumption of power in Germany (reactions to events in Austria are not useful for this analysis).[45]

First, the Nazi takeover was sufficiently prominent and controversial as to induce a wide array of rightist sources to render a judgment on a focused set of events. Second, the Nazi takeover entailed the suppression of the left but at the cost of the concurrent dissolution of all parties, including the Zentrum, Europe's largest Catholic party. Thus, elimination of the threat from the left both raised important normative issues and starkly posed the costs and benefits of ending democracy. Throughout 1933, a number of regional CEDA newspapers (such as the *Diario de León*, *El ideal Gallego*, *Diario de Valencia*, and *Diario de La Rioja*) criticized the new Nazi authorities for

43. Preston (1978: 100, 122) appreciates the left's perception that the CEDA's rise to power was "synonymous with the establishment of fascism," but acknowledges that the "CEDA may not have been a fascist organisation in the terms of post-1945 academic definition" and avoids applying the term to the CEDA except with such qualifiers as "quasi." The specter of monarchism in the 1930s at times appears to render Spain less relevant to analysis of post-1945 events. However, not only should (ruling) monarchism be understood as a subtype of authoritarianism, but also the fact that interwar Spanish rightists eventually defected to a non-monarchical authoritarian formula ensures this case's comparative relevance.

44. Montero (1977, 2: 67, 39–88).

45. Many rightists in Spain (like elsewhere) were convinced that Dollfuss's 1934 crackdown was in response to a Socialist coup attempt. Consequently, support was expressed even by conservatives defending constitutionalism. Semolinos Arribas (1985: 179–285) analyzes extensive treatment of the Nazis in the Spanish press.

amoral materialism (and in that sense even socialism) and racialism, and for violating political liberties and suppressing the Catholic Zentrum party. But more typically, Gil Robles and other CEDA leaders condemned National Socialism (and fascism) not for authoritarianism but for being unreligious or even antireligious and excessively statist, and hence inappropriate for ideological transplantation to Spain.[46]

The many regional CEDA newspapers that praised the Nazis did so for emphatically instrumental reasons, although they were organs of an avowedly clerical party and might be presumed to have ethical motivations. They did not defend or justify Nazi behavior on ethical grounds, asserted no philosophical affinity with fascism or National Socialism, typically did not discuss the origins and details of Nazi ideology, and could hardly praise its economic successes, which took several years to materialize.[47] Instead, the major virtue they perceived in the Nazi project was the suppression of the German left. *La gaceta del norte* portrayed events in Germany as a positive and "spiritual reaction" to threatening Marxism and socialism. *El noticiero* also discussed fascism in terms of preexisting leftist threats, and *El Castellano* and *El pueblo Manchego* defended Nazi anti-Semitism by insisting that Jews played a central role in Marxist movements. *El pueblo Manchego* insisted that "Marxism is the enemy" and that "it is necessary to impose the principle of authority on all social classes."[48] This closely paralleled praise for Nazism by the Spanish Economic Union, the peak industrial employers' association. The Economic Union lauded Nazism not because of its economic success and despite its repression but rather the opposite: despite the Nazis' early economic problems and because Nazism had eliminated the left organizationally:

> But if no good can be seen in Hitler's economic policies, his hostility toward Marxist socialism is crystal-clear, and the persecution to which he has subjected that movement is indisputably effective. The ease with which the organizations and power of the famous German socialism have been dissolved is incredible. The scant resistance which socialism has offered to the dictatorships everywhere is curious. In Germany, after having sent into flight the

46. In Luis Lucía's words, "Millions of men can march in front of me wearing shirts of whatever color and saluting with the most outlandish gestures. . . . They are force, but force isn't reason"; CEDA (1933: 10). On Gil Robles, see also Tusell (1974: 206).

47. This discussion draws on material from newspapers affiliated with the CEDA's provincial affiliates, a neglected resource, consultation of which was valuably recommended by José Ramón Montero and Javier Tusell.

48. *La gaceta del norte*, February 25, 1933, p. 1; *El noticiero*, August 26, 1933, p. 1; *El Castellano*, July 5, 1933, p. 3; *El pueblo Manchego*, October 12, 1933, p. 2, July 21, 1933, p. 1, and April 3, 1933, p. 1. Also *El correo de Andalucía*, March 16, 1933, p. 12.

most prominent revolutionaries and having suppressed the newspapers of the Marxist party, Hitler has achieved the absolute submission of all the German workers' organizations, reorganizing them into a "German Workers' Front."[49]

These commentators did not glorify the violent means by which this goal was secured, as "ideological" fascists (like the tiny Falange) might.[50] Instead, these papers typically downplayed Nazism's sanguinary nature and limited praise only to the destruction of the leftist "common enemy." They understood repression as neither unacceptable nor aesthetically pleasing but as a potentially constructively employed instrument in a complex situation. Even *Ideal* (Granada), which condemned fascism in theory and book-burning in practice, suggested that "fascism is the heroic defense of a people who will not resign themselves to falling into the hands of Marxist barbarity. It is the desperate defense of civilized principles, and appears when no other solution is possible, with its inevitable violence."[51] *La gaceta del norte* called for regimes to use state power to suppress ideas such as those advocating conflict between classes.[52] These rightists understood political rights as assets that might have to be sacrificed as part of a greater net gain. They were neither ideological fascists nor linear products of a monarchical cultural history. Their hedging reflected outcome-oriented and context-specific calculations.

Access to Exit Options

Nearly from the Republic's start, rightists also sought to maintain access to effective vehicles for exiting democracy. The Carlists constantly maintained an armed force, and Alfonsine monarchists approached Mussolini's regime in 1933–34 to secure arms and funding for a coup. But prominently absent until 1936 was the extensive support for extramilitary forces that was visible in Italy in 1919–22, in Weimar, and even in France in the late interwar period.[53] Especially absent was a large fascistic paramilitary force. The PSOE's Luis Araquistain argued that Spanish fascism was deprived of the needed social base of unemployed war veterans. In the same vein, Payne

49. *Economia Española*, 1 (May 1933), pp. 42–43. See also 1 (April 1933), p. 129. Cabrera (1983: 269–70) quotes a 1932 Economic Union circular to its affiliates noting that neither democratic nor fascist governments were avoiding the Depression crisis.

50. At least rhetorically: Payne (1961: 51–52).

51. *Ideal*, March 11, 1933, p. 3; May 9, 1933, p. 3; May 21, 1933, p. 3.

52. *El noticiero*, June 10, 1933, p. 1; *La gaceta del norte*, January 13, 1933, p. 1.

53. Mazzetti (1979), Gil Pecharromán (1994: 265–66). To call the JAP, the CEDA's youth wing, a party militia exaggerates its power and discipline.

contends that initial support for the Falange withered when that party proved insufficiently muscular, not particularly Catholic, and excessively socially reformist.[54] But both latifundistas' maintenance of local enforcers and the rapid creation of coercive structures at the start of the civil war suggest that rightists had the means to create a paramilitary force when the need presented itself.[55]

The crucial difference regarding Spain in this matter is the military. Unlike in Weimar Germany, the army was not merely highly political and generally rightist in orientation but also large. Rightists attempting to maintain access to an effective exit vehicle did not need to generate an entirely new Freikorps structure. They simply had to protect the strength of the state security apparatus and cultivate as conservative an orientation within it as possible. They did both assiduously. Conservatives vigorously opposed the dissolution of major units or discharge of key officers. Center-right governments in 1934–35 "strengthen[ed] the armed forces and guarantee[d] their bulwark against the revolutionary left" by reorganizing command structures to empower sympathetic officers.[56] Not leaving such an important matter to national politicians, many local conservatives cultivated close personal relations with military and Civil Guard unit commanders, publicly feting them and holding memorials for those who fell in the course of (internal security) service. In 1931–36, conservatives at various levels made major investments in maintaining an amply powerful and conservative coercive apparatus.

Political Outcomes in Democracy, 1934–36

Conservatives' Basic Preferences under Center-Right Governments

Between 1931 and 1933, the right experienced a remarkable electoral revival. In 1931, the conservative *La vanguardia* remarked that "the forces which defended our social interests . . . suffered a serious collapse." Rightists ended up being best represented in the Republic's first parliament by the secular-conservative Radicals and a vocal but small group of Catholic conservatives. But in 1932 and 1933 the Radicals retained their strength

---

54. Araquistain (1934: 470) and Payne (1961: 59, 61, 69–70), who also described the *center-right* government's partial suppression of Falange paramilitary activity in 1934.

55. When the 1932 PSOE congress raised calls for dissolution of the Civil Guard, Wenceslao Carrillo responded that this would accomplish nothing "if other forces are created which continue in the service of the caciques"; PSOE (1934: 341).

56. Payne (1987: 80–81; 1993: 238–39), Preston (1978: 167).

while the Catholic CEDA grew rapidly, championing "Religion, Country, Order, Family, Work, and Property."[57] Conservative resistance was not limited to electoral and legislative arenas. Local employers fought wars of attrition over wages, attempted to weaken unions, and whenever possible undermined and sabotaged the already-cumbersome land reform. In November 1933, center-right and right parties won nearly two-thirds of the parliament. The governments they formed were led by the secular conservative Radicals and initially supported by the CEDA from outside the cabinet (eliciting outcry from hard-line monarchists).[58]

These governments responded vigorously to civil violence and enacted policies far closer to the policy preferences of both secular and Catholic conservatives than Azaña's policies were. These governments undermined much of the first *bienio*'s work, restoring state funding to the Catholic Church hierarchy, easing restrictions on religious education, overturning important portions of the 1931–33 labor market legislation, reversing numerous provisions of the land reform, and tolerating an employers' offensive. The massive agricultural laborers' strike in mid-1934 was defeated by a government crackdown and firm support for the owners.[59] Constitutional revisions favorable to the right were also considered. The shift to the right was so profound that even social-Catholic aspirations for the rural sector were rejected; despite the CEDA's occasional use of social-Catholic rhetoric, in the end it failed "to live up to its promises of killing revolution by kindness."[60]

These governments also zealously suppressed civil violence, including during the anarchosyndicalist uprising of December 1933 and the 1934 revolt organized by working-class organizations in 1934, which for all practical purposes attempted to nullify the 1933 elections. This revolt was triggered by the CEDA's formal entry into the cabinet in October 1934 and broke out in various regions. But the ill-planned uprising was particularly concentrated in the Asturian mining region, where "rank-and-file militancy . . . impelled the local PSOE leaders to proceed with the revolutionary movement." It took military units eight days to retake Oviedo and more to

57. *La vanguardia* (Barcelona), May 13, 1933, p. 3; *El debate*, April 29, 1931, p. 1.

58. The left was unimpressed with the CEDA's official support of a Republican government. But, in Carr's (1982: 628) words, "Gil Robles could have been a Spanish Parnell and reduced government to impotence." Lerroux (1945: 190) insisted the CEDA's decision delivered a measure of stability to the regime.

59. Malefakis (1970: 335–42), Tuñón de Lara (1985: ch. 9).

60. Robinson (1970: 205). On Giménez-Fernández's social-Catholic proposals, see Malefakis (1970: 347–55). The most famous criticisms of these came from monarchists, but the governing parties themselves did not need the monarchists to legislate, and killed reform on their own.

mop up miners' strongholds with horrifying brutality. Rightists were deeply shocked by these highest levels of civil violence during the Republic, but most concluded that the government responded effectively. Paul Preston notes Francisco Franco's satisfaction at the time "that a conservative Republic ready to use his services could keep the Left at bay."[61] These policies were likely to stick at least until the next election, largely because the conservative coalition was cohesive despite its many disputes. The venerable, corrupt Radicals were not at all the functional equivalents of the hermaphroditic Zentrum of the Weimar Republic; Lerroux's break with the Socialists was definitive, and by 1933 "the conservative orientation of [R]adicalism was affirmed in a clear way."[62]

But unthreatening outcomes in democracy could not be predicted beyond the next election, especially since the Socialists were radicalizing at the national level. This process had begun even before the 1933 elections and intensified after it. Largo Caballero and many local PSOE/UGT leaders supported rhetorically fiery, quasi-revolutionary proposals regarding property ownership and the means for enacting them.[63] The new militancy made itself evident in the June 1934 rural strike and the October 1934 "revolution." Paradoxically, the costs of excluding this newly militant left were never so low as in 1934–35, since the rural strike exhausted and shattered many local units of the FNTT and the events of October only reinforced the preexisting imbalance of coercive power. And while the left's organizational capacities were decimated, the center-right and right deepened their control of the state's security apparatus.

The Right's Basic Preferences under the Popular Front

Had the PSOE been politically isolated, as French Communists were after 1947, its radicalization might not have been threatening. But the events of 1934–35 inspired a new alliance between the left and the center-left parties, whom the CEDA termed the PSOE's "accomplices." This meant that the left as a whole loomed large when elections were called for February 1936.[64] From the start, substantial uncertainty hung over exactly what the Popular Front would do were it to win power. The Front contained centrists, reformists, Socialist maximalists, and Stalinists; it was not clear where its center of gravity lay or how stable that was. Its electoral manifesto was per-

---

61. Preston (1978: 128; 1994: 107). Robinson (1970: 191) notes rightist criticism of commuted death sentences for several revolt participants.
62. Ruiz Manjón (1976: 394).
63. Preston (1978: 105).
64. Juliá (1979), Tusell (1971, I: 214).

ceived as highly ambiguous and a poor indicator of likely behavior in office, particularly because its members could not agree to a common policy on an issue as basic as expropriation of the land. Institutional revisions were proposed, especially to alter the conservative supreme court.[65] The degree to which outcomes were perceived as contingent on proximate events is reflected in General Franco's comment before the vote that, in Preston's words, "everything now hinged on *what* the Popular Front did *if* it won the elections."[66]

Subsequent events clarified ambiguities in directions deeply disturbing to the right. The Front won the election with 47 percent of the vote, to the right's 45 to 46 percent. Centrists and Left-Republicans formed governments backed by the PSOE from *outside* the cabinet, leaving the "fundamental force in the coalition" apparently free of responsibility and restraint.[67] The cabinet resumed the land reform and other first *bienio* projects and made few or no significant concessions to rightists. But the most notable threats to the right emerged *desde abajo*, from below, from gradually escalating direct action and violence. What Payne terms the "ominous Spring" (February to July 1936) emerges in historiographical treatments as chaotic, in part because many of the most important events took place at the local level, distant from the lagging attentions of the (increasingly censored) national press. Violence was not exclusively directed against the right, but most was. More important, government policy was often one of tolerance.[68] The differences between 1936 and 1931–33 were dramatic:

- In 1931–33, the left coalition was prominently committed to moderate legislation; in 1936 the right perceived the PSOE's (much less the PCE's) commitment to the Front's ostensibly moderate election program as very shallow.
- In 1931–33, the extent of the left's ambitions over property distribution was uncertain; by 1936, the PSOE had spent over two years calling for

65. Cierva (1969: 609, 659), Bassols Coma (1981: 59–62). We might reasonably conclude that the Popular Front also would have called for a reversal of any protective upper house the constitution or second *bienio* might have created. The PSOE publicly declared itself dissatisfied with the Front's 1936 common program; Tusell (1971: 184, 199, 214).

66. Preston (1994: 114), emphasis added.

67. Juliá (1979: 161).

68. Payne (1970: 185–214). There was a prominent attempt to assassinate the PSOE's Jiménez de Asúa, and the Falange initiated frequent clashes. Leftist activists were aware of the government's leniency; see Benito Pabón's remarks in Payne (1993: 315). The PSOE had always manifested a mixed judgment of working-class violence. Jiménez de Asúa had vigorously defended the peasants tried for the Castilblanco violence against Civil Guards and prominently adhered to social-psychological theories that downplayed individual responsibility for certain acts.

an overthrow of the rural property regime and was cooperating with the revolutionary CNT and PCE.

- In 1931, Socialist leaders proclaimed they were committed to the legislative process; by 1936, they called for rule by decree.
- In 1931–33, rightists could reasonably hope that the Socialists would be able to discipline their rank-and-file; by 1936 many rightists believed leaders of the left could not bring direct action to a stop even if they wanted to.

It is difficult to exaggerate the significance of the events in 1936. In some areas, wage-related strikes spread and local authorities required employers to hire assigned workers. Beginning in March a "great wave of farm seizures" assumed awesome dimensions. By July it had already accomplished the transfer of an estimated 5 percent of total cropland. In Badajoz, some sixty thousand peasants, "more than half of the adult male rural population," may have been involved. Gabriel Jackson concludes that "[t]he months of June and July witnessed truly revolutionary events in both city and countryside. . . . Property lines and authority melted . . . in the countryside of western and southern Spain, a profound agrarian revolution was indeed beginning."[69] Maximalist socialists all along intended to tie the government's hands: "We must settle the agrarian problem by ourselves in such a way that the . . . government need only give legal form to realities which the peasant organizations have already created."[70] Violence and intimidation accompanied the strikes, the land invasions, and the "spontaneous socialization" that some workers adopted toward shopkeepers' inventories.

Rates of political killing appear to have exceeded those of 1919–22 in Italy and occurred in the climate of acute interclass hostility and thinly veiled intimidation, which pervaded many factories and the vast agricultural spaces of the south and southwest. Payne suggests that because many large landowners "deserted their properties after the elections . . . it was the rural middle classes, not the latifundists, who bore the brunt of the harassment, violence, and property destruction." In these areas, "the machetes were gleaming," to use James Scott's evocative description of rural class tensions elsewhere.[71] Political trends in democracy were particularly bleak because many rightists concluded that the challenge from the left threatened to inflict irreversible harm on core rightist interests. Even if conservative parties won the next elections (due no later than 1940), by then it might have been impossible to

69. Malefakis (1970: 368–70), Jackson (1965: 220–23). Payne (1993: 341) provides the 5 percent estimate. For business reactions to these events, see Cabrera (1983: 287–306).

70. Quoted in Malefakis (1970: 365–66).

71. Payne (1970: 191), Scott (1985: 254). Malefakis compiled statistics on the violence in 1936, published in Linz (1978b: 188).

reverse the effects of mass expropriation, for example. This explains why defection from democracy made sense even though the right won nearly 46 percent of the vote in 1936 (to the Popular Front's 47 percent) and thus had excellent prospects for winning in the future.[72]

By the spring and summer of 1936, rightists in Spain found both their core interests over property and their safety under accelerating assault in democracy. Compared to that certain defeat, even an authoritarian project that imposed risks of regime/opposition conflict and repression could appear preferable.

"Attending Democracy's Funeral": The Right's Regime Preferences, 1934–36

Rightist Acquiescence, 1934–35

The pattern of contingent protections from the end of 1933 to the start of 1936 and then the gradual disappearance of any protection explains a dramatic switch in regime preferences in the same period. In 1934–35, openly pro-authoritarian groups remained very weak. Preston and others speculate that Gil Robles conspired to carry out a coup while he was minister of defense.[73] But this suspicion may conflate active support for a coup or an actual attempt to mount one, for which there is no evidence, with hedging—maintaining close relations with rightist military commanders and explicitly (if privately) considering the conditions under which a coup might be necessary and how it might be carried out—which clearly did occur. The absence of a coup was not for lack of opportunity. Control of the military by the center-right government meant exclusion was far easier to impose in 1934–35 than in 1931–33 (or for that matter after February 1936). It was also not due to a lack of efforts by exclusionary entrepreneurs. Some strategic actors had for years attacked the CEDA's Republic-supporting role in 1933–35, reorganized to broaden their appeal, and campaigned incessantly: "Calvo Sotelo spoke at meetings up and down the country, but his movement failed to attract the C.E.D.A.'s masses." Nor was the left unthreatening in 1934–35; Juliá emphasizes that even the "moderate part of the right, the legalists, the accidentalists" believed that Spain was threatened by Marxist hordes.[74]

---

72. Franco argued the coup prevented "what might have been irreparable"; Fundación Nacional Francisco Franco (1987: 18).

73. Preston (1978: 129–30), Jackson (1965: 172–73n7), Payne (1993: 238–39).

74. Robinson (1966: 182), Juliá (1979: 56).

What was key was that in 1934–35, rightists had no *motive* to relocate decision-making power even to conservative authoritarian rulers, who at best could generate marginal policy improvements over existing conservative governments in democracy, at the price of heightened risks to security. Control of the state apparatus gave rightists their best opportunity yet to exclude the left, but also the least motive, just as when French conservatives returned to office in 1938. Gil Robles used just such terms to dismiss the notion that he favored a coup while in the government: "Why would I become Minister of Defense to start a coup d'état? What need did I have of the army in order to win? . . . Even if I had thought about such a thing, even if the army would have forgotten its duty—which it did not—what need did I have of that? Who doubts that all of Spain is with us . . . those, like ourselves, who have Spain as a whole with them, have enough power, with the backing of the citizenry, with votes."[75]

One important piece of evidence supports the notion that defection from democracy was not yet occurring as late as the start of the 1936 election campaign. Rightist leaders negotiating joint multicandidate slates themselves believed that authoritarian sentiments did not predominate among their voters. The monarchists acquiesced to only a modest minority of slots, and the fascist Falange was not accommodated at all. These leaders' beliefs were ratified when rightist voters overwhelmingly rejected the few stand-alone pro-authoritarian candidate slates.[76] Capable of operating comfortably in the world of hedging—between reliable support and outright defection—rightist leaders maintained close ties to the military, granted hundreds of thousands of licenses for private guns (some of which the Popular Front would later confiscate), and appear to have consulted several foreign embassies to test those countries' likely reaction in the event the Popular Front won the upcoming election and was then overthrown.[77] But they did not defect, yet.

Measuring Defection from Democracy in 1936

It is tempting to suggest that defection was not the first preference of rightists. Franco was among many who preferred that the Popular Front government itself suppress workers' direct action and union "agitation."[78]

---

75. *El debate,* July 2, 1935, p. 2.
76. The Falange ran separately and received less than 1 percent of the vote nationwide. Carlist monarchists running separately in Castellón and Santander won under 10 percent of the vote.
77. Payne (1993: 306), Valls (1992: 228).
78. Preston (1994: 120–21).

Indeed the first preference of many rightists was surely for a Republic governed by parties of the right. I could go further and make the equally valid claim that many rightists' *truly* first preference would have been for Spain to have a thoroughly moderate working class. Crucially, none of these options was on offer in the summer of 1936. The Popular Front had won the election and was not inclined to block workers. It was not even clear that its leaders could have delivered on any such inclinations. Rightists confronted an unhappy choice, between outcomes as they were in democracy under the Popular Front or a military coup with the various risks that that entailed.

Many on the right concluded that military rule was the least worst choice available. Defection was often grudging and to all appearances took cognizance of the risks of authoritarianism as well as its potential benefits. Cambó's diary later articulated this from wartime exile: "I am anti-fascist, anti-dictatorial, but, in the face of anarchy, as a lesser evil, force must be used."[79] A number of conservatives who cannot be accused fairly of long-standing authoritarian sympathies endorsed military intervention to restore public order. Among these conservatives were Cambó, Miguel de Unamuno, and Lerroux, who later wrote that "if power is in the middle of the street, I will fall into line with the soldier who goes to pick it up to save the country from anarchy."[80] Such statements suggest the somewhat different claim that many rightists might have been satisfied with a brief military interlude aimed at suppressing violent direct action and restoring state authority. But for our purposes this is a distinction without a difference: it is an induced preference for an antidemocratic solution to the problems in 1936. Ramón Serrano Suñer, Franco's brother-in-law and a politician straddling the line between the CEDA and the Falange, insists that momentum for the coup would never have built up without violence in the spring of 1936.[81] But there is every reason to believe that many rightists would have reacted similarly had the Popular Front forces simply legislated all the expropriation of property that occurred through direct action.

Most studies that touch on the subject conclude that the civilian right massively backed the coup. How can we measure this? We can imagine that it took time for rightists to form firm expectations about the likely trajectory of events under the Popular Front. After the election's first round

79. Cambó (1982: vol. 2, p. 21). A decade earlier, Cambó (1925: 89) argued that Italian fascism attracted support when "there awoke in the bourgeoisie the instinct to preserve its wealth, [when] there ignited among intellectuals the desire to protect their culture from barbarianism."

80. Vincent (1996: 247), Lerroux (1945: 570).

81. Interviews in Madrid, 1993 and 1995.

showed the Popular Front ahead, some rightist leaders pressured Prime Minister Manuel Portela and Franco (then chief of the general staff) to annul the elections, but Franco was among those who waited to see exactly what Popular Front rule would be like. A letter to Franco from one of his correspondents suggested this period's emphasis on hypothetical if-then calculations by addressing what would happen "[I]f you and your comrades at any time feel that the circumstances which you mention come about and you are pushed to a rising."[82] By the summer, many of the right's most feared if-then "circumstances" were materializing, and the right became what it had not been at any point since 1931: an activated constituency for a coup. While a conservative military coup was obviously not guaranteed to succeed, it at least held out a reasonable chance for rightists to secure their basic preferences, whereas they appeared certain to experience economic and perhaps political extinction in democracy. The Popular Front governments were painfully aware of the unreliability of the right's regime preferences; in Casares Quiroga's words, "After five years the Republic still needs to defend itself from its enemies."[83] The right was defecting from democracy for rational reasons; for equally rational reasons, the left would resist.

There are no concrete indicators of regime preferences in the spring of 1936. But nearly all scholars identify massive rightist sympathy for the July coup. After the February elections, Gil Robles, *El debate*, and most of the *cúpula*—the national leadership—of the CEDA publicly urged rightists to respect the election results and the legally constituted authority they produced, and Gil Robles insisted neither he nor the CEDA could be the vehicle for an exclusionary bid against the left.[84] As a result, rightists searching for such a vehicle had to look elsewhere. Proscription in April forced the Falange underground, depriving researchers of official data on its membership, but scholars have agreed that that affiliation expanded exponentially in the spring and summer. In Payne's words, the "swing toward 'fascism' by the Spanish Right was definitely beginning." In May, the rightist *Ya* surveyed its Madrid readers' preferred candidate for president, and the Falange's José Antonio topped the poll, an outcome inconceivable even a few months earlier.[85] The conservative *La vanguardia* asked:

---

82. Payne (1987: 81–82), Preston (1994: 114).

83. *DSC* 29 (May 19, 1936), p. 693; Payne (1993: 325).

84. *El debate*, February 19, 1936, p. 1; February 26, 1936, p. 1; March 6, 1936, pp. 1–2; March 15, 1936, p. 1; and May 3, 1936, p. 1.

85. Payne (1961: 98, 107); also Jackson (1965: 198), Robinson (1970: 254). The government blocked publication of the results of the *Ya* poll, which were circulated outside Spain and published by Bravo Martínez (1940: 180–81). The four leading candidates were Primo de Rivera (38,496 "votes"), Calvo Sotelo (29,522), Gil Robles (29,201), and Lerroux (27,624).

How many votes did the Fascists have in Spain in the last election? Nothing: a ridiculously small amount. . . . Today, on the other hand, travelers returning from different parts of Spain are saying: "There everybody is becoming a fascist." What kind of change is this? What had happened? What has happened is simply that it is no longer possible to live, that there is no government. . . . Fascism is . . . the sinister shadow projected across the land by democracy itself, when its internal decomposition turns it into anarchy.[86]

Growth of the Falange was accompanied by coordination between local CEDA affiliates and local military units.[87]

Perhaps most poignantly, "mainstream" conservative leaders acknowledged the massive defection of their own rank-and-file. In June, Maura wrote that "[t]here could not fail to be a reaction. This has taken shape in the alarming form of what is called 'fascism.' People have joined that movement en masse." Gil Robles acknowledged that "a violent spirit is growing in non-Marxist ranks" and support for exclusion "is growing, augmenting, and winning in immense sectors of Spanish opinion." Like others at the time, Gil Robles recognized that his once-mighty party was not simply being outflanked; in Robinson's words, he "knew . . . the CEDA was disintegrating."[88] Recognition of this had direct consequences even before the coup. In April, rightist party leaders selected joint slates for new elections in two provinces, and nearly half of the (formerly CEDA) spots on the Granada slate were turned over to the Falange, while the initial new list in Cuenca was made up of Primo de Rivera, General Franco, an ex-Agrarian, and only one CEDA candidate. Primo de Rivera, although later disqualified, appears to have been the top vote-getter for the slate.[89] By the summer of 1936, plotters detected massive sympathy for a conservative coup on the part of civilian rightists. The inclusion of many conservative republican Radicals in the coup coalition inspired Franco to urge that the uprising and war effort initially downplay monarchical intentions. In this sense, the true backbone of the revolt was not the army (as Calvo Sotelo thought) or agrarian elites (as several analyses of interwar Europe suggest) but the muscular middle strata whose extensive and intense support propelled the military finally to act.

If defection from democracy is difficult to measure, how did conspirators detect latent support? As in other cases, "civilian pressure to intervene

86. Payne (1993: 448n47).

87. For developments in one region, see Valls (1992: 228–33).

88. Maura's series began on June 18; see Jackson (1965: 216). For Gil Robles' remarks, see *El debate*, April 24, 1936, pp. 1–2; *El debate*, March 15, 1936, p. 1; and Robinson (1970: 259, 292).

89. Gil Robles (1968: 558–70).

in the political process . . . was conveyed to military officers through the medium of personal contacts, public manifestos, and newspaper editorials."[90] Plotters initiated contact with a variety of rightist groups and were promised support in the event of a coup by civilians such as Calvo Sotelo, portions of the CEDA youth sector, the Carlists, and the Falange. Serrano Suñer insists that as events unfolded "everyone simply knew" that a military coup would attract the support of most on the right. Plotters' assessments of support in their local areas had a decisive influence on behavior. Serrano Suñer remembers that a regular feature of conversation in conspiratorial circles was that the uprising would face stiff odds in left-dominated regions. While the revolt was swift and complete in conservative areas like Navarre and Old Castile, few garrisons in leftist bastions risked "pronouncing" to begin with. Insofar as General Emilio Mola calculated that the coup would fail in places like Madrid and that columns would need to fight a brief campaign of conquest, the coup was not inherently botched: it was going to have to be a (mini-) civil war all along.[91] Plotters knew a coup's prospects were poorer than two years before when the right controlled the state; they launched one anyway.

High risks in democracy predetermined only one outcome: the right hedged. The conservatives were not inherently either prodemocratic or pro-authoritarian; they adapted to circumstances. Those circumstances ensured that the Second Republic did not consolidate, because the members of at least one major group were not reliably prodemocratic, not even (not especially) in their own eyes. Hedging did not predetermine support for the 1936 coup or a breakdown in any other specific form. The great majority of conservatives did not respond to pro-authoritarian appeals when their parties lost the 1931 elections to a moderate left, or when the Socialists radicalized but the right held office, and may not even have done so when the Popular Front first took office in 1936 under conditions of substantial uncertainty. It was only when highly threatening political outcomes materialized that rightists clamored for a coup. In one sense, Robinson and Preston, usually portrayed as historiographical opponents, are both correct. Many rightists initially accepted the Republic as Robinson contends, but only provisionally, and then they rebelled against it, as

---

90. Stepan (1971: 95).

91. Serrano Suñer interview, Madrid, 1995. Robinson (1970: 279–80) shows that the plotters disagreed over whether mass support was required to carry out a coup or only to stabilize exclusionary rule afterward, and suggests that Mola believed the coup would be wider than it was.

Preston argues. But they did so in reaction to the behavior and choices of the left as Robinson claims, even if there was no "Red plot," as Preston emphasizes.[92]

The evidence is not persuasive that international demonstration effects (IDEs) played a key causal role in these events. As in other cases, rightists repeatedly proved capable of sharply distinguishing their situation from events abroad. While one Jesuit magazine warned that republicanism was not right for Spain though perhaps it was for the United States, where "people know how to be democrats," other "accidentalists" cited Catholic *ralliement* to France's democratic Third Republic. While some *cedistas* admired Italy and Nazi Germany as authoritarian models, the CEDA leadership modeled the party in part on the German Zentrum, a victim not a proponent of dictatorship, and Gil Robles, Luis Lucía, and Federico Salmón rejected fascism and Nazism as ideologies.[93] Perhaps most clearly, the specter of communism did not inspire rightists to a panicked reaction against all left agendas. Luis Lucía's *Diario de Valencia* sharply distinguished the Largo Caballero wing from the PSOE moderates. After the 1934 revolt, *El debate* appealed for a crackdown not on all leftist organizations but only those promoting violent revolution.[94] In the wake of that uprising, Left-Republican newspapers such as *El defensor de Granada* continued to publish without interruption, and *La humanitat*, an Esquerra organ in Barcelona, reappeared days after the Catalan "revolt," whereas PSOE and PCE newspapers were suspended until 1936. Under the Popular Front, rightist leaders once again distinguished between PSOE moderates and radicals.[95] In general, rightists were often painfully aware of international contrasts rather than parallels. The Lliga's *La veu de Catalunya* editorialized that "we prefer that Catalonia resemble Norway, for example, and not the Venezuela of General Castro or General Gómez." But they also knew that they faced a left unlike that faced by the right in some other countries; in this spirit,

92. Robinson (1970), Preston (1978).

93. Vincent (1996: 152), Robinson (1970: 75), Tusell (1974: 172, 179).

94. *Diario de Valencia,* July 28, 1933, p. 1; *El debate,* October 31, 1934, p. 1. Lines were blurred at times, including in the arrest of Azaña in 1934. But even this vindictive act was justified by (erroneous) accusations of active participation in the revolt, and Azaña was acquitted by the heavily conservative supreme court.

95. *El debate,* February 12, 1936, p. 2, and February 19, 1936, p. 2, categorized Popular Front supporters who wanted a stable Republic versus a revolution; the latter included the PCE and only "part of" the PSOE. Gil Robles (1968: 617–19) encouraged talks with Prieto to feel out the possibility of a government ranging from moderate *cedistas* to moderate Socialists; also *El debate,* April 24, 1936, p. 1. Preston (1978: 192–93) suggests that Gil Robles merely "tolerated" these talks in the (equally remote) hope they might split the PSOE. But even this portrays Gil Robles as making important operational distinctions between Socialists.

the conservative Republican *La noche* regretfully acknowledged that "here we are not English."[96]

Strategic Action and Leadership Opportunities in 1936

Until the coup was launched, the Popular Front government relied almost exclusively on a strategy of attempting to make an authoritarian project less attractive to the right rather than making expected outcomes in democracy more so. The Front vigorously suppressed the Falange and resumed reassigning suspect military officers to peripheral commands.[97] The amnesty of those arrested in 1934 restored much of the left's organization. And while the government did not provide arms to trade unions—whose activists proposed to reformat as militias—neither did it disarm leftist "action groups." Prieto warned that "[i]f reaction dreams of a bloodless *coup d'état* like that of 1923, it is entirely mistaken. If it supposes that it will find the regime defenceless, it is deluding itself. To conquer it will have to surmount the human barrier with which the proletarian masses bar its way."[98] The larger and more militant leftist groups were, the more costly it would be to exclude them.

But the larger and more militant the leftist groups were, the more threatening they were in democracy. The government transmitted numerous signals that policy trends highly disadvantageous to the right were likely to continue and intensify. Moreover, government tolerance of direct action eroded the security-related risk advantage that democracy would otherwise have offered. As a result, authoritarianism offered the prospect of a net *increase* in rightists' safety. Prieto was one of the few leaders of the left to argue publicly that civil violence "only suffered by the upper classes" could provoke disaster. The conservative *La veu de Catalunya* warned in June and July that "[w]hat has to happen is that the government end the disorder. . . . It is not possible for matters to continue indefinitely in this manner."[99]

96. *La veu,* July 18, 1936, p. 1, and June 4, 1936, p. 1; *La noche* (Barcelona), July 2, 1936, p. 8, and July 3, 1936, p. 8.

97. Palacio Atard (1970).

98. Robinson (1970: 275); Araquistain (1934: 470). The fact that the left suffered the least optimal overall outcome in 1936 has invited speculation that maximalist socialists either (a) underestimated the right's capacities to conduct a coup (b) overestimated the left's capacities to resist one, or (c) misestimated the degree to which leftist actions would provoke a coup. The nature of strategic action in democratic breakdowns may deny government leaders crucial information, since plotters attempt to conceal their plan's membership, magnitude, and schedule.

99. Linz (1978b: 194); *La veu de Catalunya,* June 17, 1936, p. 10, and July 7, 1936, p. 8. Also *La noche* (Barcelona), July 6, 1936, p. 10, July 9, 1936, p. 8, and July 13, 1936, p. 10, and *Ren*

Calvo Sotelo's assassination suggested that not even rightists protected by visibility and parliamentary immunity were safe.

Rightist plotters could anticipate segmental support for a successful coup. The coup was not merely an epiphenomenal product of the emergence of a coup constituency. Among officers associated with the Unión militar Española (UME), plotting began soon after the February 1936 elections. General Mola assumed leadership of the main cabal, which government surveillance forced the plotters to repeatedly renew and retool even as negotiations proceeded among diverse conspiratorial strands. Supply was shaped by more than just demand.[100] But demand was crucial. The plot's architects had witnessed or experienced the failure of socially isolated military projects in 1930–31 and 1932; Preston argues that Franco was profoundly influenced by both episodes.[101] They thus took steps not only to secure the unity of the military but also to influence mass rightist choices. The coup's midlevel "technicians" sought leaders with credibility among civilians. They formulated a program to be released at the outset of the coup, promising what amounted to radically different political outcomes than those expected in democracy. And the plotters moved to take advantage of the "ideal psychological moment" provided by rightist outrage over Calvo Sotelo's assassination.[102]

Only when the coup had been activated in Spanish Morocco and the northern garrisons did the Popular Front indicate it would move political outcomes in democracy in the right's direction by quickly appointing a more centrist prime minister and apparently even offering to name Mola to the cabinet. This was not so much too little as too late; its intended recipients dismissed the gesture as an insincere tactic.

What could left leaders have done to prevent the coup? Another pair of historical opponents can be said to be correct. Rightist defection might have been averted had the left and right acted and interacted differently, as Chapaprieta suggested when he argued that "peace was possible." But no obvious changes in the Popular Front's behavior could have induced

---

ovación (Barcelona), July 16, 1936, p. 1, which editorialized that "without control of the masses, or of the security forces, nor of the organized workers' movement, the outcome of the current situation appears tragic, unless it is avoided by a patriotic spirit which is put before all else, to save Spain and the Republic from the abyss at which we stand."

100. Olaya Morales (1979: ch. 11).

101. Several of the UME plotters had been associated with Sanjurjo's putsch. Franco appears to number among those who believed some measure of social support was imperative; Payne (1993: 83n27), Preston (1994: 113, 130).

102. Robinson (1970: 286), Preston (1994: 137). Both Sanjurjo and Franco were well known and respected among civilian rightists, which is why they had been featured as conservative parliamentary candidates.

rightists to abandon *hedges*, in no small part because by 1936 many rightists concluded that left leaders lacked not only the desire but also the capacity to control their rank-and-file. In that sense, true "peace" was "not possible," as Gil Robles claimed.[103] Left leaders had no tools with which to persuade rightists that outcomes in democracy would be so moderate that it was worth abandoning hedges against the risk of another radical surge.

What role did opinion leadership play in the right's defection? Gil Robles eventually secretly ordered cadres to cooperate with the plot and funneled CEDA campaign funds to its organizers, but in public, where opinion leadership presumably takes place, he urged acceptance of the 1936 election results and new government until late in the Republic's final phase, when the Falange were already overflowing with new members. If the CEDA's opinion leadership caused rightists to provisionally accept democracy before 1936, how can we explain massive defection that year? Claims that radical-right opinion leaders were the cause of defection have the opposite burden, of explaining why these leaders did not have that effect before February 1936. Actors' comparisons of alternatives provide a more consistent explanation: the right's payoff structure changed dramatically in 1936, inspiring rightists at the mass level to "jump the rails," defecting to a political project that would seek their policy preferences in an authoritarian context. Unwilling to run fast enough to keep ahead of its rank-and-file, the CEDA was eclipsed by leaders who were. Julio Gil Pecharromán argues that Calvo Sotelo's "influence" among "the rightist masses grew with the deterioration in the social and political situation." This interpretation invests influence in the changing situation, not Calvo Sotelo. Even organizational leadership played no obvious crucial role in the coup.[104]

Actors on the right were not the only ones for whom the answer to the question, "Democracy with whom?" was crucial to the selection among possible decision rules. Maximalist socialist leader Largo Caballero remarked in 1936 that "Marxism is the enemy of the class struggle. . . . Marxism wants classes to disappear, wants there to be only one class." Unfortunately, the only way maximalists saw to achieve this was to eliminate the bourgeoisie

    103. For example, Goicoechea in *ABC*, February 29, 1936, p. 23; Lerroux (1945: 226). Both *La veu de Catalunya*, June 4, 1936, p. 1, and one of General Mola's first 1936 secret circulars portrayed the government as "prisoners" of working-class organizations; Robinson (1970: 279). Even Jackson (1965: 196) concludes that Azaña's 1936 government was simply "*desbordado*, 'swamped,' by its own masses."

    104. Gil Pecharromán (1994: 269). CEDA propaganda had made Gil Robles a type of *caudillo*, but he insisted he would not lead a coup. Calvo Sotelo was spectacularly killed before the revolt began. The coup was nominally led by General Sanjurjo, who immediately died in a plane crash. The plot was organized by the efficient but uncharismatic Mola, who also soon died. Only gradually did Franco rise in the Nationalist firmament. This was a coup in search of a leader, not the other way around.

in a class struggle. In this way, both socialists and rightists preferred democracy. They simply preferred it without each other.[105] This pattern was not immutable, however. As we will see, if interwar rightists recognized that "here we are not English," their successors in the 1970s would say, sometimes explicitly, that "now we are not that previous Spain."

105. The 1934 leftist revolt, while attempting to overthrow a legally elected parliamentary majority, did not reflect a systematic aversion to democracy. The PSOE maintained participatory intraparty decision-making. Local PSOE and UGT members elected delegates who in turn debated issues at congresses, voted to establish party policy, elected their leadership, and selected electoral candidates. As late as June 1936, the PSOE conducted a nationwide balloting among its members to fill vacancies in national party offices; see Contreras (1981: 123–69), Jackson (1965: 221–22).

5

Democratic Transition and Consolidation in Spain, 1976–1986

> Members of the government have recently proclaimed the need to make political pacts. . . . But we encounter a few problems. . . . With whom should the government pact? . . . Pact yes, but with whom?
>
> ADOLFO SUÁREZ, June 1976

By the mid-1970s, Spanish rightists' regime preferences had shifted from pro-authoritarian to prodemocratic. Within the regime leadership, this shift in regime preferences meant the emergence of "soft-liners" and full-fledged democratizers, who carried out what must rank with the fall of the Berlin Wall as the most celebrated post-1945 transition to democracy. Moreover, after 1977 these conservatives, to all appearances, were committed to democracy, abandoning ambivalent regime discourses and access to coercive instruments. It is generally agreed that Spain developed a consolidated democracy at least by the early 1980s. In this chapter I argue that conservatives made this shift because they perceived that democracy not only posed few threats in 1976–77 but also represented a predictably low risk, since the Spanish left was likely to be predictably moderate. Rightists appear to have based such predictions on the belief that deep-running social-structural changes that occurred under Franco—especially the massive expansion of the middle class—had undermined the social bases of left radicalism. My argument in this chapter neither assumes that authoritarianism is a necessary stage in economic development nor that "modernization" has specific determinative effects on democracy. It simply contends that Spanish rightists believed that industrialization, middle-class predominance, and greater economic security in general had changed fundamentally the answer to the question, "Democracy with whom?" I support this argument with voting and survey data as well as two sets of interviews. I first analyze the transition in 1976–77 and then consolidation after 1977.

The Spanish transition, like many other major events, is more difficult to demarcate in time than one might assume initially. For many, it began with King Juan Carlos's appointment of Prime Minister Adolfo Suárez in mid-1976; for others, with the crowning of the king six months earlier or with tepid reforms in early and mid-1976. The transition can be said to have ended in 1977 (the year of the first elections), 1978 (with the adoption of the constitution), or 1982 (when the left entered office). Throughout this extended period, diverse forces engaged in intense signaling and interaction, involving demonstrations, strikes, arrests, releases, and conversations, as they jockeyed for advantage and institutional and electoral support. Western European governments and parties intervened to promote successful democratic implantation. The evident complexity of these years has raised important questions regarding what role memory and international actors have played, why the party system developed as it did, what influenced constitutional forms, and what explains rates of participation after 1977.[1]

Among these and other possible questions, I focus on a narrow but crucial one: what explains rightists' induced preferences for democracy rather than authoritarianism in 1976 and afterward? While the extended transition was complex, two specific decisions in 1976 were critical. Raymond Carr and Juan Pablo Fusi conclude that "what the first Suárez government achieved seems extraordinary": dominated by "soft-liners" and backed by many senior regime figures, it established contacts with the opposition and by November 1976, proposed a sweeping political reform bill to the Francoist legislature, which was then to be submitted to the people in a referendum.[2] Rejection at either stage would indicate support for authoritarian maintenance. The Cortes approved the reform by a vote of 425 to 59, with 13 abstentions. In the referendum campaign afterward, pro-authoritarian leaders campaigned for a "no" vote, while Socialists and Communists urged abstention. But 77 percent cast ballots, and of them 94.2 percent voted for reform. Since left voters made up a heavy concentration of abstainers and only 2.6 percent cast "no" votes, we can conclude that the vast majority of center-right and right voters supported a transition.

There can be little doubt that these decisions were deliberate rather than "unintended."[3] In many cases, the shift in regime preferences was accom-

1. For example, McDonough, Barnes, and López Pina (1998).
2. Carr and Fusi (1979: 218).
3. Two contrary claims have been made about the Cortes vote. First, Cortes members may not have understood what the reform would lead to. But then the strident objections of

plished within the lifetime of numerous older rightists who had backed the 1936 coup (people eighteen years old in 1936 were fifty-eight years old in 1976) or involved a shift by younger rightists who at the very least had been educated under Francoist rule. Continuing after 1977, only marginal numbers of these same voters cast ballots for pro-authoritarian parties; center-right parties and governments did not cultivate privileged partisan ties with the military; and all significant conservative organizations rejected and condemned the 1981 coup attempt. It was this commitment, even when the Socialists won an absolute majority in 1982, that enabled the left to campaign and then legislate without fears of mass segmental defection from democracy.

Explaining the Decisions to Democratize

Despite extensive scrutiny of the transition, there is still no widespread agreement as to what explains the crucial decisions that initiated and sustained it, decisions that remain perplexing. One influential set of interpretations suggests that the regime elite only grudgingly abandoned authoritarianism in the face of prohibitively costly societal resistance, exclusion from the European Common Market, or internal regime decomposition. In contrast, culturalist theories explain the transition in terms of increasingly prevalent, sincere prodemocratic norms. Within the terms of this latter interpretation, some in Spain have argued that the passing of generations was crucial, since those who had experienced the events of 1936–39 were too embittered to compromise. But theorists of "democratic learning" have argued that it is precisely firsthand experience with costly violence that makes actors more willing to compromise.[4]

In this chapter I argue that the Spanish right committed to democracy as a result of weighing the payoffs of regime alternatives. The right shifted strategy between the 1930s and the 1970s because the calculatory contexts of 1936 and 1976 were dramatically different. In the 1930s, the right had

---

proauthoritarian rightists become inexplicable, and Share (1986: 110–12) shows that Cortes members understood the law meant competitive party elections. Others have argued that a clearly reformist bill was approved by reactionary Francoist legislators only as the result of the Suárez government's threats and bribes, reviving images of Laval manipulating French parliamentarians to abandon constitutional forms in 1940. As with 1940, this image underestimates the preexisting popularity of the course of action eventually chosen. Most Cortes members had already voted for the mildly reformist associations law earlier in 1976 without unusual arm-twisting, and all those who voted against the Political Reform had also voted against that earlier law; see Sánchez Navarro (1990: 21).

4. Prominent examples of these approaches include works by Maravall (1982), Pérez-Díaz (1993), Bermeo (1992), and Aguilar Fernández (1996).

been preoccupied for decades with social-revolutionary impulses discernible among industrial workers and millions of desperate landless laborers. In mid-1936, conservatives perceived full-blown threats in democracy to their basic preferences over safety, property, and the Catholic Church. In the face of this, conservative military rule compensated for its inevitable risks of violence with vastly more favorable policies than were on offer in democracy. By the late 1960s and early 1970s, conservative forecasts of likely outcomes in democracy had changed dramatically.[5] Conservatives became convinced that the prospective democratic electorate was highly unlikely to generate property-threatening policies or extensive civil violence. Crucially, this forecast was not based on tactical behavior by left parties. The PCE in these years tacked closer to the center, but if anything the PSOE radicalized (at least rhetorically) in the lead-up to the transition, proclaiming itself a Marxist party for the first time.[6] Instead, the right believed left leaders would be hemmed in by the fact that the social bases of the radical left had been powerfully eroded by changes in Spain's social structure, income and educational levels, and to a lesser extent the effects of the civil war. This meant that the right could expect to secure its basic preferences over both policy issues and safety in democracy—even in the event of electoral alternation—without having to incur the risks of exposure to repression inherent even under a sympathetic authoritarian regime. Conservative authoritarian rule became a solution to a problem that no longer existed.

This calculus was only strengthened by events in democracy after 1977. Conservative perceptions that moderation of the left was enduring and not merely contingent were confirmed by important differences between events that occurred between the interwar period and the initial years of post-Franco democracy. In 1931–33, moderate-left party and union leaders fended off bottom-up pressures for more radical land reform, worker control, and nationalization measures. In contrast, democracy after Franco generated sharply declining worker mobilization and bottom-up pressures to moderate, not radicalize. The one major attempt at radicalization of the left, in 1979, failed for lack of rank-and-file support. And the party that emphatically dominated the left portion of the spectrum, the PSOE under Felipe González, had socioeconomic ambitions largely limited to the indus-

5. The regime-endorsing 1966 referendum is not by itself persuasive evidence that authoritarian support was strong at that time, since the regime continued to vigorously punish opposition. It is no more credible that only 1.8 percent of the population opposed the further elaboration of Francoism, than that 93 percent in 1947 favored the regime's initial institutionalization, the *Caudillo*'s dominance, and monarchical restoration. Both must be discounted in the same way as the 1924 Italian and 1933 German elections.

6. Juliá (1990).

trial modernization and welfare-state policies already begun under Franco and expanded under the democratic center-right. This left moderation explains why the right committed to democracy after 1977 despite the failure of initial pacting, the center-right's lengthy exclusion from office (1982–96), and institutions that were in many ways loss-concentrating.

Rightists also did so despite what was, if anything, a *decline* in the costs of excluding the left. For this reason, approaches that explain democratic stability in terms of rising costs of authoritarianism are sharply challenged by the Spanish case. Similarly, as we will see, heightened sensitivity to the costs of civil war does not constitute a persuasive answer to the question of why rightists defected from authoritarianism to democracy. This overall argument contains a counterfactual causal claim: had perceived risks in democracy remained high, the Spanish right should have either continued to prefer authoritarianism or at least hedged heavily in democracy, even if all other events were somehow to be held constant. Interviews conducted with two samples of conservative actors permit a rare opportunity for testing the plausibility of a counterfactual claim of this kind.

Sources of Data on Conservative Beliefs about Regime Alternatives

Regime preferences can be established through survey data from before, during, and after the 1976–77 transition, voting results beginning in 1976, and data on organizational membership. These measures consistently reveal high levels of support for democracy over authoritarian alternatives. However, available data are limited concerning actors' expectations of likely outcomes under regime alternatives. This limitation is striking because most influential theories of the transition contain at least implicit claims about the perceptions of the authoritarian leadership around the time of Franco's death—for example, claims that rising costs of exclusion impelled democratization. These theories are therefore largely speculative.[7] Some data exist in politicians' speeches, articles, and statements to the press, although oral and written records, produced either contemporaneously or since, generally address specific events rather than the possible consequences of available options. Existing interview and survey data are also very limited in this regard.[8] I developed a supplementary source

7. Share (1986: ch. 2) very effectively reviewed a number of them.
8. Both Martinez's (1993) interviews of business leaders and the Centro de Investigaciones Sociológicas (CIS) Study 1112 (September 1976) of small- and medium-sized business owners revealed support for liberalization and democratization. But neither solicited assessments of the likely results of alternatives. Most interviews with transition leaders have been concerned with establishing the record of events after the transition was initiated. I thank DATA, S. A., for survey materials dating to before the 1976 referendum vote.

of evidence for this study: interviews with two sets of rightists. The first set of interviews was with seventeen transition leaders, including nearly all civilians in the transition cabinet (though not Suárez) and several other prominent elite advocates of the transition (Manuel Fraga, Miguel Primo de Rivera, Laureano López Rodó, and an anonymous participant who played perhaps the most decisive single role in civil-military relations in this period):[9]

Interviews with Suárez Cabinet Members and Other Transition Leaders

Fernando Abril, Agriculture
Leopoldo Calvo-Sotelo, Public Works (also prime minister 1981–82)
Eduardo Carriles, Treasury
Manuel Fraga, former minister and leading conservative transition figure
Ignacio García López, minister of the Francoist ruling party
Landelino Lavilla, Justice
Laureano López Rodó, former commissar of the Plan and former minister of Foreign Affairs
Francisco Lozano Vicente, Housing
José Lladó, Commerce
Rodolfo Martin Villa, Interior
Aurelio Menéndez Menéndez, Education and Science
Alfonso Osorio, vice-president of the Government
Carlos Pérez de Bricio, Industry and Energy
Alvaro Rengifo Calderón, Labor
Miguel Primo de Rivera, sponsor of the Law of Political Reform in the Cortes
Andrés Reguera, Information and Tourism
The anonymous participant

Fifty interviews were also conducted in May to June 1995 with a sample of owners of small retail businesses (*autónomos*) in Madrid, selected in coordination with local retail business associations.[10] These retailers had supported Franco but generally favored democracy in 1976 and since. It is not assumed that owners of small retail businesses in general or these

---

9. Interviews were requested from the fifteen living civilian members of Suárez's first cabinet. Manuel Fraga responded to half the questions but would not respond to the remainder; his responses are included for the questions he addressed. Many of the members of Suárez's cabinet had been civil servants under the old regime; some had also served as heads of large state-owned industries (Osorio, Lozano Vicente, Reguera) or were technical experts in state service (Abril, Lladó). Several had served in the Francoist Cortes prior to their entry into Suárez's cabinet. Six had served in Arias Navarro's last cabinet. The leader interviews were conducted May 1993 to May 1995.

10. The interviews are described in the Appendix.

business owners in particular were representative of the middle class of the 1970s. But *autónomos* were considered one of the pillars of "sociological Francoism," and as a category European small retailers are well known for conservative political sympathies, a stereotype the interviewees overwhelmingly fulfilled. Yet forty-six of the fifty interviewed voted to democratize in 1976, compared to two who voted against it (but said they wavered between ambivalence and generally favoring reform) and two who reported being entirely ambivalent. Since 1977 all but one consistently supported prodemocratic parties. The contrast with the 1930s could hardly be starker.

Conducting interviews raised two important questions. The first is the selection bias obvious in limiting study to actors who supported Franco but later supported democratization. The sample at the very least should have included actors who supported Francoism and opposed the transition, if not actors who filled all four cells of the two-by-two table suggested by these either-or options in two periods. This problem is not mitigated by the fact that the transition's opponents represented less than 3 percent of the 1976 electorate. This error in the original research design is addressed later by examination of the published views of several prominent reform opponents. The second concern is that interviews conducted twenty years after an event might introduce into the research even involuntary revisions of the beliefs actors once held. The format of the interview sessions was designed to address this, and there are three reasons to believe that interviewees' responses were broadly valid. First, many of the interviewees' responses are politically controversial in the post-1977 political climate, and the respondents have had few incentives to revise their memories in these directions. Second, the interviewees proved willing to admit error in certain of their predictions. Third, the interview materials are accompanied by contemporary statements and available survey evidence whose contents are less detailed and nuanced but run parallel in content.

The Background to Transition

The three and a half decades after the civil war witnessed at least four major developments: the institutionalization of conservative authoritarianism, substantial socioeconomic change, integration into the international economy, and gradual political liberalization by the 1960s. In the course of the civil war and in its immediate aftermath, the Nationalist forces disarticulated nonrightist parties and unions. Behind the lines alone, Nationalist forces executed an estimated forty thousand people during the war for political reasons and another thirty thousand in its wake.[11] Hundreds of thousands more were imprisoned, many for years. Franco emerged within the senior Nationalist ranks to lead a regime that imposed a lengthy initial period of severe repression and economic autarchy. This regime preserved property claims and other orthodox economic interests, but the economy stagnated at distressingly low levels, at times involving extensive hunger in the southern countryside. Given its ties to the Axis powers, the regime also attracted, in the wake of World War II, important sanctions by the victorious Allies, including exclusion from the United Nations.[12]

However, the regime soon improved its internal and international situations. The regime's political factions or "families" were organized into the ruling *Movimiento Nacional,* although Richard Gunther aptly terms the later Francoist order a technocratic "no-party state." Stanley Payne describes it as an early case of bureaucratic authoritarianism.[13] The 1960s witnessed some political liberalization, which was neither linear nor uninterrupted. What Juan Linz terms "semiopposition" groups participated in limited debate, while centrists, socialists, and even communists were less thoroughly persecuted than before and operated locally and discreetly, although they remained organizationally feeble and under strict surveillance.[14] Economic liberalization was even more dramatic. Import-substitution industrialization produced limited growth, and agriculture fell in relative terms from accounting for 40 percent of the economy to approximately 25 percent. In a crisis of rapidly mounting deficits and inflation in 1959, a cabinet in which technocrats held key economic posts implemented a liberalizing stabilization plan. Charles Anderson describes the abandonment of the autarchic model as made up less of grand strategy than numerous small adjustments.[15] While this produced neither a "free" domestic market nor open trade, it injected competition into numerous areas of economic life, in addition to the regime's strict safeguarding of public order and traditional religious mores.

Just as profound was the change in Spain's international situation. The regime ingratiated itself with a West in search of anti-Soviet allies, and Spain joined several international conventions and signed key agreements with the United States.[16] Ultimately it became the recipient of both extensive

11. Compared to some thirty-five thousand to sixty thousand executed by Republicans. Payne (1987: 209–28) reviews estimates.
12. Cierva (1978: 25–43). On the old regime, see Payne (1987).
13. Gunther (1980), Payne (1987: 450), Linz (1970).
14. Linz (1973).
15. Anderson (1970: chs. 4–5).
16. Liedtke (1998).

foreign investment and the world's largest tourist flow. By 1970, Spain—still firmly under authoritarian rule—had gained full membership in the United Nations, International Monetary Fund, and World Bank, and achieved associate status with the European Common Market, a status that granted Spanish business many of the economic benefits of membership without open competition in their home market. Spain's economy grew quickly in this period and came to resemble developed European economies much more closely.

The economic expansion had social effects unforeseen by many of the architects of growth. This may not have been strictly true in all cases: just as the social Christian Manuel Giménez-Fernández had wanted "fewer poor and fewer rich" in 1935, the Three-Year Plan of Economic and Social Development produced by Laureano López Rodó in 1964 aimed for "a social diffusion" of property ownership.[17] But market opportunities also drew millions of women into the workforce and flooded the country with visitors and media from Europe's democracies. Mass industrialization and the emergence of an increasingly important service sector meant sweeping changes in places of residence, education and skills, incomes, and standards of living, culminating in a significant expansion of the middle class. Expanding opportunities elicited a "rural exodus" of landless laborers; over 1.5 million people emigrated from rural Andalucía alone between 1951 and 1975. All these changes were accompanied by modest but tangible advances in welfare-state provisions. José Maria Maravall concludes that the "changes in the social structure were very deep."[18]

Franco's final years witnessed growing levels of protests by students and workers; the security forces attacked but could not eliminate Basque separatist violence, and in 1974 authoritarianism collapsed in Portugal. Franco's advancing age and ill health in these years posed urgent questions about the country's future, but no major decisions—beyond Prince Juan Carlos becoming heir to the throne in 1969—could be made until Franco's death in 1975. Even then, Carlos Arias Navarro, Franco's last prime minister and the king's first, attempted unsuccessfully to navigate a course between hardline resistance and profound change. After Suárez's elevation to the position, it came as a shock to many when the regime's leadership abandoned authoritarianism within eighteen months and, crucially, with broad support from conservatives.

17. Comisario del Plan de Desarrollo Económico y Social, *Summary of the Spanish Economic and Social Development Plan, 1964–1967* (Madrid: IMNASA, 1964), p. 39.

18. Maravall (1973: 442). On the welfare state and agrarian social structure, see Esping-Andersen (1994) and Pérez-Díaz (1974).

Forecasting Political Outcomes under Francoism without Franco

Before voting in 1976, what political outcomes did rightists forecast under authoritarian rule in the second half of the 1970s? Contrary to much speculation, there is substantial reason to conclude that rightists believed a strategy of authoritarian maintenance for many years after Franco's death not only was feasible but also did not even risk severe repression or an internal collapse of the regime. Francoism had entrenched a policy formula generally favorable to rightists. And actors had strong bases for predicting broad continuity under authoritarianism after Franco's death. Indeed, Juan Carlos's coronation, the reappointment of Franco's last prime minister, and the appointment of Suárez in 1976 were all publicly regretted by those who feared these events would result in stifling continuity. The regime's policies were designed and administered by a durable technocratic elite that remained very much present. Moreover, international sanctions were far lower in the mid-1970s than had been the case for years after World War II. Spain's regime had successfully integrated into the world economy and tapped most benefits of Common Market membership without having to sacrifice authoritarianism in the process. There is scant evidence that authoritarian maintenance after 1976 would have triggered relevant economic or other international sanctions.[19] Francoism also had a consistent record of applying harsh coercion only to its opponents; gradual liberalization permitted ever-greater selectivity. By the 1960s, citizens not considered potential opponents enjoyed a number of liberties that paralleled democratic political rights, though always at the regime's discretion. Rightists' risks from repression were substantially *lower* by the first half of the 1970s than in preceding decades.

Finally, there were few prospects of exposure to violence between a *continuista* regime and its opponents. The issue of the balance of domestic coercive power deserves to be clarified given arguments both about the effects of capitalist development on democracy in general and about rising protest in Spain in particular.[20] There can be little doubt that both the "costs of suppression" and rightist citizens' risks of exposure to regime/opposition violence in the mid-1970s, while perhaps slightly higher than ten years earlier, were unambiguously *lower* than in 1936 and for some time afterward, when rightists supported authoritarian implantation and

19. Share (1986: 47–52).
20. Maravall (1982: 14) influentially emphasized the causal importance of "popular pressure 'from below'." Also, Maravall and Santamaría (1986: 72, 77–79) and Tezanos (1989).

stabilization. The 1936 coup faced extraordinary obstacles both in the Popular Front government's control of the military command structure and in its massive workers' organizations. The right required unprecedented mobilization and violence to exclude the left in 1936. This situation was not recreated at any point in the subsequent four decades. By 1939, the Franco regime was in command of an unchallenged security system while the opposition was shattered in Spain and in disarray in exile. It was precisely a sense of security that permitted the regime's modest liberalization, starting in the 1950s.

What Linz describes as the "limited pluralism" tolerated by the regime permitted a gradual increase in the level of activity and discourse critical of authoritarianism, even within the regime's broad ranks (the "semiopposition"), and an important expansion of the "island of democratic culture" that had been "preserved under the dictatorship" even in its early phases.[21] One result was a gradual growth in the number of strikes, marches, protests, and petitions. But Spain's authoritarian rulers assiduously maintained control over the means by which they could prohibit activity when they wished to.[22] The regime's exceedingly steep advantage in coercive capacities remained essentially unchanged from 1939 or 1945 to the 1970s. Few observers voiced serious doubts about the military's discipline. And the regime's opponents had no significant capacities for mass mobilization. PSOE membership may have been below ten thousand at the beginning of 1976, and the fact that membership expanded rapidly that liberalizing year underscores the degree to which activity depended on repression being eased. Even the Communists, long considered the strongest opposition group, should not be overestimated.[23]

This interpretation was shared by many on the left. In 1974, Luís García San Miguel, after considering "realistically the power which the rival forces dispose of," concluded that "for the moment it would be difficult to create a situation of violent confrontation in Spain." Three years later, even after dizzying PSOE and PCE growth, *Zona abierta* editors believed "the possibility of convoking people in the streets to topple the security forces of the state is practically null." Ignacio Sotelo acknowledged that the left was

21. Linz (1970; 1973), López Pintor (1985: 121).

22. As Gallo (1974: 355–56) puts it, individual opponents like Tierno Galván enjoyed access to public forums by the "gracious permission of the regime." Opposition activists were to a certain extent tolerated in the media and unions, but no comprehensive opposition organ was allowed to emerge and the PCE could do nothing to prevent repeated arrests of Comisiones Obreras (CC.OO.) leaders.

23. Mujal-León (1983: 141). On membership estimates, see Mateos (1993: 433–34) and Gillespie (1989a: 288–89, 314). PCE support for guerrilla warfare after 1939 ended in complete failure. Only the Basque ETA possessed even small arms on any scale.

"incapable and afraid" of a strategy of mass mobilization, and negotiated from a "clear situation of inferiority": "the democratic forces were too weak to question the established institutional order."[24] This parallels pretransition conclusions of numerous scholars, that opposition forces were quite weak. In Donald Share's later words, "There was no reason . . . obliging the franquist regime to vacate power."[25]

Consistent with this, the rightists interviewed, as well as conservatives at the time, found the notion of authoritarianism after 1976 feasible and even acceptable.

Transition Leaders' Perceptions

The transition leaders were asked a series of questions concerning their assumptions, held in the years surrounding Franco's death, regarding "a government which intended not to legalize other political parties and to maintain itself without elections for an indefinite period after Franco's death." In brief, most of the leaders did not believe such a regime would have been threatened by internal decay, lack of support from the military, civilian opposition, events in Portugal, or European sanctions.

In one of their points of broadest agreement, fifteen of the seventeen leaders reported that before the transition, they had been aware that very few regime personnel manifested strong pro-authoritarian ideological commitments. The Francoist ruling party had always been an awkward amalgam, and in a description generally accepted by the other interviewees, Fernando Abril labeled it "decaffeinated" by the 1970s, one whose members lacked authentic, energizing faith in any morality justifying indefinite authoritarian prolongation. But these leaders also believed this did not diminish authoritarianism's ability to reproduce itself. Fifteen of the seventeen reported they had believed that most colleagues were professionally ambitious and career-minded, and that a reputable *continuista* authority would have found sufficient capable and disciplined staff.[26] Nor

24. García San Miguel (1974: 105–06); *Zona Abierta* quoted in Share (1986: 41); Sotelo (1980: 179, 182, 189). Toharia's (1989: 62) survey evidence suggests that only a modest minority believed "opposition groups . . . could have overthrown the regime had they tried."

25. Share (1986: 208), Linz (1973: 182).

26. Only Primo de Rivera had believed they would not; the anonymous participant said it would find "some." Rengifo reported that ideological commitment existed "in parts" of the regime apparatus. The anonymous participant stated that he was not in a position to assess ideological characteristics of personnel outside the military. Whether Franco himself was a necessary condition for authoritarian maintenance is a separate matter. Like all causal claims, the notion that Franco was indispensable contains counterfactual hypotheses that must be plausible in order for the claim to be so. This notion contains at least three implausible assumptions. First, it implies that Franco was crucial to the authoritarian project in 1936. But the coup

had these leaders detected an erosion of military support. The armed forces' relationship with the Franco regime was complicated by issues of status, funding, and politicization. But fourteen of the seventeen leaders said they had believed in the mid-1970s that most members of the military would obey a *continuista* leadership. Most had believed that the military's *cúpula* or top leadership actively preferred *continuismo*, and that most military officers below that level were fundamentally apolitical and would not spark significant opposition to regime maintenance through the medium term under any imaginable circumstances.[27] These responses suggest that in the early and mid-1970s, many members of the Francoist leadership believed that dynamics internal to the regime, while variegated, did not constitute a substantial obstacle to the prolongation of authoritarianism.

Events external to the regime were more complex. It was not always easy to identify which sectors supported the regime or how intensely. The Catholic Church backed the Nationalists in the civil war, but the nature of its relationship with the regime afterward (even before Vatican II) has been debated. Patterns and intensity of support among more diffuse groupings such as business, middle classes, and civil servants are even more difficult to determine. But the leaders interviewed reported that by the mid-1970s they detected scant popular support for neo-Francoism. They were aware of a heavy erosion of sympathy among traditional, especially middle-class, supporters: thirteen of sixteen respondents to questions on this matter said they believed in the first half of the 1970s that not even an "important minority" of the population considered *continuismo* desirable after Franco's death. Abril had believed some mass support was "possible"; only Leopoldo Calvo-Sotelo and Alvaro Rengifo had perceived a notable measure of mass support.[28] All were keenly aware that the erosion of sectoral support would

---

coalition formed without any singular leader and the *caudillo* mythology began to be created only after the military rose and Franco was gradually elevated to chief. Second, the notion implicitly claims that rightists would have supported a transition had Franco died in 1945 or 1955. But evidence presented in the counterfactual scenario later in this chapter directly undermines this implicit claim; also, Payne (1987: 294–95, 328–31, 347–49, 380) describes monarchist schemes to replace Franco with an alternative authoritarian formula in the 1940s. Finally, the notion suggests that had Franco lived many years more, rightist support would have remained intact. Yet numerous indicators suggest that support for democracy was growing among rightists while he was alive. What is plausible is the much narrower claim that some of the regime elite delayed acting on their pro-reform preferences out of loyalty to a leader they knew was aged and ill and only a temporary obstacle to change.

27. García López was "ambivalent" as to likely military support Fraga and Reguera had believed that while the military would be loyal for some years, many younger officers would not support maintenance forever. Studies emphasizing the end of ideological monolithicism in the military include those by Gallo (1974: 361), Payne (1987: 93–94), and Caparrós (1983: 27–29).

28. Lozano Vicente, Menéndez, and Osorio had believed some citizens would support a slower transition but not an indefinite *continuista* project.

have made a *continuista* regime reliant on repression to a far greater degree than any time since the late 1950s, converting authoritarian rule, in Carlos Pérez de Bricio's words, into an essentially "military regime." They found such a regime highly unpalatable; López Rodó said that it was "unthinkable" for him to participate in one.

But fourteen of the seventeen leaders reported they had assumed that the regime possessed sufficient coercive capacities so that societal resistance could not have "threatened stability" for years at the very least.[29] Nearly all of them underscored the profound imbalance between the regime's coercive resources and what Alfonso Osorio termed the "few capacities" available to regime opponents. Rodolfo Martín Villa, Suárez's interior minister, found strikes and demonstrations "worrying" but insisted that the threat of overthrow "was never particularly serious." An important minority had believed mass opposition would have been impossible to contain over the long haul.[30] But even they emphasized that a threat to regime stability would have taken years to materialize. This conforms to contemporaneous assessments by Gonzalo Fernández de la Mora and several of the interviewees (Eduardo Carriles, Landelino Lavilla, Osorio, and Andrés Reguera) as members of the *Tácito* (Tacitus) group that supported liberalization from a broadly Christian Democratic perspective. In October 1973, the latter wrote that an authoritarian regime "could keep this society almost subject or silenced, but of course could not depend on it or penetrate it. It runs the risk of being an outsider, an alien, an invader . . . which the society would expel *if it could.*"[31]

Over three-fourths of the leaders also said that the Portuguese 1974 military coup was not an "important" influence on their 1976 decision.[32] Most had believed events in Portugal were propelled by factors absent in Spain: the exhaustion of state security forces in external wars and the strength of extreme-left groups in a less prosperous society. Most thus believed the 1974 revolution neither signaled that *continuismo* was inherently doomed nor had the capacity to inspire similar events in Spain. Fraga insisted the situation in Portugal was fundamentally different and had "nothing to do

---

29. The terms "social resistance," "the people," and "citizens" were used in the interviews to describe in general terms prospective domestic opponents of neo-Francoism. By the time of the interviews, this interpretation was profoundly at odds with public discourses emphasizing the power of popular pressure.

30. These were Carriles, García López, Menéndez, Reguera, and also Abril, who says he had known since mid-1976 that "the day would come" when the political situation could no longer be "controlled" by authoritarian rulers, but had no fixed notion of when that would be.

31. Fernández de la Mora (1986: 33, 38), Tácito (1975: 117). Powell (1990) discussed Tácito.

32. Calvo-Sotelo, Carriles, López Rodó, and Osorio said it was.

with Spain."[33] The effects of international demonstration effects are ambiguous, here as elsewhere. As Carlos Huneeus notes, the Portuguese revolution was invoked by both reformers *and* hard-liners within the Franco regime, and initially inspired regime leaders to crack down on perceived liberalizers. Indeed, every leader interviewed remembered Francoist colleagues who used events in Portugal to buttress arguments *against* democratization.[34]

Finally, transition leaders almost unanimously reported that they did not support democratization out of hopes of entering the European Common Market.[35] Most had been interested in joining specific Western organizations but not for economic benefits, which, they emphasized, Spain already enjoyed due to trade agreements, including with the Common Market. Rather, they wished to number among what Leopoldo Calvo-Sotelo and Osorio termed the politically "modern" West, and relegated economic objectives to a categorically secondary role. Echoing others, Calvo-Sotelo remarked, "Did we say, 'How do we get in? Well, let's do it by becoming democrats.' No. . . . We already wanted to be democrats and pluralists, and then, as an extra, we can also enter Europe. . . . It's not exactly as if we resignedly accepted democracy as the price to be paid [to enter]." Among the political benefits sought via formal membership was reinforcement of a democratization strategy they already favored, a benefit of membership that was a consequence and not a cause of preferring democratization.

These leaders had believed democratization was not their only choice. While *continuismo* was bound to be complex and difficult, they had believed it would have been feasible at least for the medium term, because careerism, institutional (especially military) discipline, and a steep imbalance of coercive power would allow an authoritarian project to overcome what was precisely its well-defined lack of ideological cohesion or popular support.

Small-Business Owners

The owners of small retail businesses who were interviewed believed authoritarian outcomes were likely to remain tolerable after Franco's

33. CIS Study 1069, conducted in October 1974, indicated that most middle- and upperclass Spaniards surveyed viewed the early Portuguese events with indifference or even "sympathy."

34. Huneeus (1981: 265–66).

35. Lavilla said that entry had even been "one of many elements" informing his decisions. Fraga believes entry was an important motive for economists and members of the business community.

death.[36] They generally approved of policies under Franco, such as low indirect (and negligible direct) taxes and toughness against crime. They were also aware of shortcomings, although they perceived them as far less onerous than did actors on the left. They were nearly unanimous in referring to Francoist Spain's lack of integration with Europe and freedom (*libertades*), both of which they ideally wished their children to enjoy. But they also perceived repression as remarkably benign considering its intensity in certain quarters. These findings are consistent with 1978 survey evidence.[37] A strong majority agreed that under Franco there were limits to what one could say about politics aloud (*en alta voz*); "one had to be careful." But forty-eight of the fifty reported they had no personal experience with selective actors of repression (arrests, police warnings, etc.), and most said they had felt able to speak freely about national politics with friends. They did not believe their experience was fortuitous, and rather that repression was consistently directed toward the regime's active opponents. "Why should I have had any trouble? I never did anything wrong. I never stuck my nose into politics." "Our family was normal, apolitical." "If you didn't get involved in politics [*meterse en la política*], they would leave you alone."

Nor had these rightists perceived that they had or soon would risk exposure to significant violence between the regime and its opponents. When asked whether the "opposition" had the capacity either to overthrow the regime or "to challenge the regime's control of the streets," three-fourths said they had believed it probably could not, and described the opposition as "very weak" prior to the transition.

They reported that at the time, they associated authoritarianism after Franco with broad continuity in these themes. The vast majority had assumed Juan Carlos would become head of state after Franco's death and that he would maintain generally advantageous policies and avoid more arbitrary repression. In this sense, their assessment of what the then-prince was likely and especially *unlikely* to do in power went a large part of the distance toward answering the question, after Franco, what? Consistent with survey data suggesting Franco's death caused "worry" only among a minority, these conservative actors in the early and mid-1970s found the prospect and fact of Franco's death devoid of the wide-ranging concerns for the

36. The issues most salient to them included the level of consumer activity, taxes, and street crime. A notable minority also considered moral issues important, particularly the status of "hard work" in society and the visibility of prostitution in their neighborhoods.

37. The 1978 data show some 41 percent of Alianza Popular (AP) voters agreeing that the Franco years "were a period in which there was much repression" and 49 percent that there had been a "lack of liberty." Around 60 percent of Union of Democratic Center (UCD) voters agreed, as did over 90 percent of left voters; Linz et al. (1981: 590).

future that appear to have been generated during numerous authoritarian successions.[38]

Both sets of interviewees reported holding beliefs in the mid-1970s that were substantially politically incorrect by the standards of post-1977 political discourse, specifically that authoritarianism had the power to resist "people power" for years after Franco's death. Regime leaders generally had accepted that Arias Navarro's tepid reform strategy failed and that the regime faced a stark choice between profound reform and feasible intensified repression. Rightist citizens believed authoritarianism after Franco imposed tangible complications but was in principle quite bearable. One may contest the validity of these perceptions but nonetheless acknowledge that if they are sincere and representative, the right's choice for democracy over exclusion remains perplexing since left/right violence was bound to be lower in 1976 than in 1936 when rightists chose exclusion over democracy.

Forecasting Political Outcomes in a Prospective Democracy after 1976

The right's decision can be explained by the fact that the risks it perceived in democracy had collapsed between the 1930s and the 1970s. Given the regime's historiography and living memories of the interwar Republic, conservatives had reason to be averse to democracy. The regime consistently warned that communism would be the beneficiary of liberalization. As late as October 1975, Franco told a crowd in Madrid's Plaza de Oriente that "everything which has been going on in Europe is due to a Masonic-leftist conspiracy of the political class in collusion with Communist-terrorist subversion."[39] Yet citizens developed forecasts, audible already in the early 1970s, that defied both regime propaganda and linear projections of the past. Rightists' forecasts of "Democracy with whom?" could not draw on recent electoral outcomes or legislative debates and apparently were grounded instead in an analysis of social structure that outlined broad contours of likely political orientations in democracy. Interwar rightists attributed left radicalism to propertyless poverty; rightists in the 1970s believed social change had rendered prospective voters far less susceptible to revolutionary appeals.

This "theory," including as it helped many rightists understand their lived experiences, permitted them to update whatever may have been their

---

38. For example, López Pintor (1982: 102–3).
39. *Boletín oficial de las cortes* (*BOC*) 70 (June 3, 1961), p. 14,627; Payne (1987: 615).

impression of the Second Republic.[40] It allowed them to reject the cata-strophist warnings of the Francoist media and educational system. Rightist survey respondents said they admired and "trusted" Franco in the mid-1970s. But they also heavily discounted his prognosis about democracy. Fernando Henrique Cardoso argues that authoritarian rulers' "reiteration of the same arguments about threats to national security will become less convincing" if political conditions change sufficiently.[41] The new Spain had undergone sufficient change: both samples of interviewees had perceived that relocating political decision-making powers to the prospective electorate was unlikely to generate radical changes in the basic political economy and other salient policies. This sidesteps extensive debate over how moderate versus radical the socialist PSOE or other parties were in and after 1976–77. The key here is how rightists *perceived* the left as a whole, and they concluded that any agitatorial leaders or organizations would be hemmed in by deep-running social change.

Most of the leaders interviewed report having predicted that generally moderate parties would dominate any new democracy: a broadly left or social-democratic party (or parties), a preponderant "center" (described by Pérez de Bricio as liberal), and a conservative party. It was difficult to predict the relative strength of these forces. Osorio remembers Suárez saying in 1976 that "[w]e're going to win and govern for twenty years," but López Rodó feared poor economic performance that year could push more voters to the PSOE and PCE.[42] Several of the transition leaders insisted they had not been able to predict the contours of the future party system at all; in García López's words, "[W]e didn't have the remotest idea." But every leader reported they had believed, prior to the transition, that democracy was unlikely to generate important threats to property, in part because they had expected the PCE to represent only a limited minority. Only the anonymous participant and Calvo-Sotelo had believed that a relatively important Communist party might emerge, earning perhaps one-third of the vote, according to the latter. While predictions about pressures for regional autonomy were diverse, these actors had expected no severe threat to the Catholic Church. And they report unanimity in having predicted that "dis-

---

40. Asked to identify the sources of their impressions of likely ideological orientations, the leaders emphasized their extensive direct contact with diverse types of citizens. Primo de Rivera was a mayor; Martín Villa (like Suárez), a provincial governor; and Calvo-Sotelo and Rengifo worked in the private sector in the early 1970s. Osorio suggested that numerous leaders formed impressions on the basis of extensive anecdotal evidence or *encuestas primitivas*. Several stated that in García López's words, "it was a matter of pure intuition" both that most Spaniards in the early 1970s rejected the revolutionary left and that most rightists preferred democracy.

41. Cardoso (1979: 49).

42. Osorio (1980: 155), López Rodó (1993: 255).

order" or violent social conflict (*enfrentamientos sociales*) were improbable. Then-Interior Minister Martín Villa remarked that "disorder . . . is the fear of any ruler who is at least moderately prudent," but he had assessed it as unlikely.

Small-business owners reported more modest capacities for predicting. They expected democracy to result in greater civil and political rights, which they welcomed. They also expected more international contact and hence especially travel, educational, and work opportunities for their children. But nearly all these mass actors insisted that prior to the transition, they had been unable to predict any other specific political outcomes in democracy. A number described the situation as one of "uncertainty" (*incertidumbre*); one echoed Adam Przeworski: "the one thing you cannot know in a democracy is what's going to happen." Several suggested that this inability to forecast originated in a lack of democratic experience: "I had never known anything other than Franco."[43] These responses appear to jeopardize an explanation emphasizing actors' forecasts.

But while unable to stipulate what lay *within* the range of likely political outcomes, they easily identified major events that they had confidently believed lay *outside* that range. Both predicting-by-including and predicting-by-excluding converged on the same result: a forecast that political radicalism was highly unlikely in any new democracy.[44] Forty-six of the fifty retailers said they had believed property ownership would not be threatened under democracy, and all but two had excluded significant levels of social violence as a serious possibility. Forty-seven had believed left parties described as more radical than "moderate socialist" ("radical" or "revolutionary") would not become among the largest: "They might be radical, but then they wouldn't be strong." Eighty-eight percent said they had not been surprised in 1977 by the modest share of the vote won by the Communist party (9.2 percent). Their willingness to report an erroneous prediction concerning a conservative party in the same election suggests this is a sincere description of their past expectations.[45]

A distinct matter is how the interviewees perceived political risks in democracy over the longer term. Given their lack of direct experience with

43. One respondent, visibly frustrated with the questions, turned one back on the interviewer: "What if I asked you who the next president of the United States would be, could you answer?"

44. Political leaders appeared to be more comfortable with predicting-by-including, perhaps because knowledge of history and other countries facilitates describing what were only hypothetical possibilities locally.

45. Thirty-nine of the fifty said they had been surprised by the equally modest success of Fraga's conservative AP. This answer suggests they did not feel the need to fabricate retrospectively a more accurate prediction in order to avoid admitting error.

Table 5.1 Assessments by Spanish Transition Leaders of Why Extensive Social Conflict Was Unlikely in a New Democracy

Fernando Abril	Development of welfare state, more social equality, no "social basis" for violence
Leopoldo Calvo-Sotelo	Wealth, enrichment even of workers who had housing, cars, and a welfare safety net
Eduardo Carriles	Completely changed social context
Manuel Fraga	Widespread access to home ownership, cars, welfare state
Ignacio García López	Material growth, decline of social differences, rise of education, welfare state
Landelino Lavilla	Social and economic changes
Laureano López Rodó	Economic changes, rise in educational levels
Francisco Lozano Vicente	Increased wealth, welfare state, disappearance of hunger, growth of middle class
José Lladó	No longer a justification for conflicts, owing to welfare state and a new distribution of wealth
Rodolfo Martín Villa	Socioeconomic changes, education and economic mobility, increased income of all
Aurelio Menéndez	Increase in education, growth of middle class, which has less "wounds" and grievances than workers
Alfonso Osorio	Social-structural change, inherent moderation of enlarged middle class
Carlos Pérez de Bricio	Social changes, working-class prosperity
Miguel Primo de Rivera	Exposure to Europe, experience of war, more education, economic change, less inequality
Andrés Reguera	Social and economic changes
Alvaro Rengifo	The trauma of the civil war
Anonymous participant	The trauma of the civil war

left unions, parties, and leaders, it is difficult to imagine that these actors' predictions could concern anything but the short term, pending further information. And yet they report that at the time of the 1976 referendum, they had reasons—in a sense, theories—for believing that moderation of the left was relatively predictable into the future. The transition leaders were asked *why* they had believed threatening political outcomes were unlikely in a prospective democracy after Franco's death. Their responses concerned both socioeconomic issues and the effects of the civil war, but converged on emphasizing an enduring basis for left moderation.

A strong majority of the transition leaders interviewed connected expected low levels of political conflict in a new democracy to the transformed social and economic conditions that were present in Spain at the time. José Lladó's response was typical: he had believed that social conflict "did not seem necessary. Levels of material well-being were quite high." Most of the leaders generally agreed with the statement that "when someone has something to conserve, it makes them [more] conservative." Several emphasized that welfare-state benefits were among the items workers "had"; Calvo-Sotelo described the expansion in social programs in the transition years as "the price to be paid for social peace." The respondents especially considered interclass conflicts unlikely even if leftist organizations and politicians attempted to activate working-class radicalism, because no social basis existed for such "agitation." In describing the Spain of the 1970s, many distinguished from earlier periods, particularly the interwar Republic. Calvo-Sotelo remembers that in the early 1970s, "[w]e had confidence that the social situation was no longer like the miserable, traumatic conditions of the Republic and of the 1940s." Osorio insisted that "[h]unger disappeared from Spain, and social confrontations, too. The problems which existed in the war, before the war, in the epoch of the Republic and the Civil War, did not exist anymore, or in the same way, by the time of Franco's death. . . . There was a middle class which did not exist before, or which, if it did exist, was very small. . . . And the proletariat had diminished considerably. . . . Spain had changed, was different economically and socially, and being different economically and socially, conditions of violence did not exist anymore."

These opinions conform closely to analyses expressed in scattered statements in the 1970s. A number of articles published by the *Tácito* reform group in the early 1970s described the growth of the middle class as generating nothing less than "a different country, a new society." Implicit in their claim that lingering social inequalities remained the single "greatest danger to social peace" was the notion that the relative compressing of the class structure had already diminished the social bases of strife. Thus, *Tácito* regularly argued that authoritarianism had largely outlived its usefulness or purpose (at least implying that it had once been useful).[46] Reform figure José Maria Areilza declared in early 1976 that "for the first time, there exists a social structure in which the middle- and upper-working class show conservative tendencies, because they live in a consumer society." Antonio Garrigues Walker assured those who might fear "that in a regime of liberties our cause would be lost," that the vast expansion of the middle class meant any new democracy would be a "bourgeois democracy." That year (and still prior to the Cortes vote), Emilio Botin, a leading banker, calculated the Communists would not be a dominant force.[47]

Last, but certainly not least, Adolfo Suárez in 1976 similarly explained political conflict in the 1930s in terms of "the traditional specter of roaming [*vagabundeando*] hunger in our cities, the resistance of the powerful to the just demands of the masses, the absence of a solid state which guaranteed

46. Tácito (1975: 72, 115–19, 145–48).
47. Areilza in Menéndez del Valle (1989: 726); interview with Garrigues Walker, Madrid, 1993, and Garrigues Walker (1976: 160); Botín's in *El país*, August 1, 1976, pp. 24–25.

the political game, and a class struggle to the death." He thus argued that the social bases of such conflict no longer existed:

> We are the tenth largest industrial nation. We have achieved acceptable standards of living. And despite bitter daily problems, we have eliminated the phantasms that could have most threatened orderly coexistence. The Spain in which we live today is a different one, in its structures, in its economy, and in its demography. . . . The advances made on a material level are today the basis for being optimistic about peaceful coexistence . . . across Spain, there exist today the necessary conditions for pluralism to be integrating and not disintegrating.[48]

In José Casanova's words, many regime leaders had "internalized the economic determinist logic of the theories of development," at least to the point of connecting modernization to moderation.[49]

These cognitive maps enabled rightists to forecast predictable moderation on the left even without direct knowledge of leftist organizations or leaders. These forecasts even survived episodes when the main left parties, in the lead-up to the Cortes and referendum votes, sent as many radicalizing as moderating signals. The PCE projected a somewhat more liberal image than in previous decades and denounced violence. But in April 1976, PSOE leader Felipe González held a lengthy meeting with Fidel Castro in Havana, and in early December, the PSOE proclaimed itself a Marxist party for the first time.[50] Yet rightist calculations about likely behavior by the left

---

48. *Diario de sesiones de las cortes* (hereafter *DSC*) 27 (June 8–9, 1976), p. 106.

49. Casanova (1983: 957) quotes López Rodó in 1969: "To achieve a $1000 [income] per capita is our number one objective; the rest, social or political, would come naturally later." In many ways these conclusions were also arrived at by social scientists attempting to establish "partisan" orientations before Franco's death, research that generally converged on finding a profound erosion of the left-most portions of Spain's historic political spectrum. This finding was consistently replicated in self-placement surveys conducted by the state-run CIS beginning in December 1976, as well as in DATA's national survey study conducted prior to the legalization of most political parties. De Miguel (1976), Centro de Investigaciones Sociológicas (1977: 120), Linz et al. (1981: e.g., 14, 189), López Pintor (1982: 108). Tezanos et al. (1973) was among the researchers connecting partisan orientations to changes in social structures. He and his coauthors used survey responses to argue that revolutionary left traditions "form part of a world already surpassed in our country, surpassed precisely—and this is what is important—in its social base." The "drastic diminution of the rural proletariat" and other changes were so extensive as to "situate us in a substantially different context than just thirty years ago." In particular, members of the greatly expanded white-collar "new middle class" largely rejected doctrinaire left formulas and at most supported socialism of a strictly moderate ("Nordic") variety. In contrast, Fernández de Castro and Goytre (1974: 248–71) emphasized continuity in the "conflictual intensity of social relations."

50. Juliá (1990).

in a new democracy apparently formed on the basis of impressions of the left's social bases and not the organized left's public postures.

Views connecting social transformation to moderation of the left were also held by many conservatives at the mass level. To determine why the owners of small retail businesses who were interviewed had believed left radicalism was unlikely in a new democracy, they were asked a somewhat less hypothetical question: why was an "average person in the street" in Madrid in the 1970s less likely to have revolutionary political orientations than a worker in Madrid "in previous decades"? Responses almost invariably concerned one of two developments. Sixteen (32 percent) of the fifty believed the civil war was a moderating influence. "No one wanted another war"; "people wanted peace [*tranquilidad*], not more war." And half the business owners explained worker moderation in terms of social-structural change, in particular, the end of "hunger," widespread access to the ownership of housing, cars, and (most commonly!) refrigerators, and the development of welfare-state (particularly unemployment) benefits.[51] They shared the image of a watershed separating the socioeconomic situation before the 1950s from the period after that: "Many people had nothing [before]." "[Later,] everyone ate, not like before, after the War." "Things had already begun to change: [a worker] already had Social Security, and things were going better." Most references were to conditions and people in the neighborhood around the shopkeeper's store or in the city of Madrid.

These perceptions meant that the right confronted a dramatically different situation in 1976 and afterward than it had in 1936; parallels and crucial differences are summarized in Table 5.2.

Victor Pérez-Díaz writes that "[a]t the end of the Francoist regime, the Spanish working class was a great unknown quantity."[52] Certainly observers in 1975–76 lacked reliable survey data on partisan orientations. But impressions of workers appear to have been plentiful nonetheless, and Charles Powell notes that "[b]y the early 1970s, even Spaniards who had supported the regime . . . had begun to believe that their socio-economic interests could be safeguarded in a democratic context as well as—or even better than—in an authoritarian one."[53] As the political spectrum narrowed dramatically, the exclusion of the left generated benefits that were less and less able to compensate for the risks to which authoritarian rule inevitably

---

51. A significant number emphasized the contrast between joblessness with and joblessness without benefits.

52. Pérez-Díaz (1993: 236).

53. Powell (1990: 253).

Table 5.2 Right's Perceptions of Likely Outcomes in Democracy, 1936, 1976, and after 1977

	1936	1976	After 1977
Largest left party had substantial prospects for winning?	Yes	Yes	Yes
PSOE the largest party on the left?	Yes	Expected to be socialist/social democratic	Yes
Large revolutionary groups to PSOE's left?	Yes	Expected not to be	No
Perceived social basis for large radical left movements?	Yes	No, though somewhat uncertain	No
Estimated likelihood of widespread (e.g., class-based) civil violence	Very high	Expected to be low	Very low
Left leaders perceived to be under extensive pressure from rank-and-file to radicalize?	Yes	Expected not to be	No
Fundamental revision of property regime perceived to have large constituency?	Yes	No	No

exposed even rightists. Exclusion was less costly than forty years earlier but was a solution to a problem that no longer existed.

Perceptions of a Different Spain in 1976: Testing the Causal Claim

If the interviewees were representative of the Spanish right by the mid-1970s, and if their forecasts crucially influenced the emergence of both elite and mass "soft-liners" within the right's ranks, how can we explain the small minority who voted "no" in 1976? Their forecasts of likely outcomes under *continuismo* appear to have been comparable to those of the reformers.[54] But they formed dramatically different perceptions of democracy. Blas Piñar, Antonio Izquierdo (editor of *El alcázar*), and Fuerza Nueva argued that democracy would linearly replicate the 1930s' assaults on

54. Blas Piñar later condemned Juan Carlos precisely for betraying a continuity Piñar had anticipated and presumed.

national unity, the church, property, and order. "In the coming elections, marxism will win"; "This Communist Party will again have the opportunity it had in 1931–1939." Throughout the second half of 1976, the *continuista* press warned that democracy in Spain would result in catastrophe, largely because competitive party politics inevitably leads to conflict, violence, and communism, as in Ulster, terrorist-ridden Italy, Lebanon, Chile, and Portugal.[55] It is worth asking why these hard-liners did not do what reformers did: link change in social structure or culture to change in likely political behavior. But this does not obscure the fact that in both cases regime preferences varied with predictions: rightists who detected high risks in democracy opposed the transition while rightists who detected low risks favored it. It is also important that the overwhelming majority of rightists appear to have forecast low political risks in democracy and that those predictions were validated by events after 1977.

Are there further ways to test for causal influence? James Fearon suggests that the credibility of a causal argument can be strengthened when its implicit counterfactual claim is found credible or defensible.[56] Our argument contains one obvious counterfactual claim: had the rightists who perceived low risks in democracy instead perceived high risks, they should have opposed the transition. The perceptions and choices of *continuistas* appear to be consistent with this. The interviews offered a more extensive opportunity to test this claim, if only imperfectly. The transition leaders were asked whether they would have supported a transition to democracy "as rapid and complete as the one you supported in 1976" had they served in a government in a country in which democracy appeared highly risky. Since most leaders had attributed low risks in democracy in the 1970s to the development of a relatively mature industrial society, this high-risk setting was described as being characterized by widespread severe poverty, no welfare-state benefits, and several million rural landless laborers. Of the thirteen who answered this question, two said their regime choice would have been the same even in that altered context (although of these two, one would have felt "more hesitation"). The remaining eleven said they either would not have supported a transition or would have supported one stretched only over ten years or more. One emphasized that the regime's leaders had no intention of exposing themselves and their values to a very hostile political environment: "we would not have taken ourselves to the guillotine." García López insisted few of his regime colleagues would have

---

55. Izquierdo (1981: 79–80), Piñar (1979: 47); *Fuerza nueva,* June 13, July 3, August 7, and August 28, 1976. Franco Salgado-Araujo (1976: 343, 349, 375) recounted Franco's comparable 1960s views of democracy's likely consequences.

56. Fearon (1991).

favored a shift to such a conflict-prone democracy: "A transition would not have been possible. . . . On the basis of what support?"[57]

The small-business owners were asked a question designed to require somewhat less hypothetical conjecture: would they have voted for "a rapid and complete transition to democracy" had a referendum been held not in 1976 but 1955 or 1960 (depending on the age of the respondent)?[58] Only 22 percent said they would have supported democratization under those circumstances with the same degree of confidence as in 1976. Sixty-four percent responded that they either would have voted against a rapid and complete transition or would have been more hesitant to support one: "I would have been afraid"; "we were not mature yet. Any atrocity could have occurred in those times"; "there were guarantees in the 1970s. [Back] then, I do not think so."[59]

We cannot assume that reactions to hypothetical scenarios reliably indicate the choices people would have made in different contexts, but these responses nevertheless serve three useful functions. First, the business owners' responses strongly suggest not only that the payoff matrix was decisive but also that they believe social-structural change was more important than the civil war in moderating the left, since the latter had already occurred in 1955 or 1960, whereas sweeping socioeconomic reform had just begun. Second, these responses fail to support theories of "democratic learning", which suggest that actors reshape present behavior after realizing the consequences of their conduct in a previous decision situation. The responses to these counterfactual scenarios suggest that rightists, while believing democracy was preferable in 1976–77 (and since), simultaneously believe authoritarianism may well have been appropriate to conditions that (more) closely approximate those of 1936. Osorio echoed many others when he said he would have backed the 1936 coup, and that between 1936 and 1976, "I did not change. Spain changed." This is not the language of learning. It is important to note that it is also not the language of nostal-

57. Three leaders were too uncomfortable with the question to answer it. The majority answer parallels an account by a senior general interviewed by Mérida (1979: 34, 38); he defended the 1936 coup but argued that a coup after the transition was unnecessary because "the circumstances today are not the same as before."

58. The leaders' question concerned a generic "country" (which might have been taken to be Spain but did not have to be) so as to permit sincere responses on the part of interviewees sensitive to the strongly controversial nature of any answer that identified concrete conditions in which they would have been "antidemocratic" in 1976 or since. Pretest interviews suggested that business owners found this scenario too abstract to form any opinion but that they readily engaged with the still-hypothetical shift of the referendum to a concrete historical situation as they had otherwise known it.

59. The remainder either would not answer a hypothetical question of this kind or said they did not know what attitude they would have had at that time.

gia; previous regime preferences were deemed inappropriate to transformed circumstances. Polling commissioned by the Suárez government confirmed that many rightist citizens continued to admire Franco but no longer preferred Francoism.[60]

Finally, these responses allow us to consider the influence of norms. Inscribed norms or values might be expected to shape people's reactions to both actual *and* hypothetical decisions. But most interviewees' support for democracy was not able to survive even the thought experiment of relocation to a context in which the answer to "Democracy with whom?" had changed in such a way as to reverse the payoff matrix. In 1976, Miguel Primo de Rivera used universalistic terms when he insisted that "we need to pass from a personal regime to a regime of participation."[61] But these responses suggest that rightists supported a "regime of participation" *by the Spanish people as they were perceived in this period* over a "personal" one *led by neo-Francoists*. When the values of the italicized terms in the previous sentence were changed sufficiently, respondents' regime preferences changed as well. Pure observation of direct causal links is inevitably impossible; given that limitation, these data represent a substantial approximation of process-tracing in this matter.

As a result of the values that did obtain in those terms, most rightists were broadly receptive to regime change by 1976. That year's referendum sparked public campaigns that exposed voters to competing opinion leaders. Reformers dominated the state media, but the antidemocratic message was supported by what *La vanguardia Española* characterized as "a vigorous campaign. . . . The extreme Right . . . made clear that it is a relevant force."[62] Both sides combined ideational and outcome-oriented appeals. Blas Piñar and other neo-Francoists unabashedly insisted that Franco would have voted "no" and warned of the dangers of democracy. Democratizers argued that authoritarianism after Franco was a "*callejón sin salida*" (dead end) while violence and communism were unlikely in democracy and "political reform is change without risk."[63] In the end, reform supporters included the vast majority of rightists, since the bulk of non-

---

60. For example, DATA Study 259, p. 45.

61. *DSC* 29 (November 16–18, 1976), p. 7.

62. *La vanguardia Española* (Barcelona), December 14, 1976, p. 7.

63. See, for example, *ABC*, December 14, 1976, p. 3, and December 15, 1976; *Arriba*, December 14, 1976, pp. 5, 7, and December 15, 1976, p. 6. Suárez also had already used the phrase *cambio sin riesgo* in his June speech supporting the Ley de Reuniones. In his December 14 television and radio address, reprinted in *ABC*, December 15, 1976, p. 6, Suárez argued that "the language of violence is no longer—thank God—the language of our people" and that extremists and the violent "are not in any way representative of the spirit [*sentir*] of the Spanish people."

voters were responding to the PCE's and PSOE's call for abstention. The results underscored the exceedingly small constituency available to pro-authoritarian rightists as they entered the new democracy.

Democratic Consolidation after 1977

> If unemployment reaches 1½ million or 2 million, then the party—democracy, that is—is over.
>
> CARLOS FERRER, employers' association head, 1978

During the twenty-five years after its transition to democracy, Spain witnessed not only long-term economic growth but also a deep recession in the late 1970s, enduringly high unemployment, important mutations in the party system, sustained Basque terrorism, fluctuating levels of political participation, and a change in lifestyles and life experiences nearly unimaginable from the vantage point of the 1930s. But studies have revealed consistent rightist support for democracy throughout. Can this be explained by conservatives' perceptions of regime alternatives after 1977? Crucially, it was soft-liners' forecasts of moderation of the left, and not hard-liners' fears of revolution, that were confirmed. A compact political spectrum made it impossible for authoritarianism to offer improvements in overall political outcomes sufficient to compensate for the loss of political rights, regardless of routine events in democracy—in other words, even when the economy experienced hard times, pacts failed, the right lost national office, and institutions were largely win- and loss-concentrating. Przeworski's characterization was reversed: rightists associated authoritarianism with greater ex ante uncertainty than democracy. The collapse of political risks under democracy had laid the basis for the consolidation of that regime.

The initial prognoses were not all optimistic. Writing in 1980 in the midst of deepening problems, Raymond Carr speculated that the right might prove as susceptible to a reversal as in the 1930s:

> It is at least arguable that a section of the middle classes welcomed the Second Republic in 1931 as a better safeguard for their interests than the discredited monarchy; and similarly that, in 1976, those same classes saw in a democratic system a better prospect for stability than decrepit Francoism. Will they, when their interests are threatened or perceived to be threatened, turn against the new democracy as they did in the days of the Second Republic?

The leader of the Confederación Española de Organizaciones Empresariales (Spanish Confederation of Business Organizations CEOE), Carlos Ferrer, Catalan politician Jordi Pujol, and several PCE figures were among those expressing concern that economic dislocation could undermine support for democracy.[64]

Yet exclusionary rightist projects were unable to attract significant segmental support. Nearly all conservatives cast ballots for centrist regional parties; Fraga's Alianza Popular (Popular Alliance [AP]), which maintained an unambiguously prodemocratic posture in election campaigns, the constitutional debate, and toward the 1981 coup; and Suárez's Unión del Centro Democrático (Union of the Democratic Center [UCD]), which was, like the French UDF, a coalition of conservatives, Christian Democrats, liberals, and moderate social democrats. Pro-authoritarian rightist parties attracted even fewer votes than *continuismo* did in the 1976 referendum: 0.6 percent in 1977, 2.1 percent in 1979, and less than 1 percent in 1982, after which the extreme right essentially disappeared organizationally. The February 1981 coup attempt, which in its confusing opening hours raised the specter of success, was overwhelmingly rejected. There was no notable pattern of rightists courting the military or supporting paramilitary forces.

Survey data, voting results, and the interviews conducted with small-business owners in Madrid were used to establish regime preferences and beliefs about regime alternatives after 1977.

Predicting Political Outcomes under a New Authoritarian Regime

Rightists' forecasts of the most likely authoritarian alternative to democracy after 1977 were rendered complex by considerable discontinuity in authoritarian leadership, caused by Franco's death and the defection to the democracy's founding coalition of the king, many other prominent regime figures, and the liberal-monarchist and Catholic "families" of the Francoist elite. Two other Franco-era mainstays were the most likely sources of any new authoritarian challenge: right-Falangists and military leaders. A number of retired and active military personnel were well known as *continuistas*. And the most vigorous and well-known civilian pro-exclusionary voices were those of Blas Piñar and his *Fuerza Nueva*, armed with a parliamentary forum in 1979–82 and sympathetic national newspapers such as

---

64. Carr (1980: 180); Pujol and Sánchez Ayuso in *DSC* 29 (October 27, 1977), pp. 1092, 1112; the CC.OO.'s Camacho in *Mundo obrero*, June 7, 1979, p. 1, and *El país*, October 16, 1979, p. 51; interview with Ferrer Salat, Barcelona, 1993, and Ferrer in *Cinco días*, October 4, 1978.

El alcázar. It is thus not quite correct to say that no "national" or "major" party or leader attempted to delegitimize democracy after 1977. These groups relentlessly blamed democracy for crime, terrorism, unemployment, corruption, drugs, and what they considered the squalor of rule by parties and the left.[65] Carr suggested in 1980 that "there is no alternative model of an anti-democratic political system of the right available as there was in the 1930s." But these exclusionary entrepreneurs drew on the substantial authoritarian strands of Spain's political culture, held large public rallies in Madrid's Plaza de Oriente on the anniversary of Franco's death, and declared Blas Piñar a new *Caudillo.* Latin American authoritarian models were also prevalent; John Coverdale cites concerns that "a Videla will come," Felipe González discussed the possible appearance of "a Pinochet," and Felipe Agüero describes plotters' interest in the coups in Chile in 1973 and Turkey in 1980.[66]

The reputations of exclusionary entrepreneurs made some very rough predictions possible. Any new exclusionary regime was likely to be vigorously anticommunist, generally economically conservative, and opposed to regional autonomy. It was unclear how the rest of Europe would react to an authoritarian regression: it had imposed moderate sanctions on the Colonels' Greece in 1967, but had extended trade privileges to Franco. The United States had supported anti-Soviet conservative authoritarianism in Spain before and presumably would have under Ronald Reagan as well. Conservatives' degree of personal safety may have been more difficult to predict. There was no reason to believe Falangist/military repression would target rightists, nor any guarantee it would not. Nor would it necessarily be able to insulate them from an uncertain amount of regime/opposition violence. Some observers predicted fierce left resistance to a coup, but the PCE's Santiago Carrillo believed citizens were conditioned into passivity.[67] Socialist- and communist-affiliated organizations grew quickly after the transition, to sizes larger than during the Second Republic. But they rapidly lost most of that membership, much as Philippe Schmitter and Guillermo

---

65. Linz and Stepan (1989: 49; 1996: 99). Blas Piñar was famous; *continuismo* was a well-known point of view; and media platforms like *El alcázar* were readily available. To explain Piñar's lack of influence over people's regime preferences in terms of his party's vote-share (i.e., his lack of influence over their votes) incurs a severe endogeneity problem in the causal argument. For brief discussions of post-1977 antidemocratic rightist politics, see Gilmour (1992) and Ellwood (1987: 176–83).

66. Carr (1980: 181); Coverdale (1982: 232); *DSC* 29 (October 27, 1977), pp. 1120–21; Agüero (1995: 167). Foreign models suggested that authoritarianism was not viable (Portugal in 1974) and that it was viable (Chile, Uruguay, and Argentina after the mid-1970s), that democracy was harmless (most of Western Europe) and that it was not (Chile 1970–73, Argentina, 1973–76, and "revolutionary" Portugal).

67. Carrillo (1983: 9–10).

Table 5.3 Approximate Membership in Unions Affiliated with Leftist Parties in Spain in the 1930s and after Franco

Second Republic	1978	1983
UGT: 1 million (1932)	UGT: 2.2 million	UGT: 600,000?
CNT: 500–800,000 (Spring 1936)	CC.OO.: 1.8 million	CC.OO.: 375,000
PCE: 50,000 (Spring 1936)		C.N.T.: 25–50,000
Total: ≈1.7 million	4 million	≈1 million

Sources: Gillespie (1989a: 336–37), Cruz (1987: 59–60), Taboadela Alvarez (1992), Comisiones Obreras, "Secretaría de organización, evolución de la cotización a la C.S. de CC.OO.," n.d., Madrid.

O'Donnell describe a "popular upsurge" soon followed by people's "withdraw[al] from intense activism."[68] In contrast to Dietrich Rueschemeyer, Evelyne Stephens, and John Stephens's suggested progression, Spanish working-class organizations were smaller and weaker in the 1980s than the 1930s, as shown in Table 5.3.[69]

A series of interview questions aimed at establishing the small-business owners' reactions to the most prominent and substantial (though not the only) plot after 1977, the 1981 coup attempt. Several retailers said they had not been afraid of violence in 1981 because they believed the coup would be contained, but 60 percent reported their predominant reaction to the coup was fear for their safety. Just over half of these were concerned primarily with the possibility of widespread violent conflict between the coup and its opponents: "If there was a coup, there would be resistance. There would be a war" (or "another war"). "Whenever there is violence, there are problems" (*líos*). Many reported concerns over repression by a new regime. A substantial number of the latter were concerned about this not because they projected past experience onto the likely conduct of the 1981 *golpistas* but precisely because they did not. A majority of the retailers emphasized they knew almost nothing about the policy preferences or attitudes toward repression of the 1981 coup leaders: "We were entering a tunnel, and we didn't know what we would find at the other end." "Because we didn't know who they were, we couldn't trust them." So diffuse was the coup project's political reputation that over two-thirds of respondents preferred to describe its leaders as "military men" (*militares*) rather than Francoists or rightists (*derechistas*). This result matches existing survey data

68. O'Donnell and Schmitter (1986: 56).
69. Taboadela Alvarez estimates CNT membership in the *late* 1980s at thirty thousand. Members of the Union Sindical Obrera (USO) are not included; Fishman (1990: 193) noted that by 1980 the USO was unofficially linked to the UCD and attempted to appeal to "center-right workers."

showing the lack of name recognition and the unpopularity of major coup figures.[70] From the late 1970s on, it was authoritarianism that connoted substantial uncertainty.

Assessing Political Outcomes in Democracy after 1977

Post-1977 democracy was marked by substantial political predictability. Studies of the party system make clear that the new democracy was characterized not only by the containment of almost all political violence to the Basque dispute but also by sustained centripetal tendencies in party politics. Moderation was ensured into the future by bottom-up pressures on the left completely unlike those that drove intra-left dynamics in 1931–33. In 1977, like afterward, extreme-right and self-styled "revolutionary" left parties such as the Revolutionary Labor Organization (ORT) and the Labor Party (PTE) won only marginal support. The staunchly conservative AP and the Communists each won under 10 percent. Moderates predominated: the center-right UCD, Felipe González's center-left PSOE, and smaller centrist parties together averaged 69 percent of the vote in 1977 and 1979. Self-placement surveys revealed a comparable left/right distribution, which was not so much bell-shaped as steeply pyramidal. This made it imperative to compete for the mass of center-straddling voters; Richard Gunther, Giacomo Sani, and Goldie Shabad describe the prevalent strategy by which parties chose to "focus attacks primarily on neighboring parties toward the center . . . [and] to ignore groups toward the extremes."[71]

Moderation on the left was particularly dramatic. After 1977 the PSOE widened its lead over the PCE at the same time it was moving steadily toward the center. Gunther, Sani, and Shabad remark that as early as 1979, the PSOE's proposed policies "were quite similar to those of the UCD." Particularly after their electoral defeat that year, the PSOE leadership moved to appropriate even more of the UCD's centrist position and middle-class electorate by assuming what amounted to a social democratic posture. They abandoned Marxism, by 1982 barely mentioned nationalizations, and replaced socialism as their main goal with "modernization."[72] Moreover, the

70. Sixty-four percent of the respondents remembered having recognized the name of Jaime Milans de Bosch; 44 percent, the name of Alfonso Armada; and 12 percent, the name of Antonio Tejero before 1981. Half the sample said they believed the *golpistas* had no program for running the country; roughly one-fourth believed they were simply attempting to restore institutional and personal privileges they had enjoyed before 1977.

71. Gunther, Sani, and Shabad (1988: 267–68), Penniman and Mujal-León (1985).

72. Gunther, Sani, and Shabad (1988: 281, 407), Williams (1989).

Table 5.4 Percentage of Votes, 1977–2000

	Extreme Left	PCE/IU	Socialists	Center	AP/PP
1977	1.0	9.3	34.8	38.8	8.4
1979	1.1	10.8	30.5	39.4	6.5
1982	1.7	4.0	48.1	15.2	26.4
1986	2.2	4.9	44	16.5	25.6
1989	1.9	9.1	40.1	14.1	25.8
1993	1.7	9.6	39.4	7.9	34.8
1996	1.4	10.5	37.9	6.3	38.9
2000	1	5.5	34.1	6.8	44.6

PSOE was consistently averse to lasting and especially national alliances with the Communists, although they formed several municipal majorities. The PSOE's aversion was the case even though the PCE was more moderate at the time of transition than in the 1930s and made great efforts to cooperate in the 1977 pacts, constitutional negotiations, and much early legislation. Once the political contours of the transition were established, the PCE-oriented Workers' Commissions (Comisiones Obreras [CC.OO.]) and PSOE-affiliated UGT union federations, rather than assume the socially revolutionary postures of unions in the Second Republic at least after 1933, concentrated on achieving better pay and working conditions and used political processes to urge the expansion of social services. Discussion of workers' self-management (*autogestión*) essentially disappeared after the transition. Carles Boix argues that the PSOE did not become a neoliberal party. But that it had profoundly moderated is undeniable.[73]

Campaign rhetoric rarely reflected this clustering around the center. Social and economic conservatives in the AP, the Catholic Church, and the main employers' associations regularly criticized the UCD for conceding too much to the left. And conservative election-time exhortations were epitomized by Suárez's 1979 televised speech charging that the PSOE's apparent moderation cloaked a Marxist agenda.[74] But to portray these as expressions of fundamental differences would be to ignore the great deal of overlap existing in both party constituencies and policy proposals after 1977. Placing the political conflicts of this period in the historical perspective of the Second Republic makes it easier to see that the political competition after 1977 was carried out within a far narrower range. A

73. Fishman (1990), Boix (1998).
74. Gunther, Sani, and Shabad (1988: 269–70) emphasized that all parties used such tactics. Osorio (1980: 329) remembered Suárez saying that "in the end I have the right as a captive audience; what are they going to do other than vote for me if they want to survive?"

substantial literature has analyzed the growth of welfare-state programs, expanded spending during the recession of the late 1970s, growth in educational commitments, notable fiscal reform in the direction of greater redistribution, deepening regional autonomy, and other goals traditionally sought by the left.[75] But especially the PSOE also freely accepted moderate limits on all these policies and even sharper ones on others, such as worker participation. Reformism was bounded sharply on the left. As a result, the UCD and PSOE overlapped heavily on tax and spending matters and fiscal reforms, property rights and nationalization questions, the role of the church in education, and workers' "control" of industry. And events powerfully reinforced perceptions that moderation of the left was predictable. Some left moderation was clearly tactical, as during the negotiations over the legalization of parties and electoral rules; also, the PSOE and PCE, which together had won 38 percent of the 1977 vote, accepted two of seven seats on the subcommittee drafting the constitution, while the UCD had three and the centrist Catalans and conservative AP had one each.[76]

Clearly unlike 1931–33, the PSOE and PCE were under far more intense pressure by their rank-and-file to avoid revolutionary appeals. Whereas moderation by the PSOE and UGT leaders during the Republic's first *bienio* defied rank-and-file preferences, the PSOE's march toward the center was clearly driven by party leaders' assessments of where crucially needed voters already lay. Whether or not one accepts their assessments, "González was strongly influenced by arguments about the rise of the 'new middle class' in Spanish society."[77] These dynamics can be discerned readily in the PSOE's strategizing in 1977–82 and the PCE's brief attempt to radicalize in 1979. Research before, during, and after the political transition emphasized that traditional "workerist" (*obrerista*) appeals would fragment the left and that the social democratization of the PSOE had electoralist virtues.[78] The potential left electorate was complex, including not only white-collar employees but also blue-collar workers in the automobile and other sectors as well as remaining agricultural laborers susceptible to more militant appeals. There was also substantial room for disagreement over what exactly moving toward the center entailed. But the socialist sociologist José Félix Tezanos concluded from surveys of the white-collar "new middle classes" in the first half of the 1970s that left parties had to adopt relatively moderate positions in any future elections. In the lead up to the 1977 vote,

75. For example, Esping-Andersen (1994), Albi Ibáñez (1990).
76. Gunther (1985: 51).
77. Gillespie (1989b: 69).
78. For example, Tezanos (1983: 45, 72–78).

PSOE research found that most workers were put off rather than attracted by symbols of past left radicalism such as the red flag and the word "revolution."[79]

It is in this context that Felipe González and Alfonso Guerra shifted the PSOE further toward the center, after the shock of the 1979 election defeat, on the eve of which Suárez demagogically but effectively referred to the PSOE's "Marxist" program. González insisted the party demote the status of Marxism and defer to his electoralist priorities. Resistance from the party's left wing forced the convocation of the PSOE's extraordinary congress of 1979, at which González emerged as the unchallenged leader. Richard Gillespie contends that the 1979 debate was not so much about Marxism as political sociology. Social democratizers such as González (who rejected that label) argued that social change had made imperative a cross-class coalition and hence a more nuanced platform. One can term this a tactical decision driven by party elites, but in the Downsian model, parties move in anticipation of *voters'* preferences; the Downsian model is structurally driven and not elite driven. The PSOE became a serious contender for national governance with a social democratic platform of the type with which conservatives elsewhere in the region had proved they could easily coexist.[80]

The 1979 events are often compared to the German Social Democrats' 1959 Bad Godesberg shift, but both cases can be misinterpreted easily. The 1979 showdown in Spain was not a cause but a consequence of the PSOE's move toward the center; the leadership called for official programmatic change, not to avoid provoking a frightened right into a coup but to enable the PSOE to attract middle-class votes from the UCD. The fact that the main center-left party sought to shift voters directly from the electorate of the main center-right party demonstrates how far the PSOE had already traveled in the left/right space. As Gillespie understatedly observed, "[I]ts pronounced moderation was doing the PSOE no electoral damage at all." In contrast, the activists who rejected González and joined the PCE in forming Izquierda Unida languished at the electoral margins.[81]

Also unlike 1931–33, bottom-up pressures also constrained any militant behavior by groups aligned to the left of the PSOE leaders. The PCE's electorate was limited to around 10 percent of the vote, and its one major

79. Interview with Tezanos, Madrid, 1995. Much of the PSOE's pretransition survey work was conducted through the Instituto de Técnicos Electorales, in which Tezanos and Alfonso Guerra were involved.

80. Gillespie (1989a: 219–399, 345–54), Share (1985). For samples of the ongoing debate, see González in *El socialista*, May 13, 1979, pp. 4–5; Sotelo (1980: ch. 7); and Enrique Gomáriz, "La Sociología de Felipe González," *Zona abierta* 20 (1979), pp. 61–76.

81. Gunther, Sani, and Shabad (1988: 264–65), Gillespie (1989a: 365–68).

attempt to mobilize political protest during the extended transition was undermined by lack of mass support. It had been isolated and frustrated by the PSOE's frequent and often back-room cooperation with the UCD in 1977–78, and used the dilution of workers' participation proposals in the 1979 Workers' Statute as a pretext for an attempt at radicalization and mass demonstrations designed to flex the extraparliamentary muscle of workers in general and the CC.OO. and PCE in particular. This effort figures in few analyses of the transition because it failed rapidly in the fall of 1979. Discussions at the time and interviews since make it clear that the leaders of the CC.OO. and PCE recognized that the effort failed because of lack of rank-and-file support, both at demonstrations and then in the April–May 1980 work councils elections, where the CC.OO. suffered sharp setbacks. In a 1980 meeting, PCE head Carrillo remarked that the Socialists had counted "on the 'conservative' tendencies which the crisis caused among large sectors of workers," and that events "show us their calculation reflected a certain reality."[82]

Consistent with this, Robert Fishman's research shows that during the extended transition, plant-level union leaders came under intense pressure for moderation from rank-and-file workers themselves.[83] Direct action was similarly limited. Several small-scale land invasions sponsored by the Sindicato de Obreros del Campo occurred in Andalucía, but the violent strikes, sizable land invasions, and widespread workplace intimidation of the 1930s did not have meaningful counterparts after 1977. This was not for lack of models: workers had not only the lore of their unions but also the prominent and massive land invasions in neighboring Portugal in 1975 for inspiration.[84] In sum, in the 1930s, left moderation was the result of leaders' tactics, which flew in the face of rank-and-file resistance, and for that reason alone was unpredictable. After 1977 moderation by leftist organizations was consistent with rank-and-file preferences.

Small-Business Owners

Rightists at the mass level formed beliefs broadly consistent with these events. The business owners expressed dissatisfaction with diverse outcomes after 1977, including terrorism; the proliferation of crime, drugs,

82. See Partido Comunista de España (1980: e.g., 13); interview with the CC.OO.'s Julian Ariza, Madrid, 1994. These sources attribute lack of support to workers' fear of unemployment.

83. Fishman (1990: 238–41) found that 72 percent of the plant-level labor leaders interviewed reported that "the lack of willingness of the workers to support strikes with the determination which would be necessary" was the primary reason limiting union demands.

84. *El país,* October 14, 1979, pp. 38–39; Bermeo (1986).

and other social ills; and the prolonged recession and rising unemployment; and consequently reduced consumer spending in their neighborhoods and stores. As Linz and Alfred Stepan emphasize, "[T]he economic situation of Spain deteriorated sharply during the transition and did not improve until three years *after* consolidation," which they date to 1982.[85] Like other small-business owners, most of the retailers interviewed were well-defined center-right or conservative voters. Three patterns of voting were most common: 28 percent reported voting consistently for the right (Fraga's Alianza Popular/Partido Popular [AP/PP]) since 1977; 60 percent for the center-right and right (typically UCD in 1977–79 and AP/PP since).[86] But despite much dissatisfaction, these conservatives did not believe democracy's political outcomes threatened their core interests and values. They credited Suárez's UCD with very effectively handling the political aspects of the transition (although several criticized the legalization of the PCE). But most were sharply critical of a number of the UCD's economic and social policies, including welfare-state spending and rising tax burdens, as well as what they considered to be excessively lenient policies toward drugs, prostitution, crime, and immigration. Their economic complaints paralleled those of the major voice of employers' interests, the (CEOE), although three-fifths voted for Suárez in 1977–79.

Rightists clearly did not linearly project the past (interwar) conduct of the PSOE. Above all, they were not threatened by the prospect of a PSOE government. Although they generated harsh criticism for economic mismanagement and corruption after 1982, most saw the PSOE as relatively moderate. Over two-thirds of the interview group believed the PSOE was not truly "radical" even in the democracy's initial years. Several said the PSOE's initial apparent militancy was "more a matter of talk than reality," "depending [on] whom [González] was talking to." Like most voters, they saw the PSOE as fundamentally moderate even before the 1979 extraordinary PSOE congress; a 1979 national survey (preceding the extraordinary congress) found that only 18 percent of voters believed the PSOE was "Marxist," while twice as many (including nearly half of PSOE voters) described it as "social democratic." And, consistent with the surveyed views of most of the business community, fully 88 percent of the retailers considered the PSOE not radical when it emerged in polls as Spain's largest party in 1981–82.

85. Linz and Stepan (1989: 44; 1996: 113).
86. One respondent in the first category voted for Blas Piñar in 1979; eight, for the PSOE in 1982 only; four, for the PSOE in 1977–82. Two would not report their votes; none reported voting for the PCE. Pérez-Díaz's (1985) survey of business people found that nearly three-fourths voted for the AP, Convergència i Unió (CiU), or Partido Nacionalista Vasco (PNV) in 1982, while less than 5 percent voted for the PSOE; also Martínez (1993: 147–55).

Jonathan Marcus notes that in 1982 "[m]any observers [in Spain] commented that the differences between the PSOE programme and the policies of the previous UCD administration were largely a matter of degree rather than of kind."[87]

Left-right convergence meant these conservatives could react without fear to the disintegration of the UCD and the weakness of the AP/PP as the 1982 elections approached. Only 12 percent said they were "very worried" or "somewhat worried" when the PSOE won the 1982 election.[88] Several explicitly recognized that only modest distances separated the UCD from the incoming PSOE: "We thought things would continue more or less the same" policy-wise. "The PSOE wasn't bringing in Marxism" (*no se llevaba marxismo*). These views are consistent with Robert Martinez's finding that the concerns of business executives and leaders of employers' associations over an all-PSOE government *declined* between 1981 and 1982, with only one-fifth expecting significant nationalizations to result.[89] Because rightists perceived that the political spectrum was relatively and predictably compact, even the strong likelihood of repeated PSOE reelections through the 1980s and early 1990s appeared unthreatening. This perception of low risks was only reinforced by the PSOE's record in office, most obviously its emphatic priority of reducing inflation rather than unemployment.

The differences are stark between 1936 and 1982:

- The center-left was allied with revolutionary parties in 1936 but not 1982.
- In 1936, fundamental revision of Spain's property regime was a major part of the PSOE, PCE, and CNT's political projects, whereas by 1982 the PSOE had abandoned essentially all references to nationalization of any form of property.
- In 1936, rightists perceived left leaders as under extensive radicalizing pressures from their rank-and-file; by 1982, the PSOE leadership's assessments of voters had driven it toward the center.
- In 1936, major parties and unions within the left electoral alliance and parliamentary coalition had lengthy records of encouraging or tolerating class-based direct action; in 1982 this was not the case.
- In 1936, detailed programs for worker participation in industry and more extensive social spending were absent only because their need was

87. Tezanos (1983: 74), Marcus (1983: 283).
88. Of these six, four said they had been concerned about property ownership in 1982 and two, with tax levels.
89. Martinez (1993: 165–69); also Pérez-Díaz (1985) and the 1982 Mercado poll cited by Gillespie (1989a: 366).

largely obviated by the PSOE, PCE, and CNT's commitment to extensive property distribution; by 1982, the PSOE proposed growth in welfare-state spending and taxes largely in line with what the center-right UCD had already been implementing.

The pattern of the 1970s and 1980s had substantial consequences for the calculus of hedging and defection. The fact that a left government's policies were not so different from the center-right's preferred policies meant that rightists could not reasonably expect substantial policy improvements if the PSOE government were to be replaced even by an "ideal" conservative authoritarian government. The *autónomos* were asked whether any set of authoritarian rulers could have provided plausible solutions to three problems they considered salient: crime, taxes, and overall economic problems (recession, inflation, and unemployment). Like most Spaniards, they believed economic problems were common across Western Europe and largely the result of oil shocks.[90] They thus had no reason to believe exclusion would generate improvement. "What are the *militares* going to do? Lower the price of oil in the world?"

Only 12 percent of the retailers believed the recession, unemployment, and inflation of the late 1970s and 1980s could have been solved by a hypothetical authoritarian government substantially more effectively than under the democracy. Twenty-eight percent believed authoritarian rulers might lower tax loads by curbing the left's social programs and rising spending by regional governments. But even they believed this at best could reduce spending and taxes only modestly; 62 percent of the interview group did not believe exclusionary rules of the game would lead to lower taxes at all. These responses do not reflect a generalized inability to identify problems that a regime change could address: forty-two of the fifty retailers believed rightist authoritarianism would be able to reduce rates of crime. But crime was not sufficient to compensate for the risks they associated with authoritarianism. In sum, they believed democracy was preferable even in hard times because authoritarian alternatives were predictably even worse. This belief helps us to place in perspective Peter McDonough, Samuel Barnes, and Antonio Lopéz Pina's finding that Spaniards in the 1980s reported rising levels of satisfaction with democracy in the present *and* favorable estimations of how life had been under Franco, which risks revealing a "creep-

90. DATA Study 262, conducted in early 1977, showed that the oil shock was by far the single most common factor cited to explain the economic problems of the early transition period. Respondents, including those characterized as conservatives and Christian Democrats, also cited strikes, a lack of investor confidence, and the Europe-wide recession.

ing nostalgia" that could work against democracy.[91] While such views bear monitoring, it is possible that this is an example of actors positively evaluating the appropriateness of different regimes to different circumstances, with authoritarianism in this case relegated to conditions, to all appearances, firmly confined to the past. A rationalist approach to democratic consolidation expects updating, not amnesia, among current democrats who once backed another regime.

(Little) Office-Holding (Failed) Pacts, and (Loss-Concentrating) Institutions

Given this payoff matrix, conservatives formed reliable prodemocratic regime preferences regardless of routine events in democracy: although pacts failed, rightist parties were shut out of office, despite an institutional context that both concentrated wins and losses and evolved over time.

Exclusion from Office, 1982–96

Rightist support for democracy was not based on dominance of political office, because in a sharp contrast with postwar Britain, Germany, Italy, and France, the right in Spain was electorally weak in the crucial years of transition and consolidation. Beginning in the fall of 1979, popularity of the center-right UCD began to decline sharply, and by 1982 the UCD had disintegrated and most conservatives were absorbed into Fraga's AP, whose profound image problems limited the party to just over one-fourth of the vote for the next decade.[92] This weakness meant not only a PSOE victory in 1982 but also relatively foreseeable Socialist victories for some time into the future. The PSOE's governing style was far from inclusive, and yet core conservative interests and values were sufficiently reflected in the moderate policies of the PSOE as to make defection predictably unattractive.

Quasi-Westminster Institutions

The PSOE's moderation was not the result of institutional constraints. While the negotiation of the 1978 constitution was consensus-oriented, the

---

91. McDonough, Barnes, and López Pina (1986: 743–44, 756n9). As late as the 1980s, 57 percent of the business executives surveyed by Martinez (1993: 142) expressed total or qualified approval of Franco, and only 27 percent expressed disapproval.
92. Hopkin (1999) analyzed the UCD's degeneration.

Table 5.5 PSOE Shares of Votes and Lower House Seats, 1980s

	1982	1986	1989
Share of votes (%)	48.1	44.1	39.6
Share of seats (%)	57.7	52.6	50.0

resulting institutions were in many ways not the type of stakes-reducing designs Arend Lijphart and Przeworski favor. Gunther has pointed out that the electoral law employs numerous districts small enough to have "strikingly unproportional" effects.[93] This manufactured ("unearned") majorities for the PSOE throughout the 1980s—as shown in Table 5.5—precisely when conservatives, it is generally agreed, became committed to democracy.

PSOE governments could not be effectively checked by the weak Senate. Moreover, the constructive vote of no-confidence designed to stabilize cabinets can also manufacture governments from parliamentary minorities, as occurred in 1977–82; this created the risk for conservatives that the left could rule this way too. The trend toward federalism might have dispersed power but it only became truly important in the 1980s, when the right's vote was too depressed and fragmented to stop the PSOE from dominating almost all regional administrations. Even if institutions had provided protection to conservatives, they could not have relied on them: democracy itself had just been achieved through legal mechanisms of revision, and the new system soon embarked on myriad technical revisions and a gradual federalizing of the state.

A Mixed Record on Pacts

The right was also not protected by pacts. Despite stereotypes, pacts were not a consistently successful feature of Spain's transition. Negotiations produced the 1977 electoral law and the 1978 constitution, as well as the best-known accord in transitions theorizing alongside Punto Fijo: the Moncloa pacts. But it is easy to exaggerate this trend. First, the original rightist decisions to democratize in 1976 occurred when left parties neither offered assurances nor were in any position to promise future rank-and-file compliance. Pacting and "consensus politics" occurred only *after* democratization became the preferred strategy of the right and in no way can be said to have "served to re-establish democracy."[94] Second, the Moncloa pacts in

93. Gunther (1989: 840).
94. Capo Giol et al. (1990: 93).

the fall of 1977 were a set of essentially economic agreements: the left agreed to limits on wages, public spending, and credit, while the UCD government agreed to implement income tax reform, reorganize welfare-state programs, and initiate administrative reforms.[95] This may have been important to preventing further deterioration of the economy.

But the Moncloa pacts failed to institutionalize compromise as the generalized strategy of major political groups. In 1977, the UGT had to be compelled by the leadership of the PSOE to accept the specific provisions of the Moncloa pacts. Employers signed on only reluctantly, and Carlos Ferrer Salat, head of the CEOE, insisted that the UCD had to "stop wanting to reach agreements with everyone." The conservative AP refused to sign the political portions of the pacts. The UCD failed to comply with many of its obligations under the pacts as it drifted to the right economically. A year later the CC.OO. issued an "emphatic 'no' to a social pact."[96] Even more striking, when the wage provisions of the Moncloa pacts came up for renewal in 1978, the Suárez government's repeated rounds of meetings (culminating in Fernando Abril's *jornada de reflexión*) failed to achieve a compromise between unions and employers. The government finally imposed wage limits by decree. Beginning the year after that, employers and the UGT came to several agreements, but the CC.OO. remained aloof for a further two years.[97] In other words, socioeconomic "consensus" strategies failed as early as democracy's second year, a fact Coverdale is among the few authors to emphasize. Political pacting expired six months after that. After the adoption of the 1978 constitution, Suárez remarked that "the consensus had ended" and the PSOE joined him in assuming a more competitive posture.[98] From then on, major legislation was increasingly imposed by the UCD and other conservatives; the PCE and CC.OO. responded to the contentious Workers' Statute bill with a campaign of strikes and demonstrations.[99] None of this is meant to denigrate agreements reached after the transition had already been initiated. But it is to emphasize that political pacts did not factor into rightists' decisions in 1976; they did not reflect a consistent or even preponderant pattern of interparty compromise; and

95. Tamames (1995: 148–64) discusses the pacts' terms.

96. Gillespie (1989a: 334–35); interview with Ferrer Salat, Barcelona, 1993, and Ferrer Salat in *Catalunya Express*, October 5, 1977; CC.OO. in *Gaceta de derecho social*, October, 1978, p. 18.

97. That is, until the June 1981 tripartite wage and price agreement. The saga of the 1978 negotiations can be followed in *El país*, September–December 1978. Fishman (1990) discussed the 1979–80 UGT/CEOE accords. Camacho and Redondo's reactions to the 1978 decree can be found in *Mundo obrero*, December 21, 1978, p. 3.

98. *DSC* 3 (March 30, 1979), p. 41; Coverdale (1982: 236–38).

99. The UCD and AP united to defeat most of the left's amendments to the Workers' Statute. Strikes and demonstrations greeted the UCD's policy for Galicia; *El país*, November 23, 1979, p. 1.

they did not create, beyond the terms of the constitution, the "mutually satisfactory procedural arrangements" for future contests and negotiations that are often understood to be the seminal contribution of pacts.[100] And yet rightists neither defected from democracy nor hedged against risk. This is consistent with their perception of low political risks in democracy both before the first pact was conceived and after later negotiations failed.

Exclusionary Entrepreneurs in the 1981 Coup Attempt and Beyond

The long series of actions, transactions, and events that made up the extended transition, lasting from 1976 at least until the PSOE's 1982 election, benefited from the skill and wisdom of leaders and the restraint of various actors. But it was more important that conservatives perceived overall political outcomes in democracy as predictably preferable to those likely under even favorable authoritarianism. This perception placed powerful constraints on pro-authoritarian leaders after 1977 and created generous margins of maneuver for leaders and parties that pursued conservative policy goals within a strictly democratic framework. The change in the strategic situation since 1936 became clear in 1981.

In 1977–81, several conspiracies emanated from *grupúsculos* ("grouplets") in the military, culminating in the 1981 coup attempt. Spain's leaders responded with alacrity, and it was quickly suppressed. But a wide number of observers concluded that, in Fusi's words, the "attempted military coup ... underlined the fragility of democracy in Spain." Many credited Juan Carlos with having "saved" democracy on the night of February 23, 1981, by resisting the plotters' appeals and arm-twisting senior officers into obedience. The putsch did reveal a fragility in one aspect of the new democracy: a small number of pro-exclusionary actors had access to a disturbing quantity of coercive resources.[101] But the events of February 1981 also focus attention on the heavily prodemocratic distribution of regime preferences, including among the overwhelming majority of conservatives surveyed.[102]

---

100. O'Donnell and Schmitter (1986: 47).

101. Agüero (1995: ch. 6–7), Fusi (1982: 222). Preston (1986: 199) writes that "only [Juan Carlos] stood between Spanish democracy and its destruction." An editorial in *Diario 16*, March 2, 1981, p. 3, claimed that "[w]ithout King Juan Carlos, the night of February 23 would have been the saddest in two generations of Spaniards. . . . The King saved us."

102. Blas Piñar largely justified the coup attempt and some civilian members of Fuerza Nueva appear to have participated in the plot (*Diario 16*, March 2, 1981, p. 8; *Cambio 16*, March 9, 1981, p. 33). But rejection was the norm among rightists. See CIS Study 1273 conducted at the end of February 1981 and DATA's March 1981 survey, cited in Linz and Stepan (1989: 45).

This distribution helped ensure the coup's failure and suggested authoritarianism's inherent implausibility. It does not diminish the heroism that the king demonstrated on the night of February 23 to suggest that in this sense it was not democracy but the coup that was fragile. As David Gilmour puts it, "If it is difficult to see what the plotters wanted, it is even harder to know who—apart from *El alcázar* and its readership—would have supported them."[103]

None of the transition leaders interviewed for this study report that they believed in 1981 that even a coordinated military action would have won any segmental support or, even if successful in seizing power, would have been able to control Spain for more than a few weeks or, at most, months. Calvo-Sotelo, in the Cortes during the attempt, remembered thinking at the time that within forty-eight hours of any initially successful coup, millions would be in the streets demonstrating against it. He captured the dramatic but calamitous nature of the coup by describing it as "the Waterloo of Francoism": a possibility for short-term advance on a road that could not, in the end, lead to victory.

By the late 1970s and 1980s, and because influential groups in democracy did not pose threats to the right's core interests and values, conservatives calculated that relocating political decision-making power even to favorable authoritarian leaders could not solve their most salient problems. If anything, authoritarian rules of the game instead would reduce their payoffs, at the very least because of higher risks to their safety. In this sense, while King Juan Carlos saved what would have been an unknown number of lives in February 1981, it was the Spanish people who saved the regime by turning their backs on any form of dictatorship. Rational choices that had once led conservatives to support a coup and decades of authoritarian rule had now led them to democratic consolidation.

103. Gilmour (1985: 247). Colomer (1995: ch. 5) uses to great effect his analysis of the plotters' (faulty) assumption that the king's second preference (after no coup) was to join an attempt. As it turned out, his second preference was to resist it.

6

Political Risks and Regime Outcomes in Europe before 1940

> If one does not want to stumble into danger and then have to
> backtrack, it is imperative to take very careful account of the level of
> political education which has been achieved by the various groups of
> our country.
>
> GIOVANNI GIOLITTI, 1902

In this chapter I extend the argument to France, Britain, Germany, and
Italy, from France in the 1870s through the interwar period. In these countries, in these years, rightists' strategies toward democracy depended on
their assessments of risks under that regime. I continue to reify both the
"right" and successive "moments" when paradigmatic conservatives perceived regime alternatives in specific ways. As in the Spanish cases, there
are costs of forcing so many events into a relatively simple framework, but
there are also substantial benefits. The focus on the right in modern West
Europe holds more or less constant one and a half "legs" of the rationalist
decision-making triad—actors' basic preferences and their beliefs about
one of the two regime options they face ("Authoritarianism under whom?")
while permitting variation in their evaluation of the other regime option
("Democracy with whom?"). As in Spain, variation in the political risks the
right perceived in democracy, determined by rightists' beliefs about the
likely behavior of the left, induced variation in the right's strategy toward
democracy. Consequently, the cases covered in this chapter join Spain
in highlighting the striking contrast between, on the one hand, cases in
which the right believed the left was predictably moderate—and hence

democracy was low risk—and, on the other, cases in which the right perceived the left as fundamentally unpredictable and democracy as highly risky. The effects of this are relatively straightforward. Where the left was unpredictable, the right's regime-related payoff matrix could easily reverse as the result of readily identifiable and plausible scenarios in democracy. For example, if rightist parties held office, or if the left was in power but tactically moderate, conservatives could secure property, income, and safety in democracy, making that regime preferable even to an authoritarian regime that also secured the right's policy interests but inevitably imposed at least some (even if low) risks of repression. But if the left radicalized and won power, such an authoritarian alternative would be preferable to democracy.

These high risks did not deterministically inspire the right's defection from democracy. But since conservatives could not forecast whether their core interests and values would be better served in democracy or under the most likely authoritarian alternative—since they could know their present but not their future regime preferences—they had powerful incentives to maintain access to vehicles for exiting democracy. In contrast, when the right perceived the left as predictably moderate, democracy was predictably the better choice and the right had incentives to abandon hedges and commit to democracy. As in Spain, conservatives often (though not always) traced moderation of the left to diffuse property ownership and widespread economic security and traced susceptibility of the left to radicalization to class-based disputes. Once again, our analysis does not rely on the validity of these connections made by rightists, and simply links the risks the right perceived in democracy, whatever their origin, to the right's strategy toward that regime.

Variation in both independent and dependent variables can be connected to specific cases. After initial uncertainty, conservatives in the early French Third Republic perceived the left portion of the political spectrum as predictably moderate. They abandoned exit vehicles and committed to democracy. But the right perceived the left as fundamentally unpredictable in interwar France, Italy, Germany, and Spain. In these cases, rightists believed the left could easily polarize to radical positions within a socialist party (Italy), in a socialist party in conjunction with growing revolutionary parties to its left (Germany, France), or both (Second Republic Spain). In France and Germany, the right's policy interests were threatened; in Spain and to a lesser extent Italy, rightists' policy interests *and* their safety were threatened in democracy. In France, diverse contingent protections ensured that the right's payoff matrix did not reverse before the 1940 German invasion, so the right did not defect. But it hedged, and democracy "deconsolidated" (a term considered at more length in Chapter 8). In three other cases I cover in this chapter, however, the right developed incentives not only to hedge but also to defect to support an authoritarian takeover. In interwar Italy, Germany, and Spain, unlike interwar France, contingent protections disappeared at specific times, triggering the right's defection from democracy. In all three cases, it is worth noting, the right defected to an authoritarian project that not only appeared very likely to secure their interests in property, income, and workplace authority but also had a track-record of consistently insulating rightists from the repressive coercion directed against leftist organizations and activists.

In contrast, and despite what is typically portrayed as an unpropitious ideological context, the pattern of the early French Third Republic was paralleled in interwar Britain. As early as the mid-1920s, British conservatives (like their counterparts in the Low Countries and Scandinavia) perceived the left half of the political spectrum, at the level of party leaders and of the rank-and-file, as predictably moderate. They could predictably secure their basic preferences in democracy without risking even modest threats to their safety under authoritarian rule, and they committed to democracy. Differences in the right's perceptions of the left and the right's resulting regime strategies are summarized in Table 6.1.

These outcomes defy competing assumptions in important ways, particularly influential (if often implicit) assumptions concerning ideational factors such as national or regional political cultures, "diffusion," and international demonstration effects (IDEs). Assumptions concerning enduring national political cultures suggest we should expect only gradual changes in regime preferences; factors such as IDEs and a regional political culture logically suggest synchronization across space. Instead, rapid discontinuities occurred in several cases. And as it would be again in the post-1945 years, divergence between cases was apparent in the periods covered in this chapter. The French right committed to democracy between the 1880s and 1914 even while many other European rightist sectors did not. Between the wars, the French right began to hedge, the right in Italy, Germany, and Spain defected to authoritarianism, but interwar British conservatives committed to democracy. In these pre–World War II cases, rightist sectors proved capable of rejecting what are generally portrayed as pro-authoritarian regional zeitgeists and IDEs.

Variations in the right's strategies also do not conform to variations in left/right balances of organizational or coercive power. The right in interwar Germany, Italy, and Spain hedged and then defected from democracy despite the fact that traditional conservative forces were weakened substantially and working-class organizations had achieved unprecedented levels of organizational mobilization and political power. On the rightist side of the left/right power balance, agrarian elites were certainly stronger in some cases than others, but "[b]y the 1920s and 1930s, landed elites almost everywhere were a spent political force." This is reflected in the fact

Table 6.1 The Right's Perceptions of the Left and Right Regime Strategies, before 1940

	Early Third Republic, France (1880s–1914)	Interwar France	Weimar	Italy	Spain	Britain
Main left party moderate in power?	Yes	Yes	Yes	No (local government)	Yes 1931–33, no 1936	Yes
Significant revolutionary organization to left of socialists?	No	Yes: PCF	Yes: KPD	Yes: PCI	Yes: CNT, PCE	No
Right believed property redistribution had significant mass constituency?	No	Uncertain	Yes, especially during Depression	Yes	Yes	No, especially by 1920s
Moderate left leaders perceived as under mass pressure to radicalize?	No, though increasing in first decade after turn of the century	Yes: bottom-up strikes, losses to PCF	Yes: rapid rise of KPD 1930–32	Yes: local revolts, competition with PCI	Yes: local violence, losses to CNT, PCE	No: pressures to moderate during 1926 strikes

Table 6.1—cont.

	Early Third Republic, France (1880s–1914)	Interwar France	Weimar	Italy	Spain	Britain
Right perceived extensive class-based civil violence/"disorder"?	No	1936–38 strikes, factory occupations	Revolts, 1918–23; fears growing during Depression	Land invasions, factory occupations	Widespread land invasions, intimidation/violence	No
Right perceived social basis for left radicalism?	No	Urban workers	Urban workers, unemployed in Depression	Landless agricultural laborers, urban workers	Landless agricultural laborers, urban workers, and miners	Possibly unemployed in Depression?
Right's Regime Strategy	Commitment to democracy	Hedging: support for paramilitary *ligues*	Hedging: freikorps, Home Guards, Nazis; defection: 1930–32	Hedging: militias, *squadre*, defection: 1920–22	Hedging: military ties, Falange; defection: 1936	Commitment to democracy

that no authoritarian overthrow in this period was traditionally monarchist; instead, interwar authoritarian projects were based primarily on unprecedented mobilization among the middle classes.[1] Moreover, many interwar rightist sectors were denied the effective and conservative military available in Spain, either because the armed forces were less inclined to intervene proactively in politics (Italy and France) or because they were unusually weakened (Weimar). Yet in these cases, rightists assembled substantial paramilitary forces from scratch.

On the union side of the left/right equation, the historic highs achieved by Spain's left union sector in the interwar years were matched in the other cases in which the right nonetheless defected. The Italian socialist union expanded from 250,000 at the end of World War I to 2.3 million in 1920. In Germany, the socialist-aligned labor federation claimed nearly 5 million union members at its peak and the socialist-dominated Reichsbanner "militia," some 3 million. It was also in the interwar years that the right in France began hedging, even as membership in the French union federation quintupled to 4 million in 1937. Even massive working-class organizations could not ensure democratic stability in the face of a united and authoritarian right, a fact apparent to many on the left. Leaders of the Social Democratic Party of Germany (SPD), for example, did not believe they could challenge the (weakened) Weimar military in a coercive contest.[2] This pattern makes it all the more striking that in two cases covered in this chapter, conservatives prominently committed to democracy not where the left was too strong to exclude but instead where the left was quite weak organizationally. In France from the 1880s to the 1910s, left unions remained divided and relatively marginal, and in interwar Britain, the Depression and a schism within Labour helped cut the rate of union affiliation among workers nearly by half between 1919 and 1933.[3] As we will also see, patterns of neither pacts nor institutional designs persuasively explain the right's commitment versus hedging.

In each section I present data concerning the right's beliefs about the left's likely behavior in democracy, grounded in rightists' rudimentary "theories" about the nature of the left. Second, I present evidence concerning the right's predominant strategy toward democracy, commitment or hedging, or in some cases defection to authoritarianism.

1. Luebbert (1991: 278), Blackbourn and Eley (1984).
2. Harsch (1993: 104, 175). The statistics are from Jackson (1988: 219–20) and Horowitz (1963: 141).
3. Bain and Price (1980: 39).

The First French Consolidated Democracy (1871–1914)

> It is France which, on the continent, remains the mother of
> democratic, moderate, and bourgeois parliamentarism.
>
> JOSEPH BARTHÉLEMY, *La crise de la démocratie contemporaine*, 1931

The French launched a successful experiment in universal male suffrage
in the 1870s. Reading backward from France's collapse in 1940 might
suggest that the French Third Republic was precarious from its founding.
But there is overwhelming reason to conclude that, with the important
caveat of female disenfranchisement, France had a consolidated democracy from the 1880s to World War I. Consolidation occurred despite a transition that other explanatory approaches would consider so unpropitious
it might be said to foreshadow Weimar's transition: the new regime was
born of defeat in war, its leaders accepted a resented treaty imposing ter-
ritorial losses and financial indemnities, amidst a working-class revolt suppressed with probably over twenty thousand dead, soon followed by a
depression. French political culture recalled only failed democratic experiments and constitutional instability, and pro-authoritarian opinion leaders
and foreign models (including Bismarck) were prolific.

The Commune and other events initially presented French conservatives
with substantial uncertainty. Adolphe Thiers, provisional president of the
new republic, expressed concern that urban workers' anarchical passions
had been reduced "to powerlessness, not to calm," and remarked of Leon
Gambetta, leader of the left-wing Radicals: "We would like to know were he
is going, what he wants, what he is." The arch-conservative Broglie
described the Radical threat as "latent."[4] Yet democracy soon presented
socioeconomic conservatives with low political risks. Although the most
likely authoritarian alternative almost certainly would have been relatively
hospitable to these actors, such a regime's modest room for improving
democracy's already agreeable policies made it the predictably worse
choice.[5] As a result, the broad mass of conservatives soon abandoned
hedges.

How can we measure and explain the right's low risks in democracy? It
is not persuasive to attribute these to office-holding, assurances, and institutions. In successive elections a hegemonic moderate republican center
increasingly marginalized both remaining monarchists and the Radicals.

---

4. Brabant (1940: 311), Halévy (1930: 117), Grubb (1996: 106).

5. The military remained sufficiently conservative that some republican leaders felt the
need to monitor officers' views; Ralston (1967: 64).

While fluid factions and shifting names make it difficult to specify parties in this period, Alain Bomier-Landowski's estimates suggest that the left properly understood never even came close to competing for a majority.[6] Conservatives were also offered diverse assurances. The broader republican leadership favored a "pragmatic republicanism, drained of radical content," and quickly demonstrated their intolerance for the kind of challenge to the social order represented by the Commune.[7] Despite their name, even the Radicals almost always postponed decisive action. And Thiers helped design institutions to safeguard rightist interests.[8] But these protections were not reliable. Election results might fluctuate. Assurances were of limited value when Radicals were seen as personally highly variable; Gambetta proudly took possession of the epithet of "opportunism" and described his strategy of tactically moderating demands while awaiting more propitious circumstances. Finally, the original institutional design in many ways concentrated wins and losses and more important, was regularly challenged and several times changed. Gambetta said he voted for the 1875 constitution only because it could be amended. Indeed, his Radicals soon proposed weakening the Senate and by 1884 helped revise portions of the constitution and the Senate's electoral rules, and in 1885 and 1889 the lower house's electoral law. Rightists thus saw protective institutions as anything but reliable. Broglie expressed concern that republicans might undermine the Senate and presidency; the latter was indeed emasculated after the *seize mai* events.[9] Since the Radicals functioned as a Revision Party, electoral results and institutions were intertwined.

Instead, conservatives perceived low risks in democracy because they believed the left was predictably moderate, largely for reasons having to do with socioeconomic structures. Elections did more than put moderates in office: they revealed just how sociologically isolated Communal politics were and how moderate the left's center of political gravity was. This can be seen in policy outcomes. Even more than bureaucratic reform and trade, the centerpiece debates early in the Third Republic were over pocketbook issues and religion. Above all, all significant parties participated in a moderate consensus not only against civil violence but on fundamental political economy, a consensus that lasted to the interwar period. Fiscal policy was relatively orthodox, and core conservative economic interests, especially private property, were never seriously threatened. On the contrary, especially small-property ownership was systematically reinforced by both

6. Bomier-Landowski (1951). For example, Socialists *plus* Radicals—many of whom were not radical—did not account for one-fifth of the 1889–93 legislature.
7. Nord (1995: 15).
8. Thiers (1915: 259), Grubb (1996: 89).
9. Chapman (1962: 68–69, 172).

rhetoric and diverse public policies. It is in this sense in particular that studies such as Sanford Elwitt's accurately describe the first several decades of the Third Republic as conservative or bourgeois.[10] Because of this consensus, core conservative economic interests were in no way threatened even when office passed to the Radicals at the turn of the century.

Under Radical-led governments, the social policies of the socialist minister Alexandre Millerand during 1899–1902 represented the outer limits of what the Republic would plausibly produce, instead of being the first steps of a more threatening left agenda. Unlike Weimar, for example, where relatively doctrinaire working-class parties regularly won 35 to 45 percent of the vote, France's (frequently divided) socialists averaged around 10 percent until 1914.[11] Just how far the moderate socioeconomic consensus stretched became evident when the Radicals in office avoided expansive social legislation, recoiled from the socialists' economic agenda and anti-militarism, and responded to increasingly frequent strikes with decisive repression. The socialist Edouard Vaillant poignantly noted that "[t]he Right begins for us much further Left than you would think." The Third Republic thus experienced what Giovanni Giolitti attempted so unsuccessfully in Italy: the integration of the system's critics into the political machinery. Alternations in office thus did not lead to particularly wide swings in political outcomes. It is possible to acknowledge real differences of opinion between, say, Radicals and *modérés*, and yet recognize that Henri de Jouvenal was not exaggerating badly when he remarked that "[t]here is little difference between" the competing center-left and center-right presidential candidates in 1906. In Jacque's Chastenet's words, the Republic was "no longer aristocratic but very bourgeois."[12]

Even the left and center's challenge to the Catholic Church's budgetary privileges and educational role was suffused with moderation, although it generated considerable vitriol on both sides both up to and after the 1905 separation of church and state. Stathis Kalyvas makes clear how extensive and ugly this debate was at various points. But while the Radicals insisted (through the 1930s) that they were separated from the right by the "abyss of secularism," events between 1871 and 1905 are not of the same magnitude as the anticlerical whirlwind in Spain in the spring of 1936. Secularization in France was phased in piecemeal, many measures were "applied

---

10. Elwitt (1975).

11. Farrar (1991). As Berstein (1980–82: 288) says of the Radicals in a later period, "For middle classes, a middle doctrine."

12. Stone (1985), Weber (1968: 39), Chastenet (1952: 243). While Hoffmann's seminal 1956 essay is certainly right that the Third Republic was based on an enduring social alliance between the well-off, moderate peasants, and middle classes, Stone (1996: 6) emphasizes that this consensus was "constantly criticized and renegotiated."

with leniency," and its culmination was profoundly telescoped in time. Separation of church and state occurred thirty-four years after democratization, in the absence of either maximalist anticlerical campaigns or an antirepublican crusade by the Catholic Church.[13]

Like in interwar Spain, French conservatives frequently traced political orientations to socioeconomic structures. Louis Chevalier argues that in the first half of the nineteenth century, France's middle and upper classes saw urban workers as shading off into the quasi-criminal "dangerous classes." Figures like Jules Méline later attributed socialism to the miseries of "disinherited classes" concentrated in working-class Paris, the northern textile regions, and other industrial cities.[14] But early in the Third Republic the question, "Democracy with whom?" called to conservative minds diverse elements of moderation. The "new social strata" (*couches sociales*) that Gambetta championed were recognized as provincial middle and lower-middle classes whose center of political gravity did not extend far toward socialism.[15] Above all, France's rural sector was dominated generally by politically moderate, small-holding tenant and sharecropping peasants. Robert Paxton makes clear that widespread conservative confidence in the small-holding rural sector reached to the interwar period. Leading conservatives were sufficiently confident of this situation that the socialist Jean Jaurès accused them of using "rural democracy like a sturdy tree trunk to support themselves in resisting the upward thrust of the workers."[16] Herman Lebovics's analysis highlights rightists' beliefs about the deep roots of moderation even when they feared it had come under strain. Conservatives concluded that rural desperation and possible future radicalization could be averted through cooperatives and expanded credit. What is striking is that even if steps were needed to shore up the political moderation of small farmers, the contrast with other sectors remains stark. Few would have suggested at the time that urban workers could be made conservative by such modest means. It was not unusual for one conservative report to describe peasants as "a class we have considered up until now immune to socialist blandishments, a class we considered the rampart of the social order." One can agree with Tony Judt that there is no one-to-one correspondence between small-holding (or tenancy) and conservatism, and with Eugen Weber that many peasants had zero-sum conflicts with rural elites, yet recognize at the same time that France's rural social structure was much less conducive to revolutionary politics than great-estate Apulia and the Po

13. Herriot in April 1932, quoted in Larmour (1964: 117); Kalyvas (1996: 122–28).
14. Chevalier (1958), Lebovics (1988: 91–92).
15. Stone (1996).
16. Paxton (1997: 29), Lebovics (1988: 171).

Valley or Andalucía and Extremadura, and that most French peasants played what was by socialist standards a conservative role. More important, many conservatives believed that.[17] The conservative response was commitment to democracy.

Given initial monarchism, Boulangism, and the Dreyfus affair, how can we conclude that conservatives were committed to democracy from the mid-1880s until 1914? This question is particularly important in light of enduring arguments concerning the precariousness of the Third Republic in this period. While this is likely to remain a subject of debate for some time, there is substantial evidence that the fragility of the early Third Republic is more initial impression than reality; specifically, there is substantial reason to conclude that the right abandoned the infrastructure of exit. It is possible to maintain an exaggerated emphasis on monarchism in this period, which prevents us, as Lebovics emphasizes, "from focusing upon the birth of a republican conservatism."[18] The 1875 constitution famously passed the first parliament by one vote, giving rise to enduring notions that the Third Republic was an accidental result of the rivalry between competing monarchical dynasties, nondemocrats who only "habituated" to democracy with time. But in Guy Chapman's view, it is "nonsense" to conclude that support for democracy was therefore extremely contingent (or even nonexistent). Given electoral trends, the next parliament would have easily passed the basic law had the first refused. Extensive evidence suggests that despite the clear commitment of hard-core monarchists and sectors within the Catholic Church to hold out and await restoration, it is easy to exaggerate true monarchist loyalties.[19] Among other indicators, ostensibly monarchist deputies regularly began supporting conservative republican governments relatively soon. By the time the Vatican officially abandoned the monarchical project in France and "rallied" to the republic, it validated what was already a migration into democracy of socioeconomic conservatives, especially at the mass level. Pro-authoritarian opinion leaders like Paul de Cassagnac had very limited followings; closer to (and

17. Lebovics (1988: 121, 115–16): "With unity and energy we can dam up this rising flood which has submerged the cities, but from which there is still time to save the countryside." Judt (1979: ch. 9), Weber (1976: ch. 15). Also, see deputy Latrade in Halévy (1930: 142–43).

18. Lebovics (1988: 3), Elwitt (1975: 12).

19. Chapman (1962: 61–62). Rustow (1970) presents an influential version of the accident-and-habituation interpretation. But local and by-elections in the fall of 1871 already revealed massive defections to conservative republicanism. Broglie thus urged his allies to run as conservative republicans and attempted to delay the second national elections as long as possible, knowing they would probably result in monarchist defeat. In other words, monarchism in 1871 was in many cases a moniker not an ethic, and republicanism was resolved upon far more quickly than habituation would normally be understood to take place. See Grubb (1996: 89), Offen (1991: 154–56).

after) the turn of the century, the Action Française, if too young to be called politically moribund, was ineffective "as a *political* group," as Eugen Weber emphasizes.[20]

None of this is to deny that antidemocratic hopes and conspiracies survived and circulated among militant elites within old monarchist families, the church, and perhaps sectors of the military. But these actors lacked what made democracies truly precarious elsewhere: a large segmental mass constituency that generally favored abolishing representative democracy and using coercive violence to exclude significant other segments of the population from political life. Thus, leading antidemocrats acknowledged their lack of a mass base.[21] This lack of a base is visible in the cases of Boulangism and the multifaceted backlash to Dreyfus, both of which *were* significant movements. While the latter was partly anti-Semitic and both harbored impulses for populist reforms of the Republic, neither movement was backed by an evidently antidemocratic, mass segmental following. Thus, for example, many of the financiers of Boulangism were monarchist, but the following that made it politically relevant cannot be compared easily to the mass segmental support for exclusion that was evident in Weimar in 1932 or Spain in the summer of 1936. On the contrary, evidence suggests that average Boulanger voters were normally committed to the emphatically democratic Radicals, not the extreme right.[22] In these years, the Radicals regularly invoked the rhetoric of "Republican defense," but they did this typically to fend off challenges to laic laws, not to democracy.

Despite national traditions, church practices, and readily accessible IDEs, conservative regime preferences in this period were by most measures reliably prodemocratic, decades before the same could be said of Britain.[23] While Lebovics usefully compares the Republic's governing alliance of iron, cotton, and wheat to Germany's iron and rye, it is crucial that in this period French conservatism's was a project within democracy. The right committed to democracy not as a defensive maneuver because the left was strong and threatening, but because it was neither. As Thiers reassured one conservative, "Frightened people will fall back on the monarchy. . . . The idea

20. Grubb (1996: 83), Sedgwick (1965), Offen (1991: 206–07), Weber (1962: viii).

21. Maurras and Dutrait-Crozon (1908) thus pinned their hopes on military and government elites. Ralston (1967: 222–24) finds no evidence of serious military plots throughout the Dreyfus Affair, and Weber (1968) emphasized that the nationalist "revival" had shallow social roots.

22. Irvine (1989), Nord (1986: 5, 262, 298, 304–07).

23. Conservative republicans discovered discourses and symbols as needed, for example, affiliating themselves with 1789 (against 1793) and referring to Catholic accommodation to democracy in Switzerland and the United States; e.g., Grubb (1996: 305).

of a *conservative republic* reassures them, rallies them, and will give them to us."[24]

Interwar Divergences (1918–39)

> Europe was flooded by dictatorships.
>
> CARLO SFORZA, *European Dictatorships*, 1931

Despite common stereotypes, interwar Europe generated considerable variety in regime outcomes, nothing approaching a systematic lurch to authoritarianism. While the right in Italy, Germany, and Spain defected to authoritarianism, the French right hedged but did not defect, and conservatives in Britain (like in the Low Countries and Scandinavia) committed to democracy.

Interwar France

From the turn of the century to the interwar years, the risks French conservatives perceived in democracy rose dramatically. This meant that *if* contingent protections were present in democracy, overall outcomes in that regime would be more attractive than those under a conservative authoritarian regime. But they might also be less attractive as the result of plausible and readily identifiable events in democracy. All three contingent factors were present (rightist office-holding, left tactical moderation, and protective institutions) to prevent highly threatening outcomes from materializing in democracy through to the 1940 German invasion, and the right did not defect. But because conservatives could know their present but not their future regime preference, they hedged. The commencement of hedging after decades of commitment to democracy demonstrates that such commitment is not irreversible; if political risks grow sufficiently, once-reliable support can degenerate to the point where actors seek access to exit options.

For the French right risks in democracy rose because of both rapid interwar growth in working-class parties and expanding alliance possibilities with the center-left, which ended the historic isolation of working-class political formations. It is difficult not to connect rising Socialist and then Communist votes to changes in existing voters' partisan preferences and to the growing industrial population that accompanied accelerating economic

24. Grubb (1996: 89), emphasis in the original.

Table 6.2 Leftward Movement of the French Electorate: Percentage of Vote in Selected Elections, 1893–1936

	1893	1914	1928	1936
Radicals ("Radical Socialists")	22.6	18.1	17.8	14.4
Independent Socialists and Socialist Republicans	—	3.9	5.2	7.6
Socialist/SFIO	8.4	16.8	18	19.9
PCF	—	—	11.3	15.3
Total	31	38.8	52	57.2

growth, especially after 1906. Writing in 1899, Gustave Le Bon regarded the growth of urban industry and workers' mobilization with concern: "Can we hope that with the progress of civilization the class struggle will be attenuated? Everything leads one to believe, on the contrary, that it will become much more intense than in the past."[25] Some PCF and SFIO growth was at the expense of the Radicals, but most growth on the left was positive-sum. As Table 6.2 shows, the right's answer to the question, "Democracy with whom?" had dramatically changed since the turn of the century.

Initially, conservatives were unsure what this change would entail. The conservative *Le figaro* asked in 1924, "A left majority? Yes, but which fraction leads it? Who commands it? . . . What direction will it take?" Contingent protections were abundant. The left government elected in 1924 required centrist votes to legislate. Through the 1920s, the left half of the spectrum continued to be led by the venerable Radicals, led by Edouard Herriot and committed to property and incremental reform. *Le figaro* noted that "[e]ven in their nightmares, pessimists have at worst the possibility of an Herriot cabinet."[26] Moreover the left was not cohesive; within two years of the 1924 and 1932 electoral victories by the left, the Radicals abandoned the socialists and switched to ally in parliament with the center-right.[27]

But in the first half of the 1930s, the alliance between the Radicals, the SFIO, and eventually the PCF grew more intense, and, in part because of the effects of the Depression, relative weights within this alliance shifted steadily leftward. In 1936, the Popular Front won a majority, the SFIO was the largest

25. Le Bon (1977/1912: 334).

26. *Le figaro*, May 13, 1924, p. 1; May 9, 1924, p. 1. Berstein (1980–82: 375–86, 413) describes the gradual development of cooperation from joint electoral lists whose purely pragmatic nature both the Radicals and the socialist (SFIO) publicly emphasized.

27. As Berstein (1980–82: 11) notes, "[T]he notion of the left did not have the same meaning for the Radicals and the Socialists." See *Le temps*, May 11, 1924, p. 1; *Le Figaro*, May 13, 1924, p. 1; Berstein (1980–82: 171–74). *Le temps*, April 21, 1928, p. 1, expressed concern that another left government would be so internally divided it could not govern coherently.

left party, and the PCF was nearly as large as the Radicals. Many rightists believed that slippage to the left would continue.[28] This leftward movement had substantial policy implications; if earlier in the Third Republic the left had threatened the Catholic Church but not basic political economy, now it offered assurances over religion but mounted a substantial class-based challenge. The 1936 election initially was met by relative calm among conservatives.[29] But it was followed swiftly by massive strikes, factory occupations, and "disorder" in major cities. It is difficult to determine exactly to what extent conservatives believed social revolution was a real possibility in 1936. Richard Vinen concludes that the "French *patronat* was always rather confused about what specific kind of threat was posed by working-class disorder." But the business community's shock at the vigorous left challenge to economic control (if not formal ownership) is not in dispute. Its immediate reaction was capitulation at the tripartite Matignon talks, which business leaders insisted was "the only means of avoiding revolution."[30]

Rightists did not defect from democracy. This was not because the Matignon concessions revealed stable conservative policy preferences. As in Italy and Germany early after World War I, business quickly began to take steps to retrieve earlier positions, what Ingo Kolboom terms the "revenge of the bosses." In France they were able to do so within democratic rules of the game for three main reasons. First, the right remained politically competitive. They had well-rehearsed coalition possibilities with the switch-hitting Radicals. Moreover, while left-leaning urban workers had grown substantially more numerous, as Joseph Barthélemy wrote, "Universal suffrage is surprisingly conservative." Paxton emphasizes that the right believed the (gradually diminishing) peasant sector still delivered substantial social stability. Second, the left offered assurances of moderation. The SFIO's León Blum offered himself as a "loyal manager" operating "within the capitalist framework," the SFIO and PCF tried to end the 1936 strikes, and Popular Front legislation was strictly reformist.[31] Third, the left while

28. *Le temps*, April 26, 1936, p. 1, said the SFIO and PCF found the Radicals temporarily useful "for their knowledge of the terrain to be conquered." Many rightists believed the PCF and SFIO felt a fundamental kinship; e.g., *Le temps*, April 22, 1928, p. 1. *Le figaro*, April–May 1928, analyzed what appeared to be communism's increasing rural support.

29. For example, *Le temps* editorial in Micaud (1943: 109), Vinen (1991: 28–29). The PCF extended its celebrated *main tendue* to Catholics, and Blum was prominently not anticlerical; Jackson (1988: 259).

30. Vinen (1991: 30–33), Irvine (1979: 155–56), Osgood (1964: 191–93), Lefranc (1976: 101–18). For one business leader's view, see Gignoux (1940). Blum later insisted civil war was a real possibility, but did so at the Riom trial while justifying his actions in 1936. Georges Villiers (1978: 137), a postwar head of the *patronat*, suggested that his positive 1946 impression of Blum contrasted with his more sinister interwar one.

31. Kolboom (1986: 53), Barthélemy (1935: 194, 199), Paxton (1997: 19–21, 176) (for similar views held by Louis Marin, see Irvine [1979: 73–74]), Jackson (1988: 169). Barthélemy

in office was constrained by a Senate dominated by centrist Radicals, who undermined the Popular Front's legislation and helped induce the Radicals to once again form a coalition with the right in 1938. That new government largely reversed Matignon, crushed the 1938 general strike, and generally represented "the kind of socially conservative, economically liberal government that industry wanted established."[32]

But as in other cases, office-holding, assurances, and institutions were unpredictable reducers of risk in democracy. The working-class parties' electorates had already grown substantially and could easily grow further, especially at the expense of the Radicals. Decision rules to a degree blocked the agendas of the left but as a whole were unlikely to be seen as fixed in a country that switched to proportional representation in 1919 and back to two-round majoritarianism in 1928 and in which both the left and right were attempting to revise the constitution.[33] And assurances by the left were received skeptically by conservatives. The left's membership surges and frequent organizational amorphousness were double-edged: left parties not only were not disciplined revolutionary armies but also often were incapable of controlling and restraining their rank-and-file, as during the 1936 strikes. The Radicals and SFIO were internally heterogeneous, making it all the more difficult to guess the location or stability of the Popular Front's center of gravity. The PCF's repeated about-faces provided no basis for predicting future behavior. The risks of a bottom-up worker challenge were amply illustrated by waves of strikes when Blum's government fell in 1937, again in the spring of 1938, and again in a massive wave that fall, when the occupation of the Renault factory "took on a semi-insurrectory character."[34]

For conservatives, democracy had become ominous: short-term threats often were fended off by contingent protections, but conservatives could not predict the regime-related payoff matrix into the future. Although a conservative authoritarian regime would have exposed them to repression and regime/opposition violence, it was a plausible option in the event of the worst in democracy. The left acknowledged that exclusion would almost

---

(1931: 136) also remained convinced at least until 1931 that Italian-style disorder would be avoided owing to France's higher levels of education and income.

32. Irvine (1979: 198), Vinen (1991: 208, 223).

33. Barthélemy (1935: 194, 199) emphasized that rightists' constitutional proposals to strengthen the executive's power of dissolution and referendum were not "an attack on universal suffrage but an appeal to it."

34. Jackson (1988: 87–95, 105) discusses to what extent the strikes should be seen as "spontaneous." Christophe (1979: 189–203) describes conservative Catholics' utter distrust of the PCF's *main tendue*. Conservative leader Louis Marin believed the PCF was moderate after 1934 only because the USSR primarily feared Hitler, hardly a factor predictable over the long run. PCF chief Maurice Thorez said in 1936 that the left was not ready for revolution "at this stage." Irvine (1979: 176), Tiersky (1974: 60).

certainly have been broadly rightist. Blum warned the SFIO in 1936 that if his proved to be a "Kerensky" government, "in today's France it is not Lenin who would reap the benefit."[35]

Rightists began hedging on a scale unknown for decades. Discourses abounded about state-led corporatism, technocracy, and the need for a strong single leader. Lucien Romier commented that "the idea of dictatorship . . . is the theme today of numberless conversations of the bourgeois in our salons and on our beaches." He saw no need for IDEs: "[I]n the bourgeois mind of France, the traditional purpose of dictatorship is to re-establish good order, bring back calm and assure tranquillity to all." Fascism, while well known and flourishing in intellectual circles, was rejected as a model by most of those considering antidemocratic solutions.[36] There had been no French dictator for two generations, but both leftists and rightists proposed different rightist personalities as possible candidates.[37] Movement toward harder-line rightist politics was discernible in existing parties like the Fédération Républicaine, but more dramatic was support for the proto-authoritarian, quasi-paramilitary *ligues*. Many hundreds of thousands and possibly a million people joined Colonel de la Rocque's Croix de Feu alone. Even when the Popular Front banned the *ligues* in June 1936, they reemerged in modified form. While La Rocque later acknowledged that at each point in the late 1930s a takeover bid lacked "the indispensable minimum of support from our citizenry," he insisted on the need to maintain "an instrument capable of crushing revolution."[38] His movement's stand on democracy was profoundly ambiguous, and an exclusionary project was clearly not many conservatives' first

35. Lacouture (1977: 283). After 1934 and 1938, La Rocque and Gautherot warned that just because the left was out of office did not mean future revolution was foreclosed; Soucy (1995: 161) and Irvine (1979: 95). The military remained distinctly antirevolutionary, and conservative paramilitary groups abounded. Emmanuel Berl (1938: 35–38) remarked that the right's coercive resources were "certainly far superior to those of the Spanish bourgeoisie" at the time of the 1936 military coup. The PCF's extraordinary caution in June 1936 suggests a similar assessment.

36. Micaud (1943: 18), Taittinger in Soucy (1986: 213). René Coty specifically insisted that conditions that had fueled left *and* right extremism elsewhere in Europe did not obtain in France; (1932?) "Profession de Foi de René Coty," p. 1, in 452 AP 1 (microfilm 628 MI 1), Archives Nationales Paris. Moreover, as always, actors were exposed to competing IDEs; liberal Catholics wanted to seduce the Radicals into a moderate coalition they styled on Van Zeeland's in Belgium; Irvine (1979: 88).

37. Taittinger launched appeals to Pétain; Barthélemy (1931: 137) remarked that "[d]ictatorial candidates are not lacking." The left-of-center *Lumière* named Pierre Laval, André Tardieu, La Rocque, Pierre Taittinger, Henri de Kerillis, and François De Wendel as possibilities; Jeanneny (1976: 557).

38. Irvine (1991: 276); the Croix de Feu/PSF's membership is disputed; Irvine (1991: 280). On the Federation, see Irvine (1979).

choice. Instead, major industrialists like François de Wendel subsidized *ligues* as a hedge, a form of insurance, at the same time they were funding parliamentary parties. Although La Rocque later supported Vichy and is sometimes termed fascist, Pierre Milza argues that La Rocque's political party could have evolved into a modern conservative party. That is the point: France's situation in the 1930s induced an uncertain wait-and-see attitude that was neither defection nor commitment.[39]

François Goguel argued that Vichy demonstrated that "the opponents of the principle of democracy had maintained an infinitely stronger position in important circles and in opinion than might have been generally supposed."[40] It may be more accurate to say that Vichy revealed not an enduring link to the ancien regime but the qualitative degeneration of conservative support for democracy from the situation before 1914. France prior to the Great War was invoked as a model by some in the Second Spanish Republic and Italy before and after World War II. Yet as a *domestic* "demonstration effect" it did not have the power to inspire the interwar French right to remain committed to democracy after their answer to "Democracy with whom?" had changed.

Italy

The breakdown of Italy's democracy was the first significant one to occur between the two world wars. Rightist defection from democracy, in response to the surge of workers' political activity that began with the end of World War I in 1918, occurred so rapidly in 1919–21 that it is difficult to distinguish the creation from the (simultaneous) use of the infrastructure of exclusion. But rightists' orientations can be effectively traced to the very high risks they faced in the new democracy. Italy as a whole did not stand at the brink of revolution: the socialist Partito Socialista Italiano (PSI) was not so inclined, and the new Communist party (Partito Comunista Italiano [PCI]) was incapable of carrying it out. But a focus on the national level is misleading. Leaders like the PSI's relatively reformist parliamen-

39. For this debate, see Irvine (1991), Soucy (1995: 136–52), and Milza (1987: 138–42) among others. Jackson (1988: 252–53) argued that La Rocque's support was greatest when he led a constitutional party, but Soucy (1995: ch. 4) demonstrated that at a minimum the PSF emphasized doctrinal continuity with its precursor, and continued to "allude to antiparliamentary solutions and paramilitary scenarios." Passmore (1997: 226–36) discussed the movement's attitude toward political decision-making. Certainly its corporatist and electoral proposals would have profoundly weakened the left. Soucy (1995: 123–28) and Jeanneny (1976: 485, 565, 589, 624) discussed funding of several paramilitary-type groups. Jeanneny suggested that De Wendel's support was motivated at least in part by concern that state forces might not effectively contain a left revolt.

40. Goguel (1952: 149).

tarians had lost control of events in a number of regions. Beginning at war's end, many major industrial cities and regions of agriculture and rural industry experienced strikes over wages, hiring practices, and numerous other aspects of labor-market and workplace relations. These challenges expanded on class conflicts that had been simmering for years, in some regions for decades, helping to explain the highly varied subsequent "political ecology of fascism."[41] Whereas the Paris Commune was followed by events that made clear how low the right's risks were in democracy, the surge in working-class mobilization and confrontation in Italy demonstrated instead just how widespread was the challenge to conservatives' core interests and values, including safety in some cases.

Amidst the rapid growth of socialist union locals, escalating intimidation of employers, and frequent assaults on persons and especially property, prefects warned the central government of significant dangers of revolutionary events.[42] Landless laborers in some areas of the north and Apulia added land invasions to these repertoires; in one case, for example, Apulian laborers disarmed local security forces, seized landlords, and held off army units for three weeks. Industrial disputes received only their most dramatic expression with widespread factory occupations in the fall of 1920.[43] The threat from the left was not confined to workplaces. In the 1919 elections, the first held under proportional representation (PR) rules, the PSI emerged as the largest party, constituting 32.3 percent of the parliament, followed by the center-straddling Catholic *popolari* (Partito Popolare Italiano [PPI]) with 20.5 percent, while diverse traditional conservatives constituted only 35.5 of the parliament. In 1920, the socialists also won control of numerous local and provincial governments. In many areas, they used local powers to great effect and developed reputations among prefects as proto-revolutionary authorities; they froze rents, intervened heavily in labor markets, and expanded taxation to the point where many on the right feared it represented indirect expropriation. While wages, working hours, and hiring practices were often the languages of grievances and negotiation, the working-class challenge was understood to aim at the massive revision of economic relationships and control of the rural economy in particular. In such an atmosphere, rightists could only attach ominous meaning to such events as the official resolution from the League of Socialist Communes (municipal governments) that "the needs of the community stand absolutely above the right of private property."[44]

41. Maier (1975: 305).
42. Snowden (1986: 158–68).
43. Spriano (1964), Clark (1977).
44. Snowden (1989: 169–71), Kelikian (1986: 125–30), Corner (1975: 76–83).

Conservatives lacked even short-term protections. Parties nominally of the right formed the cabinet but did not control a parliamentary majority, and numerous conservatives concluded that the Liberals, who had facilitated retroactive legalization of the first wave of postwar land invasions and remained aloof during the factory occupations, lacked the vigor and inclination to confront decisively the workers' challenge.[45] The Catholic PPI also was not a reliable ally. As with Weimar's Zentrum, the PPI contained not only a conservative faction but also an influential wing that was determined to use social change to secure a lower-middle-class and worker base. Conservatives often lumped the PSI and PPI together as left parties, terming many *popolari* white or black Bolsheviks and considering them at best untrustworthy and more often as hostile.[46] Nor were there assurances from the left. PSI figures like Filippo Turati were reformist, but pacts were unlikely to have been of value when events "exposed the inability of union officials to keep their extremists in line." Locally, PSI units were often radical. In Ferrara in 1920, for example, they campaigned with a call for major socioeconomic change and the formation of a proletarian militia to enforce it.[47] And the right had only some institutional protections. PR reduced electoral stakes. But the Senate's blocking role was ineffective when the threat was not pending legislation but the government's loss of control over events outside the legislative process. And counting rules and horizontal separation of powers were of only limited use when the PSI won absolute majorities in a number of regions. Answering the question, "Democracy with whom?" dampened the potential protective effects on risk of any of these devices.

Rightists responded by forming local militia-type organizations of middle-class and agrarian defense, well before the rise to prominence of squads linked to Mussolini.[48] But, in Renzo De Felice's words, conservatives found in fascism a force capable of "reversing . . . the[ir] real inferiority in the agricultural zones controlled by the [workers'] league system." Squad activity was initially visible in Trieste and Venezia where nationalist issues were acute, but rapidly became concentrated where worker-employer conflict was most severe. By late 1921, squads in many regions operated "where

45. The government was perceived to tolerate threats to safety and property; see Snowden (1986: 173–74) and the exchanges in Sonnino (1975: 692, 712).

46. Snowden (1989: 110). Antonio Salandra (1969: 261) wrote in his diary in March 1922 that the PSI/PPI majority was left-leaning and that "democracy, lacking conscience and substance, will always produce by a large majority a triumph of the left."

47. Kelikian (1986: 118–22), Corner (1975: 44–45, 104–05), also Kelikian (1986: 123–24).

48. Snowden (1989: 133–35), Cardoza (1982: 197–98, 295–96). In this sense, Mussolini's fascists were not innovators, simply particularly zealous locally and then entrepreneurial in assembling a national organization.

their intervention was requested," destroying union and left-party facilities, killing or driving out socialist organizers, and in the process reducing Confederazione Generale del Lavoro (CGL) membership by over four-fifths between 1920 and 1922.[49] Because this was a response to the threat posed through violence *or* legal processes, it occurred where local laborers both had and had not initiated direct action. Local police frequently saw the squads as useful supplemental staffing for combating revolutionary activity, and when occasional prefects moved against them, local landowners and employers often succeeded in pressuring Rome to overrule or replace them.[50] The effects of squad violence were sweeping: socialist (and PPI) units, already exhausted by strikes, were shattered. This makes it difficult to establish when exactly Italian democracy should properly be understood to have broken down. One could even argue, as Maier suggests, that the 1921 election returns reflect unrepresentative distortions in provinces of brutal assaults against the left.[51]

Many analyses suggest that the fact that fascist squad structures were maintained after 1921 reveals jittery conservative overreaction. But such interpretations wrench events out of time in both directions. Local studies portray the post-1918 worker mobilization as only the most sustained in a decades-old pattern of dispute and confrontation. Thus, the emergence of owners' and employers' tactics substantially predated the rise of fascism in 1920–21.[52] In this enduring context, the squad campaigns freed owners from the left's achievements of the previous two years, but could not, unless sustained, prevent the next two years' worth. There was every reason for conservatives to conclude what became counterfactual only afterward: that had the squad structure been dismantled, the left would have remobilized and attempted an ongoing and multifaceted challenge. The year 1920 proved to be the interwar high water mark for the left only because fascism ensured it was. Thus, the PSI made significant advances in municipal elections *after* the factory occupations failed. Thus, when Mussolini, in search of respectability in Rome, signed the demobilizing "pact of pacification" with the left in 1922, local fascist leaders allied with agrarians quickly sabotaged the agreement.[53] Conservatives had not detected the disappearance

---

49. De Felice (1966: 21), Roveri (1974: 178), Kelikian (1986), Cardoza (1982), Snowden (1986, 1989). Passuello and Furegon (1981: 91) reduce local fasci to the "armed wing of the landowners."

50. Snowden (1986; 1989: ch. 5).

51. Maier (1975: 326–27).

52. Cardoza (1982: 197) quotes one businessman's 1914 concern that strikes were "a dress rehearsal for the revolution that will take place, I fear . . . when the troops are out on maneuvers and the bourgeoisie is at the seaside."

53. De Felice (1966: ch. 2), Adler (1995: 185).

of the "abyss" or "precipice" in democracy to which they regularly referred.[54] Democracy posed substantial ongoing risks of outcomes highly threatening to the right.

What sort of authoritarian alternative could these actors forecast? While a cluster of conditions at the war's end and the complex ideological atmosphere described by A. James Gregor gave birth to fascism, diverse local studies leave little doubt that its organizational crystallization and political relevance derived from its role as exclusionary entrepreneurs for many employers and owners. Anticipating Paxton's recommendation that we define fascism more by "how it works than on what it says," De Felice concludes that Italian fascism became "essentially of the right."[55] Adrian Lyttelton and Maier discuss Mussolini's assurances to owners and employers about private property and other key issues. De Felice remarks that Italy's elites believed they could "educate fascism . . . correct it . . . absorb it"; insofar as Mussolini was perceived as hemmed in by the traditional right—the Crown, the bureaucracy, the military, senior rightist politicians—this made likely policy outcomes appear only more favorable to conservatives.[56] Nor did authoritarianism pose high risks to rightists' safety: fascist violence in 1920–22 established a track-record of consistently exempting the right from violence directed against the left. Such selectivity does not suggest that fascism's sole effect was to represent elite economic interests. Fascism became a power on its own terms as well, particularly when provincial squads outnumbered conventional security forces and became largely self-sustaining. Then, they were able not only to entice or coerce membership from sharecroppers and many laborers but also to intimidate employers into modest concessions to workers. As one prefect reported, landowners "have found their concerns taken over by fascists, from whom they would like to free themselves but cannot." In the end, Anthony Cardoza concludes, fascism used the middle and upper classes as much as they used it. But Mussolini's movement clearly protected private property and made the left its main enemy. It, at least among other groups, thus attracted the support of many owners and employers at the mass level as well as leading figures in industry and especially (as Franklin Hugh Adler emphasizes) agriculture.[57]

It is perhaps more difficult to "measure" the right's deliberate defection from democracy in the Italian case than in any other. In 1932, the overwhelming majority of middle- and upper-class Protestants in Germany

---

54. For example, Sonnino (1975: 710, 741).
55. Gregor (1979), Paxton (1997: 157), De Felice (1966: 123).
56. Lyttelton (1973: 51), Maier (1975: 339), De Felice (1966: 41).
57. Kelikian (1986: 147–51, 202), Cardoza (1982: 298), Adler (1995).

voted for the Nazis or Deutschnationale Volkspartei (DNVP); the Spanish military plotters of 1936 anticipated mass conservative support for a coup and received it. In Italy, support for authoritarianism can appear more elusive. In one sense, rightists always "preferred" a conservative democracy that might deliver both advantageous policies and the lowest possible risks to safety. But since such a regime appeared unavailable, can we be sure that the Italian right preferred an enduring authoritarian regime rather than the democracy that *was* on offer? Whereas the Nazis and the DNVP and the 1936 Spanish coup were avowedly authoritarian projects, Mussolini repeatedly promised to respect the constitution and accreted power only gradually through the 1920s.[58] This was the opposite of the British path. There, monarchical forms gradually were given a democratic substance; under Mussolini constitutional vessels were filled with authoritarian content. What evidence of segmental defection do we have? The 1924 elections in which government candidates won over 60 percent of the vote often are said to demonstrate a "consensus" for fascist rule, but it remains difficult to interpret votes cast in conditions saturated with intimidation, as with Germany in 1933 and Spain in 1947.[59] It may be revealing that Mussolini, when designing the electoral law for 1924, rejected proposals requiring a slate to win 40 percent or even 33 percent in order to win the supermajority-creating "bonus," insisting the threshold be set at 25 percent. This insistence suggests that he was unsure whether he would win even a third of the vote. But even if the right's defection from democracy is disputed, none of this obscures the right's extensive hedging and willingness to use violence and exclusion to pursue its core goals. Democracy was high risk, and the right did not commit to it.

Weimar

Weimar appears to least match the theoretical argument. Nazism's hyper-nationalism and anti-Semitism imply cultural motivations.[60] The left/right

58. Sforza (1931: 24) and De Felice (1966: 532) record fascist promises. On the stump in 1924 both Mussolini and Salandra insisted on their strict constitutionalism; e.g., *I grandi discorsi elettorali del 1924* (Milan: Editrice Imperia, 1924), pp. 16, 74–75. Lyttelton (1973) offers a powerful account of the gradualist establishment of the dictatorship.

59. Party behavior is also an ambiguous indicator. Even while serving in Mussolini's government, the PPI voiced support for strict constitutionalism at its 1923 congress. Was the PPI only repulsed by repression against itself? See *Il popolo*, April 12–13, 1923, pp. 1–2; May 16–17, 1923, p. 1. Giolitti accepted the Acerbo law, but apparently partly because he was afraid to provoke further fascist violence; De Rosa (1957: 19), De Nicola (1924: 22). Liberals and others joined Mussolini's 1924 electoral list, but many simply wanted to enter a parliament that was clearly being manufactured.

60. Mosse (1964), Goldhagen (1996).

divide seems thoroughly blurred: Weimar's main fault lines are portrayed as pitting the center-straddling founding coalition against both extremes, with the "right" divided by social status, religion, economic sector, and party-political tradition. And the threat from the left seems dubious: the Social Democratic party (SPD) was one of the most gradualist in Europe. But in this section I make the case that the deepest fault line did run between left and right; that perceived high risks as early as 1918–19 caused rightists to hedge; and that by the early 1930s the vast bulk of middle- and upper-class Protestants defected to support authoritarian formulas in response to a gathering political threat, of which the rapid growth of the Communists was only the most formal indicator. Sebastian Haffner argues that what Weimar needed was "a democratic Right," but it developed an authoritarian one instead. This development cannot be explained in terms of institutional design (which was broadly stakes-reducing) or national defeat and Versailles; the question remains why *revanchisme* was not acted out within democratic rules, as occurred in France after 1871.[61]

Simply put, hedging and later defection occurred because the left portion of Weimar's spectrum was marked by a high degree of unpredictability, which accelerated after 1929. This is not always evident. Approaches that emphasize class conflict such as those of Barrington Moore and Gregory Luebbert fail to persuasively specify a revolutionary threat, especially from the reformist SPD. In this section I argue that conservatives faced daunting unpredictability on the left despite the SPD's emphasis on a gradualist welfare state and opposition to hard-left revolts. The right's perception was articulated by the burghers of the Hamburg Senate in 1917: "That our working population has remained peaceful and reasonable can be, in great measure, ascribed to the efforts of the Social Democratic leadership. . . . Those Social Democrats now sitting in the Bürgerschaft are thoroughly moderate, and for the most part belong to the furthest right wing of the party. The Senate, accordingly, is directing its efforts toward maintaining the influence of the present [SPD] leadership over the working population."[62] This statement captures two elements of unpredictability. Workers' moderation appeared to depend on the orientation of leaders, and leaders' influence over workers was itself contingent. The SPD leadership was seen as the most moderate of several different possible and plausible forms of working-class politics, and its control over workers was not seen as a predictable equilibrium.

Events at war's end underscored the susceptibility of vast sectors of workers to radical appeals. It is now easy to describe November 1918 and its

61. Haffner (1997: 62). The Republic was federal, and proportional representation avoided the manufactured majorities plurality rules would have created.
62. Comfort (1966: 65–66).

aftermath as a thoroughly "failed revolution," but the proliferation of soldiers' and workers' councils was ominous to conservatives. The 1919 "March
days" in Berlin pitted over forty thousand troops against fifteen thousand
leftist rebels and left some twelve hundred dead. Richard Comfort describes
the rallies, riots, looting, armed clashes, unreliability of existing security
forces, martial law, and eventual army occupation that Hamburg experienced on and off through to the summer of 1919.[63] Such behavior by
workers and left parties was neither geographically isolated nor soon ended
Significant riots, looting, and revolts extended into the mid-1920s. In the
1923 general strike (called in response to an attempted extreme-right
putsch), left action committees assumed provisional control in many areas,
and in the Ruhr the Communists (KPD) mobilized strikers into a "Red
Army" numbering perhaps fifty thousand, which seized power in several
major industrial cities and mining areas. Government-backed paramilitary
forces suppressed the action, killing more than one thousand.[64]

If the left/right balance of coercive power determines democratic stability, Weimar had good prospects. Leftist organizations were growing
rapidly while the right's blue line was unprecedentedly thin. The Imperial
army had largely dissolved, security forces were weak, and the Versailles
Treaty limited the new army to a small fraction of pre-1914 levels and
banned reserves. Although initially weaker than anywhere in modern
Europe, the right proliferated ambivalent regime discourses and assembled
coercive forces from scratch. Peter Fritzsche argues that many middle-class
citizens initially welcomed the change in regime in 1918.[65] But in the face
of revolutionary activity, the liberal journalist and activist Theodor Wolff
acknowledged that many feared "the mortal danger that seems to threaten
them." As James Diehl notes, instead of paramilitarization leading to
Weimar's troubles, those troubles led to the right's paramilitarization.[66] To
help stabilize the new regime against the radical left, the SPD-led founding coalition organized the paramilitary Freikorps, but these soon became
self-sustaining in various guises due to extensive rightist support. Franz von
Papen later insisted these units were crucial given both eastern frontier
issues and "the desperate German internal situation at the time." Both the
military and, as Henry Turner notes, businesses supported these units
because "at the very least they seemed indispensable for suppressing socialist activities at home."[67]

---

63. Gordon (1957: 30–33), Comfort (1966).
64. Waite (1969: 176–82), Mommsen (1996: 148–53).
65. Fritzsche (1990: 26–29).
66. Wolff (1936: 139), Diehl (1977: ix).
67. von Papen (1953: 120), Mommsen (1996: 142), Turner (1985: 9).

Fritzsche insists the Home Guards, which reached one million predominantly middle-class members early in Weimar, were paper tigers, in many cases disarmed by trade unionists in confrontations.[68] But this only highlights that middle-class/worker political lines were clearly drawn and that conservatives had ongoing grounds for seeking a stronger defense force. When the Allies forced the Home Guards to disband in 1920, many units joined a world of secret paramilitary units with extensive funding from industrialists, agrarian interests, and the army. Moreover, conservative party and economic elites maintained close relations with leaders of the diminished regular military, and at various points during the course of Weimar considered knocking at the barracks door.

Left/right tensions had two prominent high points during Weimar. In the policy disputes of the 1920s, in Germany (like France) "great social conflicts were fought out indirectly."[69] Debate was refracted through prosaic issues such as tax reform, binding wage arbitration, welfare-state programs, and industrial workdays, but in fact concerned much larger questions. The legalist and gradualist proposals even from SPD moderates like Otto Braun and Friedrich Ebert did not appear to be an end-point of left demands as they did early during the Third Republic in France or would in Germany after 1949. Instead, tax changes, social programs, wage arbitration, and worker representation on corporate boards connoted palpable if gradual movement toward effective control of the economy by the left. Thus, conservative agrarians believed they were threatened with "indirect expropriation via taxation." Versailles reparation obligations, when met, raised the issue of effectively mortgaging Germany's industrial assets.[70] And crucially, the 1923 hyperinflation was resolved by a harsh stabilization that essentially expropriated liquid assets, caused high bankruptcy rates, and imposed heavy tax increases by emergency decree. This "crisis before the crisis" meant "an extensive redistribution of wealth," which statistics suggest fell mainly on middle-class, not working-class, shoulders.[71]

Conservative parties implicated in these policies suffered massive losses rightward by 1928, well before the onset of the Depression and the rise of the Nazis. Thomas Childers shows that many small-party beneficiaries of this disaffection (such as the Business Party, which urged: "Middle Class,

68. Fritzsche (1990: 61), Diehl (1977: 32–38, 55–67), Waite (1969: 189–95).
69. Maier (1975: 305).
70. Moeller (1986: 118), Hardach (1980). Schuker (1988) emphasizes that U.S. loans outweighed reparations payments from 1919 to 1933. But this did not smooth the distributional conflicts involved in financing reparations.
71. Mommsen (1996: 184), Hughes (1988: 13–15). The redistribution was thus largely within the middle class, from creditors and owners of annuities to debtors, including the government.

Awake!"), rather than representing parochial economic interests, instead championed sharp cuts in social programs and a systematic critique of the Weimar regime. The NSDAP only later attracted these already unmoored votes.[72] As has been noted by others, the collapse of mainstream right parties was not caused by the rise of the Nazis; it was a precondition for it.

The Depression sharply heightened unpredictability on the left. Unemployment rates reaching over 30 percent were not the highest in Depression-era Europe, but political dynamics on the left were distinctive: the unemployed became the basis of the region's largest communist party. The KPD was hampered by leadership conflicts and unstable membership. But while the Socialists outpolled the KPD nearly three-to-one as late as 1928, the KPD by November 1932 was Weimar's most rapidly growing and third largest party, only a few percentage points behind the SPD, and hence plausibly poised to become the largest working-class party in the next elections. One can dismiss the Nazi canard about a KPD plot in 1933—and even accept Arthur Koestler's retrospective assessment of the KPD as a "castrated giant"—yet acknowledge that the KPD's rapid growth dramatically increased the right's risks of highly threatening outcomes in democracy. The Nazis played on such fears, with Hitler telling the Düsseldorf Industry Club in 1932 that the country was split uneasily, half nationalist and half Marxist, and that worsening unemployment was replenishing the latter.[73]

The disputes of the 1920s thus gave a distinct shape to Depression politics. Whereas most conservatives in Britain and France did not attribute the Depression to behavior by the left—and hence did not believe it could be relieved by relocating political decision-making—many on the German right attributed the emerging extremity of the political situation to welfare-state costs, reparations, high wages, and (for many sectors) free trade, all of which policies found their most consistent support in the SPD.[74] In other words, the SPD's policies were perceived as being of monumental political importance for the gathering political crisis of the early 1930s. It became possible afterward to conclude that Weimar's welfare state was merely a pre-

---

72. Jones (1988), Childers (1983: 263).

73. Koestler (1965: 48), Domarus (1992: 103–12). Mommsen (1996: 416) argues that the Boxheim documents reveal that "the NSDAP regarded an uprising by the Communist working class as well as parts of the SPD and socialist labor unions as highly probable." Several scholars have pointed out that unemployment in the Netherlands was at times higher. But there the Depression had very different political effects on the perceived nature of the left: the Socialists remained relatively moderate and the Communists stagnated below 4 percent of votes.

74. Export-oriented industries also favored servicing international loans and reparations obligations *until* the collapse of world markets. Only well into the Depression did unions voice concerns over using needed resources to pay reparations, and even then the SPD ignored them; Harsch (1993: 153–55).

cursor to the postwar mixed economy, but that does not mean that that was how it was seen (or what it was) at a time when the political situation appeared politically open-ended. What rightists understood as the political causes of the Depression, combined with its increasingly threatening political consequences, permitted them to envision dramatic improvements in a rapidly degenerating situation if only they could control decision-making.

Neither institutions, assurances, nor office-holding permitted the right to resolve the challenge by the left within democracy. It is unlikely that any SPD assurances would have had enough credibility to make a significant difference in rightists' calculations about political outcomes, since by 1932 the SPD's ability to influence workers was sharply declining. Instead, losses on its left flank began to shape the SPD's strategies.[75] Rightist control of the presidency did not make for reliable protection because of its limited powers and Paul von Hindenburg's very advanced age. And the right was never able to win an absolute majority in a system, moreover, that consistently produced razor-thin and politically ambiguous election outcomes and the highest level of voting volatility in interwar Europe, even before the rise of the NSDAP.[76] The votes from the Catholic Zentrum could have provided a parliamentary majority, but that party's promiscuous coalition strategies more consistently allied it with the SPD. The Catholics' Janus-faced posture appears to have been the result of both class and religious factors. The Zentrum's worker constituency prevented it from pursuing the right's emerging agenda, especially welfare-state cuts and protectionism. This led frustrated Zentrum conservatives (like their Italian PPI counterparts) to refer to "people whose coats are black on the outside and red on the inside." Why exactly middle-class Catholics accepted their party playing a highly ambiguous role has been the topic of debate; for our purposes the important fact is that they did and that as a result rightists did not believe the Zentrum was a reliable ally in the left-right struggle.[77] Nazi propaganda

75. Harsch (1993: 89).

76. Bartolini and Mair (1990: 323–58). In the 1932 presidential race, Hitler openly emphasized Hindenburg's age and positioned himself to represent "young Germany"; Mommsen (1996: 480). Two important examples of electoral ambiguity may suffice: Hindenburg never won an absolute majority in 1925, and shifting alliances made it impossible to read the left/right balance of forces from his 1932 reelection.

77. Moeller (1986: 137, 153–54) concludes that "[a] Center vote remained a form with ambiguous content." This characterization describes votes both for and by the Zentrum. The 1926 referendum vote made credible the threat that Catholic workers might defect leftward were the Zentrum to go to the right. See Moeller (1986: 130–35, 147), James (1986: 272), Patch (1985: 108–16; 1998: 82), and Turner (1985: 166). Burnham (1972) argues Catholics were culturally inoculated against Nazism, but events in Spain, Italy, and Austria suggest they were not inoculated against authoritarianism as such. Brustein (1996) claims that sectoral economic interests led Catholic farmers to reject Nazism, but this does not explain urban Catholic

preyed on these fears as well, routinely insisting that other right parties and the Brüning and von Papen governments could, in Joseph Goebbels's words, "no longer be seen as a bulwark by the wavering middle class."[78]

What were the political contours of the most likely authoritarian alternative to democracy? Unlike in Spain during the Second Republic, the military was profoundly weakened by treaty provisions. So, like in Italy, the right from Weimar's start constructed massive paramilitary forces; by the early 1930s the Nazi party was clearly the leading pro-authoritarian force on the right. In some ways, the NSDAP was as dubious a savior for rightists as Mussolini. Turner makes clear that big business was skeptical about its economic program right through Weimar's end-phase. But it is also easy to exaggerate Nazi "socialism." The Nazis consistently allied with right parties in municipal elections starting in 1929 and state governments in 1930–32. All "socialists" may not have left the NSDAP with Otto Strasser in 1930, but the Nazis consistently stressed their support for private property and cuts in welfare and taxes and opposition to socialization, class struggle, and economic leveling. Indeed, changes in the NSDAP's stance on property were carried out to attract owners of small farms and other floating right-of-center voters. Childers concludes that attacks on the SPD and communism were "by far the most conspicuous and consistent aspect of Nazi electoral literature."[79] Moreover, like in Italy, enduring civil violence may have paved the way for authoritarianism rather than repelling the right from it, since it permitted the Nazis to establish a track-record of overwhelmingly directing violence against the SPD and KPD and sometimes the Zentrum.[80]

---

middle-class aversion. Perhaps more plausible is that, like Catalans and Basques, German Catholics were a minority historically persecuted by the "national" right, and as such were prone to side with the left to preserve certain policy goals distinct from the right's as a whole. Certainly Zentrum leaders invoked memories of the Kulturkampf to discourage conservative farmers from defecting to the DNVP; Moeller (1986: 124–25, 148). This pattern might also explain why many minority Catholics in Prussia merely abstained in the 1925 presidential elections when they were discontented with the alliance with the left formed by the Catholic candidate Wilhelm Marx, whereas the Bavarian Catholic party, more confident in its own majority-Catholic region openly endorsed the more conservative (and Protestant) Hindenburg. See Zeender (1963). This suggests that Hitler's assurances over confessional schools and Vatican relations may thus have played a relevant role in the Zentrum's vote for the Enabling Acts; Patch (1998: 298–99).

78. Childers (1983: 209).

79. Turner (1985: 60–99, 197–201), Childers (1983: 127–28, 150, 155, 268). In other words, the traditional right hoped to pull the Nazis toward the center in one sense (curbing their violent excesses) but toward the right in another (shedding their remaining socialistic baggage).

80. Bessel (1984: ch. 6). Conservative complacency over the distribution of Nazi violence is evidenced by the shock that greeted the Night of the Long Knives, which von Papen (1953: 321, 582) described as the "first time" the rule of law was violated, though it occurred months after the repression of the left.

It is also easier to establish defection from democracy than in the Italian case. The Nazi vote quickly escalated from the low single-digit range before 1929 to 18 percent in 1930 and over 37 percent in July 1932. Brustein argues that NSDAP voters "did not envision Auschwitz, World War II, or the destruction of Germany." But while the road to Auschwitz may or may not have been twisted, the road to authoritarianism certainly was not. On the campaign trail Hitler openly promised to eliminate the constitution and assault opponents: "We shall not rest until the last newspaper is crushed, the last organization destroyed . . . and the last Marxist converted or exterminated." Support for this was generalized on the right. Nearly all middle-and upper-class Germans who had previously cast ballots for "bourgeois" or rightist parties voted for either the Nazis or the equally authoritarian DNVP in 1932. One of Richard Hamilton's most striking findings is that large shares of middle- and upper-class Berliners even defected from the iconic Hindenburg to Hitler for president in 1932.[81]

Data even permits us to identify intriguing connections between the right's fears about the left and votes for the Nazis. Jürgen Falter finds that the NSDAP's percentage of the vote rose with unemployment but not because the unemployed voted for it. Unemployment correlated negatively with the NSDAP vote cross-sectionally: counties with higher, especially blue-collar, unemployment had fewer Nazi votes. But it correlated positively longitudinally: the higher unemployment rose nationally, the higher the support for the Nazis. Richard Evans articulates one obvious conclusion: the Nazi surge resulted in large part from "a growing fear among those who were not unemployed of the political consequences of the growing radicalisation of the unemployed themselves."[82]

Defection from democracy was a daunting project. Working-class mobilization was unprecedented. Some feared the Allies would harshly sanction any new authoritarian regime. Voting Nazi meant rejecting not only models of democracy such as those in Britain and the United States, but also national authoritarian traditions such as monarchism and the ideological hegemony of Junkers and big business.[83] We thus can return to the three

---

81. Brustein (1996: 181), Fest (1974: 292, 311), Hamilton (1982).

82. Evans (1987: 16), also Falter (1986). Berman (1998: 191–92) argues that "bourgeois" economists, policy-makers, and business leaders believed unemployment was feeding both the KPD *and* the NSDAP.

83. Mommsen (1996: 169, 181). The survival of the DNVP and Turner's evidence suggests the Nazis were a coalition of most rightists *other* than Junkers and top industrialists. This interpretation is not to revive the "lower-middle-class thesis." Hamilton's (1982) data shows how far into the upper middle class Nazi voting reached. Franz von Papen (1953: 168) and the centrist Theodor Wolff (1936: 305) believed Germany could not imitate Britain because it did not have the latter's moderate left; Wolff also praised Britain's more broad-minded aristocracy.

elements that at first make Weimar appear to fit this theory poorly. The deepest political fault line was in reality a left/right divide (a fact that right-ists were not the only ones to recognize); the right understood the left to be polarizing toward radical positions, though that process was underway as opposed to accomplished; and the right was calculating, not captive to norms operating independently of events and options.[84] Breakdown of the Weimar Republic was no more structurally predetermined than that of any other democracy. But from the start Germany's high-risk interwar democracy lacked the political predictability required for consolidation.

Britain

Given the regional political culture and IDEs, Britain's conservatives between the wars should have defected from democracy. It is said they had a lengthy democratic tradition, but in reality tolerance of dissent had long coexisted with an equally vaunted elitism justifying highly restricted voting rights. Each expansion of the franchise was contested and anxiety-inducing.[85] Yet while the "right" was (as in other cases) internally varie-gated—outside the Conservative party were splinters and inside it were, as Stanley Baldwin put it, "Diamond Jubilee Diehards and Tory democrats pulling me two ways at once"—by the second half of the 1920s, rightists had developed prodemocratic regime preferences reliable into the future.[86] Conservatives did so because after initial hesitation they concluded that workers and the Labour party were predictably reformist and democracy predictably unthreatening.

After 1918, war's-end issues and Irish Home Rule were contentious and important, but economic and class-based issues were "the meat of politics in the twenty years between the Wars." The 4th Reform Act in 1918 extended the franchise to the remaining 40 percent of men and most women. Conservatives initially associated this extension with greater unpredictability, as in 1867 when some were hopeful but others fearful: "nobody knows who are to be the future governors of England."[87] A 1917 Conservative party report anticipated that electoral reform would enfranchise "young men of no fixed political opinion and over one million of these

---

84. Friedrich Stampfer, a senior SPD figure, wrote afterward (1936: 531) that a confrontation in 1930 would have pitted Hindenburg, the military, the "bourgeois parties," and the Nazis against the SPD and KPD, although the latter had real differences of their own.

85. Fforde (1990: 17, 54), Epstein (1987: 505–10).

86. Middlemas and Barnes (1969: 435). The party is termed Conservative or Tory throughout.

87. Macmillan (1966: 456), McKenzie and Silver (1968: 4). The Act left women under thirty years old off the rolls; voting ages were equalized in 1928.

would belong to the Labouring classes." Austen Chamberlain calculated the rise of the Labour party would bring with it "dangers the outcome of which it is hard to predict," and lamented that "[t]his new electorate is much less dependable and consistent than the old one was." [88] Like in France, the interwar years saw socialists become the main left party. And many conservatives clearly greeted Labour's first (minority) government in 1924 with trepidation and close scrutiny.

Election-time rhetoric could be hysterical, for example, warning that a Labour victory would "be the most important change that this country has seen since the Norman Conquest" and famously suggesting links between Labour and Bolshevism. But not only did such scare tactics often not seem to work; they also did not match many conservatives' private analyses.[89] Conservatives were protected in democracy by several devices. The right retained robust prospects for governance, angling for votes even among workers (who had so recently responded to the call of king and country), and were often able to turn electoral pluralities into parliamentary majorities because of the Labour/Liberal split. Tories were in office for seventeen of the twenty interwar years. Second, Labour was tactically moderate. The moderate leaders who consolidated a grip on Labour soon after the war took numerous steps to gain respectability; even Tory die-hards portrayed Ramsay MacDonald as Kerensky not Lenin. The posture was partly because Labour required others' votes to govern in 1924 and 1929–31; the majority-making Liberals insisted they would keep Labour "powerless for serious mischief."[90] Institutions were a more complex matter: Tories knew that first-past-the-post electoral rules might enable Labour to win power with only a plurality of votes, but the House of Lords partially constrained even Labor in power.[91]

But all these protections were unreliable. Most obviously, continuing Labour advances might easily deny the Conservatives the "working-class Tories" that kept them competitive.[92] And Tories were unsure either to what

---

88. Pugh (1978: 92–99), Chamberlain (1995: 99, 259), Cowling (1971: 181). One Conservative party chairman wanted the reform to be accompanied by a stronger House of Lords. Cooper (1954: 121) insists that in the initial postwar period "there was in Great Britain a widespread fear of revolution."

89. *Daily Mail,* January 2, 1924, p. 8.

90. Bentley (1977: 146), Koss (1976: 264–65). Labor leaders condemned Bolshevism, ruled out expropriation and direct action on the threshold of office in 1924, and in office pursued budgetary orthodoxy. On Labour signals and assurances, see Sanders (1984: 214–15), Cowling (1971: 39, 179), Marquand (1977), Lyman (1957: 99), Pimlott (1977: 39), and Ramsden (1978: 155). The king was gratified by the 1924 assurances, and numerous Tories remarked on Labour's moderation in office, e.g., Sanders (1984: 214–15).

91. Lax (1979: 380–81).

92. Sykes (1983: 670) shows that conservatives had such worries before World War I. The *Daily Mail,* June 3, 1929, p. 10, cautioned that "*the Socialist tide is still rising.*"

extent moderates like MacDonald represented the party's leadership, much less its voters, or how effective moderates' control was over the "wild men" elements of the union movement.[93] The institutional compromise could be revisited. Only twenty years earlier, the Liberals had persuaded the king to accede to the weakening of the House of Lords, amidst conservative fears that had he refused, the left would have moved to challenge the monarchy as well. Now, Labour called for abolishing the Lords and lacked only the votes to at least further weaken them. Salisbury had been aware of the contingency of institutional equilibria when he remarked: "Unless we can do something to reconcile the working classes to the [Conservative] party, then the controversy between the [then Liberal] Government and the House of Lords can only end in one way." A 1927 parliamentary debate over reform of the Lords revealed how common that awareness remained. As John Buchan put it, "There will be no revolution, no constitutional revolution, in Britain until the great bulk of the British people resolutely desire it, and if that desire is ever present what Statute can bar the way?" Duff Cooper added, "You will not stop revolution by a veto"; Lloyd George stated that in the event, "your paper Constitutions would be no good."[94] Finally, it is not credible that an authoritarian project was "impossible." The fact that force had not worked in Ireland by no means precluded it in Britain. The military hierarchy was accused of excessive elitism while British unions, unlike those in Spain and Italy, had no arms or underground experience.

Had office-holding, assurances, and institutions been the only obstacles to radical political outcomes in democracy, conservatives would have had powerful incentives to hedge. But many conservatives believed risks in democracy were low because they became satisfied that both Labour and most workers were dependably moderate. Retrospect makes it easy to exaggerate this: it is important to remember that some rightists like Lord Beaverbrook made panic a habit, and die-hards favored strengthening the Lords because they *did* fear revolutionary agendas. But Tories nonetheless generally viewed "their" left profoundly differently than did their counterparts in Italy, Spain, or Germany. They became convinced that Labour's leaders were not tactical but committed moderates. Labour purged its few quasi-revolutionaries in the 1920s and 1930s and consistently rejected rad-

93. Baldwin sought to strengthen Labour moderates in the 1920s, e.g., by abandoning campaigns against the "political levy." The *Daily Mail*, January 17, 1924, p. 8, asked "whether [MacDonald] will be able long to hold back his followers." Similarly, Churchill in the *Daily Mail*, January 18, 1924, p. 7.

94. Sykes (1983: 670). *Hansard*, July 6, 1927, columns 1316, 1360, 1329, and Lax (1979: 310–13, 396), who discusses conservatives' awareness of institutional contingency beginning in the mid-nineteenth century.

icalism in international socialist organizations.[95] The *Economist* remarked in 1923 that all major party programs "are confined well within the bounds of constitutionalism. This is a point which we are too apt to overlook, because we have learnt to take it for granted; but it is obviously a matter of supreme national importance." Diverse sources reflect this strain in interwar conservative thinking. Tories specifically concluded that workers were averse to revolutionary ends and means. Many Tories "had ceased to take the apocalyptic view of [franchise] reform" already by 1918.[96] Many explained the moderation even of Labour's urban working-class base in terms of a distinct British culture, portraying Britain as just as different from the rest of Europe as many continental Europeans considered it.[97] These Tories (like MacDonald himself) believed Labour would lose votes if it championed direct action or outright revolution. As one Conservative member of Parliament remarked on this subject in 1924, "After all, we are a bourgeois people and shall remain so until we really go downhill." Most interwar Tories appear to have anticipated Ben Pimlott's later judgment that "there is little to suggest" that "the working-class . . . was 'potentially militant.' "[98]

This view survived the 1926 General Strike and the Depression. Despite exaggerated claims that "the Conservative mind in 1926 was a study of apprehension and fear," the strike failed for lack of rank-and-file support and was seen to have dealt a profound blow to trade-union militants and to have strengthened moderates like Walter Citrine.[99] As Luebbert puts it,

95. Pimlott (1977: 178–79, 194), Chamberlain (1995: 278). Cowling (1971) is right to insist that interwar politics reorganized itself along Labour/anti-Labour lines, but this is not the same as specifying the extent of polarization.

96. *Economist*, November 24, 1923, p. 909; Pugh (1978: 105). For other conservative assessments of Labour moderation, see Macmillan (1966: 198, 234), Cooper (1954: 122), Baldwin in Ramsden (1978: 209–10), Sanders (1984: 214–15), Headlam (1992: 115), and Winterton (1953: 124).

97. For example, interview with Lord Hailsham (Quintin Hogg), London, 1997; Baldwin in Ramsden (1978: 212, 331); Salisbury in Lax (1979: 423); Duff Cooper in *Hansard,* July 6, 1927, column 1360.

98. Marquand (1977: 793), Sanders (1984: 136), Headlam (1992: 47), Pimlott (1977: 195). In contrast with the situations of the interwar PSF, PSOE, and SPD, Ramsay MacDonald believed Labour could easily lose votes on its *right* flank; Marquand (1977: 793).

99. George (1965: 23), Headlam (1992: 85), Winterton (1953: 141–42), Bridgeman (1988: 199, 210, 227), Hailsham interview. Cooper (1954: 147, 150) later wrote that the strike "brought the country nearer to revolution than it has ever been. It was difficult then, and it is impossible now, to form an accurate estimate of the danger," but at the time he was joking about it with his wife: "Diana asked me this morning how soon we could with honour leave the country. I said not till the massacres begin." Brivati (1996: 290) writes that Hugh Gaitskell believed revolution would have been unpopular and an impossibility in 1926.

we can imagine 1926 would have gone differently had trade-union leadership been different, but "to presume a genuinely revolutionary council is to posit an entirely different labour movement." And the Depression functioned very differently politically than in Germany. The split of the Labour party in 1931 permitted the formation of hegemonic center-right National governments that attracted on average nearly three-fifths of voters in the 1930s. John Ramsden remarks that "the millions who might have turned to fascism in other circumstances found themselves protected and well enough looked after by the Conservative ministers who governed Britain after 1931."[100] But low risks in democracy ran deeper than that. By the second half of the 1920s, the leaders and apparatus of the left predictably supported policies far closer to the center than to revolution. Even the left in power, unconstrained by pacts and institutions, was highly unlikely to threaten conservatives' core interests.

After 1931, debate over protectionism sharpened, and mass unemployment (with rates reaching approximately 25 percent), the Hunger Marches, and left-Labour impatience did not go unobserved or unremarked upon. But even the leftward move that the Labour rump experienced in opposition was modest by continental standards, and Clement Attlee emphasized Labour's constitutionalism, continually refused alliances with the Communists, and proposed broad budgetary orthodoxy. Hugh Dalton dismissed "all theatrical nightmares of violent head-on collisions.[101] Tory Member of Parliament Cooper thus argued that his party's 1929 "Safety First" campaign theme fell flat because "there was no apparent reason for fear." The conservative *Times* responded to the Tory defeat that year by observing "there is no ground for supposing that the country has abandoned its traditional moderation." In the next few years, Arthur Balfour invested great stock in "a people so fundamentally at one that they can safely afford to bicker; and so sure of their own moderation that they are not dangerously disturbed by the never-ending din of political conflict"; and Leo Amery expressed no fear when he assumed Labour would go on to win the elections expected in 1939.[102]

---

100. Luebbert (1991: 209). Ramsden (1978: 345–46) terms British fascism "one of the most important non-events of the decade."

101. Morgan (1984: 13–15), Pimlott (1977: 27). After 1931, Labour arguably developed a more specific rather than more expansive stance on nationalizations. Chamberlain (1995: 337) was one Conservative who feared that workers possessed resentments "more like continental class hatred than anything we have experienced in my life time." Turnbull (1973) discusses perceptions of the "hunger marches."

102. Cooper (1954: 165–66); Ramsden (1978: 292); *Times*, June 1, 1929, p. 13; Balfour (1933: xxiv); Amery (1988: 403). In 1929, Macmillan (1966: 233) concluded "the whole temper of the nation is cooler now than it was five years ago."

This lack of fear explains why when in office in the 1920s, conservatives did not redesign institutions either to block Labour's return to office or to constrain it in office. Nor did they hedge against risk in democracy by cultivating special relations with military officers or through insurance-type support for pro-authoritarian groups.[103] Relocating power to authoritarian rulers, accompanied as it would be by risks of repression and resistance by the left, was predictably suboptimal. In Weimar, the right chanced an exclusionary attempt against the largest union federation in Europe; in Britain it remained loyal to democracy even though the costs of exclusion would have been much lower, particularly after Labour's schism in 1931 and the steep decline in union organizations.[104] British conservatives developed reliable regime preferences despite both elitist traditions and pro-authoritarian opinion leaders at home and IDEs across Europe—indeed they often explicitly rejected foreign models.[105] Labour did not manifest serious fears of a coup. Despite severe effects from the Depression and a shared ideological "atmosphere," the contrast with Spain, Italy, and Germany could not have been more stark.

Conclusions

France from the 1870s to 1914 and France, Britain, Germany, and Italy in the interwar period generated outcomes unexpected by competing assumptions about regime support. In years generally considered ideologically hostile to democracy, French conservatives abandoned hedges to risk in that regime in the last decades of the nineteenth century and British conservatives did so in the interwar period. Though pacts and protective institutions may have been crucial in temporarily stabilizing new and fragile democracies, the right's pattern of commitment in these two cases versus hedging (and even defection to authoritarianism) in the others is not easily accounted for by the presence or absence of political pacts or by the level

103. This was not due to any lack of potential exclusionary leaders. Ash (1968) discusses Field-Marshal Wilson; Oswald Mosley was also well known. Die-hards favored strengthening the House of Lords, but Lax (1979: ch. 3) describes how unexcited Conservative voters—and the party leadership—were by this issue.

104. Stafford Cripps's remark that the left could "win our Socialism" only if it first secured democracy suggests a similar assessment of the coercive balance; Pimlott (1977: 177). Union membership slumped from 7.8 million in 1919 to 4.8 million on average in 1926–36; Bain and Price (1980: 39).

105. For example, the *Daily Mail* on Primo de Rivera, January 17, 1924, p. 8. Ramsden (1978: 348) undermines claims that many Tory members of Parliament admired fascism. It is simply not credible that appeasement generally indicated regime envy. If anything, British conservatives were driven by mistrust of the Nazis to refuse an aggressive alliance against the USSR.

of "stakes" embedded in institutional designs. Institutions were a particularly unlikely platform from which the right might confidently predict unthreatening political outcomes in democracy, since institutions protective of the right came under significant revision challenges from the left in France early during the Third Republic, in Britain in the early twentieth century, and in Spain between the two wars. As we will see, pacts and protective institutions became even more prominent by their absence from consolidated democracies after 1945.

And the right's hedging versus commitment is also not easily reconciled with what emerges as left/right balances of organizational power during these periods. Where left mobilization was unprecedentedly high, rightist sectors nevertheless defected from democracy in Italy, Germany, and Spain, whereas they committed to democracy in late-eighteenth-century France and interwar Britain when left-oriented unions remained or were rapidly becoming relatively weak.

Consolidation once achieved was not guaranteed. The French right resumed hedging in the interwar years, demonstrating that if risks in democracy rise substantially from low levels, it is possible for commitment to be undermined, hedging to begin, and democracy to deconsolidate, an issue dealt with at more length in Chapter 8. While this is happily the only case of deconsolidation examined here, it is a sobering reminder that the specific conditions that inform the right's commitment to democracy can be eroded, inducing the right to update or revise its strategy.

7

Political Risks and Regime Outcomes in Europe after 1945

> Economic liberalism is dead. Who is there today to defend it?
>
> LÉON BLUM, May 1945

The post-1945 period, like the interwar years, generated substantial variation in the right's strategies toward democracy. After initially wide uncertainty at war's end, conservatives in Germany and France rapidly joined their counterparts in Britain in committing to democracy. In Britain, this commitment represented continuity from the interwar years; in France, it represented the right's *re*commitment to democracy after interwar deconsolidation. In Germany after 1945, consolidation resulted from a sharp shift away from the right's interwar strategy; many actors who had previously backed authoritarian rule committed to democracy. Instead of suggesting that the Bonn Republic was therefore a dubious extension of authoritarianism, this retooling of strategies constituted a great triumph for democracy in Europe. But the Italian center-right hedged for as much as several decades after 1945, and the right in Spain continued to support authoritarianism until within at least a few years of Franco's death. It was only later that the right in these two cases converged with their conservative counterparts across the region in committing to democracy. Like in the interwar period, this pattern can be explained in terms of the right's comparisons between regime alternatives. In these five countries, the most likely authoritarian alternative to democracy was broadly rightist and likely to insulate conservatives from repression. But the right's assessment of risks in democracy varied substantially across them.

In Britain, France, and West Germany, like in post-Franco Spain, the right perceived that the range of likely political outcomes in democracy predictably excluded highly threatening events; in France this view pertained for somewhat distinctive reasons. As a result, authoritarianism appeared likely to generate policies generally favorable to conservatives while imposing only modest risks to their safety, but conservatives could expect predictably to secure both favorable policies and the lowest possible levels of safety in democracy. Democracy was thus predictably and not merely provisionally the better choice. This was the case because, as Maier notes, in many European cases "the Left too debarked differently after the second war." Left parties were often more successful after World War II than in the interwar years at winning office (including in Britain and post-Franco Spain) but acted in service to agendas that "often remained a less clearcut challenge . . . than they were after 1918."[1] Exactly why this moderating occurred on the left, and why conservatives perceived it as deep-running and not merely a precarious bundle of tactical choices, are matters beyond the scope of this study. But the net effect of the right's beliefs about the moderation of the left was that the right had powerful incentives to (continue to) foreswear access to vehicles for exiting democracy and to commit to that regime.

But the left did not "debark" after 1945 equally across the region. In France, the Communists emerged from the war greatly strengthened but were quickly and thoroughly isolated politically when the Socialists manifested rigorous anticommunism. This had crucial effects on likely political outcomes, rendering democracy a low risk for conservatives. But where the left half of the political spectrum remained fundamentally unpredictable, the right's situation and strategy were very different. As we have seen, Spanish conservatives continued to perceive workers and the left as radical until profound socioeconomic changes dramatically raised incomes and enlarged middle classes beginning in the 1960s. The result, until that process was advanced, was continued support for Francoist authoritarianism despite the plethora of regional prodemocratic models and discourses. In Italy, the Communists emerged from the war both vastly strengthened and, unlike in France, capable of allying with socialists. The resulting high perceived risks in democracy meant that conservatives' regime-related payoff matrix could easily reverse, owing to readily identifiable and plausible scenarios (indeed, routine events) in democracy, such as minor electoral shifts and alternation in office. If the left radicalized and won office, a conservative authoritarian regime could easily be preferable to democracy. As in other cases, these high risks did not trigger automatic defection.

1. Maier (1981: 331, 334).

But postwar Italian rightists could know only their current and not future regime preferences, leaving them with powerful incentives to hedge. They did so by organizing state security forces along highly politically partisan lines.

Beginning in the 1970s, Italian, like Spanish, conservatives increasingly perceived the left as predictably moderate and democracy as low risk. With this development, their forecasts converged with those of conservatives in Britain, Germany, and France; democracy was the predictably better choice. This staggered timing created the distinct trajectories summarized in Table 7.1.

The pre-1940 and post–World War II cases are illustrated in Figure 7.1.

This diverse pattern is not easily accounted for by political pacts, office-holding, or institutional designs. Conservatives were unexpectedly success-ful electorally after 1945. But this success did not protect against the victories by the left that did occur or, just as important, the distinct possi-bility of victories by the left in any given election, since in almost all cases the left too was electorally competitive. Instead of being consistently low stakes, institutions in several consolidated democracies either were quite high stakes (Britain) or were revised in the direction of marginally or even substantially higher stakes than before (France in 1958, Italy in the 1990s). Pacts as defined in transitions theorizing were rare, and there is little evi-dence that left leaders in Britain, France, or Germany after the late 1940s, Italy in the 1970s, or Spain after 1978 entered into occasional cross-aisle policy agreements in order to deter right-wing coups. Nor were pacts func-tionally replaced by credible international guarantees over outcomes in democracy. U.S. military forces did not occupy Britain or France or protect against revolutionary outcomes in Germany and Italy beyond the first postwar years, though their presence in Germany may initially have cau-tioned the KPD.[2] The country-based evidence regarding these factors, sum-marized in Table 7.2, reveals no consistent relationship with the right's regime strategies.

Finally, the right does not appear to have been locked into democracies by either domestic or international constraints on excluding the left. Above all it is not at all evident that domestic left/right balances of organizational power shifted substantially between the interwar period (when several rightist sectors hedged or defected, or did both) and the postwar period (when most committed to democracy). It is easy to exaggerate both the

---

2. For example, Major (1997: 245). U.S. authorities suspended a 1946 nationalization measure approved by referendum in Hesse; see Major (1997: 92–93) and Sassoon (1996: 159) for this and other such instances. Przeworski (1991: 24) defines pacts as "collusive agreements to stay away from dominant strategies that threaten democracy."

Table 7.1 Conservative Perceptions of the Left and Conservative Regime Strategies after 1945

	Britain	France	(West) Germany	Italy, 1945–mid-1970s	Italy, mid-1970s–on	Spain, 1945–1960s	Post-Franco Spain
Main left party moderate in power?	Yes	Yes	Yes	Yes (local government)	Yes	N/A	Yes
Significant revolutionary organization to left of socialists?	No	Yes: PCF (contained from 1947 on, then increasingly moderate)	No	Yes: PCI	No (PCI moderated)	Yes: PCE	No
Right believed property redistribution had mass constituency?	No	No	No	Yes, especially in the South	No	Yes	No
Moderate left leaders perceived as under mass pressure to radicalize?	No	No	No	Yes	No	N/A	No: pressures to moderate
Right perceived class-based civil violence/"disorder"?	No	Limited PCF sabotage in 1947	No	Land invasions in the South	No	Perceived substantial potential	No
Right's Regime Strategy	Commitment to democracy	Commitment to democracy	Commitment to democracy	Hedging; highly partisan organization of the military	Commitment to democracy	Support for authoritarianism	Commitment to democracy

N/A, not applicable.

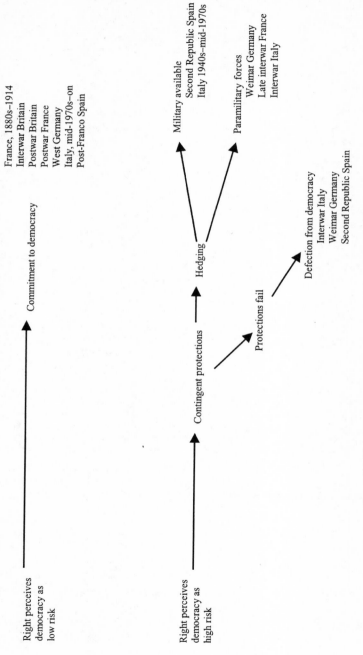

Figure 7.1 The Right's Regime Orientations in Selected Western European Cases

Table 7.2 Office-Holding, Pacts, and Institutions in Uncertain and Consolidated Democracies

	Pacts	Institutional "Stakes"[a]	Right in Office[b] (% of Time)	Outcome
Uncertain				
Interwar France	No	Moderate	64% (1918–40)	Hedging
Weimar Germany	No	Low/moderate	*	Hedging/ defection
Interwar Italy	No	Low	*	Hedging/ defection
Second Republic Spain	No	Moderate/high	41% (1931–36)	Hedging/ defection
Italy, 1945–76	Yes	Low	100%	Hedging
Consolidated				
France, 1880s–1914	No	Moderate	*	Commitment
Interwar Britain	No	High	86% (1918–40)	Commitment
Postwar Britain	No	High	64% (1945–2000)	Commitment
Postwar France	No	Low (1945–58) High (1958– on)	76% (1945–2000)	Commitment
West Germany	No	Moderate	71% (1949–2000)	Commitment
Italy, 1976–on	No	Low (until 1994) Moderate (1994 on)	83% (1976–2000)	Commitment
Post-Franco Spain	1977–78, then failed	Moderate	35% (1977–2000)	Commitment

[a] *Low stakes*: proportional representation (PR) and parliamentarism. *Moderate stakes*: semipresidentialism (Weimar); parliamentarism either with majoritarian electoral rules or with PR with a substantial threshold or small enough districts to substantially penalize small parties. *High stakes*: plurality electoral rules or presidentialism.

[b] Asterisks indicate that percentages of time "in office" could not be determined because of extremely loose or nonideological party affiliations (France), frequent government dependence on sometimes nonexplicit parliamentary support outside the cabinet (France, Italy, and Weimar), or staggered parliamentary and presidential terms (Weimar).

strength of the left and the weakness of the right emerging after 1945. Membership in left-oriented unions surged at Liberation but also often slumped at the end of a postauthoritarian "popular upsurge." Membership remained only roughly steady in some cases and grew in several northern European countries, including West Germany and several democracies already consolidated in the interwar period. But in more than one case,

Table 7.3 Approximate Blue-Collar Union Membership, Uncertain and Consolidated Democracies

	Unconsolidated Peak	Post-Liberation "Surge"	About 5 Years Later
France	3–5 million (1936–38)	6 million (1946)	<3 million (1951)
Germany	ADGB: 5.7 million (average 1919–31) KPD: 250–300,000 (1932)	4.3 million (1949)	6.1 million (1954)
Italy	2.7 million (1920)	3.7 million (1949)	≈3 million (1960)
Spain	1.5–2 million (1932–36)	4 million (1978) Consolidated	≈1 million 1950
Britain	6.1 million (average 1916–25)	4.7 million (average 1926–35)	8–9 million

Sources: Bain and Price (1980), Adams (1952), Lorwin (1954), Ehrmenn (1947), Gillespie (1989a), Crvz (1987), Taboadela Alvarez (1992), CC. OO., "Secretaría de Organización, evolución de la cotización a la C.S. de CC. OO.," n.d., Madrid.

the postsurge slump actually meant that left union membership was *lower* than that in the interwar period, as Table 7.3 suggests, even if we account for population changes (and consider different possible measures for union strength).[3]

On the other side of the power balance, in contrast, the middle classes that formed the mobilizational backbone of interwar rightist political pro-

3. The statistics in Table 7.3 represent approximate membership in predominantly blue-collar unions allied with socialist, communist, or other left parties: France (interwar: Confédération Générale du Travail [CGT]; postwar: CGT + Force Ouvrière), Germany (Allgemeiner Deutscher Gewerkschaftsbund [ADGB] + KPD unions; Deutscher Gewerkschaftsbund [DGB]), Italy (Confederazione Generale del Lavoro [CGL] + Unione Sindacale Italiana [USI]; Confederazione Generale Italiana del Lavoro [CGIL]), Britain (Trades Union Congress [TUC]), Spain (Unión General de Trabajadores [UGT] + Confederación Nacional del Trabajo [CNT] + PCE unions; UGT + Comisiones Obreras [CC.OO.]). Catholic/Christian Democratic unions, predominantly white-collar and civil service union federations, and the center-right, post-Franco USO are excluded.

In four of our five countries, interwar-to-postwar population changes only accentuated the trends in left-union strength suggested by total membership. Britain's population grew somewhat from 1921 to 1931 to 1951, for example, while France's remained broadly steady. Italy's and Spain's populations grew substantially between their interwar democracies and redemocratization (approximately 30 percent and 45 percent, respectively), accentuating the outright decline in left-union strength in Spain and in reality converting what appears to be continuity in Italy into de facto decline. The division of Germany, and the approximately one-fifth decline in population from Weimar to early 1950s West Germany, make treatment of that case distinct. Union density might be used as an alternative measure of union strength. From Weimar to West Germany, union density (percentage of potential union membership that is unionized) among blue-collar workers rose slightly. But in this case as in the others, union density, which might be understood to control for population change, is more misleading than

jects emerged intact after 1945. In terms of explicitly coercive instruments, moreover, the rapid disarming of left-oriented wartime resistance forces in France and Italy left regular militaries unchallenged; these forces remained characterized by important elements of their historic antileftism, most obviously in France, in Democrazia Cristiana (DC)–dominated Italy, and in post-Franco Spain.[4] Regime-related pressures from the United States were distinctly ambiguous in content; American behavior in Greece, Iran, and Guatemala in 1945–54 suggested that the United States was agnostic as to the regime type of its anti-Soviet allies, except perhaps Germany.

In other words, we could say of the European right what Eric Hobsbawm remarks of the revolutionary left: it had opportunities for the seizure of power in "stable industrial societies" that it did not exercise.[5] Thus, for example, the right did not even attempt to exclude the left in France in the early part of the Third Republic when socialists and unions were marginal; in Britain when Labor underwent a profound organizational crisis in 1931; in France when the communists were isolated and the socialists weakened at the onset of the Cold War; in France in 1958 when Charles de Gaulle briefly assumed sweeping powers amidst deep strategic splits among socialists; or, for the sake of argument, in Britain in the 1980s, when Labour split again and the miners' strike embittered the national discourse and generated violence that could easily have been construed as "provocation." Yet in none of these cases did the right even attempt to create a (more) favorable balance of coercive power as a hedge against future need. None of this is meant to suggest that the costs of class-based exclusion would have been low after 1945. But costs appear to have roughly leveled off in the interwar period rather than rising further, making costs of exclusion an unlikely candidate for explaining what was in several cases the profound shift in the right's strategies between these two periods.

---

useful because it does not control for change in the absolute size of the blue-collar sector. As a result, it can and does happen that union density rates can rise even as the blue-collar population *and* absolute left-union membership decline. While such a measure of density may be very useful for a variety of research purposes, it could easily give the impression that the power of the left has increased, even though available blue-collar union forces may have declined in absolute terms. Simple membership, while imperfectly coping with population change, is a superior measure for addressing relative left/right organizational power. Insofar as union density is used as a measure, it is worth noting that it varied substantially across both countries and time after 1945, from high levels in Sweden to very low ones in France, for example, and generally declining from the 1950s to the 1970s and 1980s, in some cases from already low rates, *without* corresponding variations in the right's regime strategies.

4. On France, see Ambler (1966: 278–80).

5. Quoted in Przeworski and Sprague (1986: 21).

Britain

In 1945, conservatives' worst-case scenario in democracy occurred: "a Socialist Government not merely in office but in power."[6] Labour won an absolute parliamentary majority and embarked on an ambitious systematization of the welfare state and nationalization of a series of heavy industries and the Bank of England. The left in Britain was one of the strongest in post-1945 Western Europe, averaging nearly 44 percent of the vote in a multiparty system from 1945 to 1979. Moreover, more even than in post-Franco Spain, a powerful Socialist party was reinforced in office by the win-concentrating institutional design in the region. As Kenneth Morgan remarks of the concentrated powers of the Westminster model, "[A]ny failures by the Labour government between 1945 and 1951 can hardly be blamed on pressures from the institutional framework that it inherited."[7] During periods of Labour rule, conservatives were not protected by a tradition of cross-aisle pacting. Conservatives' short-term risks were reduced somewhat by the fact that the Tories remained electorally competitive, regularly had substantial prospects for winning the next elections, and periodically held office. This competitiveness could be forecast: starting with the 1945 defeat, public opinion surveys suggested durable strong Tory support and showed the Tory party leading Labour years before the Tories' return to office in 1951. But this was a highly contingent protection since Labour was also highly competitive, actually attracting more votes even when the Tories went on to win office 1951.[8]

Instead, the right's risks in democracy were profoundly reduced, and its commitment to democracy undergirded, by a predictably compact left/right spectrum. The fact that the right perceived the left as predictably moderate meant that relocating power to any feasible set of authoritarian leaders was suboptimal, even in the event of electoral alternation in a democracy with high-stakes decision rules. Low risks in democracy meant that the right's commitment to democracy did not rely on Tories' expectations that they would win any specific upcoming election. Convergence is not meant to suggest a complete overlap between left and right; the absence of an overlap of that extent helps explain why some scholars can identify a postwar "consensus" in Britain after 1945 while for others this is a "myth." Conservatives expressed real concerns over the more militant impulses within Clement Attlee's party and governments, typically found

---

6. *Daily Mail*, July 27, 1945, p. 4.
7. Morgan (1984: 81–85). Stakes were raised slightly further when Labour abolished plural votes and reduced the House of Lords' delay power.
8. Gallup (1976a).

Nye Bevan profoundly unpalatable, and found ominous Labour's (never enacted) proposal to indefinitely extend war-time controls over production, distribution, and prices. To some economic liberals, the nationalization of (profitable) steel and road haulage companies connoted a threat to a wider range of types of property.[9] But policy convergence, symbolized rhetorically by the cross-aisle composite character "Mr. Butskell," nonetheless embodied a far greater overlap than had existed historically and especially in interwar Spain, Germany, Italy, or France.

We can examine these low risks in democracy beginning with the 1945–51 Attlee governments. All parties in the wartime national coalition had cooperated relatively smoothly in dozens of policy areas, including organizing the emerging welfare state, despite disagreements concerning the costs of state intervention. Consequently, while Labour's 1945 victory inevitably meant some leftward shifts in policies, many Tories also expected substantial continuity in many major areas.[10] Some conservatives urged expanded social policy for the reasons given by Quintin Hogg in 1943, echoing Bismarck: "if you do not give the people social reform they are going to give you social revolution." But it was also clear, including to Hogg, that by 1945 the left/right debate, and the left's challenge to Britain's existing order of things, took place within increasingly bounded parameters.[11] These boundaries were partly set by Tory centrism. The Conservatives mounted "very little significant opposition" to the first wave of nationalizations, they accepted several significant expansions of the welfare state, and their Industrial Charter accepted the nationalizations as well as full employment as a goal.[12]

Crucially, however, conservatives viewed the British (and hence Labour's) electorate as fundamentally moderate. This was true, first, at the level of its leaders. Stafford Cripps and several others spoke extravagantly of radicalism and even direct action at their moment of victory in 1945. But party leader Attlee made clear that Labour was "constitutionally-minded" in its methods, and he, Ernest Bevin, and others were widely respected as competent and responsible in core matters of legalism, the budget, European security, management of the bureaucracy, housing, and the welfare state.[13] Decisively, even Labour's organized left wing empha-

9. Rollings (1992), Ramsden (1995: 190).
10. For example, Amery (1988: 1049); Butler in *Hansard*, August 17, 1945, column 194; and *Times*, July 27, 1945, p. 5, which argued that "[t]here is no reason however why the world should look for any revolutionary change in foreign—or indeed domestic—policy."
11. *Hansard*, February 16, 1943, column 1614; interview with Hailsham, 1997. Winterton (1953: 42, 338) contrasted moderation by the left after 1945 with that in both Britain's past and the rest of Europe.
12. Morgan (1984: 104).
13. Ramsden (1995: 165), Attlee in *Hansard*, December 6, 1945, column 2562.

sized that its policy goals were not open-ended. While the large-industry nationalizations carried out after 1945 were ambitious, most Labour office-holders and activists also expected them to be the last for some time; in other words, Labour broadly shared the Tories' 1950 promise to "bring nationalisation to a full stop here and now." Moreover, as Peter Hennessy discusses the Tories had confidence that Labour planned no radical change at nationalized institutions like the Bank of England.[14]

Even more fundamental than convergence on the "elite" level were wide-spread perceptions that bottom-up pressure on the left was, if anything, centrist and hence acted to ensure Labour's continuing moderation. As in other consolidated democracies, the main center-left party faced no sub-stantial organizational competition on its left flank; diverse far-left projects consistently failed miserably. Published polling results revealed much greater from-below pressure toward the center than for Labour radicaliza-tion. In 1949–50, for example, a majority of the surveyed public opposed any further nationalizations (including specifically iron and steel national-ization), and pluralities regarded nationalization as deleterious in several sectors; in 1950 fully 78 percent of the respondents to a Gallup poll char-acterized Labour as either "too Socialist" (44 percent) or "just about right" (34 percent) while only 12 percent wished it to be more socialist.[15] Polling and electoral data informed conservatives' conclusions that the Tories were quite capable of winning swing voters back directly from the Labour column. This assessment of the electorate's moderate center of gravity was also perceived on the left; as Hugh Gaitskell asked rhetorically, "Can anyone honestly say that if the Labour Party had chosen a policy which reflected more or less the line of the Communist Party we should have received a larger vote?"[16] None of this prevented Tories from occasionally using scare tactics at election time just as it did not stop Labour from arguing the Tories would destroy the welfare state. But these charges often failed to resonate even with partisan conservatives; this must include Churchill's notorious—and notoriously unsuccessful—1945 election-eve warning that a "Socialist system" would require "some sort of Gestapo."[17]

Given the calculatory framework at the time, relocating power even to sympathetic authoritarian leaders would be suboptimal—it would heighten risks to safety while at best generating modest policy improvements. As

14. Morgan (1984: 121, 125; 1987: 288–89), Hennessy (1992: 203–04).
15. Gallup (1976a: 191, 231–32).
16. Brivati (1996: 150). The Conservative Leo Amery (1988: 1048) reacted to his party's 1945 election defeat by predicting to his diary that now Labor would be the one to suffer from initial postwar austerity, allowing the Tories to return to office soon after. Hogg wrote *The Case for Conservatism* for workers whom he believed could be wooed directly back from Labor.
17. For responses, see Amery (1988); *Times,* July 5, 1945, p. 5; and the *Economist,* cited in Morgan (1984: 38).

such, even hedging was unattractive. It is worth noting that the perceived risks in democracy were so small, even under Labour governments, that Tories did not take advantage of periods in power to rejigger institutions in their favor—for example, by restoring plural votes, restoring the Lords' two-year delay powers, or even introducing proportional representation— which would have made any future Labour absolute majorities much less likely. This calculatory framework was not undermined by events from the late 1940s through the 1990s. This explains why there was no discernible rise in support for pro-authoritarian formulas even when Samuel Beer and others connected declining satisfaction with "overloaded" democracy in the 1970s to the possible erosion of regime support.[18] Left/right differences continued to remain modest even though the consensus over nationalized industries and other specific policies eroded, and Thatcherite and Labour responses to the crisis of the late 1970s were termed "polarization." Indeed, by the 1990s Britain was ever more driven by middle-class politics and policies as the result of further change on the left, whether induced by declining working-class numbers or more "political" factors as discussed by Anthony Heath, Roger Jowell, and John Curtice.[19]

The Bonn Republic

The (West) German political spectrum gradually emerged as similarly compact. As in Britain and post-1977 Spain, party moderation was driven by bottom-up pressures, that is, from voters and not party leaders. These positive postwar developments should not obscure democracy's daunting prospects and initial uncertainties in 1945. The right lacked a democratic historical tradition. Germany had again suffered defeat, another generation of young men was "inured to violence," and public opinion polls suggest there was ample room for a new "stab in the back" theory.[20] The material situation was initially extremely bleak. Both returning soldiers and around eight million refugees arriving from the east (constituting a notable share of the Federal Republic's population by 1951) discovered a very grim existence. Price controls encouraged an important black market, and the 1948 currency reform initially was followed by further unemployment. It might be said that under these unpropitious circumstances, rightist defection was prohibited only by the Allied occupation or by the weakening of the right and the revival of union power. Or perhaps Germany is the perfect

18. Beer (1982: 114–19).
19. Heath, Jowell, and Curtice (1985).
20. Maier (1981: 330). Merritt (1995: 94) shows that nearly as many Germans surveyed in the U.S. zone attributed defeat to internal "treachery" as to the Allies' military superiority.

case for approaches that treat the war as a crucial psychological "pivot point," before which many citizens did not realize the virtues of democracy (and peace) but after which nearly all had learned crucial lessons. In this interpretation, average Germans were ideationally "immunized" by the traumas of Nazi dictatorship, war, defeat, and/or Allied "re-education."

However, these are not persuasive claims. Extensive survey research suggests that Nazism and the war did not effectively "immunize" Germans against all forms of authoritarianism. At the very least, many did not conflate all authoritarianisms into Hitlerism; for example, in 1951, one-third of respondents answered positively to the idea of restoring the monarchy.[21] Moreover, large segments did not even repel from Nazism. Notable groupings were willing to vote for former Nazi officials recruited as candidates of mainstream parties such as the Free Democratic Party (FDP) and even the Christian Democratic Union (CDU).[22] Survey research reviewed by Elisabeth Noelle and Erich Neumann and Richard Merritt shows that well into the 1950s very large (and initially growing) segments of the population positively assessed Hitler's pre-1939 regime and accomplishments. And instead of rejecting Nazism under all circumstances, significant segments—even in the monitored political context of occupied Germany—reported that they considered support for Nazism conceivable under readily identifiable lesser-of-two-evils scenarios. Asked how they would choose between Nazism and Communism, "the number opting for National Socialism increased from 19 percent in November 1945 to well over twice that many in February 1949." Such a preference meant that support for Nazism in the past was not necessarily a source of regret or shame. In 1962, 20 percent of Germans who had been at least fifteen years old in 1932 said that the political choice in 1933 may well have been between Nazism and Bolshevism, and a further 28 percent insisted that formulation was absolutely correct.[23] Unsurprisingly, Gabriel Almond and Sidney Verba, Ralf Dahrendorf, and other theorists operating on culturalist assumptions were pessimistic about West Germany's democratic prospects through the 1960s.[24]

In regard to power balances, while the Allies remained more concerned about rightist authoritarianism than perhaps in any other anti-Soviet ally,

---

21. Noelle and Neumann (1967: 196), Boynton and Loewenberg (1974).

22. Tauber (1967).

23. See Noelle and Neumann (1967: 193, 203) and Merritt (1995: 93, 97, 99), whose data generally cover the U.S. occupation zone. They show that for a decade after the war, large percentages identified 1933–39 as the most prosperous time for twentieth-century Germany. The number stating that National Socialism was a good idea badly carried out was greater than that saying it was an inherently bad idea; in the first four years after the war the former rose while the latter fell.

24. Almond and Verba (1963: 429, 495), Dahrendorf (1967).

it is not clear that they would have blocked a conservative reaction to a radical left challenge. Certainly, U.S. support for authoritarian (and recently "fascist") Spain and Portugal sent mixed messages on this score. And the domestic balance of left/right power had not obviously changed. The loss of eastern Germany undercut the Junkers, but interwar authoritarianism had relied on a middle-class base that remained intact. While union membership and densities went up somewhat (unlike in France and Italy and later, Spain), for the first postwar decade they were lower than at their interwar peak in the early 1920s. Moreover, unlike what might be expected if rightists were "locked" into democracy, there is no evidence that rightists even *attempted* to amass the coercive resources that would have been required for any overthrow attempt.[25]

Instead, from the start West German conservatives generated neither ambivalent regime discourses nor paramilitary forces. Most who had voted for the NSDAP in 1932 appear to have consistently voted for democratic center-right parties beginning with the first Land elections in 1946. But these previous votes and positive evaluations of the previous regime's record did not qualify them as possible future defectors, because by the 1940s and 1950s they were called upon to make choices about which regime was best for the present, not the past. Rapidly falling risks in democracy resulted in the marginalization of proto-authoritarian parties. This is not to deny substantial initial uncertainty. Konrad Adenauer was concerned in 1945 that the KPD would emerge from the war much strengthened and closely allied with the SPD, and the two left parties not only stole the initial march on political organizing but also at first cooperated locally and in antifascist committees.[26]

But as Major puts it, Germany (like France) experienced the rapid replacement of an antifascist with "an anti-Communist consensus." Assurances over outcomes in democracy had diverse origins. Moderation by the SPD was partly tactical; SPD leader Kurt Schumacher remarked, "We have to understand that the Left in Germany has provided the theory, but the Right the practice, of the class struggle."[27] Allied occupiers were antiradical. Institutional design was relatively low stakes, although arguably slightly less so than under Weimar, given the electoral threshold and the fact that the constructive vote of no-confidence permitted governance by pluralities. Also, conservatives were better served by the postwar party system than in

25. The SPD opposed the creation of a regular military, arguing it would again escape parliamentary control. But Drummond's (1982) analysis suggests the SPD's real concern was potential reunification and international peace.

26. Schwarz (1995: 330, 359–60).

27. Major (1997: 78, 44), Graf (1976: 67).

Weimar. The earliest postwar Christian Democratic organization contained a progressive wing shaped by the old center-straddling Zentrum. But these sectors were soon overwhelmed and outmaneuvered by conservatives flowing in from Weimar-era conservative parties. The Christian Democrats (CDU) were thus starkly different from the interwar Zentrum not only in the sense that the party emerged as a reliably center-right force but also in the sense that for the first time the interests of Germany's middle classes, businesses, and both Protestant and Catholic churches were stably united in a single force against the left.[28] And this combination was potent: from 1949 until 1961, the center-right as a whole (the CDU plus the much smaller FDP and the disappearing German Party [DP] and Bavarian Party [BP]) averaged 61 percent of the vote while the left averaged 33 percent. Uwe Kitzinger suggests that we think of the West German electorate in this period as one-third to the left and nearly two-thirds unsure whether they would vote and if so for which center-right party.[29]

But as in other cases, none of these events could be relied upon. The Allies largely exited German domestic politics by 1949–50. Pacting would not have been predictable and anyway was not typical. The 1949 constitution was the only major arrangement negotiated by all parties (and even then the SPD, FDP, and others outvoted the CDU on the matter of the electoral law), and the CDU governed strictly from the center-right, not in a cross-aisle fashion. Institutions were subject to change: electoral provisions protecting smaller parties were revised in 1953 and 1956 (and a substantial, though ultimately unsuccessful, move toward plurality rules was made in 1966–69). Electorally, while the CDU was firmly in command through much of the 1950s, the SPD had been mere points behind the CDU in 1949. Polls suggested the 1957 election would be relatively close (though it did not turn out to be), and as of 1961 the SPD was capable of forming a parliamentary majority with the centrist FDP. In the 1960s the SPD averaged 40 percent of the vote.

What was perceived as more predictable was the stable moderating of the electorate and party system. This stability eventually ensured that political outcomes in democracy were predictably unthreatening, regardless of alternation in office, the absence of political pacts, and recurrent moves toward somewhat higher-stakes decision rules. There were several measures of underlying moderation in the party system. The KPD fell below 6 percent of votes in 1949, and what had been the largest communist party in Western Europe two decades earlier became the second smallest in 1953. The next

28. For brevity's sake, the CDU and Christian Social Union (CSU) are referred to simply as the CDU. On this sector, see Pridham (1977).
29. Kitzinger (1960: 130).

year a government official remarked that there was no need to ban the KPD because the voters had already accomplished that. Beginning at least as early as mid-1947, few people polled expected Communists to govern within the next ten years.[30] And the SPD moderated beginning relatively soon after liberation. Initially that party cast an ambiguous shadow. Even while strictly repudiating an alliance (much the less an East German–style merger) with the KPD, SPD leader Schumacher insisted on the usefulness of Marxist analysis and assumed the SPD could appeal to many newly pro-letarianized, former middle-class voters without having to move toward the center. There is some reason to believe the SPD's moderating had origins in the international division of Germany, since the east had contained the strongest historic bases of the KPD and much of the SPD. But events in the western zones were not predetermined. The SPD's size and posture were shaped by complex events, and the KPD initially appeared to have strong enough bases in certain western electoral districts for Adenauer to want them diluted by more conservative wards.[31]

Whatever the cause, the SPD pursued a consistently reformist legislative strategy and began a profound moderating substantially before the cele-brated 1959 Bad Godesberg conference. It is not clear "exactly" when con-servatives perceived the left in West Germany as predictably moderate, but it was certainly largely accomplished by the time electoral alternation became a serious prospect in the late 1950s. At least some perceived the constraints on left radicalism as bottom-up, concluding from the founding 1949 election that while the CDU on its own was not hegemonic, the center-right as a whole was.[32] This was not for reasons suggested by classic social-structural analyses—because middle classes predominated—but instead because even most industrial workers eschewed radical politics.[33] The CDU's most consistent campaign strategy was to appeal to the dominant constituency opposed to radicalism with a call for "No Experiments" and a warning that the SPD would pursue substantial nationalizations.

In response to repeated defeats, the SPD soon defined itself as cross-class, and by 1952–53 there were open calls from what William Graf terms that party's "pragmatic right" for an abandonment of "all references to Marx, the concept of a planned economy, the use of the red flag, the reference to fellow party members as comrade," and so on. By 1957 the SPD's lead-

---

30. Merritt (1995: 338). Major (1997: 153–54, 233, 237, 289) discussed early projections and pointed out that General Clay was somewhat less sanguine about the KPD's potential given desperate economic conditions.

31. Graf (1976: 65–66), Adenauer (1966: 82).

32. Schwarz (1995: 431–32).

33. The number of white-collar employees and civil servants probably surpassed the number of blue-collar workers only in the 1970s.

ership did not mention socialism and reemphasized its commitment to economic competition and private property.[34] The party reconciled its differences with both the Catholic Church and the government's defense and foreign policies, casting Germany's lot unambiguously with the West. The cumulative impact of these changes was to conflate the short- and long-term goals of the SPD in the sense that feasible reformism became the end-goal. It could be argued that as early as the mid-1950s the SPD departed from the center-right most sharply not on political economy but on defense and foreign policy.[35]

But even these issues did not indicate polarization on the interwar scale. As a result, the 1959 Bad Godesberg program, like the 1979 shift by the PSOE in Spain, should be understood to represent not so much a cause as an outgrowth of the party's preexisting movement toward the center. As Donald Sassoon puts it, "Every single one of the great innovations of Bad Godesberg can be traced to a previous party statement," and the 1959 program largely repackaged multiple preexisting policy shifts. The SPD was already located so tantalizingly close to many middle-class and moderate voters that a major public relations effort might secure them. The net effect was that "[t]here was no longer a basic difference between this program and the CDU's 'social market economy.' "[36] And the strategy apparently worked: the SPD advanced from 31.8 percent of the vote in 1957 to 36 percent in 1961 and nearly 43 percent in 1969. By then alternation in office was unthreatening to core conservative interests and values. We can surmise that this would also have been the case with higher-stakes political institutions, since the CDU championed the 1966–68 bid for plurality-type electoral rules that risked absolute-majority SPD governments as much as it offered hope for CDU counterparts. In other words, it became clear to both the SPD and the center-right that (like in interwar Britain) socialists stood to gain votes by moving toward the center and not the extremes. Ronald Bunn suggests that this is what made proposals by the left such as welfare programs and co-determination so different after 1945 than in Weimar: these were clearly end-goals and not incremental steps on a readily discernible path leading to total worker control. Just as the CDU publicly reacted hyperbolically to electoral defeat in 1969, employers criticized co-determination, but it was eventually implemented in several key industries by the CDU, which after 1982 also did not reverse further expansions of the program made by the SPD in the 1970s.[37]

---

34. Graf (1976: 150), Kitzinger (1960: 133).
35. Sassoon (1996: 249–50), Drummond (1982).
36. Sassoon (1996: 254–55), Herz (1979: 250–51), Miller and Pothoff (1986: 166, 172–73).
37. Bunn (1958: 285–86).

The SPD in office from 1969 to 1982 was a thoroughly revisionist social democratic party whose left factions and impulses were no more radical than in 1945–50. By the 1990s, the SPD if anything had moderated even further in its search for the "new center." This moderating was not because the SPD restrained itself for fear of provoking an antidemocratic reaction. Conservatives did not hedge despite the facts that rightist defection was neither logistically nor ideologically inconceivable after 1945, that no pacts reassured conservatives, that electoral alternation soon became a viable possibility and then reality, and that the institutional design was not lower stakes than earlier (and the CDU tried to *raise* stakes in 1966–69). Conservatives neither hedged nor defected because stable moderation by the left made authoritarianism predictably suboptimal.

The Fourth and Fifth Republics in France

A radical threat to conservative interests and values existed on the left in postwar France, but it was thoroughly contained. Liberation opened an initial period of unpredictability. If "the Fifth Republic was born on the right," the Fourth was not.[38] The Communist party (PCF) was expected to emerge from the war as Stalinist as before and substantially stronger, whereas as Réné Rémond comments "[I]n 1945 the hour finally seemed to have arrived when 'the End' could be written to the history of the Right."[39] In November 1944, General Charles de Gaulle could only guess that "the Communists will not have a majority of the country behind them," and most respondents to an IFOP poll the next month expected either the socialist SFIO or the PCF to be the largest party in municipal elections and almost none expected it to be a party of the right or even center.[40] In early 1946, one French observer could look with envy to northern Europe where workers appeared more moderate, and the U.S. ambassador later wrote that in 1946, he had been "discouraged about the possibility of preventing the Communists from eventually taking over."[41] In the first national elections the next October, the PCF was the strongest single force, with 26 percent of the vote; together the PCF and SFIO nearly won a majority. Conservatives thus quickly focused on whether there would form a "socialo-

38. Duhamel (1980: 7).
39. Rémond (1969: 318).
40. "Compte Rendu de l'Entretien avec le general de Gaulle d'une delegation du Comité Directeur du Parti Socialiste," National Archives (hereafter abbreviated as AN), Edouard Depreux papers, 456 AP 4; *IFOP Bulletin* 8 (January 16, 1945), p. 20.
41. Dumaine (1958: 52), Wall (1991: 68).

communist block" with the capacity to generate deeply threatening political outcomes.[42] Defection was far from inconceivable; the Gaullist Michel
Debré could imagine plausible events leading to a breakdown of the new
regime.[43]

As in many other cases, rightists had several short-term protections. The
United States might have acted against a PCF takeover. Conservatives soon
effectively competed electorally; their Parti Républicain de la Liberté
(PRL) was "the dorsal fin of French conservatism," and it was not long
before the entire creature surfaced in several parties. The left offered
explicit assurances of moderation; the PCF insisted personal private property was sacred and by mid-1946 a "pause" was declared in the nationalization program.[44] And the proportional representation electoral law did not
magnify the advantages of the left, although neither the upper house nor
the presidency were strong. But in postwar France as in other cases, rightists could not predict political risks on these bases. Electoral prospects were
uncertain. Assurances meant little when the SFIO seemed ready to ally leftward and the PCF was entirely untrustworthy.[45] And institutions were in flux
during and after the lengthy constituent phase. Calls for fundamental revision appeared almost immediately after the constitution's adoption, and
the 1950s brought substantial change in electoral laws and the powers of
the upper house. Had a specific institutional formula been rightists' sole
protection against high risks, they would have retained incentives to hedge.

Conservatives developed reliable prodemocratic regime preferences
because other events made political outcomes in democracy predictably
unthreatening. Above all, the PCF was systematically isolated, leaving the
politically relevant spectrum abbreviated on the left. The initial postwar
governing formula was a PCF/SFIO/Christian Democrat coalition, which
negotiated the constitution, participated in the occupation of Germany,
restored France's colonial structure, and launched economic reconstruction. While the SFIO found this three-way arrangement advantageous at
first, by 1946 it was eroding and in 1947 domestic and Cold War disputes
led to the expulsion of the PCF. But unlike in Italy, the break was between
the PCF and *all* other parties, including the Socialists who threw their lot
in with the center and the right. The rupture was dramatically marked by

42. *Le monde*, October 20, 1945, p. 3, and November 12, 1946, p. 1; untitled electoral analysis, 1945 or 1946, in AN, Louis Marin papers, 317 AP 242; Villiers (1978: 116).
43. Writing as Fontevrault in *Les cahiers politiques*, May 1945, p. 51.
44. Vinen (1995: 115), Wall (1983: 35), Ehrmann (1957: 347).
45. When the PCF's Jacques Duclos asked another deputy, "What surprises you?" he received
as a reply, "To tell the truth, nothing surprises me coming from you." *Annales de l'Assemblée
Nationale: Débats*, August 11, 1947, p. 4235.

Prime Minister Paul Ramadier's exemplary democratic socialist condemnation of the PCF's Stalinism.[46]

The campaign of exclusion against the PCF, conducted as much by the SFIO as any party, was extraordinarily intensive and extensive. The socialist-allied Force Ouvrière split from the main union. Communists were purged from positions in the social security system, boards of nationalized companies, and the corps of prefects, the interior ministry, and the army. The other parties responded to PCF-induced labor agitation with legislation dealing harshly with sabotage. Without SFIO allies, the PCF lost control of many municipal councils and then seats in the next elections, and at the national level the other parties changed both chambers' electoral laws to reduce representation by the PCF in particular. Ronald Tiersky's description of these events as "containment" of the PCF effectively connotes both the strategy's international context and its systematic nature. In François Goguel's words, the "breach between Communists and non-Communists has now become by far the widest of all those which divide the various sectors of opinion."[47]

Whereas interwar conservatives had seen the SFIO as the "hinge of possible majorities," shading almost imperceptibly into communism, opinion polls suggested that after 1945 they perceived the two forces very differently.[48] Aware of events behind the Iron Curtain and intimate with the ways of the PCF, not just conservatives but a majority of socialists surveyed identified communism as France's main political danger. Even the SFIO's opposition in 1951–56 did not represent the "turn to the left" the PCF hoped for. An excluded PCF also appears not to have seemed a threat from outside the policy process. There is little doubt that conservatives perceived PCF leaders as potentially revolutionary.[49] But several Fourth Republic conservative deputies had believed that the industrial workers who voted for the PCF would on the whole be unwilling to answer a call for insurrection.[50] The PCF's second-in-command had said in 1944 that if the party had tried to seize power at Liberation, many of its nominal adherents would have abandoned it. It was

46. *Annales de l'Assemblée Nationale: Débats,* June 3, 1947, pp. 1875–77. Other SFIO leaders expressed equally harsh views; see Goguel (1952: 36) and Graham (1965: 175–76).

47. Wall (1983: 58–59, 63, 66–67), Tiersky (1972), Goguel (1952: 173).

48. For example, the survey of Mouvement Républicain Populaire (MRP) voters in Gallup (1976b: 42). Villiers (1978: 137) and Pinay (1984: 78) assessed specific SFIO leaders. The quote is from *Le monde,* June 4, 1946, p. 1.

49. For example, Pinay (1984: 80), Teitgen (1988: 381). *Sondages,* December 1, 1947, pp. 243–45, and December 1, 1948, p. 226; Gallup (1976b: 177).

50. Interviews with Fourth Republic conservative parliamentary deputies Olivier Guichard and Michel Maurice-Bokanowski, Paris, 1997. Mauriac (1973: 57, 182) suggests that de Gaulle believed most French Communists were not really revolutionary and had by May 1946 missed their chance to take power either legally or by force.

clear that worker support was weak for political as opposed to economic strikes. By 1948, a strong majority of the population polled believed the PCF would never come to power.[51] This was not the only instance of thorough ghettoization or "quarantine" of a party at the national level; the same occurred to the Movimento Sociale Italiano (MSI) until the 1990s and the French National Front (with 10 to 15 percent of the vote) from the mid-1980s on.

The nature of the PCF's presence in the body politic from 1947 until the 1980s was complex and much debated, but for our purposes the important point is that while it secured one-fourth of the vote, its leaders were excluded from the formal national political game *and* lacked the capacity to use force to upset that game. As a result, a moderate consensus after 1947 stretched across three-fourths of the political spectrum, which could experience a "safe" form of alternation, between coalitions ranging from the SFIO to the center-right and ones ranging from the Mouvement Républicain Populaire (MRP) to some Gaullists. All this had clear effects on political outcomes. Socioeconomic conservatives took over key economic portfolios as early as the late 1940s, and by 1951 controlled both the prime ministership and the presidency. The SFIO lacked allies for anything but moderate welfare-state policies. Jean-Pierre Rioux remarks that especially when the SFIO went into opposition in 1951, "the Right . . . was confident that it governed a bourgeois France," so much so that Michel Debré felt it necessary to take issue with the widespread notion that it was "normal" and acceptable that one-fourth of the electorate be organized out of policy-making.[52]

Conservatives' reliable prodemocratic regime preferences were well established by the time the Fourth Republic underwent crisis and change in 1958. Opposition to the Fourth Republic in no way indicated antidemocratic impulses. De Gaulle was many things but he was not in favor of exclusionary rules of the game ("Why should I, at the age of sixty-seven, begin a career as a dictator . . . ?"). A threat to democratic procedures emerged only among the most hard-line military officers and settler activists in Algeria, and surveys consistently revealed no erosion in regime support among conservatives in general. Indeed, conservatives considered democracy so low risk that redesigning democracy's institutions to a *higher-stakes* formula (majoritarian electoral rules and a strong presidency) was unthreatening.[53] Thus, the end of the Fourth Republic and the inaugura-

---

51. Wall (1983: 30), Lorwin (1954: 139–42), *Sondages*, February 1, 1948, p. 35.

52. Rioux (1987: 195); Debré (1952: 72–73); Olivier Guichard and Maurice-Bokanowski interviews, 1997. Polls suggested that by 1949 a majority believed there had already been too many nationalizations; Gallup (1976b: 136).

53. Suleiman (1994: 146, 152). Even a sizable number of PCF voters favored the new constitution. The overwhelming majority of people polled blamed the Fourth Republic's failures on such factors as cabinet instability; see *Sondages*, e.g., April 1958, pp. 29–30.

tion of the Fifth, while a case of institutional reformulation, cannot use-fully be described as one in which "unique" leadership factors "changed what appeared to be a threat to a democratic regime into a transformation that can be considered a reequilibration of democracy."[54] Subsequent events confirmed just how marginal the antidemocratic agendas were. Jean-Louis Tixier-Vignancour's 1965 presidential bid united various hard-right groups, not all of them rejectionist, and even then attracted only 5 percent of voters.

This overall calculus did not change in the following four decades. In the mid-1960s heavy majorities of voters from the SFIO rightward, when polled, said they believed the PCF's (limited) influence would either remain steady or decline further, but not grow. More important, the extent to which the PCF remained in any sense a radical party became a regular subject of debate and analysis, and pluralities of all non-PCF electorates believed their lives would not change significantly if the PCF governed.[55] The Socialists thus allied in the 1970s with a PCF that had become far more "workerist" than revolutionary. Even François Mitterrand's 1981 assumption of office with an absolute Socialist majority, with four PCF Ministers, and a limited nationalization program did not threaten the fundamental postwar political economy. This lack of threat was especially evident when economic and political pressures forced the Socialists to make a u-turn, creating the ever-more compact spectrum of the late 1980s and 1990s.[56] Such a context could not inspire rightists to hedge against risks in democracy, much less to defect from that regime. Even surges of "extreme-right" politics such as Poujadism in the 1950s and the National Front after 1983 represented controversial agendas but not essentially antidemocratic projects.

Postwar Italy

A democratic "regional political culture" was not sufficient to cause either democratization in Francoist Spain or reliable prodemocratic regime preferences among Italian conservatives. Instead, the most polarized spectrum in liberated and democratic Europe created high enough political risks in democracy to lead conservatives to hedge in a variety of ways. As a result, scholars have treated the question of consolidation in postwar Italy—and

54. Linz (1978a: 76–77, 100n11).
55. Lavau (1975). Surveys of the 1960s are reviewed by Fichelet et al. (1969: 262, 265, 275–76). Majorities, even on the center-right and right, believed the PCF had changed notably in the previous decade.
56. Hall (1987).

especially its timing—as problematic.[57] Substantial tensions occurred between left and Christian democratic factions in wartime partisan forces, and the euphoria of Liberation was accompanied by the renewal of left/right confrontations. As elsewhere in the region, traditional parties of the center and right were in disarray, and as a result the strongest organized forces that emerged in 1943–45 were the Communists (PCI), the Socialists (PSI), and the Christian Democrats (DC); the latter were led by Alcide de Gasperi and were heirs to part of the interwar *popolari*.[58]

In one way the situation was comparable to France's: Communists accounted for about one-fourth of the vote. But in 1947, as Raymond Aron put it, "[I]n France, the socialist party rallied to the anti-communist camp, in Italy to the communist one," in electoral alliances and unions. As a result, Italian conservatives remained concerned about a PCI-dominated "socialo-communist" bloc for the next two decades.[59] Such a combination would presumably have resulted in great shifts in policies toward property ownership and the status of the Catholic Church. Moreover, large sectors of the left's rank-and-file were prone to direct action. This was evidenced in factory occupations, the nationwide explosion of protest after an attempted assassination of PCI leader Palmiro Togliatti in 1948, and the extensive land invasions that erupted particularly in the south through the early 1950s. In all these cases, the PCI called for restraint, but as with the interwar PSOE, SFIO, and PCF, the PCI was hardly able to enforce doctrinal or tactical discipline on its newly swollen membership.[60] De Gasperi attempted to "parliamentarize" the DC's conflict with the PCI precisely because it could easily have been conducted in other forums. The range of distinctly possible political outcomes in democracy thus stretched considerably farther to the left than in France after 1947: a left dominated by the PCI could come to power via several readily identifiable and plausible scenarios.

Compared to this possibility, exclusion was feasible. Traditional security structures survived the war surprisingly intact and were politically reliable once Communists were purged after 1947.[61] But, as in all the cases I have

----

57. For example, Sartori (1976), Cotta (1990), Hine (1990).

58. For brevity's sake, the main socialist sector after 1945 is referred to simply as the PSI, as distinct from Giuseppe Saragat's Partito Social-Democratico Italiano (PSDI).

59. See, e.g., Sturzo (1956) and Scelba's 1945 letter in Malgeri (1976: 358, 360); Aron (1948: 224).

60. Colarizi (1984: 552–53). On perceptions of proclivities to violence, see, e.g., Sturzo (1947: 26). PCI leaders readily recognized such tendencies; e.g., Togliatti in Behan (1997: 141, 218–37), who also describes the events of 1948 in Milan. On the land invasions, see Cinanni (1979) and Ciconte (1981).

61. Pasquino (1986).

discussed, the costs of excluding the left did not alone determine rightist defection. Several factors protected the right from the materialization of radical potentialities in democracy. But they were not predictable factors. The DC was not as reliably conservative as the German CDU. Shifts by small coalition partners combined with perhaps a 5 to 6 percent gain by the left could have created PCI-dominated governments between 1946 and 1963. In 1968–87, possible combinations of left parties could account for nearly 49 percent of the parliament.[62] Rightists received some reassurance from international actors, beginning with war-time limits on arms supplies to northern partisans by the Allies, who feared the emergence of a communist army on the Greek model.[63] But most Allied troops left Italy soon after the war, and while the United States might have intervened against a PCI insurrection—although the Pax Americana did not block southern land invasions in 1943–45—it was entirely unclear what response would have greeted an election victory by the left.[64] Finally, the center-right sought protections in institutions. The DC championed proportionality, regionalism, and judicial review in the 1948 constitution to limit the left's prospective power, but by the 1950s it delayed implementation of the latter two in order to concentrate its growing power, and added a win-concentrating bonus to the electoral law for 1953 before reversing itself three years later. In other words, while institutions were generally stakes-reducing (Luigi Sturzo preferred PR for that reason), they were also seen as malleable rather than fixed.

More meaningful assurances over political outcomes would have had to come from the PCI itself. But the swift turnarounds executed by Stalinist parties such as the PCI held out little promise of reliability, and much of the PCI's moderation was clearly tactical. Conservatives regularly applied the term *doppiezza* (duplicity) and the metaphor of a Trojan horse to the PCI's behavior and strategy.[65] The PCI acknowledged this reputation when it tried to insist that certain of its reformist proposals were not merely tactical but strategic goals. Moreover, rightist concerns included violence; they knew leftist expartisans retained caches of arms, and as Simona Colarizi

---

62. A hypothetical cabinet ranging from the Partito di Unità Proletaria (PdUP) to the PSDI appears only slightly more contrived than real ones that ranged from the PSDI to the Partito Liberale Italiano (PLI) after 1947, or from the PSI to the PLI in the 1980s.

63. Lamb (1996: 230, 232).

64. The degree of flux over Allied involvement was indicated in the 1947 peace treaty and its revision; Miller (1986: e.g., 194, 240). Romero (1989: ch. 6) addresses U.S. involvement in elections and unions.

65. Di Loreto (1991: 53, 236–37) also described public DC declarations on possibilities of a PCI insurrection. On *doppiezza*, also see Amendola quoted in Behan (1997: 141–42).

put it, whereas units of the interwar PSI militated for an insurrection they were incapable of carrying out, the PCI downplayed what conservatives believed was a very real underground revolutionary apparatus.[66]

Leaders on the center-right had at least a measure of "theorizing" about what contributed to susceptibilities to left radicalism: propertyless poverty, which was less changed in Italy (and Spain) than elsewhere in the region. This notion played no small part in the DC's eventual program, described by Sidney Tarrow and almost unique among nonleft governments, of land reform in the south, aimed at creating small-holders likely to support the DC and not the PCI.[67] But so long as risks in democracy were high and center-rightists' future regime preferences could not be known ex ante, hedging was the order of the day.

The first major and striking expression of hedging was widespread rightist support for the monarchy in the June 1946 referendum. This referendum was held after conservatives had numerous reasons to detect high risks in democracy, including land invasions and PCI and PSI strength and cooperation in local elections. The 1946 referendum vote is often studied cursorily and the 45.8 percent promonarchical vote is interpreted ambiguously. But the vote is quite revealing. If the 1976 Spanish referendum posed a choice between democracy and authoritarianism, this referendum posed one between democracy without and with a major hedge. Given the monarchy's almost inevitably conservative orientation and long-standing interventionism in political affairs, both sides in the referendum campaign agreed that the monarchy would act as a conservative brake on democratic processes: prorepublicans argued that profound social change could only be achieved if the monarchy were removed, while promonarchy campaigners warned that any such step represented a risky "leap in the dark." Support for this hedge roared through conservative ranks: the average monarchist was a Christian Democrat and the average Christian Democrat (indeed a vast majority of them) voted for the monarchy.[68]

66. Colarizi (1984: 555–56).

67. Tarrow (1967: 291–315). Ginsborg (1990: ch. 4) emphasizes that industrialists who were determined to induce political stability supported this reform.

68. Given the PLI, Common Man's Front (Uomo Qualunque [UQ]), and monarchist vote totals, over three-fourths (and perhaps over four-fifths) of DC voters must have supported the monarchy. On the "leap," see Gambino (1975: 182–83), including the footnotes. Scoppola (1977) discussed De Gasperi's calculations and strategy. Many analyses portray support for the monarchy, which was disproportionately regional, as a function of the south's authoritarian traditionalist culture. But Mussolini's pre-1922 support had been weak in the south. Moreover, the monarchy received about one-third of the vote in the center and north. If the promonarchy vote was stronger in certain regions, it was because the conservative vote in the June 1946 election was as well.

In elections held the same day, nearly 15 percent of voters also supported parties to the DC's right: the Liberals, the monarchists, and the Common Man's Front (Uomo Qualunque, [UQ]), which called for an end to antifascist purges, criticized the DC both for cooperating with the left and for fearing to be a frankly middle-class or "bourgeois" party, and urged that party politics be replaced with a more administrative state. In subsequent local elections, these parties surged and the UQ beat the DC in Rome. In the face of this rightward shift, the DC felt compelled to break off the coalition with the left. This period also witnessed at least occasional relations between the right-most currents in the DC and Catholic Action on the one hand and the UQ and monarchists on the other.[69] At least in these most uncertain initial years, numerous voters cast ballots that revealed abiding skepticism about democracy without fetters.

Perhaps most crucially, hedging also can be discerned in the right's aggressive and deliberate strategies toward the distribution and organization of coercive resources. As political life revived, scattered violence was directed against workers' parties and organizations in the south. Colarizi describes the spread of the armed rightist Armata Italiana della Libertà, which may have numbered around one hundred thousand. In this era of a rising left, De Gasperi asked U.S. troops to stay on until the last possible moment in 1947. A 1948 ban on paramilitary activity left the regular military as the only major armed force in the country, and the center-right parties that dominated government beginning in 1947 swiftly created a highly partisan military, including through purges of officers sympathetic to the left.[70] Like in Spain in 1933–35, access to such an instrument meant that hedging did not require paramilitary mobilization. Such a rigorously anticommunist military as well as secretive projects such as Operation Gladio might seem to have been inspired by foreign policy concerns, since resistance to the USSR was believed to require anticommunist credentials. But whether or not the "otherness" of Italian Communists was the result of their affiliation with the USSR does not obscure the fact that the center-right designed the state's coercive apparatus in such a way that it was off limits to, and could be used against, political sectors representing up to a third of the electorate.[71] Not surprisingly, the left treated the postwar military as a profoundly problematic entity, and politicians on the left such as Pietro Nenni and Togliatti perceived rightist regime preferences as unreli-

---

69. Setta (1975: 97–98, 224), Colarizi (1984: 454–58), Kogan (1966: 72–74).

70. Colarizi (1984: 448–49, 606–07), Miller (1986: 239–40, 245).

71. Ferraresi (1992). Apparent instances of center-right and rightist politicians' tolerance or even encouragement of military involvement in domestic politics as revealed in the De Lorenzo, P-2, and other affairs are striking, but also prone to sensationalistic commentary.

able enough to engage in the self-censorship and tactical concessions that O'Donnell and other theorists identify with uncertain democracies.[72]

For several reasons, it is not a simple matter to establish when rightists' views of the postwar left changed, since electoral rhetoric remained catastrophist and politicians' professional longevity has politicized memoirs and confined private records. But there is widespread agreement that economic and religious conservatives' political risks in democracy fell gradually through the 1960s and 1970s. In the early 1960s, the DC successfully negotiated an "opening to the left" that co-opted a willing PSI, whose entry to government (despite conservative concerns) entailed almost no serious economic policy concessions. In time the "centering" extended to the PCI as well, although researchers have debated both when the PCI moderated to what amounted to democratic-socialist positions and when conservatives recognized these changes. In 1976, the "historic compromise" created tacit PCI support for a DC government, but it is not clear to what extent this reflected changed views by conservatives of the left. Survey data considered by Giacomo Sani and Giovanna Guidorossi shows that through the early 1970s most center and center-right voters said they would *never* vote for the PCI and that through the late 1970s only a bare majority of center voters— and less D` voters—believed the PCI was very different from Soviet bloc communist parties.[73] Nonetheless, Paolo Farneti suggests that Italy's party system was no longer polarized but reflected "centripetal pluralism" by the mid-1960s, and David Hine argues that "there is no doubt that the 1970s represents the watershed" in terms of PCI change and the DC leadership's acknowledgment of it. By the mid-1970s Donald Blackmer and other analysts were describing the PCI as an opposition party that accepted many of the system's features.[74]

At the very least, conservative commitment to democracy was evident in the 1990s. As with the transition from the Fourth to the Fifth Republic in France, the shift to higher-stakes electoral rules coincided with no discernible erosion of democratic support. And as the reformatted left became electable, Silvio Berlusconi failed in his attempt to rally voters with accusations that the Democratic Party of the Left remained communist and risky. The stable compacting of the spectrum had rendered exit predictably suboptimal, perhaps only a few years before the same occurred in post-Franco Spain.

72. Nenni wrote that in 1964, when talks over PSI cabinet entry coincided with the De Lorenzo affair, "[t]he parties and Parliament suddenly realized that they could be bypassed," and he had no doubt as to the political coloration of any resulting regime; quoted in Ginsborg (1990: 278).

73. Sani (1975: 474–89), Guidorossi (1984: 122–24, 133).

74. Farneti (1985), Hine (1990: 66), Blackmer (1975: 53–59).

Conclusions

The year 1945 provided a pivot point neither for the right's strategies toward democracy in Western Europe nor, therefore, for regime outcomes in the region. The pivot image might be said to fit Germany. But Britain's conservatives had already committed to democracy in the interwar period, as had France's as early as the late nineteenth century. And rightist sectors in Italy and Spain took several decades to adopt the same strategy after 1945. This pattern of extensive and enduring nonsynchronization across rightist sectors strongly suggests that national-level factors are crucial and hence that the broad multicase convergence since the 1970s on rightist commitment to democracy is the result of national developments rather than a regional political culture, for example. In terms of other possible explanations, there can be little doubt that office-holding, pacts, and protective institutions have been crucial in attracting the support of threatened sectors in a number of uncertain democracies. But there is little evidence that such devices inspired rightist sectors in Europe to abandon access to vehicles for exiting democracy, creating the conditions for democratic consolidation. Instead of an increasing proliferation of formal pacts and power-sharing arrangements, such devices have been prominently *absent* from Western Europe's post-1945 consolidated democracies. Thus, for example, just as high-stakes designs were not a requirement for defection and breakdown in earlier periods, low-stakes institutions were by no means mandatory after 1945. If anything, there have been notable examples of change in the direction of greater win- and loss-concentration, in France in 1958 and in Italy in the 1990s. Britain stands out as the most durable consolidated democracy covered here, with the highest-stakes institutional design in the region.

The right's convergence on commitment to democracy appears to correspond most closely to a distinctly *political* background condition: low risks in democracy, grounded in a predictably moderate left portion of the political spectrum. It is no coincidence that the recent decades in which the European right for the first time has uniformly committed to democracy is also the period in which the right's core interests and values have faced lower risks under inclusionary rules of the game than ever before. This and related issues are taken up in the concluding chapter.

8

Consolidation into the Future and outside Europe

> Try to imagine personal government in the United States. It is like trying to imagine a national worship of Zeus.
>
> WOODROW WILSON, *Political Science Quarterly*, 1887

In this chapter, I address the environmental factors that gave rise to political predictability in Western Europe; the future prospects for these consolidated democracies, including the possibility of deconsolidation; and the implications this analysis has for the study of consolidation in Latin America, Eastern Europe, and other regions that either are increasingly populated by still-uncertain democracies or continue to be dominated by authoritarianism.

The Emergence of Political Predictability in Western Europe

The experience of the five largest countries in Western Europe across the twentieth century supports the claim that conservative commitment to democracy in modern Europe can be traced more persuasively to "rough rigidity" in the matrix representing conservatives' payoffs from democracy and the most likely authoritarian alternative than to factors such as wealth, international demonstration effects (IDEs), or political culture. The fact that conservative perceptions of low political risks in democracy underlay this causal chain means that democratic consolidation in the region has as a necessary (pre)condition a factor that is centrally political and in that sense is easily distinguished from the social, cultural, economic, and educational "requisites" or "background conditions" emphasized by diverse existing structural theories of democratic stability. It is also easily distinguished from another centrally political factor emphasized by Göran Therborn, Dietrich Rueschemeyer, Evelyne Stephens, and John Stephens, and Ruth Collier: changing balances of power.

There can be little doubt that the shifts in the left/right balance of power that had occurred by the early twentieth century made exclusion of workers more costly than in the distant past and played a large role in converting democracy from an option that rightist forces once easily had dismissed to one that at the least had to be resisted actively and could even appear in certain circumstances as the lesser of two evils. Dankwart Rustow's image of democracy resulting from a hurting stalemate might well describe cases in which the political terrain came to resemble an armed camp in the first third of the twentieth century.[1] But in Chapters 3 through 7 I argued that trends in the balance of power cannot persuasively be credited with converting the right's provisional support for democracy to commitment to that regime, primarily because in most cases there was no important shift in left/right balances of power from the interwar period—when rightists were often only provisional democrats and in some cases were pro-authoritarian—to the post-1945 period—when more and more rightist sectors in Europe committed to democracy. The conservative sectors that provided the backbone of all the authoritarian projects in interwar Western Europe survived intact into the post-1945 period, while working-class organizational power rose in only some (predominantly northern European) cases, remained roughly steady in several others, and *fell* in France and Spain and perhaps other countries (depending on how union membership is measured). Although the costs of excluding the left almost certainly played a significant role in introducing democracy to the region, these costs appear to have roughly leveled off at interwar levels. The evidence is not persuasive that *consolidated* democracies are the result of the European right being fought to a draw.

Instead, in Spain, Britain, France, Germany, and Italy, and by all appearances also Ireland, the Low Countries, and Scandinavia, conservatives became reliable democrats because of sharp reductions in what Dahl terms the costs of toleration: they gradually came to associate democracy with low risks to their core interests and values. These low perceived risks are the result of neither pacts, which generally have been absent from consolidated democracies and were widely seen as highly malleable anyway, nor institu-

---

1. Rustow (1970: 352–53).

tions, which were often not optimal for conservatives and were surprisingly malleable as well. Instead, the fundamental moderating of the left—long before globalization and Third Way convergence late in the twentieth century—emerges, in this way as in others, as one of the most important developments in modern European history. This moderating meant that conservatives' risks in democracy were low even when center-left parties won office temporarily or for long periods, when the left failed to make specific promises of moderation (or cross-aisle pacts failed), when electoral laws and constitutional designs manufactured center-left majorities or con-centrated the power of center-left governments, or indeed when several or all of these conditions were present, as in Britain in 1945–51.

The right's commitment to democracy, in other words, is not the result of conservatism's defeat or fear but of its triumph and confidence. The twentieth century proved to be a "bourgeois" or conservative century in many more places than Britain alone. In retrospect this was a striking devel-opment. For centuries, property owners and other members of Europe's social elites harbored fears of mass-level revolts and resistance; this was true in feudal society, under absolute monarchies, and then in "mass society," given the rise of organized workers and political socialism. Arno Mayer is among many who treat perceptions of threats from below as a pervasive elite preoccupation lasting through World War I; as we have seen, they in fact endured substantially beyond that in several cases.[2] But a sea change occurred in this aspect of the region's history. Core conservative interests in "order" and existing property regimes became predictably entrenched in a popular consensus that would have been unimaginable in earlier eras. This is easily discernible in France from the 1880s or so until 1914, in Britain from the late 1920s, in France again and Germany since the early post-1945 period, and in Italy and Spain from about the mid-1970s. The fundamental properties of capitalism proved astonishingly tenacious even when the left governed, perhaps because, as Donald Sassoon remarks, "the more successful the socialists became, the more dependent they found themselves on the prosperity of capitalism."[3] As a result, conservatives have been able to safeguard their core interests in safety and policy within democracy, without having to incur the costs and risks of resorting to authoritarian projects. In its terminology if in no other way, this argument parallels the claims by Max Weber and others that a necessary condition for modern Western capitalism is forms of predictability—concerning property rights and a wide range of bureaucratic practices—that ensured capital-holders it was safe to commit to long-term capital investments.

2. Mayer (1981).
3. Sassoon (1996: xxii).

E. L. Jones and Douglass North and Robert Paul Thomas thus conceive of the economic "rise of the West" as largely a story of rigidification in a particular (thick) vein of political affairs and the increasing predictability of outcomes that this permitted: the creation of credible bounds of likely behavior toward property, income, and contracts. This increase in predictability was not only painfully gradual, nonuniform, and nonlinear, but also complex in nature. Property "rights" long existed on paper but were enforced so unenthusiastically, inexpertly, or unevenly as to inspire massive discounting of their credibility. Individual monarchs and then dynasties and entire political systems had to develop reputations for not expropriating property in ordinary times, not suddenly levying confiscatory taxes, not debasing currencies, and not repudiating public debts.[4] The emergence of consolidated democracies in the same region is a parallel story of the decidedly gradual, nonuniform, and nonlinear emergence of credible bounds confining likely political behavior in democracy, which in this region and in the twentieth century meant boundaries confining left/right contestation. Why exactly this bounding occurred remains unclear, and this study remains agnostic on the question. But an examination of the cases makes it difficult not to conclude that it was related to profound changes in the structures of socioeconomic conflict. This is not a coded allusion to modernization, since lowered levels of conflict over core conservative interests such as property can be found in rural France during the Third Republic and northern Spain between the two wars. Nor can the issue be reduced simply to property ownership, given the profound advanced industrial changes in income sources and the economic life experiences that did not so much erode traditional property structures as render them less politically salient.

Regardless of its origins, however, the "containment" of left/right conflict meant that conservatives associated inclusion and democracy with much lower risks than ever before in history. Guillermo O'Donnell, arriving at this issue along a very different pathway, has argued that a crucial precondition for democracy in the "originating countries" was the long-term accretion of interwoven rights that ensured that "governments were already constrained" and hence that inclusion "was not a jump in the void" but rather "a tempered wager." In newer democracies, in contrast, "[t]he privileged . . . saw the extension of the wager as extremely threatening."[5] O'Donnell's analysis and the one developed here can usefully be understood to converge on two points. First, democracy's prospects are improved when it "institutionalizes uncertainty" only in a technical and *not* in a sub-

---

4. Jones (1981), North and Thomas (1973).
5. O'Donnell (in press: 51–54).

stantive sense—that is, when the right calculates that many threatening political outcomes can be ruled as highly implausible in democracy, regardless of the uncertainty that inevitably governs exactly which party or coalition will win a given election. Second, the emergence of this state of affairs in Europe is the result of long and not shallow or easily replicable processes, a matter to which I return later. However, the two analyses differ in that O'Donnell's focus on interregional differences submerges intra-European contrasts; in this study I bring the latter into high relief. This is not only to better understand modern European political development but also to build confidence in our focus on declining risks in democracy. Contrasts between cases such as Britain, France, and Germany, or between Spanish cases separated by time, are what enable us to conclude confidently that it is variations in conservatives' perceived risks in democracy that correspond most closely to variations in the right's orientations toward democracy, rather than zeitgeists, levels of wealth, or national or regional political cultures.

The Future of Advanced Industrial Democracies

Contrasts within Western Europe are not always present: convergence in predictability has led to convergence in consolidation since the 1970s. Must this convergence continue? Commentators in the past century have generated at least three major images of the likely trajectory of modern democracy: pessimistic, cyclical, and optimistic. I will address pessimistic and cyclical notions first. Traditionally, pessimism about democracy's prospects often stemmed from convictions that democracy is a degenerate form of government; more common recent versions have focused on specific new lines of sociopolitical conflict poised to undermine democracy, such as the "overload" theories of the 1970s.[6] Cyclical theories sometimes have departed from the assumption that forms of governance, like organic entities, inevitably mature and die. Perhaps more common recently, if generally unspoken, are images of a "cycle of regime rise and decline," suited to a postutopian era in which no good time is expected to last forever.[7] Insofar as cycles involve downturns, this image also suggests that contemporary consolidated democracies eventually will be confined parenthetically within other, also cycling, eras of authoritarianism.

The theory of democratic commitment I developed here remains agnostic as to what exactly caused macroshifts in the levels of political pre-

6. For example, Huntington (1974).
7. Gunther, Diamandouros, and Puhle (1995: xi).

dictability in democracy, and focuses on the consequences of such shifts. But it nonetheless constitutes a valuable starting point for a discussion about the durability of currently consolidated democracies, based on its argument about the "constant causes" that have consistently renewed the right's contemporary democratic commitment. Specifically, the theory provides no basis for predicting that currently consolidated democracies must end, ever. The theory argues that key shifts in political contexts, shifts that cause sharp variations in the political risks actors detect in democracy, in turn have profound consequences for those actors' strategies toward democracy. The theory therefore can help to lead us back along the causal chain to a point where we can predict that commitments to democracy will remain intact unless a contextual shift occurs, of that kind and on that scale. The erosion of the right's commitment to democracy would be predicted only by a theory which generates the underlying prediction that the right is going to perceive political spectra as highly susceptible to (re)polarization. It is unclear what exactly causes national political spectra to remain and appear reliably compact. But by the same standard, existing theorizing offers no specific reason to believe that repolarization is either occurring or inevitable. Religious/secular and urban/rural disputes have largely disappeared in Western Europe. Predictions of new or revived lines of polarization have been repeatedly frustrated by events. For example, acute new conflict dimensions have not yet accompanied the transformation from industrial to postindustrial societies. At least so far, the material/postmaterial cleavage has failed to assume substantially conflictual forms. For several possible reasons, the economic insecurity associated with globalization and welfare-state retrenchment, if anything, has to date, coincided with further left/right convergence. There is no guarantee that these or other lines of dispute will not become more acute. But compactness has proved resilient for several decades.

Possibilities for Deconsolidation

By the same standard, however, the theory developed here offers no strong grounds for concluding that democracy is inherently self-perpetuating. At least in that sense it does not validate Enlightenment notions of democracy's inevitability and hence irreversibility, or other teleological sentiments of the kind that O'Donnell identifies in prominent existing theorizing about consolidation.[8] Given the high incidence of regime changes, schol-

---

8. O'Donnell (1996).

ars have rarely argued explicitly that regimes are path-dependent, but it is often suggested that democracy becomes habitual or otherwise self-perpetuating after a certain amount of time (which Robert Dahl suggests may be twenty years).[9] Moreover, Juan Linz and Alfred Stepan, among others, have argued that because of ontological differences in the nature of support for democracy and authoritarianism, support for the latter tends to degenerate whether authoritarian regimes "succeed" or "fail," whereas support for democracies can withstand either outcome.[10] This claim anticipates a teleology toward ever-more common democracy. It thus runs the risk of leaving support for authoritarianism theoretically underdetermined, and shares the turn-of-the-twentieth-century optimism about democracy's prospects that was apparent during the high point of Samuel Huntington's first democratization wave. Of course, that wave was followed by a great flourishing of both new and familiar forms of exclusionary rule in interwar Western Europe, Eastern Europe, East Asia, and the Middle East; both interwar and post-1945 Latin America; and postcolonial Africa. This record recommends caution in assuming that the Third Wave is relegating authoritarianism to backwaters before rendering it obsolete.

The theory developed here permits us to identify the general conditions that would lead to the erosion of commitment to democracy. Because commitment to democracy is a response to ongoing events—because its causes are constant—renewal in these causes is required to maintain commitment. We can make explicit the counterfactual claim underlying this analysis of contemporary Europe. If in cases that we considered consolidated here, the right had instead perceived political spectra as prone to polarization, the right would have hedged and not committed to democracy; these regimes would not have consolidated after all. The perception of high risks in these democracies in the future would lead to the same outcome. This scenario is not merely hypothetical. Interwar France joins Chile and Uruguay as a crucial cautionary tale in this regard. In Chapter 6 I argued that the bulk of French conservatives committed to democracy beginning in the 1880s and remained committed roughly until the First World War, when class-based polarization and rising political risks in democracy led them to begin hedging a reversal in their own regime preferences, as a result of rising possibilities of highly threatening outcomes in democracy. Happily, this is the only example of deconsolidation examined here (the analysis concluded that France in 1958 and Italy in the 1990s were *not* cases of deconsolidation, as should be expected given the fact that neither

9. Rustow (1970), Dahl (1989: 315).
10. Linz and Stepan (1996: 77–81).

involved the high risks in democracy that erode commitment to democracy).[11]

However, while I argued in the preceding section that there is no theoretical reason to believe that polarization and its attendant high risks are inevitable after decades of left/right compactness, there are also no grounds for concluding that dramatically increased political risks are impossible. Although several predicted acute political conflicts have not materialized, advanced industrial countries potentially contain multiple bases for polarization. As in interwar France, class is one basis, including as the concept of class may be redefined in the course of contemporary capitalism's diverse transformations. As a thought experiment—the point of which is not prediction—it is also worth considering the religious/secular divide in contemporary United States. Although no specific current trend suggests such an extrapolation would be valid, *if* we extrapolate over the next twenty-five years both the past quarter-century's growth of Christian conservative subcultures and the articulation and elaboration of secular critiques of politicized evangelicalism, a striking situation would emerge. In it, one political camp would aim to substantially reorganize public as well as private educational content; reproductive policies; tax codes; marriage and divorce laws; enforced standards of decency in publishing, broadcasting, and public behavior; possibly gender roles; and numerous other aspects of both public and private daily life. The other camp would vigorously oppose all these changes. Perceived threats would become acute if each side was large enough to compete for single-party control of national legislative and executive power. Each would presumably insist that the other side's position on these issues was intrusive, even invasive, and that its own core values should not have to be submitted to the other's political control. A defense of core interests and values on such terms constitutes the antidemocratic choice, however reluctantly and regretfully it may be arrived at. No current trend in currently consolidated democracies suggests either this or another comparable rise in risks in democracy. But the constancy of the cause of democratic commitment not only means that democratic consolidation did not have to emerge where it did—as it has not emerged elsewhere—but also means it does not have to endure.

11. Linz (1978: 87) considers 1958 "a violation of the condition of regime continuity." Gunther, Diamandouros, and Puhle (1995: 15, 394) suggest that "the regime" deconsolidated in Italy in the early 1990s. But the latter acknowledge that "widespread support for democracy in Italy remained unshaken." Evidence strongly suggests the same is true of France in 1958. While both cases involved a crisis of specific decision rules (and/or parties) *within* a democratic regime, in neither case were the defining characteristics of democracy violated, since democracy cannot be reduced to historically specific institutional formulas or written constitutions. In my understanding, neither involved deconsolidation.

Prospects for Consolidation in Later Third Wave Democracies

As Huntington suggests, a theory of consolidation in Europe "could yield lessons for the third wave."[12] In Chapter 3 I argued that a wide range of events can inspire rightists to find democracy provisionally preferable to any specific authoritarian alternative. For example, the right may be temporarily deprived of coercive means, perhaps by international sanctions or credible threats of intervention, as in Haiti in 1994. Or rightists may expect to shape policies by holding office, or while out of office may be protected by assurances, explicit or implicit. But in all these cases, rightists who perceive radicalization of the left as distinctly possible have incentives to hedge against that risk and the associated possibility of a reversal in their own regime preferences. Movements and governments of the left that are aware of such hedging, in response, may engage in the self-censorship and agenda limitation that O'Donnell and Philippe Schmitter identify with uncertain democracies.[13] Commitment and consolidation in these cases occur only when conservatives conclude that politically relevant movements of the left, even ones with populist or radical histories, have become reliably unthreatening. At one level, this might appear an optimistic "lesson": consolidation in Latin America and other regions does not depend on cultural and economic developments that seem either out of reach or undesirable for reasons quite apart from sour grapes. On the other hand, the theory also suggests that even a systematic effort by prodemocratic international actors, pact-makers, and institutional (re)designers has the vice of its virtues: actors know that what can be done in the short term can often be undone in a similar time frame. These devices can contribute to *provisional* support for democracy, which is no small achievement. But *commitment* to democracy requires much greater political predictability than they can supply. My knowledge of cases outside Europe precludes addressing here the question of how distant that standard might be in specific cases or even entire regions. But it may be useful to return to economic predictability as a point of comparison.

James Mahon concludes that even after Latin American governments took extensive steps beginning in the 1980s "to convince investors that . . . liberal rules are solidly in place," hedged investment portfolios reflected investors' enduring skepticism that these policies would prove politically sustainable, and lenders remained aloof.[14] Parallel skepticism may prevent

12. Huntington (1991: 270).
13. O'Donnell and Schmitter (1986: 23, 41).
14. Mahon (1996: 162–63, 166), Maxfield (1997: 35–36).

the right's commitment to democracy for the foreseeable future. Such skepticism is suggested by Ernest Bartell's data showing that Chilean business leaders in 1987–88, even those who expected political outcomes in Chile's then-prospective democracy to be relatively favorable in the short term, continued to associate the left with striking degrees of unpredictability. Bartell concludes that their stated "concern during a period of market-led economic improvement about something as fundamental as property rights, in retrospect, indicates the degree of uncertainty with which even relative optimists faced the transition to democracy."[15] While conservatives' perceived risks in Chile may well have declined in the succeeding decade, Venezuela, Colombia, Peru, and Ecuador have generated events likely to maintain high perceived risks, including occasional land invasions, widespread sympathy for episodic rebellions, and discernible support for populist political rhetoric and redistributory agendas. These leave the impression that neoliberal or orthodox economic policies are the result more of international constraints than deep-running domestic policy preferences.[16] In such contexts, the right's perceived risks may remain high despite years of flamboyantly moderate conduct by left leaders. In the face of the possibility of a reradicalization of the left, the right has incentives to continue to value what O'Donnell terms its "unreliable, but indispensable, military guardians." Timothy Sisk records comparable fears among whites in transitional South Africa.[17]

In yet other regions, political spectra may be expanding rather than contracting, further diminishing already limited conditions propitious for the emergence of commitment to democracy. For example, the rise of Islamist movements in the Middle East and North Africa since the 1980s may be serving as the functional equivalent of the rise of socialism in Europe during the late eighteenth and early nineteenth centuries. The organizational elaboration of these Islamist movements may raise the costs of excluding them from political decision-making but simultaneously raise the risks that traditional elites and secular allies associate with democratization. The result may be not inclusion but unprecedented mobilization aimed at enforcing exclusion; Algeria would be the terrible paradigmatic case. Of course, here, as in Europe, polarization only has narrow (if important) determinative effects. It destroys the basis for *committed* democratic support but leaves actors capable of crafting provisional support, including through such devices as credible pacts, protective institutional designs, and power-sharing agreements. In Jordan, Morocco, and perhaps the Gulf

---

15. Bartell (1995: 64).
16. Haggard and Kaufman (1992).
17. O'Donnell (1992b: 47), Sisk (1995).

states, monarchy may yet be used as post-1945 Italian monarchists intended, as a type of hedge against risks in democracy.[18] For the moment, most regimes in the region are far from being quasi-democratic even in this way. The absence of sustained democratization in this region and enduring democratic uncertainty in several other regions accentuates both Western Europe's relative distinctiveness and our need to closely examine the long-term processes that undergird contemporary events.

18. Anderson (1991).

Appendix: Interviews on the Spanish Right's Beliefs in the 1970s and 1980s

In Chapter 5 I presented evidence from interviews with two types of actors: seventeen leaders of the 1976–77 transition project and a sample of fifty generally conservative small-business owners. The interviews were designed to establish what had been the interviewees' assessments of likely political outcomes under alternative regimes in the mid-1970s and, in the case of the business owners, through the mid-1980s as well. Transition leaders were initially approached by a letter from the Fulbright Commission in Madrid. Each letter was followed up by a telephone call. A majority of these requests resulted in interviews; Adolfo Suárez declined and Marcelino Oreja was unavailable. The initial (pretest) group of small-business owners was selected through business associations representing different retail sectors. Selected owners were approached in their places of business. Of the full sample, somewhat less than half agreed to be interviewed.[1] All business owners were guaranteed anonymity. Leaders also were offered anonymity, but only one wished to remain anonymous. Almost half of the interviews with the leaders were conducted in their homes, especially for those who were in semi- or full-retirement. Most interviews with the business owners were conducted in back rooms at their place of business. The interview sessions with the small-business owners lasted between 1½ and 2¾ hours; those with the transition leaders ranged from 50 minutes to 3½ hours (the last of these was with Calvo-Sotelo and was spread over three sessions).

---

1. Most who declined cited a lack of time; several cited an aversion to discussing controversial subjects, particularly relating to the pre-1977 period.

Challenges arose from the fact that the interviews were conducted twenty years after the events in question. The formats were designed to address involuntary revision of memories and also willful revision to bring stated prior beliefs into line with current political orthodoxies. First, the interview session with each transition leader was designed to evoke the environment in which the leader's past private beliefs were formed and held, and therefore began with an account of family background, formal education, and career up to the mid-1970s, arriving only gradually at explicit discussion of regime-related beliefs beginning in the 1970s.[2] Second, at least every other (and in many cases, every) question was accompanied by a reminder that each question's intention was to establish the interviewees' perceptions at the time, not their judgment since the mid-1970s. There is reason to believe that these devices helped reduce involuntary revision. Above all, many of the interviewees specifically contrasted the perceptions or beliefs they held at the time with opinions of the same events they have formed since.

Transition leaders who were politically active at the time of the interviews (Martín Villa was a member of parliament, for example) might have been the most likely to engage in voluntary revision of stated past beliefs. Interviewees therefore were asked to discuss a number of their past predictions about likely outcomes in a then-prospective democracy. In particular, transition leaders were asked about their past expectations of the likely electoral appeal of Fraga's Alianza Popular (AP) in 1977, a topic on which they were relatively likely to have made an inaccurate prediction at the time.[3] A majority acknowledged surprise at the time at the poor showing of the AP. This and other examples of willingness to admit error in past predictions suggest the credibility of their claim to have more accurately predicted, for example, the PCE's electoral weakness in the same election.

Interview sessions varied somewhat in structure, but each addressed each of the following topics:

- Personal experience with arrest, surveillance, and other forms of repression under Franco
- Assessment of economic and other salient policies under Franco

---

2. Michael Mann, at the time visiting the Fundación Juan March, recommended this strategy, which necessarily extended the length of each interview but leaves the impression of having notably influenced the quality and reliability of responses. Interviewees often expressed pleasure at discussing events they had not thought about for years.

3. Many conservatives and scholars assumed in the mid-1970s that a staunchly conservative party would attract a substantial vote by drawing on what was termed *franquismo sociológico*. In fact, the AP won less than 10 percent of the vote in June 1977.

- The likelihood that Juan Carlos would succeed Franco as head of state and broadly continue his policies and strategy of repression
- Estimation of the opposition's mobilizational capabilities in the early to mid-1970s
- Estimation of the military's discipline, willingness to support an authoritarian project after Franco, and ability to maintain power
- The prospects for private property in a new democracy
- The likelihood that significant civil violence (*conflictos sociales*) would appear in a new democracy
- The types of parties likely to attract the most votes
- Expected likely leaders of the government in a new democracy
- What groups were understood to have provided the social basis for "radical left" politics in Spain's past.

In addition, leaders were asked questions concerning the willingness of colleagues to serve a neo-Francoist project, the influence of Portugal on their decisions, and the influence of European Common Market sanctions versus entry. Business owners also were asked about a series of topics regarding events after 1976:

- The degree of radicalism of the PSOE from the transition to the early 1980s
- The likelihood that the PSOE would win the 1982 elections and the degree of concern this had caused them
- The likelihood that PSOE governments would generate challenges to property, confiscatory taxes, or tolerance of class-based violence
- The likely leaders and policies of any authoritarian regime after 1977
- The likelihood that authoritarian leaders after 1977 could solve a series of named problems
- The desirability and feasibility of the 1981 coup.

References

Abraham, David. 1986. *The Collapse of the Weimar Republic.* 2d ed. New York: Holmes and Meier.

Adams, John Clarke. 1952. "Italy." In *Comparative Labor Movements*, edited by Walter Galenson. New York: Prentice-Hall.

Adenauer, Konrad. 1966. *Memoirs, 1945–53.* Chicago: Henry Regnery.

Adler, Franklin Hugh. 1995. *Italian Industrialists from Liberalism to Fascism.* Cambridge: Cambridge University Press.

Agüero, Felipe. 1995. *Soldiers, Civilians, and Democracy: Post-Franco Spain in Comparative Perspective.* Baltimore: Johns Hopkins University Press.

Aguilar Fernández, Paloma. 1996. *Memoria y olvido de la Guerra Civil Española.* Madrid: Alianza Editorial.

Albi Ibáñez, Emilio, ed. 1990. *La hacienda pública en la democracia.* Barcelona: Ariel.

Alexander, Gerard. 2001. "Institutions, Path Dependence, and Democratic Consolidation." *Journal of Theoretical Politics* 13: 249–70.

Almond, Gabriel. 1956. "Comparative Political Systems." *Journal of Politics* 18: 391–409.

Almond, Gabriel, and Sidney Verba. 1963. *The Civic Culture.* Princeton: Princeton University Press.

Álvarez, Juan. 1936. *Las Guerras Civiles Argentinas y el problema de Buenos Aires en la república.* Buenos Aires: Editorial "La Facultad."

Ambler, John Stewart. 1966. *The French Army in Politics, 1945–1962.* Columbus: Ohio State University Press.

Amery, Leo. 1988. *The Empire at Bay: The Leo Amery Diaries, 1929–1945*, edited by John Barnes. London: Hutchinson.

Anderson, Charles W. 1970. *The Political Economy of Modern Spain.* Madison: University of Wisconsin Press.

Anderson, Lisa. 1991. "Absolutism and the Resilience of Monarchy in the Middle East." *Political Science Quarterly* 106: 1–15.

Araquistain, Luis. 1934. "The Struggle in Spain." *Foreign Affairs* 12: 458–71.

Aron, Raymond. 1948. *Le grand schisme.* Paris: Gallimard.

Ash, Bernard. 1968. *The Lost Dictator: A Biography of Field-Marshal Sir Henry Wilson.* London: Cassell.

Avilés Farré, Juan. 1976. "La derecha republicana, 1930–1936." *Revista de estudios sociales* 16: 77–117.

Bain, George Sayers, and Robert Price. 1980. *Profiles of Union Growth: A Comparative Statistical Portrait of Eight Countries.* Oxford: Basil Blackwell.

Balcells, Albert. 1968. *El problema agrari a Catalunya, 1890–1936: La qüestió rabassaire.* Barcelona: Editorial Nova Terra.

Balfour, Earl. 1933. "Introduction." In *The English Constitution,* by Walter Bagehot. Oxford: Oxford University Press.

Baloyra, Enrique. 1988. "Public Opinion about Military Coups and Democratic Consolidation in Venezuela." In *Democracy in Latin America: Colombia and Venezuela,* edited by Donald Herman. New York: Praeger.

Barker, Ernest, ed. 1946. *The Politics of Aristotle.* London: Oxford University Press.

Bartell, Ernest. 1995. "Perceptions by Business Leaders and the Transition to Democracy in Chile." In *Business and Democracy in Latin America,* edited by E. Bartell and Leigh Payne. Pittsburgh: University of Pittsburgh Press.

Barthélemy, Joseph. 1931. *La crise de la démocratie contemporaine.* Paris: Recueil Sirey.

———. 1935. *Valeur de la liberté et adaptation de la république.* Paris: Recueil Sirey.

Bartolini, Stefano, and Peter Mair. 1990. *Identity, Competition, and Electoral Availability: The Stabilisation of European Electorates, 1885–1985.* Cambridge: Cambridge University Press.

Bassols Coma, Martin. 1981. *La jurisprudencia del tribunal de garantías constitucionales de la II República Española.* Madrid: Centro de Estudios Constitucionales.

Bates, Robert, Avner Greif, Margaret Levi, Jean-Laurent Rosenthal, and Barry Weingast. 1998. *Analytic Narratives.* Princeton: Princeton University Press.

Beer, Samuel. 1982. *Britain against Itself.* New York: W. W. Norton.

Behan, Tom. 1997. *The Long Awaited Moment: The Working Class and the Italian Communist Party in Milan, 1943–1948.* New York: Peter Lang.

Bell, Daniel. 1973. *The Coming of Post-Industrial Society.* New York: Basic.

Ben-Ami, Shlomo. 1978. *The Origins of the Second Republic in Spain.* Oxford: Oxford University Press.

Benavides, Domingo. 1973. *El fracaso social del Catolicismo Español.* Barcelona: Editorial Nova Terra.

Bentley, Michael. 1977. *The Liberal Mind, 1914–1929.* Cambridge: Cambridge University Press.

Berl, Emmanuel. 1938. *Frère bourgeois: Mourez-vous? Ding! Ding! Dong!* Paris: Bernard Grasset.

Berman, Sheri. 1998. *The Social Democratic Moment: Ideas and Politics in the Making of Interwar Europe.* Cambridge: Cambridge University Press.

Bermeo, Nancy. 1986. *The Revolution within the Revolution: Workers' Control in Rural Portugal.* Princeton: Princeton University Press.

———. 1992. "Democracy and the Lessons of Dictatorship." *Comparative Politics* 24: 273–91.

Bermeo, Nancy, with José García-Durán. 1994. "Spain: Dual Transition Implemented by Two Parties." In *Voting for Reform,* edited by Stephan Haggard and Steve Webb. Oxford: Oxford University Press.

Bernstein, Peter L. 1996. *Against the Gods: The Remarkable Story of Risk*. New York: Wiley.

Berstein, Serge. 1980–82. *Histoire du parti Radical*. Paris: Presses de la Fondation National des Sciences Politiques.

Bessel, Richard. 1984. *Political Violence and the Rise of Nazism: The Storm Troopers in Eastern Germany, 1925–1934*. New Haven: Yale University Press.

Blackbourn, David, and Geoff Eley. 1984. *The Peculiarities of German History*. Oxford: Oxford University Press.

Blackmer, Donald L. M. 1975. "Continuity and Change in Postwar Italian Communism." In *Communism in Italy and France*, edited by Donald L. M. Blackmer and Sidney Tarrow. Princeton: Princeton University Press.

Blinkhorn, Martin. 1975. *Carlism and Crisis in Spain*. Cambridge: Cambridge University Press.

Boix, Carles. 1998. *Political Parties, Growth and Equality*. Cambridge: Cambridge University Press.

Bomier-Landowski, Alain. 1951. "Les groupes parlementaires de l'assemblée nationale et de la chambre des députés de 1871 à 1940." In *Sociologie electorale*, edited by François Goguel and Georges Dupeux. Paris: Armand Colin.

Boron, Atilio. 1992. "Becoming Democrats? Some Skeptical Considerations on the Right in Latin America." In *The Right and Democracy in Latin America*, edited by Douglas Chalmers, Maria do Carmo Campello de Souza, and Atilio Boron. New York: Praeger.

Boynton, G. R., and Gerhard Loewenberg. 1974. "The Decay of Support for Monarchy and the Hitler Regime in the Federal Republic of Germany." *British Journal of Political Science* 4: 453–88.

Brabant, Frank. 1940. *The Beginning of the Third Republic in France*. London: Macmillan.

Bravo Martínez, Francisco. 1940. *Historia de Falange Española de la J.O.N.S.* Madrid: Editora Nacional.

Bridgeman, William. 1988. *The Modernisation of Conservative Politics: The Diaries and Letters of William Bridgeman, 1904–1935*, edited by Philip Williamson. London: Historians' Press.

Brivati, Brian. 1996. *Hugh Gaitskell*. London: Richard Cohen.

Brustein, William. 1996. *The Logic of Evil: The Social Origins of the Nazi Party, 1925–1933*. New Haven: Yale University Press.

Bryce, James. 1921. *Modern Democracies*. New York: Macmillan.

Buchanan, James M., and Gordon Tullock. 1962. *The Calculus of Consent*. Ann Arbor: University of Michigan Press.

Bueno de Mesquita, Bruce. 1996. "Counterfactuals and International Affairs." In *Counterfactual Thought Experiments in World Politics*, edited by Philip E. Tetlock and Aaron Belkin. Princeton: Princeton University Press.

Bunn, Ronald F. 1958. "Codetermination and the Federation of German Employers' Associations." *Midwest Journal of Political Science* 11: 278–97.

Burnham, Walter Dean. 1972. "Political Immunization and Political Confessionalism: The United States and Weimar Germany." *Journal of Interdisciplinary History* 3: 1–30.

Cabrera, Mercedes. 1983. *La patronal ante la II República*. Madrid: Siglo XXI.

Calero, Antonio M. 1976. *Movimientos sociales en Andalucía (1820–1936)*. Madrid: Siglo XXI.

Callaghy, Thomas. 1988. "The State and the Development of Capitalism in Africa: Theoretical, Historical, and Comparative Reflections." In *The Precarious Balance:*

State and Society in Africa, edited by Donald Rothchild and Naomi Chazan. Boulder: Westview.

Cambó, Francesc. 1925. *El torno del fascismo Italiano*. Barcelona: Editorial Catalana.

———. 1982. *Meditacions: Dietari (1936–1946)*. Barcelona: Editorial Alpha.

Caparrós, Francisco. 1983. *La UMD: Militares rebeldes*. Barcelona: Editorial Argus Vergara.

Capo Giol, J., R. Cotarelo, D. Lopez Garrido, and J. Subirats. 1990. "By Consociationalism to a Majoritarian Party System: The Rise and Decline of the Spanish Cortes." In *Parliament and Democratic Consolidation in Southern Europe*, edited by Ulrike Liebert and Maurizio Cotta. London: Pinter.

Cardoso, Fernando Henrique. 1979. "On the Characterization of Authoritarian Regimes in Latin America." In *The New Authoritarianism in Latin America*, edited by David Collier. Princeton: Princeton University Press.

Cardoza, Anthony. 1982. *Agrarian Elites and Italian Fascism: The Province of Bologna, 1901–1926*. Princeton: Princeton University Press.

Carr, Raymond. 1980. *Modern Spain, 1875–1980*. Oxford: Oxford University Press.

———. 1982. *Spain, 1808–1975*. 2d ed. Oxford: Clarendon.

Carr, Raymond, and Juan Pablo Fusi. 1979. *Spain: Dictatorship to Democracy*. London: George Allen and Unwin.

Carreras, Francesc de. 1983. "Los intentos de reforma electoral durante la Segunda República." *Revista de estudios políticos* (nueva época) 31–32: 165–97.

Carrillo, Santiago. 1983. *Memorias de la transición*. Barcelona: Ediciones Grijalbo.

Carsten, F. L. 1966. *The Reichswehr and Politics: 1918 to 1933*. Oxford: Clarendon.

Casanova, José. 1983. "Modernization and Democratization: Reflections on Spain's Transition to Democracy." *Social Research* 50: 929–73.

Castillo, Juan José. 1979. *Propietarios muy pobres: Sobre la subordinación política del pequeño campesino en España (La Confederación Nacional Católico-Agraria, 1917–1942)*. Madrid: Ministerio de Agricultura/Servicio de Publicaciones Agrarias.

CEDA. 1933. "Hombres nuevos y política nueva." N.p.: CEDA.

Centro de Investigaciones Sociológicas (CIS). 1977. *La reforma política/La ideología política de los Españoles*. Madrid: CIS.

Chamberlain, Austen. 1995. *The Austen Chamberlain Diary Letters*, edited by Robert Self. Cambridge: Cambridge University Press.

Chapman, Guy. 1962. *The Third Republic of France: The First Phase, 1871–1894*. London: St. Martin's.

Chastenet, Jacques. 1952. *L'enfance de la troisième, 1870–1879*. Paris: Hachette.

Cheibub, José Antonio. 1998. "Political Regimes and the Extractive Capacity of Governments." *World Politics* 50: 349–76.

Chevalier, Louis. 1958. *Classes laborieuses et classes dangereuses à Paris pendant la première moitié du XIXe siècle*. Paris: Plon.

Childers, Thomas. 1983. *The Nazi Voter*. Chapel Hill: University of North Carolina Press.

Christophe, Paul. 1979. *1936: Les Catholiques et le Front Populaire*. Paris: Desclée.

Ciconte, Enzo. 1981. *All'asalto delle terre del latifondo*. Milan: F. Angeli.

Cierva, Ricardo de la. 1969. *Historia de la Guerra Civil Española: Perspectivas y antecedentes, 1898–1936*. Madrid: Editorial San Martín.

———. 1978. *Historia del Franquismo: Aislamiento, transformación, agonía (1945–1975)*. Barcelona: Planeta.

Cinanni, Paolo. 1979. *Lotte per la terre nel mezzogiorno, 1943–1953*. Venezia: Marsilio.

Clark, Martin. 1977. *Antonio Gramsci and the Revolution That Failed*. New Haven: Yale University Press.

Cohen, Youssef. 1985. "The Impact of Bureaucratic-Authoritarian Rule on Economic Growth." *Comparative Political Studies* 18: 123–36.

———. 1994. *Radicals, Reformers, and Reactionaries: The Prisoner's Dilemma and the Collapse of Democracy in Latin America*. Chicago: University of Chicago Press.

Colarizi, Simona. 1984. *La Seconda Guerra Mondiale e la repubblica*. Milan: TEA.

Coleman, James. 1990. *The Foundations of Social Theory*. Cambridge: Harvard University Press.

Collier, David, and Deborah Norden. 1992. "Strategic Choice Models of Political Change in Latin America." *Comparative Politics* 24: 229–43.

Collier, David, and Steven Levitsky. 1997. "Democracy with Adjectives." *World Politics* 49: 430–51.

Collier, Ruth. 1999. *Paths Toward Democracy*. Cambridge: Cambridge University Press.

Colomer, Josep. 1995. *Game Theory and the Transition to Democracy: The Spanish Model*. Brookfield, Vt.: Edward Elgar.

Comfort, Richard. 1966. *Revolutionary Hamburg*. Stanford: Stanford University Press.

Confederación National de Trabajo. 1978. *El Congreso Confederal de Zaragoza*. Madrid: Zero.

Contreras, Manuel. 1981. *El PSOE en la II República: Organización e ideología*. Madrid: Centro de Investigaciones Sociológicas.

Cooper, Duff. 1954. *Old Men Forget*. New York: E. O. Dutton.

Corner, Paul. 1975. *Fascism in Ferrara*. Oxford: Oxford University Press.

Cotta, Maurizio. 1990. "The 'Centrality' of Parliament in a Protracted Democratic Consolidation: The Italian Case." In *Parliament and Democratic Consolidation in Southern Europe*, edited by Ulrike Liebert and Maurizio Cotta. London: Pinter.

Coverdale, John. 1982. "Inflation and Democratic Transition in Spain." In *The Politics of Inflation*, edited by Richard Medley. New York: Pergamon.

Cowles, Virginia. 1953. *Winston Churchill*. New York: Harper and Brothers.

Cowling, Maurice. 1971. *The Impact of Labour: 1920–1924*. Cambridge: Cambridge University Press.

Cruz, Rafael. 1987. *El Partido Comunista de España en la Segunda República*. Madrid: Alianza Editorial.

Cucó Giner, A. 1970. "Contribución a un estudio cuantitativo de la C.N.T." *Saitabi* 20: 181–202.

Dahl, Robert. 1956. *A Preface to Democratic Theory*. Chicago: University of Chicago Press.

———. 1971. *Polyarchy*. New Haven: Yale University Press.

———. 1989. *Democracy and Its Critics*. New Haven: Yale University Press.

Dahl, Robert, and Charles E. Lindblom. 1953. *Politics, Economics, and Welfare*. New York: Harper and Row.

Dahrendorf, Ralf. 1967. *Society and Democracy in Germany*. Westport, Conn.: Greenwood.

Dawes, Robyn. 1988. *Rational Choice in an Uncertain World*. New York: Harcourt Brace Jovanovich.

Debré, Michel. 1952. *La république et ses problèmes*. Paris: Nagel.

De Felice, Renzo. 1966. *Mussolini il fascista: La conquista del potere, 1921–1925*. Turin: Einaudi.

De Miguel, Amando. 1976. "Spanish Political Attitudes, 1970." In *Politics and Society in Twentieth-Century Spain*, edited by Stanley Payne. New York: Franklin Watts.

De Nicola, Enrico. 1924. *Discorso elettorale (Aprile 1924)*. Rome: Camera dei Diputati.

De Rosa, Gabriele. 1957. *Giolitti e il fascismo: In alcune sue lettere inedite*. Rome: Edizioni di Storia e Letteratura.

———. 1988. *Il Partito Popolare Italiano*. Bari: Laterza.

Diamond, Larry. 1992. "Economic Development and Democracy Reconsidered." *American Behavioral Scientist* 35: 450–99.

Diehl, James. 1977. *Paramilitary Politics in Weimar Germany*. Bloomington: Indiana University Press.

Di Loreto, Pietro. 1991. *Togliatti e la "doppiezza": Il PCI tra democrazia e insurrezione, 1944–49*. Bologna: Il Mulino.

Di Palma, Giuseppe. 1990. *To Craft Democracies*. Berkeley: University of California Press.

Domarus, Max. 1992. *Hitler: Speeches and Proclamations, 1932–1945: The Years 1935 to 1938*. London: I. B. Tauris.

Downs, Anthony. 1957. *An Economic Theory of Democracy*. New York: Harper and Row.

Drummond, Gordon D. 1982. *The German Social Democrats in Opposition, 1949–1960*. Norman: University of Oklahoma Press.

Duhamel, Olivier. 1980. *La gauche el la Ve République*. Paris: Presses Universitaires de France.

Dumaine, Jacques. 1958. *Quai d'Orsay (1945–1951)*. London: Chapman and Hall.

Eckstein, Harry. 1966/1961. "A Theory of Stable Democracy." Reprinted as Appendix in *Division and Cohesion in Democracy: A Study of Norway*. Princeton: Princeton University Press.

———. 1988. "A Culturalist Theory of Political Change." *American Political Science Review* 82: 789–804.

Ehrmann, Henry W. 1947. *French Labor from Popular Front to Liberation*. New York: Oxford University Press.

———. 1957. *Organized Business in France*. Princeton: Princeton University Press.

Ellwood, Sheelagh. 1987. *Spanish Fascism in the Franco Era*. New York: St. Martin's.

Elster, Jon. 1986. "Introduction." In *Rational Choice*, edited by Jon Elster. New York: New York University Press.

———. 1989. *Nuts and Bolts for the Social Sciences*. Cambridge: Cambridge University Press.

———. 1993. "Constitution-Making in Eastern Europe: Rebuilding the Boat in the Open Sea." *Public Administration* 71: 169–217.

Elwitt, Sanford. 1975. *The Making of the Third Republic: Class and Politics in France, 1868–1884*. Baton Rouge: Louisiana State University Press.

Epstein, Klaus Werner. 1987. *The British Constitutional Crisis, 1909–1911*. New York: Garland.

Erro, Davide G. 1993. *Resolving the Argentine Paradox*. Boulder: Lynne Rienner.

Esping-Andersen, Gösta. 1994. "Budgets and Democracy: Towards a Welfare State in Spain and Portugal." In *Developing Democracy*, edited by Ian Budge and David McKay. London: Sage.

Evans, Richard J. 1987. "Introduction." In *The German Unemployed*, edited by Richard J. Evans and Dick Geary. London: Croom Helm.

Falter, Jürgen W. 1986. "Unemployment and the Radicalisation of the German Electorate, 1928–1933: An Aggregate Data Analysis with Special Emphasis on the Rise of National Socialism." In *Unemployment and the Great Depression in Weimar Germany*, edited by Peter D. Stachura. London: Macmillan.

Farneti, Paolo. 1985. *The Italian Party System*. London: Frances Pinter.

Farrar, Marjorie Milbank. 1991. *Principled Pragmatist: The Political Career of Alexandre Millerand.* New York: Berg.

Fearon, James D. 1991. "Counterfactuals and Hypothesis Testing in Political Science." *World Politics* 43: 169–95.

Ferejohn, John. 1991. "Rationality and Interpretation." In *The Economic Approach to Politics,* edited by Kristin Renwick Monroe. New York: HarperCollins.

Fernández de Castro, Ignacio, and Antonio Goytre. 1974. *Clases sociales en España en el umbral de los años 70.* Madrid: Siglo XXI.

Fernández de la Mora, Gonzalo. 1986. *Los errores del cambio.* Barcelona: Plaza y Janes.

Ferraresi, Franco. 1992. "A Secret Structure Codenamed Gladio." In *Italian Politics: A Review,* edited by Stephen Hellman and Gianfranco Pasquino. London: Pinter.

Fest, Joachim. 1974. *Hitler.* New York: Harcourt Brace Jovanovich.

Fforde, Matthew. 1990. *Conservatism and Collectivism, 1886–1914.* Edinburgh: Edinburgh University Press.

Fichelet, Monique, Raymond Fichelet, Guy Michelat, and Michel Simon. 1969. "L'image du Parti Communiste Français d'après les sondages de l'I.F.O.P." In *Le communisme en France et en Italie.* Paris: Armand Colin.

Fishman, Robert. 1990. *Working-Class Organization and the Return to Democracy in Spain.* Ithaca: Cornell University Press.

Franco Salgado-Araujo, Francisco. 1976. *Mis conversaciones privadas con Franco.* Barcelona: Editorial Planeta.

Fritzsche, Peter. 1990. *Rehearsals for Fascism: Populism and Political Mobilization in Weimar Germany.* New York: Oxford University Press.

Fundación Nacional Francisco Franco. 1987. *"Apuntes" personales del generalísimo sobre la república y la guerra civil.* Madrid: Fundación Nacional Francisco Franco.

Fusi, Juan Pablo. 1982. "Spain: The Fragile Democracy." *West European Politics* 5: 222–35.

Gallo, Max. 1974. *Spain under Franco.* New York: E. P. Dutton.

Gallup, George, ed. 1976a. *The Gallup International Public Opinion Polls: Britain, 1937–1975.* New York: Random House.

———. 1976b. *The Gallup International Public Opinion Polls: France, 1939, 1944–1975.* New York: Random House.

Gambino, Antonio. 1975. *Storia del dopoguerra dalla liberazione al potere DC.* Bari: Laterza.

Garrido González, Luis. 1979. *Colectividades agrarias en Andalucía: Jaén (1931–1939).* Madrid: Siglo XXI.

Garrigues Walker, Antonio. 1976. *Una política para España.* Madrid: Unión Editorial.

George, Margaret. 1965. *The Warped Vision.* Pittsburgh: University of Pittsburgh Press.

Gibson, Edward. 1992. "Conservative Electoral Movements and Democratic Politics." In *The Right and Democracy in Latin America,* edited by Douglas Chalmers, Maria do Carmo Campello de Souza, and Atilio Boron. New York: Praeger.

Gibson, James. 1996. "A Mile Wide But an Inch Deep(?): The Structure of Democratic Commitments in the Former USSR." *American Journal of Political Science* 40: 396–420.

Gignoux, C.-J. 1940. "La France économique et financière." In C.-J. Gignoux, Georges Henri Rivière, Germain Bazin, and Bernard Champigneulle. *La France en guerre.* Paris: Plon.

Gillespie, Richard. 1989a. *The Spanish Socialist Party.* Oxford: Clarendon.

———. 1989b. "Spanish Socialism in the 1980s." In *Southern European Socialism,* edited by Tom Gallagher and Allan Williams. Manchester: Manchester University Press.

Gilmour, David. 1985. *The Transformation of Spain: From Franco to the Constitutional Monarchy.* London: Quartet.

Gilmour, John. 1992. "The Extreme Right in Spain: Blas Piñar and the Spirit of the Nationalist Uprising." In *The Extreme Right in Europe and the USA,* edited by Paul Hainsworth. New York: St. Martin's.

Gil Pecharromán, Julio. 1994. *Conservadores subversivos: La derecha autoritaria Alfonsina (1913–1936).* Madrid: Eudema.

Gil Robles, José María. 1968. *No fue posible la paz.* Barcelona: Ariel.

Ginsborg, Paul. 1990. *A History of Contemporary Italy: Society and Politics, 1943–1988.* London: Penguin.

Goguel, François. 1952. *France under the Fourth Republic.* Ithaca: Cornell University Press.

Goldberg, Arthur S. 1969. "Social Determinism and Rationality as Bases of Party Identification." *American Political Science Review* 63: 5–25.

Goldhagen, Daniel Jonah. 1996. *Hitler's Willing Executioners.* New York: Knopf.

Gordon, Harold J., Jr. 1957. *The Reichswehr and the German Republic, 1919–1926.* Princeton: Princeton University Press.

Graf, William David. 1976. *The German Left since 1945.* Cambridge: Oleander.

Grafstein, Robert. 1991. "Rational Choice: Theory and Institutions." In *The Economic Approach to Politics,* edited by Kristin Renwick Monroe. New York: HarperCollins.

Graham, Bruce D. 1965. *The French Socialists and Tripartisme, 1944–1947.* London: George Weidenfeld and Nicholson.

Gregor, A. James. 1979. *Young Mussolini and the Intellectual Origins of Fascism.* Berkeley: University of California Press.

Green, Donald P., and Ian Shapiro. 1994. *Pathologies of Rational Choice Theory.* New Haven: Yale University Press.

Grubb, Alan. 1996. *The Politics of Pessimism: Albert de Broglie and Conservative Politics in the Early Third Republic.* Newark: University of Delaware Press.

Guidorossi, Giovanna. 1984. *Gli Italiani e la politica.* Milan: Franco Angeli.

Guizot, François. 1974/1849. *Democracy in France.* New York: Howard Fertig.

Gunther, Richard. 1980. *Public Policy in a No-Party State: Spanish Planning and Budgeting in the Twilight of the Francoist Era.* Berkeley: University of California Press.

——. 1985. "Constitutional Change in Contemporary Spain." In *Redesigning the State: The Politics of Constitutional Change,* edited by Keith Banting and Richard Simeon. Toronto: University of Toronto Press.

——. 1989. "Electoral Laws, Party Systems, and Elites: The Case of Spain." *American Political Science Review* 83: 835–58.

Gunther, Richard, and Roger Blough. 1981. "Religious Conflict and Consensus in Spain: A Tale of Two Constitutions." *World Affairs* 143: 366–412.

Gunther, Richard, Giacomo Sani, and Goldie Shabad. 1988. *Spain after Franco: The Making of a Competitive Party System.* Berkeley: University of California Press.

Gunther, Richard, P. Nikiforos Diamandouros, and Hans-Jürgen Puhle, eds. 1995. *The Politics of Democratic Consolidation: Southern Europe in Comparative Perspective.* Baltimore: Johns Hopkins University Press.

Hacking, Ian. 1990. *The Taming of Chance.* Cambridge: Cambridge University Press.

Haffner, Sebastian. 1997. *The Meaning of Hitler.* London: Phoenix.

Haggard, Stephan. 1990. *Pathways from the Periphery.* Ithaca: Cornell University Press.

Haggard, Stephan, and Robert Kaufman. 1992. "Introduction." In *The Politics of Economic Adjustment,* edited by Stephan Haggard and Robert Kaufman. Princeton: Princeton University Press.

Halévy, Daniel. 1930. *La fin des notables.* Paris: Grasset.

Hall, Peter. 1987. "The Evolution of Economic Policy under Mitterand." In *The Mitterand Experiment,* edited by George Ross, Stanley Hoffmann, and Sylvia Malzacher. New York: Oxford University Press.

Hamilton, Richard. 1982. *Who Voted for Hitler?* Princeton: Princeton University Press.

Hardach, Karl. 1980. *The Political Economy of Germany in the Twentieth Century.* Berkeley: University of California Press.

Hardin, Russell. 1982. *Collective Action.* Baltimore: Johns Hopkins University Press.

——. 1995. *One for All: The Logic of Group Conflict.* Princeton: Princeton University Press.

Harsch, Donna. 1993. *German Social Democracy and the Rise of Nazism.* Chapel Hill: University of North Carolina Press.

Hartz, Louis. 1955. *The Liberal Tradition in America.* New York: Harcourt Brace and World.

Headlam, Cuthbert. 1992. *Parliament and Politics in the Age of Baldwin and MacDonald: The Headlam Diaries, 1923–1935,* edited by Stuart Ball. London: Historians' Press.

Heath, Anthony, Roger Jowell, and John Curtice. 1985. *How Britain Votes.* Oxford: Pergamon.

Hechter, Michael. 1987. *Principles of Group Solidarity.* Berkeley: University of California Press.

Hennessy, Peter. 1992. *Never Again.* London: Jonathan Cape.

Herz, John H. 1979. "Social Democracy versus Democratic Socialism: An Analysis of SPD Attempts to Develop a Party Doctrine." In *Eurocommunism and Eurosocialism,* edited by Bernard Brown. New York: Cyrco.

——. ed. 1982. *From Dictatorship to Democracy.* Westport, Conn.: Greenwood.

Herzog, Don. 1998. *Poisoning the Minds of the Lower Orders.* Princeton: Princeton University Press.

Higley, John, and Richard Gunther, eds. 1992. *Elites and Democratic Consolidation in Latin America and Southern Europe.* Cambridge: Cambridge University Press.

Hine, David. 1990. "The Consolidation of Democracy in Post-War Italy." In *Securing Democracy,* edited by Geoffrey Pridham. New York: Routledge.

Hirschman, Albert O. 1977. *The Passions and the Interests.* Princeton: Princeton University Press.

——. 1991. *The Rhetoric of Reaction.* Cambridge: Belknap-Harvard.

Hoffmann, Stanley. 1963. "Paradoxes of the French Political Community." In *In Search of France.* Cambridge: Harvard University Press.

Hopkin, Jonathan. 1999. *Party Formation and Democratic Transition in Spain.* New York: St. Martin's.

Horowitz, Daniel L. 1963. *The Italian Labor Movement.* Cambridge: Harvard University Press.

Huber, John, and Ronald Inglehart. 1995. "Expert Interpretations of Party Space and Party Locations in 42 Societies." *Party Politics* 1: 73–111.

Hughes, Michael. 1988. *Paying for the German Inflation.* Chapel Hill: University of North Carolina Press.

Huneeus, Carlos. 1981. "La transición a la democracia en España." In *La transición a la democracia en el sur de Europa y América Latina*, edited by Julián Santamaría. Madrid: Centro de Investigaciones Sociológicas.

Huntington, Samuel P. 1970. "Social and Institutional Dynamics of One-Party Systems." In *Authoritarian Politics in Modern Society*, edited by Samuel P. Huntington and Clement Moore New York: Basic.

——. 1974. "Postindustrial Politics: How Benign Will It Be?" *Comparative Politics* 4: 163–91.

——. 1991. *The Third Wave*. Norman: University of Oklahoma Press.

Inglehart, Ronald, and Dusan Sidjanski. 1974. "Dimension gauche-droite chez les dirigeants et électeurs Suisses." *Revue Française de science politique* 24: 994–1025.

Irvine, William D. 1979. *French Conservatism in Crisis: The Republican Federation of France in the 1930s*. Baton Rouge: Louisiana State University Press.

——. 1989. *The Boulanger Affair Reconsidered*. New York: Oxford University Press.

——. 1991. "Fascism in France and the Strange Case of the Croix de Feu." *Journal of Modern History* 63: 271–95.

Irwin, William J. 1991. *The 1933 Cortes Elections: Origins of the Bienio Negro*. New York: Garland.

Izquierdo, Antonio. 1981. *Yo, testigo de cargo*. Barcelona: Editorial Planeta.

Jackson, Gabriel. 1965. *The Spanish Republic and the Civil War*. Princeton: Princeton University Press.

Jackson, Julian. 1988. *The Popular Front in France: Defending Democracy, 1934–38*. Cambridge: Cambridge University Press.

James, Harold. 1986. *The German Slump: Politics and Economics, 1924–1936*. Oxford: Clarendon.

Jeanneny, Jean-Noël. 1976. *François de Wendel en république: L'argent et le pouvoir, 1914–1940*. Paris: Seuil.

Jones, E. L. 1981. *The European Miracle*. Cambridge: Cambridge University Press.

Jones, Larry Eugene. 1988. *German Liberalism and the Dissolution of the Weimar Party System, 1918–1933*. Chapel Hill: University of North Carolina Press.

Judt, Tony. 1979. *Socialism in Provence, 1871–1914*. Cambridge: Cambridge University Press.

Juliá, Santos. 1977. *La izquierda del PSOE (1935–1936)*. Madrid: Siglo XXI.

——. 1979. *Orígenes del Frente Popular en España (1934–1936)*. Madrid: Siglo XXI.

——. 1984. *Madrid, 1931–1934: De la fiesta popular a la lucha de clases*. Madrid: Siglo XXI.

——. 1990. "The Ideological Conversion of the Leaders of the PSOE, 1976–1979." In *Elites and Power in Twentieth-Century Spain*, edited by Frances Lannon and Paul Preston. Oxford: Clarendon.

Kalyvas, Stathis. 1996. *The Rise of Christian Democracy in Europe*. Ithaca: Cornell University Press.

Karl, Terry Lynn. 1990. "Dilemmas of Democratization in Latin America." *Comparative Politics* 23: 1–21.

——. 1997. *The Paradox of Plenty*. Berkeley: University of California.

Kelikian, Alice A. 1986. *Town and Country under Fascism: The Transformation of Brescia, 1915–1926*. Oxford: Clarendon.

Kitzinger, Uwe W. 1960. *German Electoral Politics: A Study of the 1957 Campaign*. Oxford: Clarendon.

Knight, Jack. 1992. *Institutions and Social Conflict*. Cambridge: Cambridge University Press.

Koestler, Arthur. 1965. In *The God That Failed*, edited by Richard Crossman. New York: Bantam.

Kogan, Norman. 1966. *A Political History of Postwar Italy*. New York: Praeger.

Kolboom, Ingo. 1986. *La revanche des patrons: Le patronat face au Front Populaire*. Paris: Flammarion.

Koss, Stephen. 1976. *Asquith*. London: Allen Lane.

Krasner, Stephen D. 1984. "Approaches to the State." *Comparative Politics* 16: 223–46.

Lacouture, Jean. 1977. *Leon Blum*. Paris: Seuil.

Lake, David. 1992. "Powerful Pacifists: Democratic States and War." *American Political Science Review* 86: 24–37.

Lamb, Richard. 1996. *War in Italy, 1943–1945*. New York: De Capo.

Lannon, Frances. 1987. *Privilege, Persecution, and Prophecy: The Catholic Church in Spain, 1875–1975*. Oxford: Clarendon.

Larmour, Peter J. 1964. *The French Radical Party in the 1930's*. Stanford: Stanford University Press.

Lavau, Georges. 1975. "The PCF, the State, and the Revolution: An Analysis of Party Policies, Communications, and Popular Culture." In *Communism in Italy and France*, edited by Donald L. M. Blackmer and Sidney Tarrow. Princeton: Princeton University Press.

Lax, Andrew Julian. 1979. "Conservatism and Constitutionalism: The Baldwin Government, 1924–29." Ph.D. dissertation, King's College, London.

Le Bon, Gustave. 1977/1912. *Psychologie du Socialisme*. Paris: Les Amis de Gustave Le Bon.

Le Bon, Gustave. 1918. *La psychologie des foules*. Paris: F. Alcan.

Lebovics, Herman. 1988. *The Alliance of Iron and Wheat in the Third French Republic, 1860–1914*. Baton Rouge: Louisiana State University Press.

Lefranc, Georges. 1976. *Les organisations patronales en France*. Paris: Payot.

Lerroux, Alejandro. 1945. *La pequeña historia*. Buenos Aires: Editorial Cimera.

Levi, Margaret. 1988. *Of Rule and Revenue*. Berkeley: University of California Press.

Lewin, Leif. 1988. *Ideology and Strategy: A Century of Swedish Politics*. Cambridge: Cambridge University Press.

Liedtke, Boris. 1998. *Embracing Dictatorship: U.S. Relations with Spain, 1945–53*. London: Macmillan.

Lijphart, Arend. 1977. *Democracy in Plural Societies*. New Haven: Yale University Press.

———. 1984. *Democracies*. New Haven: Yale University Press.

Lijphart, Arend, and Carlos H. Waisman. 1996. "The Design of Democracies and Markets." In *Institutional Design in New Democracies*, edited by Arend Lijphart and Carlos H. Waisman. Boulder: Westview.

Linz, Juan J. 1970. "An Authoritarian Regime: Spain." In *Mass Politics*, edited by Erik Allardt and Stein Rokkan. New York: Free Press.

———. 1973. "Opposition in and under an Authoritarian Regime: The Case of Spain." In *Regimes and Oppositions*, edited by Robert Dahl. New Haven: Yale University Press.

———. 1978a. "Crisis, Breakdown, and Reequilibration." In *The Breakdown of Democratic Regimes*, edited by Juan Linz and Alfred Stepan. Baltimore: Johns Hopkins University Press.

——. 1978b. "From Great Hopes to Civil War." In *The Breakdown of Democratic Regimes*, edited by Juan Linz and Alfred Stepan. Baltimore: Johns Hopkins University Press.

——. 1998. "Democracy's Time Constraints." *International Political Science Review* 19: 19–37.

Linz, Juan, Manuel Gómez-Reino, Francisco Andrés Orizo, and Darío Vila. 1981. *Informe sociológico sobre el cambio político en España, 1975–1981*. Madrid: Euramérica.

Linz, Juan, and Alfred Stepan. 1989. "Political Crafting of Democratic Consolidation or Destruction." In *Democracy in the Americas*, edited by Robert Pastor. New York: Holmes and Meier.

——. 1996. *Problems of Democratic Transition and Consolidation*. Baltimore: Johns Hopkins University Press.

——. eds. 1978. *The Breakdown of Democratic Regimes*. Baltimore: Johns Hopkins University Press.

Linz, Juan, and Arturo Valenzuela, eds. 1994. *The Failure of Presidential Democracy*. Baltimore: Johns Hopkins University Press.

Lipset, Seymour Martin. 1959. "Some Social Requisites of Democracy: Economic Development and Political Legitimacy." *American Political Science Review* 53: 69–105.

Loewenstein, Karl. 1935a. "Autocracy vs. Democracy in Contemporary Europe, I." *American Political Science Review* 29: 571–93.

——. 1935b. "Autocracy vs. Democracy in Contemporary Europe, II." *American Political Science Review* 29: 755–84.

López Pintor, Rafael. 1982. *La opinión pública Española del Franquismo a la democracia*. Madrid: Centro de Investigaciones Sociológicas.

——. 1985. "La opinión pública y la transición: Una mirada retrospectiva." *Revista de occidente* 54: 113–22.

López Rodó, Laureano. 1993. *Claves de la transición: Memorias IV*. Barcelona: Plaza y Janes.

Lorwin, Val R. 1954. *The French Labor Movement*. Cambridge: Harvard University Press.

Luebbert, Gregory M. 1986. *Comparative Democracy*. New York: Columbia University Press.

——. 1991. *Liberalism, Fascism, or Social Democracy*. New York: Oxford University Press.

Lustick, Ian. 1996. "History, Historiography, and Political Science." *American Political Science Review* 90: 605–18.

Lyman, Richard. 1957. *The First Labour Government: 1924*. London: Chapman and Hall.

Lyttelton, Adrian. 1973. *The Seizure of Power: Fascism in Italy, 1919–1929*. Princeton: Princeton University Press.

Macarro Vera, José Manuel. 1982. "Causas de la radicalización socialista en la II República." *Revista de historia contemporánea* 1: 178–224.

——. 1985. *La utopía revolucionaria*. Seville: Monte de Piedad y Caja de Ahorros de Sevilla.

Macmillan, Harold. 1966. *Winds of Change, 1914–1939*. New York: Harper and Row.

Mahon, James E., Jr. 1996. *Mobile Capital and Latin American Development*. University Park: Pennsylvania State University Press.

Maier, Charles S. 1975. *Recasting Bourgeois Europe: Stabilization in France, Germany, and Italy in the Decade after World War I*. Princeton: Princeton University Press.

——. 1981. "The Two Postwar Eras and the Conditions for Stability in Twentieth-Century Western Europe." *American Historical Review* 86: 327–52.

Mainwaring, Scott. 1992. "Transitions to Democracy and Democratic Consolidation." In *Issues in Democratic Consolidation: The New South American Democracies in Comparative Perspective*, edited by Scott Mainwaring, Guillermo O'Donnell, and J. Samuel Valenzuela. South Bend: University of Notre Dame Press.

Major, Patrick. 1997. *The Death of the KPD: Communism and Anti-Communism in West Germany, 1945–1956*. Oxford: Clarendon.

Makin, Guillermo A. 1983. "The Military in Argentine Politics, 1880–1982." *Millennium: Journal of International Studies* 12: 49–68.

Malefakis, Edward. 1970. *Agrarian Reform and Peasant Revolution in Spain*. New Haven: Yale University Press.

Malgeri, Francesco, ed. 1976. *Luigi Sturzo: Scritti inediti (Vol. 3, 1940–1946)*. Rome: Edizioni Cinque Lune.

Maravall, José María. 1973. "Modernization, Authoritarianism, and the Growth of Working-Class Dissent: The Case of Spain." *Government and Opposition* 8: 432–54.

——. 1982. *The Transition to Democracy in Spain*. New York: St. Martin's.

——. 1994. "The Myth of the Authoritarian Advantage." *Journal of Democracy* 5: 17–31.

Maravall, José María, and Julián Santamaría. 1986. "Political Change and the Prospects for Democratic Transition." In *Transitions from Authoritarian Rule*, edited by Guillermo O'Donnell, Philippe Schmitter, and Laurence Whitehead. Baltimore: Johns Hopkins University Press.

March, James, and Johan Olsen. 1976. *Ambiguity and Choice in Organizations*. Bergen: Universitetsforlaget.

Marcus, Jonathan. 1983. "The Triumph of Spanish Socialism." *West European Politics* 6: 281–86.

Marquand, David. 1977. *Ramsay MacDonald*. London: Jonathan Cape.

Martinez, Robert. 1993. *Business and Democracy in Spain*. New York: Praeger.

Mateos, Abdón. 1993. *El PSOE contra Franco: Continuidad y renovación del socialismo Español, 1953–1974*. Madrid: Editorial Pablo Iglesias.

Mauriac, Claude. 1973. *The Other De Gaulle: Diaries, 1944–1954*. New York: John Day.

Maurras, Charles, and H. Dutrait-Crozon. 1908. *Si le coup de force est possible*. Paris: Nouvelle Librarie Nationale.

Maxfield, Sylvia. 1989. "National Business, Debt-Led Growth and Political Transition in Latin America." In *Debt and Democracy*, edited by Barbara Stallings and Robert Kaufman. Boulder: Westview.

Mayer, Arno. 1981. *The Persistence of the Old Regime*. New York: Pantheon.

Mazower, Mark. 1998. *Dark Continent: Europe's Twentieth Century*. New York: Vintage.

Mazzetti, Massimo. 1979. "I contatti del governo Italiano con i conspiratori militari spagnoli prima del Luglio 1936." *Storia contemporanea* 10: 1181–94.

McClosky, Herbert, and Alida Brill. 1983. *Dimensions of Tolerance*. New York: Russell Sage.

McDonough, Peter, Samuel Barnes, and Antonio López Pina. 1986. "The Growth of Democratic Legitimacy in Spain." *American Political Science Review* 80: 329–63.

McDonough, Peter, Samuel Barnes, Antonio López Pina, Doh C. Shin, and José Álvaro Moisés. 1998. *The Cultural Dynamics of Democratization in Spain*. Ithaca: Cornell University Press.

McKenzie, Robert, and Allan Silver. 1968. *Angels in Marble*. London: Heinemann.

Meaker, Gerald H. 1974. *The Revolutionary Left in Spain, 1914–1923*. Stanford: Stanford University Press.

Menéndez del Valle, Emilio. 1989. "Política exterior y transición democrática en España." In *La transición democrática Española*, edited by José Félix Tezanos, Ramón Cotarelo, and Andrés de Blas. Madrid: Editorial Sistema.

Mérida, María. 1979. *Mis conversaciones con los generales: Veinte entrevistas con altos mandos del ejército y de la armada*. Barcelona: Plaza y Janes.

Merritt, Richard. 1995. *Democracy Imposed: U.S. Occupation Policy and the German Public, 1945–1949*. New Haven: Yale University Press.

Micaud, Charles A. 1943. *The French Right and Nazi Germany, 1933–1939*. Durham: Duke University Press.

Middlemas, Keith, and John Barnes. 1969. *Baldwin*. London: Macmillan.

Mill, John Stuart. 1958/1861. *Considerations on Representative Government*. Indianapolis: Bobbs-Merrill.

Miller, James Edward. 1986. *The United States and Italy, 1940–1950*. Chapel Hill: University of North Carolina Press.

Miller, Susanne, and Heinrich Potthoff. 1986. *A History of German Social Democracy*. Leamington Spa U.K.: Berg.

Milza, Pierre. 1987. *Fascisme Français*. Paris: Flammarion.

Moe, Terry. 1979. "On the Scientific Status of Rational Models." *American Journal of Political Science* 23: 215–43.

Moeller, Robert G. 1986. *German Peasants and Agrarian Politics, 1914–1924: The Rhineland and Westphalia*. Chapel Hill: University of North Carolina Press.

Molas, Isidre. 1972. *Lliga Catalana*. Barcelona: Ediciones 62.

Mommsen, Hans. 1996. *The Rise and Fall of Weimar Democracy*. Chapel Hill: University of North Carolina Press.

Monroe, Kristin Renwick. 1991. "The Theory of Rational Action." In *The Economic Approach to Politics*, edited by Kristin Renwick Monroe. New York: HarperCollins.

Montero, José Ramón. 1977. *La CEDA*. Madrid: Ediciones de la Revista de Trabajo.

——. 1988. "Las derechas en el sistema de partidos del Segundo Bienio Republicano." In *La Segunda República Española: Bienio rectificador y Frente Popular, 1934–1936*, edited by J. L. García Delgado. Madrid: Siglo XXI.

Moore, Barrington. 1966. *Social Origins of Dictatorship and Democracy*. Boston: Beacon.

Morgan, Kenneth O. 1984. *Labour in Power, 1945–1951*. Oxford: Clarendon.

Mosse, George. 1964. *The Crisis of German Ideology*. New York: Grosset and Dunlap.

Mujal-León, Eusebio. 1983. *Communism and Political Change in Spain*. Bloomington: Indiana University Press.

Myers, David J., and Robert E. O'Connor. 1998. "Support for Coups in Democratic Political Culture." *Comparative Politics* 30: 193–212.

Noelle, Elisabeth, and Erich Peter Neumann, eds. 1967. *The Germans: Public Opinion Polls, 1947–1966*. Allensbach: Verlag für Demoskopie.

Nord, Philip G. 1986. *Paris Shopkeepers and the Politics of Resentment*. Princeton: Princeton University Press.

——. 1995. *The Republican Moment: Struggles for Democracy in Nineteenth-Century France*. Cambridge: Harvard University Press.

North, Douglass. 1990. "A Transaction Cost Theory of Politics." *Journal of Theoretical Politics* 2: 355–67.

North, Douglass, and Robert Paul Thomas. 1973. *The Rise of the Western World*. Cambridge: Cambridge University Press.

North, Douglass C., and Barry R. Weingast. 1989. "Constitutions and Commitment: The Evolution of Institutions Governing Public Choice in Seventeenth-Century England." *Journal of Economic History* 49: 803–32.

O'Donnell, Guillermo. 1973. *Modernization and Bureaucratic-Authoritarianism.* Berkeley: Institute of International Studies.

——. 1979. "Tensions in the Bureaucratic-Authoritarian State and the Question of Democracy." In *The New Authoritarianism in Latin America,* edited by David Collier. Princeton: Princeton University Press.

——. 1992a. "Transitions, Continuities, and Paradoxes." In *Issues in Democratic Consolidation: The New South American Democracies in Comparative Perspective,* edited by Scott Mainwaring, Guillermo O'Donnell, and J. Samuel Valenzuela. South Bend: University of Notre Dame Press.

——. 1992b. "Substantive or Procedural Consensus? Notes on the Latin American Bourgeoisie." In *The Right and Democracy in Latin America,* edited by Douglas Chalmers, Maria do Carmo Campello de Souza, and Atilio Boron. New York: Praeger.

——. 1996. "Illusions about Consolidation." *Journal of Democracy* 7: 34–51.

O'Donnell, Guillermo. In press. "Democratic Theory and Comparative Politics."

O'Donnell, Guillermo, and Philippe Schmitter. 1986. "Tentative Conclusions." In Guillermo O'Donnell, Philippe Schmitter, and Laurence Whitehead. *Transitions from Authoritarian Rule.* Baltimore: Johns Hopkins University Press.

O'Donnell, Guillermo, Philippe Schmitter, and Laurence Whitehead, eds. 1986. *Transitions from Authoritarian Rule.* Baltimore: Johns Hopkins University Press.

Offen, Karen. 1991. *Paul de Cassagnac and the Authoritarian Tradition in Nineteenth-Century France.* New York: Garland.

O'Gorman, Hubert J. 1975. "Pluralistic Ignorance and White Estimates of White Support for Racial Segregation." *Public Opinion Quarterly* 39: 313–30.

Olaya Morales, Francisco. 1979. *La conspiración contra la república.* Barcelona: Producciones Editoriales.

Ortega y Gasset, José. "Ideas de los Castillos." In *Obras Completas: El Espectador (1916–1934).* Madrid: Revista de Occidente.

Osgood, Samuel. 1964. "The Front Populaire: Views from the Right." *International Review of Social History* 9: 189–201.

Osorio, Alfonso. 1980. *Trayectoria política de un ministro de la corona.* Barcelona: Planeta.

Palacio Atard, Vicente. 1970. "El gobierno ante la conspiración de 1936." In *Aproximación histórica a la Guerra Española (1936–1939),* edited by Palacio Atard, Ricardo de la Cierva, and Ramón Salas Larrazábal. Madrid: Universidad de Madrid.

Partido Comunista de España (PCE). 1980. *Los comunistas en el movimiento obrero: Reunión de militantes obreros comunistas, Madrid, 17–18 Mayo 1980.* Madrid: PCE.

Partido Socialista Obrero Español (PSOE). 1934. *XIII Congreso del Partido Socialista Obrero Español de 6 al 13 de Octubre de 1932.* Madrid: Gráfica Socialista.

Pasquino, Gianfranco. 1986. "The Demise of the First Fascist Regime and Italy's Transition to Democracy: 1943–1948." In *Transitions from Authoritarian Rule,* edited by Guillermo O'Donnell, Philippe Schmitter, and Laurence Whitehead. Baltimore: Johns Hopkins University Press.

Passmore, Kevin. 1997. *From Liberalism to Fascism: The Right in a French Province, 1928–1939.* Cambridge: Cambridge University Press.

Passuello, Mario, and Nevio Furegon. 1981. *Le origini del fascismo a Vicenza.* Vicenza: Neri Pozza Editore.

Patch, William L., Jr. 1985. *The Christian Trade Unions in the Weimar Republic.* New Haven: Yale University Press.

———. 1998. *Heinrich Brüning and the Dissolution of the Weimar Republic.* Cambridge: Cambridge University Press.

Paxton, Robert O. 1997. *French Peasant Fascism: Henry Dorgère's Greenshirts and the Crisis of French Agriculture, 1929–1939.* New York: Oxford University Press.

Payne, Leigh. 1994. *Brazilian Industrialists and Democratic Change.* Baltimore: Johns Hopkins University Press.

Payne, Stanley. 1961. *Falange: A History of Spanish Fascism.* Stanford: Stanford University Press.

———. 1970. *The Spanish Revolution.* New York: W. W. Norton.

———, ed. 1976. *Politics and Society in Twentieth-Century Spain.* New York: Franklin Watts.

———. 1987. *The Franco Regime, 1936–1975.* Madison: University of Wisconsin Press.

———. 1993. *Spain's First Democracy: The Second Republic, 1931–1936.* Madison: University of Wisconsin Press.

Penniman, Howard, and Eusebio Mujal-León, eds. 1985. *Spain at the Polls, 1977, 1979, and 1982.* Durham: Duke University Press.

Pérez-Díaz, Victor. 1974. *Pueblos y clases sociales en el campo Español.* Madrid: Siglo XXI.

———. 1985. "Los empresarios y la clase política." *Papeles de economía Española* 22: 5–37.

———. 1993. *The Return of Civil Society: The Emergence of Democratic Spain.* Cambridge: Harvard University Press.

Pérez Yruela, Manuel. 1979. *La conflictividad campesina en la provincia de Córdoba, 1931–1936.* Madrid: Ministerio de Agricultura/Servicio de Publicaciones Agrarias.

Pimlott, Ben. 1977. *Labour and the Left in the 1930's.* Cambridge: Cambridge University Press.

Piñar, Blas. 1979. *Hacia la III República?* Madrid: Fuerza Nueva.

Pinay, Antoine. 1984. *Un Français comme les autres.* Paris: Belfond/Jean-Cyrille Godefroy.

Polanyi, Michael. 1966. *The Tacit Dimension.* Garden City: Doubleday.

Popkin, Samuel. 1991. *The Reasoning Voter.* Chicago: University of Chicago Press.

Popper, Karl. 1949. *The Open Society and Its Enemies.* London: Routledge and Kegan Paul.

Powell, Charles T. 1990. "The 'Tácito' Group and the Transition to Democracy, 1973–1977." In *Elites and Power in Twentieth-Century Spain*, edited by Frances Lannon and Paul Preston. Oxford: Clarendon.

Preston, Paul. 1978. *The Coming of the Spanish Civil War.* London: Methuen.

———. 1986. *The Triumph of Democracy in Spain.* London: Methuen.

———. 1994. *Franco: A Biography.* New York: HarperCollins.

Pridham, Geoffrey. 1977. *Christian Democracy in Western Germany: The CDU/CSU in Government and Opposition, 1945–1976.* London: Croom Helm.

Przeworksi, Adam. 1986. "Some Problems in the Study of the Transition to Democracy." In *Transitions from Authoritarian Rule: Comparative Perspectives*, edited by Guillermo O'Donnell, Philippe Schmitter, and Laurence Whitehead. Baltimore: Johns Hopkins University Press.

———. 1988. "Democracy as a Contingent Outcome of Conflicts." In *Constitutionalism and Democracy*, edited by Jon Elster and Rune Slagstad. Cambridge: Cambridge University Press.

———. 1991. *Democracy and the Market.* Cambridge: Cambridge University Press.

Przeworski, Adam, Michael Alvarez, José Antonio Cheibub, and Fernando Limongi. 1996. "What Makes Democracies Endure?" *Journal of Democracy* 7: 39–55.

Przeworski, Adam, and John Sprague. 1986. *Paper Stones.* Chicago: University of Chicago Press.

Pugh, Martin. 1978. *Electoral Reform in War and Peace, 1906–18.* London: Routledge and Kegan Paul.

Rae, Douglas. 1969. "Decision Rules and Individual Values in Constitutional Choice." *American Political Science Review* 63: 40–53.

Ralston, David B. 1967. *The Army of the Republic: The Place of the Military in the Political Evolution of France, 1871–1914.* Cambridge: MIT Press.

Ramsden, John. 1978. *The Age of Balfour and Baldwin, 1902–1940.* London: Longman.

———. 1995. *The Age of Churchill and Eden, 1940–1957.* London: Longman.

Rémond, René. 1969. *The Right Wing in France: From 1815 to de Gaulle.* Philadelphia: University of Pennsylvania Press.

Rioux, Jean-Pierre. 1987. *The Fourth Republic, 1944–1958.* Cambridge: Cambridge University Press.

Robinson, Richard A. H. 1966. "Calvo Sotelo's *Bloque Nacional* and its Manifesto." *University of Birmingham Historical Journal* 10: 160–84.

———. 1970. *The Origins of Franco's Spain: The Right, the Republic, and Revolution, 1931–1936.* Pittsburgh: University of Pittsburgh Press.

Rollings, Neil. 1992. "'The Reichstag Method of Governing'? The Attlee Governments and Permanent Economic Controls." In *Labour Governments and Private Industry,* edited by Helen Mercer, Neil Rollings, and Jim Tomlinson. Edinburgh: Edinburgh University Press.

Romero, Federico. 1989. *Gli stati uniti e il sindacalismo Europeo, 1944–1951.* Rome: Edizioni Lavoro.

Rose, Richard, William T. Mishler, and Christian Haerpfer. 1998. *Democracy and Its Alternatives.* Baltimore: Johns Hopkins University Press.

Roveri, Alessandro. 1974. *Le origini del fascismo a Ferrara, 1918/1921.* Milan: Feltrinelli.

Rueschemeyer, Dietrich, Evelyne Huber Stephens, and John Stephens. 1992. *Capitalist Development and Democracy.* Chicago: University of Chicago Press.

Ruiz Manjón, Octavio. 1976. *El Partido Republicano Radical, 1908–1936.* Madrid: Tebas.

Rustow, Dankwart. 1970. "Transitions to Democracy." *Comparative Politics* 2: 337–63.

Salandra, Antonio. 1969. *Il diario di Salandra,* edited by G. B. Gifuni. Milan: Pan.

Sánchez Navarro, Ángel J. 1990. "La transición política en las cortes de Franco: Hacia la ley para la reforma política (1975–1976)." Madrid: Instituto Juan March, Centro de Estudio Avanzados en Ciencias Sociales.

Sanders, Robert. 1984. *Real Old Tory Politics: The Political Diaries of Sir Robert Sanders, Lord Bayford, 1910–35,* edited by John Ramsden. London: Historians' Press.

Sani, Giacomo. 1975. "Mass-Level Response to Party Strategy: The Italian Electorate and the Communist Party." In *Communism in Italy and France, edited by* Donald L. M. Blackmer and Sidney Tarrow. Princeton: Princeton University Press.

Sani, Giacomo, and Giovanni Sartori. 1983. "Polarization, Fragmentation, and Competition in Western Democracies." In *Western European Party Systems,* edited by Hans Daalder and Peter Mair. Beverly Hills: Sage.

San Miguel, Luis G. 1974. "Para una sociología del cambio político y la oposición en la España actual." *Sistema* 4: 89–107.

Sartori, Giovanni. 1987. *The Theory of Democracy Revisited.* Chatham, N.J.: Chatham House.

Sassoon, Donald. 1996. *One Hundred Years of Socialism: The West European Left in the Twentieth Century.* New York: New Press.

Schmitter, Philippe, and Terry Lynn Karl. 1991. "What Democracy Is . . . And Is Not." *Journal of Democracy* 2: 75–88.

Schuker, Stephen A. 1988. "American 'Reparations' to Germany, 1919–33." Princeton: Studies in International Finance.

Schwarz, Hans-Peter. 1995. *Konrad Adenauer.* Vol. 1. Providence: Berghahn.

Scoppola, Pietro. 1977. *La proposta politica di De Gasperi.* Bologna: Il Mulino.

Scott, James. 1985. *The Weapons of the Weak.* New Haven: Yale University Press.

——. 1990. *Domination and the Arts of Resistance.* New Haven: Yale University Press.

Sedgwick, Alexander. 1965. *The Ralliement in French Politics, 1890–1898.* Cambridge: Harvard University Press.

Selborne, William. 1987. *The Crisis of British Unionism: Lord Selborne's Domestic Political Papers, 1885–1922,* edited by George Boyce. London: Historians' Press.

Seligson, Mitchell A., and John A. Booth. 1993. "Political Culture and Regime Type: Evidence from Nicaragua and Costa Rica." *Journal of Politics* 55: 777–92.

Semolinos Arribas, Mercedes. 1985. *Hitler y la prensa de la II República.* Madrid: Siglo XXI.

Setta, Sandro. 1975. *L'uomo Qualunque.* Bari: Laterza.

Sforza, Carlo. 1931. *European Dictatorships.* New York: Brentano's.

Share, Donald. 1985. "Two Transitions: Democratisation and the Evolution of the Spanish Socialist Left." *West European Politics* 8: 82–103.

——. 1986. *The Making of Spanish Democracy.* New York: Praeger.

Shepsle, Kenneth, and Mark S. Bonchek. 1997. *Analyzing Politics: Rationality, Behavior, and Institutions.* New York: W. W. Norton.

Shubik, Martin. 1982. *Game Theory in the Social Sciences.* Cambridge: MIT Press.

Shugart, Matthew, and John Carey. 1992. *Presidents and Assemblies.* Cambridge: Cambridge University Press.

Silone, Ignazio. 1962. *La scuola dei dittatori.* Milan: Mondadori.

Silver, Allan. 1971. "Social and Ideological Bases of British Elite Reactions to Domestic Crisis in 1829–1832." *Politics and Society* 1: 179–201.

Simon, Herbert A. 1976. "From Substantive to Procedural Rationality." In *Method and Appraisal in Economics,* edited by Spiro Latsis. Cambridge: Cambridge University Press.

Sisk, Timothy D. 1995. *Democratization in South Africa.* Princeton: Princeton University Press.

Skidmore, Thomas. 1967. *Politics in Brazil, 1930–1964.* New York: Oxford University Press.

Skocpol, Theda. 1973. "A Critical Review of Barrington Moore's Social Origins of Dictatorship and Democracy." *Politics and Society* 4: 1–34.

Snowden, Frank. 1986. *Violence and Great Estates in the South of Italy: Apulia, 1900–1922.* Cambridge: Cambridge University Press.

——. 1989. *The Fascist Revolution in Tuscany, 1919–1922.* Cambridge: Cambridge University Press.

Sonnino, Sidney. 1975. *Carteggio, 1916–1922,* edited by Pietro Pastorelli. Bari: Laterza.

Sotelo, Ignacio. 1980. *Un socialismo democrático.* Madrid: Taurus.

Soucy, Robert. 1986. *French Fascism: The First Wave, 1924–1933.* New Haven: Yale University Press.

———. 1995. *French Fascism: The Second Wave, 1933–1939.* New Haven: Yale University Press.

Spearman, Diana. 1939. *Modern Dictatorship.* London: Jonathan Cape.

Spooner, Mary Helen. 1994. *Soldiers in a Narrow Land: The Pinochet Regime in Chile.* Berkeley: University of California Press.

Spriano, Paolo. 1964. *L'occupazione delle Fabbriche.* Turin: Giulio Einaudi Editore.

Stampfer, Friedrich. 1936. *Die vierzehn Jahre der ersten deutschen Republik.* Karlsbad: Verlagsanstalt "Graphia."

Stepan, Alfred. 1971. *The Military in Politics.* Princeton: Princeton University Press.

Stone, Judith F. 1985. *The Search for Social Peace: Reform Legislation in France, 1890–1914.* Albany: State University of New York Press.

———. 1996. *Sons of the Revolution: Radical Democrats in France, 1862–1914.* Baton Rouge: Louisiana State University Press.

Sturzo, Luigi. 1947. *Lettere a Democratici Cristiani, Settembre 1946–Ottobre 1947.* Rome: Società Editrice Libraria Italiana.

———. 1956. *L'apertura a sinistra e l'unificazione socialista.* Naples: Edizioni Politica Popolare.

Suleiman, Ezra N. 1994. "Presidentialism and Political Stability in France." In *The Failure of Presidential Democracy,* edited by Juan Linz and Arturo Valenzuela. Baltimore: Johns Hopkins University Press.

Sykes, Alan. 1983. "The Radical Right and the Crisis of Conservatism before the First World War." *Historical Journal* 26: 661–76.

Taboadela Alvarez, Obdulia. 1992. "La afiliación sindical: Hacia una aproximación del sistema de representación de intereses en el sindicalismo Español contemporánea." Ph.D. dissertation, Universidad Complutense, Madrid.

Tácito. 1975. *Tácito.* Madrid: Ibérico Europea.

Tamames, Ramón. 1995. *La economía Española, 1975–1995.* Madrid: Temas de Hoy.

Tarrow, Sidney. 1967. *Peasant Communism in Southern Italy.* New Haven: Yale University Press.

———. 1995. "Mass Mobilization and Regime Change: Pacts, Reform, and Popular Power in Italy (1918–1922) and Spain (1975–1978)." In *The Politics of Democratic Consolidation: Southern Europe in Comparative Perspective,* edited by Richard Gunther, P. Nikiforos Diamandouros, and Hans-Jürgen Puhle. Baltimore: Johns Hopkins University Press.

Taylor, Michael. 1987. *The Possibility of Cooperation.* Cambridge: Cambridge University Press.

Teitgen, Pierre-Henri. 1988. *"Faites entrer le temoin suivant": 1940–1958, De la résistance à la V' République.* Rennes: Ouest-France.

Tezanos, José Félix. 1983. *Sociología del socialismo Español.* Madrid: Editorial Tecnos.

———. 1989. "La crisis del Franquismo y la transición democrática en España." In *La transición democrática Española,* edited by José Félix Tezanos, Ramón Cotarelo, and Andrés de Blas. Madrid: Editorial Sistema.

Tezanos, José Félix, Jesús López Aparicio, José Luis Rodríguez, and Rafael Dominguez. 1973. *Las nuevas clases medias.* Madrid: Editorial Cuadernos para el Diálogo.

Therborn, Göran. 1977. "The Rule of Capital and the Rise of Democracy." *New Left Review* 103: 3–41.

Thiers, Adolphe. 1915. *Memoirs, 1870–1873*. London: George Allen and Unwin.

Thompson, David. 1946. *Democracy in France*. London: Oxford University Press.

Tiersky, Ronald. 1974. *French Communism, 1920–1972*. New York: Columbia University Press.

Tilly, Charles. 1978. *From Mobilization to Revolution*. New York: Random House.

———. 1986. *The Contentious French*. Cambridge: Belknap.

Tocqueville, Alexis de. 1969. *Democracy in America*. Garden City: Doubleday.

Toharia, José Juan. 1989. *Cambios recientes en la sociedad Española*. Madrid: Instituto de Estudios Económicos.

Tsebelis, George. 1990. *Nested Games*. Berkeley: University of California Press.

Tuñón de Lara, Manuel. 1985. *Tres claves de la Segunda República*. Madrid: Alianza.

Turnbull, Maureen. 1973. "Attitude of Government and Administration Towards the 'Hunger Marches' of the 1920s and 1930s." *Journal of Social Policy* 2: 131–42.

Turner, Henry Ashby. 1985. *German Big Business and the Rise of Hitler*. New York: Oxford University Press.

Tusell, Javier. 1971. *Las elecciones del Frente Popular en España*. Madrid: Editorial Cuadernos para el Diálogo.

———. 1974. *Historia de la Democracia Cristiana en España*. Madrid: Editorial Cuadernos para el Diálogo.

Valenzuela, J. Samuel. 1992. "Democratic Consolidation in Post-Transitional Settings." In *Issues in Democratic Consolidation: The New South American Democracies in Comparative Perspective*, edited by Scott Mainwaring, Guillermo O'Donnell, and J. Samuel Valenzuela. South Bend: University of Notre Dame Press.

Valls, Rafael. 1992. *La derecha regional Valenciana (1930–1936)*. Valencia: Edicions Alfons el Magnànim.

Villiers, Georges. 1978. *Temoignages*. Paris: Editions France-Empire.

Vincent, Mary. 1996. *Catholicism in the Second Spanish Republic: Religion and Politics in Salamanca*. Oxford: Clarendon.

Vinen, Richard. 1991. *The Politics of French Business, 1936–1945*. Cambridge: Cambridge University Press.

———. 1995. *Bourgeois Politics in France, 1945–1951*. Cambridge: Cambridge University Press.

von Papen, Franz. 1953. *Memoirs*. New York: E. P. Dutton.

Waite, Robert G. L. 1969. *Vanguard of Nazism: The Free Corps Movement in Postwar Germany, 1918–1923*. New York: W. W. Norton.

Waldner, David. 1999. *State Building and Late Development*. Ithaca: Cornell University Press.

———. Forthcoming. "Regimes." In *International Encyclopedia of the Social and Behavioral Sciences*, vol. *Public Policy*, edited by Kenneth Prewitt and Ira Katznelson. Amsterdam: Elsevier Science.

Wall, Irwin M. 1983. *French Communism in the Era of Stalin*. Westport, Conn.: Greenwood.

———. 1991. *The United States and the Making of Postwar France, 1945–1954*. Cambridge: Cambridge University Press.

Wallsten, Thomas S. 1990. "Measuring Vague Uncertainties and Understanding Their Use in Decision Making." In *Acting under Uncertainty*, edited by George M. von Furstenberg. Boston: Kluwer.

Weber, Eugen. 1962. *Action Française*. Stanford: Stanford University Press.

——. 1968. *The Nationalist Revival in France, 1905–1914.* Berkeley: University of California Press.

——. 1976. *Peasants Into Frenchmen.* Stanford: Stanford University Press.

——. 1994. *The Hollow Years: France in the 1930s.* New York: W. W. Norton.

Weber, Max. 1949. *The Methodology of the Social Sciences.* New York: Free Press.

——. 1978/1920. *Economy and Society.* Berkeley: University of California Press.

Weingast, Barry R. 1996. "Off-the-Path Behavior: A Game-Theoretic Approach to Counterfactuals and Its Implications for Political and Historical Analysis." In *Counterfactual Thought Experiments in World Politics,* edited by Philip E. Tetlock and Aaron Belkin. Princeton: Princeton University Press.

Western, Bruce. 1997. *Between Class and Market: Postwar Unionization in the Capitalist Democracies.* Princeton: Princeton University Press.

Whitehead, Laurence. 1989. "The Consolidation of Fragile Democracies." In *Democracy in the Americas,* edited by Robert Pastor. New York: Holmes and Meier.

Wiarda, Howard. 1981. *Corporatism and National Development in Latin America.* Boulder: Westview.

Williams, Allan M. 1989. "Socialist Economic Policies: Never off the Drawing Board?" In *Southern European Socialism,* edited by Tom Gallagher and Allan Williams. Manchester: Manchester University Press.

Williamson, Oliver. 1983. "Credible Commitments: Using Hostages to Support Exchange." *American Economic Review* 73: 519–40.

Wilson, Woodrow. 1887. "The Study of Administration." *Political Science Quarterly* 2: 197–222.

Winterton, Earl [Edward]. 1953. *Orders of the Day.* London: Cassell.

Wolff, Theodor. 1936. *Through Two Decades.* London: William Heinemann.

Woodward, E. L. 1963. *Three Studies in European Conservatism.* Hamden: Archon.

Wylie, Laurence. 1957. *Village in the Vaucluse.* Cambridge: Harvard University Press.

Zeender, John. 1963. "The German Catholics and the Presidential Election of 1925." *Journal of Modern History* 35: 366–81.

Ziegler, Rolf. 1998. "Trust and the Reliability of Expectations." *Rationality and Society* 10: 427–50.

Zimmermann, Ekkart. 1985. "The 1930's World Economic Crisis in Six European Countries." In *Rhythms in Politics and Economics,* edited by P. M. Johnson and W. R. Thompson. New York: Praeger.

Index